PERSPECTIVES™ ON
MARKETING

THE AGENCY PERSPECTIVE
JASON I. MILETSKY

THE CLIENT PERSPECTIVE
MICHAEL HAND

COURSE TECHNOLOGY
CENGAGE Learning™

Perspectives on Marketing
Jason I. Miletsky and
Michael Hand

Publisher and General Manager, Course Technology PTR: Stacy L. Hiquet

Associate Director of Marketing: Sarah Panella

Manager of Editorial Services: Heather Talbot

Marketing Manager: Mark Hughes

Acquisitions Editor: Mitzi Koontz

Series Editor: Jason I. Miletsky

Project Editor: Kate Shoup

Editorial Services Coordinator: Jen Blaney

Copy Editor: Kate Shoup

Interior Layout: Shawn Morningstar

Cover Designer: Mike Tanamachi

Indexer: Katherine Stimson

Proofreader: Melba Hopper

Library of Congress Control Number: 2008935080
ISBN-13: 978-1-59863-871-4
ISBN-10: 1-59863-871-8

Course Technology, a part of Cengage Learning
20 Channel Center Street
Boston, MA 02210
USA

Cengage Learning is a leading provider of customized learning solutions with office locations around the globe, including Singapore, the United Kingdom, Australia, Mexico, Brazil, and Japan. Locate your local office at: **international.cengage.com/region.**

Cengage Learning products are represented in Canada by Nelson Education, Ltd.

Printed in Canada
1 2 3 4 5 6 7 11 10 09

For your lifelong learning solutions, visit **courseptr.com.**
Visit our corporate Web site at **cengage.com.**

*I'd like to dedicate this book to Snuffleupagus.
I always believed in you….*

—JASON MILETSKY

*To my wife and best friend, Doreen.
Thanks for the continued support.*

—MICHAEL HAND

ACKNOWLEDGMENTS

First, I'd like to thank everyone at Cengage Learning, including Mitzi Koontz, Mark Hughes, and my editor, Kate Shoup, who really did an outstanding job. I'd especially like to thank Stacy Hiquet, who worked with me to make the entire *Perspectives* series a reality. While I'm at it, I'd also like to thank everyone at Cengage Learning who worked with me on my earlier book, *Principles of Internet Marketing*. I know I became a lot harder to work with once *Perspectives* got under way, and I appreciate you all putting up with me!

Thanks, too, to Michael Hand, my counterpart in this book. Who would have known that two decades after Mr. Franzetti's business class, we'd be writing a book together? Congrats, Mike! I'm already looking forward to the next one.

Of course, I couldn't have done any of this without the great cast of clients I've worked with over the years, the team at PFS, and especially my business partner and the best damned PR guru I know, Deirdre Breakenridge.

As in all of my books, I want to thank everyone and anyone who's given me encouragement, believed in me, or even just been patient when work and writing have kept me from seeing them as often as I might have wanted to. This includes my parents; assorted uncles, aunts, and cousins; Cindi; Jackie; Chris; and everyone I've promised to stay in better touch with but haven't. Lastly, thanks to everyone at Eros Café in Rutherford, NJ, and the café in the Barnes & Noble in Clifton, NJ, who let me sit there for endless hours and kept me jacked up on Diet Pepsi while I wrote this.

—JASON MILETSKY

Acknowledgments

Being completely honest, writing a book was no simple task. When I signed on to do this project, I grossly underestimated the time it would take to pull it off and the support you need to get it done. First, thank you to my writing partner, Jay Miletsky. You continue to amaze me with your creative energy and passion to take on more. You have been a great friend through the process and I am proud to have my name on the cover next to yours.

Next, a sincere thanks to our editor, Kate Shoup—the real brains behind making this book come to life. I owe you more than one box of chocolate. Also, thank you to the team at Cengage Learning for taking a chance on a first-timer.

It is impossible to remember where you learned what you know after 15+ years of life in the "real world," but there are some people I would like to call out for their role in my journey. My deepest gratitude to Randall Tallerico, Tom Jump, Jeff Gooding, CJ Fraleigh, Jill Cooley, Erv Frederick, Rob Ole, Randy Ransom, Sue Pinter, Ernie Savo, Mike Wege, Lauren Reynolds, Eric Snyder, Veronica Villasenor, and Marie Tzan. Professionally, you have helped me frame the way I think and challenged me when I needed it most in both business and life. No career is built without help.

As the book clearly states, no client can perform without strong agency support alongside them. Thanks to the amazing teams at Momentum Detroit, McCann Detroit, Zipatoni, Upshot, Arc WW, Market Vision, GM Planworks, Tracy Locke, GMR, Keystone, and TPN. Special thanks to Amy J. for the ongoing encouragement and Kerry for the constant check-ins during the homestretch.

Last, but certainly not least, thank you to my family. Ben, Kyle, and Abby: I love each of you more than life itself. Now that this book is finished, I will have more time for playing football, writing songs, and watching Dora. Most of all, thanks to my amazing wife. You are an incredible person and I thank you for the sacrifice of time you've made during the past nine years while I've figured things out. I owe you more than one Saturday morning to sleep in. You are an inspiration for the entire family and I love you.

—MICHAEL HAND

ABOUT THE AUTHORS

Jason Miletsky is CEO and executive creative director at PFS Marketwyse, a leading New Jersey agency specializing in helping mid- to large-sized companies bridge the gap between traditional and Internet marketing. An industry veteran, Jason heads up a creative team of marketing professionals focused on developing brands and generating awareness through traditional, online, and integrated efforts. His marketing work has included successful consultation and campaigns for companies including Hershey's, AmerisourceBergen, Emerson Electric, JVC, and The Michael C. Fina Company. Jason has authored eight books, including *Perspectives on Marketing* and *Perspectives on Branding*, as well as his new college textbook, *Principles of Internet Marketing*. Jason speaks publicly at seminars, companies, and universities on topics including marketing, brand-building, and various Internet-related topics. He has been a featured speaker for the Institute of International Research (IIR), National Association of Broadcasters (NAB), Strategic Research Institute (SRI), New Jersey Institute of Technology (NJIT), Pratt, and others. Jason is a graduate of Brandeis University (1994), and currently lives in Nutley, NJ.

Michael Hand has more than 15 years of experience on the client side for some of America's biggest and most powerful brands. His career path has led him from the world of product introductions at BMW of North America, to licensing and promotions at M&M/Mars, to media operations and advertising development at General Motors, before spearheading retail strategy and brand activation at the Miller Brewing Company. Most recently, he oversaw consumer promotions, and Hispanic- and sports-marketing efforts at The Hershey Company in Hershey, PA. Hand has been recognized by the In-Store Marketing Institute as a "Person to Watch" for his role in retail brand-building and he has been a featured speaker on connecting with the U.S. Hispanic population for the American Marketing Association and Sports Sponsorship Symposium. Michael is a former student-athlete at Colgate University and has served on the Board of Directors for the American Liver Foundation in Wisconsin. He currently resides in central Pennsylvania with his wife and three children.

TABLE OF CONTENTS

Part Two
The Foundations   91

Part Three
Getting to Work   **163**

Part Four
Evaluation   307

Part Five
Just for Fun   343

Closing Remarks   361
Index   363

Introduction

Walk down the aisles of any bookstore or library and you're bound to see plenty of books written by two or more authors. But sit down and read through it, and it's doubtful you'll be able to tell which author has contributed which information. They've collaborated, shared notes, and have ultimately written the book from a single voice.

But is that the best way to learn about a given topic? Sure, the authors are usually recognized experts in their field and can draw from some unique experiences and insights, but each book only takes into consideration a single viewpoint—one perspective that the reader is supposed to accept as true. That might make for an interesting read, but it only tells half the story. The importance, value, and methodology of marketing, for example, may look dramatically different when seen through the eyes of a representative for a marketing agency than through the eyes of a representative for a client. Each may be an expert when it comes to the art of marketing, but their approach—and even their fundamental beliefs—could be quite opposite, simply because they work on different sides of the fence.

That's what makes the books in the *Perspectives* series so different from any other books on the shelves. Each offers a true 360-degree learning experience that gives you the opportunity to learn by providing two distinct and often opposing viewpoints. It's a rare chance to get both sides of the story so that you, the reader, can get a more complete understanding of the given topic.

In order to make a series like this work, though, the authors for each book need the freedom to write in their own voice and provide their own opinion, even at the risk of conflicting with their co-author. Therefore, it's important to note that **the authors of this book have not collaborated on their work during the course of their writing**. In fact, neither author will even have a chance to read their co-author's submissions until after the book has been completed. This is what makes *Perspectives* books such a unique concept, and a true opportunity to get both sides of the story.

In *Perspectives on Marketing*, Jason I. Miletsky represents the agency perspective, while Michael Hand speaks on behalf of the brand. Through a total of 101 questions divided into five distinct parts, Jason and Michael give their expert opinions on important topics including the dynamic of the client/agency relationship, the foundations of brand-building and marketing, campaign execution, evaluating success, and measuring ROI. Part how-to book, part philosophical debate, *Perspectives on Marketing* covers all the topics that anyone involved in marketing would need in order to vastly improve their knowledgebase and skill set.

We hope you have as much fun reading *Perspectives on Marketing* as we had working on it. Sometimes the authors whole-heartedly agreed with each other. In other instances, they couldn't have been more different. There's no question, however, that it's eye-opening to see the different perspective each author provided. But the perspectives don't end in this book. We want to hear your point of view, as well. Visit the blog site for this book at PerspectivesOnMarketing.com to comment on select content, read questions and answers that don't appear in this book, and let us know whose perspective you agree with more.

JASON MILETSKY

Like 95 percent of people who have actively pursued a career in marketing, I grew up being more interested in the commercials on TV than in the TV shows themselves. As a kid in the 1970s, I don't remember many of the shows that I watched (except a few cartoons here and there), but I very distinctly remember Mr. Whipple and his crusade against those confounded toilet-paper squeezers, the Asian drycleaner who tried in vain to protect his "ancient Chinese secret," Rosie's paper-towel heroics, those silly guys who couldn't keep their chocolate and peanut butter apart from each other...the list goes on.

Between high school and college, I continued to be enamored by ads, along with any movie that used advertising as basic premise. (Not that there were many; in fact, the only ones I really remember are *Crazy People* with Dudley Moore and *Nothing in Common* with Jackie Gleason and Tom Hanks.) Of course, I'd find myself doing what every other creative guy would do when we saw an ad we didn't like: immediately coming up with my own ideas of how the ad *should* have been done. I'd always have a clever tagline at the ready— because, of course, it was just that simple. Target audiences? Demographics? Test markets? *Brand-building?* Please. How tough could marketing be?

We all know where that story ends. It ends on the first day on the payroll, when the real world of marketing is revealed: the world behind the ads. All of a sudden, nothing was as easy as it seemed. Mikey may have liked it and Marvin may have been messy, but they only got that way after endless creative meetings left an army of ideas on the war-room floor, internal political games were played to perfection between the client and agency, markets were measured, and strategies developed. There was, in fact, a complex and captivating business behind the creativity.

In writing this book from the agency perspective, I've given my viewpoint on topics ranging from concept and development to achieving success and measuring ROI. My favorite parts, though, were those dealing with the agency/client relationship. After all, that's where the *real* creativity comes into play!

I've tried to be brutally honest (at times to my own detriment) and to avoid giving the vague, canned answers that marketers are so famous for. Do I speak on behalf of every agency out there? Of course not. There will probably be many who disagree with points I make here and there. There will be some, I'm sure, that will secretly agree with certain arguments I make but will never admit it out loud (especially to their clients). But after all these years in the trenches, I'm confident that I've represented the majority of agency people and their own views of the wild, wacky world of marketing. And I've learned that far more than just the creative aspects of marketing, it's that wackiness that makes the field truly come alive.

I sometimes find it hard not to smile when I guest-lecture to a college class of marketing majors and one or two students approach me after class to tell me about their great ideas for one of the brands my agency works with. It seems they always have a tagline at the ready. Because of course, it's just that simple.

MICHAEL HAND

When I graduated from Colgate University, after barely squeezing out the required GPA, I had little to no idea where I would go next. I had a sales job offer in Cleveland, a customer-service job offer in Phoenix, and—thank God—a marketing job offer based in New Jersey. I also had a stack of rejection letters so high I could wallpaper my off-campus apartment with them.

These three opportunities did not require me to draft a long "pros and cons" list of which to choose for my future. It was very clear that the job in marketing was the right one for me. The thing about marketing is, I have always been in love with the idea of taking a product (any product) and convincing a prospective consumer that they absolutely must have it—not from a salesman-like angle, but from the perspective of building a story around it and making the product seem bigger than life. I have always loved storytelling and finding ways to build an emotional connection between a consumer and an inanimate object.

As time has marched forward, I have begun to realize that I am wired differently than other people. I never simply walk through the grocery store at a leisurely pace, filling my basket with whatever items actually make my list; I watch consumers and see how they react when they approach the shelf. I examine the small kids in the cereal aisle picking out that one *special box* because it has a "cooler prize inside." My wife hates going shopping with me because I turn a simple in-and-out trip into a half hour of marketing research.

It doesn't stop at the store level; as a kid, I would watch football games on Sunday afternoon—and while I could tell you every player's stats on the field and college of origin (useless trivia remains a lifelong interest), I could also recite the names of the Miller Lite All-Stars, Budweiser Clydesdales, and Wrigley Doublemint Twins. I was enamored with the action between the plays as much as the action on the field. To this day I look at the logos that fill stadiums and seek ways to better integrate brand messages seamlessly into the action. Marketing, unlike most other professions, never turns itself off.

So why take on this project and write this book? I may have more than 15 years of experience working the sidelines for some of the biggest clients in the world across product categories ranging from cars to candy and light bulbs to beer, but trust me: I am *not* trying to pass myself off as the "all knowing expert." What I continue to learn is that the game of marketing never ends, and there is always more to learn. I am proud of the work I have put out into the market during this span of time and even more proud of the relationships I have built with people along the way. I will not sit here and tell you that this book is going to completely open your eyes to a whole new way of thinking; what I hope this book *does* do is provide you with a basic road map of what is going on inside a client's head throughout the marketing process.

If you read my answers to one of the questions in this book and think I have completely missed the mark, that is fine by me. I know for sure some marketers will disagree with many of my comments. To be candid, I hope they do. My intention while writing was not to speak on behalf of clients the world over; I simply wanted to have a conversation with you, the reader, and tell you what was on my mind in a way that would balance the true challenges of finding marketing success with both consumers and agency partners. I have tried to find a balance that could make the information readable for the folks new to this crazy world, while also sparking debate among seasoned veterans. If my style gets a bit heavy on traditional thinking at times, sorry about that; move on to the next question, and you might get a very different impression. I simply wanted to answer with candid thoughts that would spark additional conversation. I also wanted to make sure that readers understood some of the "behind the scenes" challenges taking place in corporate conference rooms across America every day.

Being a good marketer takes more than book smarts and an MBA from a top-flight business school; it takes a balance of knowledge, patience, understanding, personal skills, and commitment. You could use that same exact list to describe what it takes to be a good father or a world-class athlete. That is the beauty of marketing: It mirrors real life.

PART ONE
The Relationship

Q: · What Makes an
· Agency a Good Agency?

Jason Miletsky

The Agency Perspective

↳ Any time this question comes up, the knee-jerk answer is "creativity." But saying that creativity defines an agency is like saying a logo defines a brand—it's too simplistic, it's too obvious, and it doesn't paint the complete picture.

That's not to say that creativity isn't a key ingredient, because it absolutely is. But there's a world of difference between creative and *smart* creative. Smart creative involves defining a concept with a marketing purpose—specifically related to the client and its needs. At least once a week, I remind our art directors and designers that we are not creating art for the sake of art, and we're not designing for the refrigerator door. Everything we do, every idea, every design, every brush stroke—all of it has to have a sound and reasonable marketing rationale behind it. Aesthetics alone don't cut it; neither do wild, out-of-the-box ideas that may raise eyebrows but not the bottom line. Creativity provides true value to the client only if it can send an effective message to the intended audience and has the potential to generate a positive ROI. Agencies may be jam-packed with creative, artistic people, but this is a business, not an art school. Our job is to market effectively, not just beautifully.

Smart creative is only part of the story, though. Good agencies are also insightful strategists that understand who and where the audience is and how it can be reached. More often than not, good agencies do this with minimal research and limited time, as clients are almost always under ridiculous pressure to get creative launched quickly and show results immediately. Timelines usually don't leave a lot of room for doing the amount of research that's really necessary, and data compiled by the client is often spotty and questionable at best. A good agency will be able to think just as creatively when it comes to outlining strategy (based on little or no data and within specific budgets) as it does when developing concept and design. What avenues work best? How long should we wait between touch points? Which marketing methods are worth the expense? How do we expect the audience to respond? A good agency will consider all of these issues—and about a million more—when developing effective marketing strategies.

Service, of course, is another key factor—one that I can't emphasize strongly enough. Perhaps more than any other client/vendor situation, agencies form true relationships with the companies they represent. Agencies act as their clients' outside perspective, representing the eyes and ears that gauge how people outside a client's walls perceive their brand. It's the agency's job to give clients new insights into their audience and feed them new ideas. At the same time, agencies need to accept criticism when clients don't like our ideas or agree with our strategic approach. Once again, this is a business; good agencies don't take criticism personally, complain internally that the client is "stupid," or consider a client's negative reaction as an affront to their art.

We need to communicate our thoughts clearly and often, letting clients know that we're on the case, that we care about their needs, and that yes, we are staying on schedule. Strong project management on the part of the agency will often be the determining factor in whether the relationship with the client works or falls apart; as such, a good agency will put an equal amount of resources into its project-management department as it puts into its creative department. Most marketing efforts, regardless of the creative concept and strategic plan, will involve numerous moving parts, all of which need to be organized and accounted for by the agency in order to build client confidence.

Finally, really good agencies look out for their clients' best interests before looking out for their own. This is actually pretty rare, no matter what the agency says in its sales pitch. It's common for agencies to push designs that may work for the client but will work for the agency's own portfolio a little more, or to develop strategies that may allow them to bill a little extra or extend billing a few more months. Similarly, we may turn into yes-men, agreeing to everything the client wants to do, even when we know it's a mistake, because we don't want to risk losing the account. The best agencies promote ideas that may be better for the client than for the agency, are willing to speak up for what's best for the brand, and are confident that making selfless decisions will result in a more successful, profitable relationship in the long run.

MICHAEL HAND
THE CLIENT PERSPECTIVE

If you look up the word "agency" in the dictionary, you would see a definition somewhat like the following: "An organization, company, or bureau that provides some service for another." (This one's from Dictionary.com.) You can find little to argue with in that definition—an agency certainly does provide some "service." The definition, however, tells you nothing about what makes one of these organizations, companies, or bureaus better than the next.

When answering the "good agency" question, most client folk tend to fall into one of two camps. The first camp focuses its answers around great creative idea development; the second focuses on superior account/customer service. I, however, am of the belief that truly great agencies supply that special mix of both. (I know, great answer, I'm really going out on a limb with that one.) Strong creative without a great account team to manage the delivery of the idea and the expectations of the client will fail every time. Likewise, the strong account team that is not balanced with sound creative thinking will be left with no programs to execute and support.

In fact, I'd take this notion further to assert that the very best agencies demonstrate strong interaction across multiple disciplines:

- **Account service:** Every client wants good chemistry with its agency, and that has to start at the account level. Indeed, I believe *everything* starts with strong account service. The account team—the group that plays the ever-important roles of telephone operator and office psychologist—represents the front line of defense and acts as the face of every agency-client interaction. This group must make sure everything that is discussed with the client is speedily conveyed to the home office, lands in the right hands, and is communicated accurately and in detail. (This last point is the key to avoiding questions from the associate design director like, "Did they not like green, or simply that *shade* of green?") In addition, this group must be able to talk the client off the ledge when things are not really as bad as they seem (or as bad as the client wants to make things out to be). While most clients expect the creative team to be a bit odd in demeanor and character, that's not the case with the account team. Clients rarely expect the creative team to stand up in their wedding or attend the funeral for a loved one, but you damn well better believe that clients want an account team whose company they enjoy enough to share dinner, drinks, and the occasional weekend activity. When you have the wrong person as your point of contact with the client, the relationship is doomed from the start.

- **Strategic planning and development:** Most clients will tell you that not only do they have all the research they need to build rock-solid plans, they actually have everything planned out. I can tell you first-hand, however, that they are typically wrong. Most clients have great product data and can tell you more than you ever need to know about the ingredient content and how best to run production lines. What most clients don't have is a truly unbiased look at who their consumer is and how they should go to market. Don't get me wrong—clients have a very good idea who they want to talk to and what message they want to communicate, but they could always use a little help to make sure their information is accurate and their assumptions work beyond the walls of the corporate headquarters building. For this reason, agencies should be solid in strategic planning and development.

The best strategic-planning groups are not only gurus in their chosen field (advertising, promotion, interactive, etc.), they also bring cross-category exposure to the best-in-class model. That is, they can present unique ways of looking at data that they gathered while working with another client. In this way, they can serve as a conduit for, say, clients that are giants in consumer packaged goods to learn from telecommunications brands, clients that are automotive manufacturers to learn from soft-drink peddlers, and so on.

- **Creative:** Creative is always crucial to an agency's DNA. Every client wants to hear big ideas and talk about super-creative ways to go to market— even when a good number of those ideas will likely scare a client and won't get executed as originally intended. Let's be clear: No agency has ever lost an account because it was *too* creative. The issue here is reality. Most clients come to the table with their own ideas and simply want somebody to agree with those ideas and then execute them with excellence. The best creatives I have encountered are those teams that can tightly tie the brand insights/ strategy work into an idea, making it appear obvious to the client (and ultimately the consumer). These strong creative teams can also embrace an idea that is not their own and find ways to make it better before it ends up in the market. The worst creatives, on the other hand, are either so arrogant that they will fight over every copy point and utterly disregard constructive feedback or totally unimaginative, taking everything at face value and simply executing what they are handed. Creative teams need to be left alone to conceptualize and ideate, but they also need to find ways to get the client involved in this process. Clients will support and fight for ideas with much greater passion if they are part of the development phase.

- **Project managers and production staff:** Typically, this is the most overlooked group at agencies. It doesn't always get highlighted in mid-year reviews, and rarely drives the agency's compensation model. But this group more than earns its pay in that it is behind every good agency-client link. Nobody thanks these guys for getting work out the door on time and within budget, but they get raked over the coals if they run up the bills and start missing deadlines. The best agency teams have rock-solid people who make sure things get done behind the scenes. When the phone rings at 4:30 p.m. on a Friday afternoon, they're usually the ones who get stuck working over the weekend to get a project out the door. They do it without a direct thank you, and they do it without complaint (some of the time).

- **Accounting and legal:** In order for any client-agency relationship to work, these two groups must stay on top of things. I personally know this area is going well if I (as the client) never hear a word from them or from my finance team. The legal guys need to keep everybody out of trouble and make sure that every contract-negotiation period runs smoothly, and the accounting guys must ensure that billing is always clean and easy. With respect to billing issues, clients hate the phone calls and time it takes to clear these up. Submit bills in a timely fashion, make sure purchase-order numbers are written on the top of each one, and don't wait until a year after a project shuts down to send the final invoice. By then, most clients have moved the money and closed the accounting line; you are only going to piss people off. How much trouble do you want to stir up over a $525 fee for photocopies and shipping charges 12 months after the fact?

- **Leadership:** Leadership at the agency's highest level needs to be involved in client interaction. Every client wants to feel that their business is important to an agency. It's a fact: The team at the top needs to spend a little time each quarter massaging clients' egos. They need to do more than just pop in for the Christmas party (even if they plan to pick up the bar tab) or casually sit through the annual review; there needs to be some real dialogue on the state of the business. More than likely, the client has selected the agency due in part to expertise of this leadership group. And while clients anticipate that the executives who pitched on behalf of the agency will eventually exit the relationship to move on to the next pitch, it helps if you don't make it so obvious.

As you can see, a lot goes into answering this question. But to sum up, the best of the best recognize these unique functional areas and worry more about personal relationships than made-up acronyms for a proprietary process developed to track ROI.

Q: WHAT MAKES A CLIENT A GOOD CLIENT?

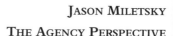

JASON MILETSKY
THE AGENCY PERSPECTIVE

I think this might be more easily answered by considering the opposite: What makes a client a bad client. The truth is that in any relationship, issues are going to come up. There are going to be times when agencies and clients don't see eye-to-eye. But a client would have to display egregiously poor behavior for an agency to sever the relationship.

The biggest issue is the abuse of anyone who works at the agency, outside of key executives. Yes, we are the agency, and yes, the client pays the bills—but no, that does not give any client the right to berate anyone on the account team. In the years since I founded my agency, I've thankfully run into this issue, where a client verbally abused one of the project managers to the point the project manager was brought to tears, only twice. As far as I'm concerned, no matter what the reason is, the first time you make one of my employees cry is the last time we do business together. There's just no reason for it. As the CEO, I have no problem with an angry client letting loose on me—vent all you want, call me every name in the book, and then we'll figure out a solution to whatever problem we face. But never *ever* attack one of the managers who has dedicated himself or herself to your account, no matter what the reason.

Obviously, those are extreme cases. But lack of respect can manifest itself in other ways besides boorishness. Bad clients tend to forget that this is a relationship, and that they hired the agency for a reason—not to be their lackeys, but to provide insight, consultation, and a different point of view. Maybe it's ego, or maybe they've never learned to let go of the reins, but bad clients will forget that the agency has something valuable to add, setting the strategy and creative themselves and leaving us with little more to do than micromanaged execution.

Another trait that makes a client a bad client (and I apologize if my answer to this question is turning into a bitch session, but I have to admit, it is somewhat cathartic) is when the client doesn't "get it." This is especially true of small companies or companies where the person heading up marketing efforts also happens to own the company. Very often, these people think they understand marketing, but the truth is they don't. They don't really get the need for planning in advance, for understanding the audience, or for setting a strategy. They think negative space in marketing material is a waste, and that every free inch of paper presents an opportunity to add more copy or make their logo larger. They don't see a difference between their target market and their barber, and they seek out feedback on everything marketing-related from everyone they come across and then urgently pass that feedback on to the agency as though it held any sort of relevance. And worst of all, these non-marketing marketers have no sense of how long it takes or how hard it is to execute a successful campaign, are more demanding, require more hand-holding than true marketing professionals, keep a stranglehold on the budget, and typically will have no ability to pull the trigger on even the smallest decision without a monumental struggle.

Finally, bad clients forget that they have to put personal feelings aside and do what's best for the account. Tell us the truth; we can take it. I'd rather you tell me point-blank you don't like an idea, or aren't happy with a strategy we're proposing, than have you smile and tell us how great everything is only to find out later that the account is suddenly up for review. As long as you're smiling, we'll think you're happy. In dealing with my own employees, I've always believed that if I don't tell them what's wrong, it's not fair of me to expect them to fix whatever issues I may have with them. They're not mind-readers. The same rule holds true for clients and agencies. There will be problems—we accept that. And there will be times you're not happy with our ideas. But good clients will tell us how they feel and respect us enough to handle it. Bad clients will spare our feelings at the risk of injuring the relationship.

Agencies are bound to run into bad clients now and then, but fortunately those clients make up the minority. For agencies hungry to grow and anxious to produce quality work, any client that doesn't fit into any of the aforementioned descriptions can be considered a "good" client—and these do, in fact, comprise the majority in the marketing landscape.

MICHAEL HAND

THE CLIENT PERSPECTIVE

┗┓ Although being a good client always ends up being more difficult than it needs to be, I think it comes down to one simple principle: no bullshit. Let's face it, people just want to know where they stand. They want clear direction that they can believe in. This is a job, not a hobby; agency teams don't enjoy spending countless hours of fruitless labor chasing ideas that will never see the light of day. Agency teams also want to be treated like equals. Just because you are the client does not mean that your time is more valuable or that you are more important.

Here are a few keys to being a good client:

- **Communicate and focus:** Right from the start, you need to have a plan. It may be a scope of work, it may be a calendar of activities, or it may be something else. Regardless of what it is, clients need to stay on task. Relationship struggles pop up when the workload gets too intense and when proposed projects get erased from the board for a whole new set of priorities. Business is always in a state of flux, but rarely do you get *really* big surprises. Keep the agency team informed of changes in overall direction and corporate strategy from the start. When you get that first call that the Chief Marketing Officer (CMO) is not quite sure where the big idea is headed, loop your partners in. They will appreciate the fact that they were able to see changes coming rather than having a new direction pop up out of nowhere (because that will inevitably require folks to work weekends and start the process over again). Just as the biggest issue facing married couples is communication, so, too, is communication key to any successful long-term client-agency partnership.

- **Objectives:** Don't just talk about objectives; set them. It's not much more complicated than that. When expectations are established and people know how they are going to be judged, it takes the unknowns out of the equation. Do you want to sell more widgets? Do you want to distribute more samples or simply drive more awareness? Whatever it is, do your best to quantify what you want to deliver and then measure against it.

- **Senior leadership:** The client's senior leadership can make or break any client-agency relationship. Corporate leaders should be exposed to the agency and should have a clear connection to the plan you are trying to implement through the agency's work. This group needs to provide stability. It needs to be able to motivate people and provide sound strategic anchoring. Most folks (not all, but most) in these chairs have paid their dues; people tend to forget that. They have worked their own way up through the ranks and they demand a bit of respect; they feel they have earned it. Also, every good client must remind their leadership team that nothing happens overnight. (Actually, many things happen overnight, but hopefully you get my point.) Keeping expectations in check is critical.

■ **Agency reviews:** You need to get these on the schedule, and they should be held on a regular basis. Nothing is worse for an agency than thinking everything is going fine and then finding out it is not. The best clients conduct and provide regular feedback sessions (and remain open to feedback in return). If your agency touches multiple parts of your business, don't just have the marketing team take a survey. Instead, share the review criteria in advance and obtain feedback from employees company-wide. For example, talk with sales and/or customer teams to get a sense of their interactions. If these interactions are limited, then at least hear what they think of the work outputs they have seen and find out whether they think those outputs are helping to make a difference in the outside world. If the feedback dialogue is slow to occur and nothing is getting accomplished, consider bringing in a third-party consultant to counsel and spark the conversation. I personally believe you can get this organized by yourselves (just lock the client and agency teams in a room and make them talk to each other), but then again, this is too critical a step to take chances on. If you place a real value in the long-term relationship with a client, placing this in the budget—perhaps as a shared expense—is critical.

■ **Celebrate the wins:** Things will go bad (or at least get stressed) at some point, and when they do, most clients will find some fault in the work of the agency roster. I can't explain why; it just happens. In some cases, this "blame" will be justified, but in other cases, it will not be. This is not, however, the point I want to make here. Rather, my point is to celebrate the victories with as much passion as when you analyze the missteps. A simple cocktail hour near the agency's office or a Friday-morning bagel delivery to say thank you goes a really long way. People want to feel like part of a team. The best clients have a way of embracing even the team who handles the agency's FedEx deliveries from the mailroom (and if the client doesn't, well, they should not expect their advertising boards in the morning delivery pouch on the day of the "big" meeting).

Q: • WHAT ARE THE MOST IMPORTANT • ELEMENTS OF A NEW BUSINESS PITCH?

JASON MILETSKY

THE AGENCY PERSPECTIVE

So there we are, at the front of the conference room. The computer is hooked up to the projector and the PowerPoint presentation that we slaved over is on the screen. Across the table sit three representatives for the client we're pitching. Each has a glass of water in one hand, a pen in the other, and a note-book turned to a fresh sheet of paper on the table. Two of them are smiling, looking forward to what we're about to show them; the third is fidgeting in his seat, clearly not happy to be there.

Does it matter what's in our PowerPoint deck? Of course. We need to demon-strate that we're an established, experienced agency, that we know the client's marketplace, that we understand their pain, and that we're strategic and creative enough to effectively market their brand. We need to prove that we'll bring something unique to the table. But all of that is expected—necessary, but expected. If we didn't know our stuff, we wouldn't have been invited to pitch in the first place. What we *really* need to do is bond with the three people we're presenting to.

One of the themes you'll pick up on throughout this book (in my answers, at least) is that the agency/client relationship is exactly that—a relationship. After all the slides in your deck have been shown and you've demonstrated that you understand their brand, the client still has to *like* you as people. You're going to be seeing a lot of each other, so you're going to have to enjoy working together. And your ability to do that is not something you can demonstrate in a PowerPoint presentation.

You're an agency! Keep it loose and fun. Agencies can't be creative if they're uptight. Keep the pitch more conversational and less like a structured presenta-tion. Ask the client questions about their brand, their needs, their past successes and previous struggles. But also delve into personal matters in a non-threatening, friendly way to find areas of commonality with each client representative—sports teams you're fans of, where you grew up, favorite authors you have in common—anything to show them that working with you will be enjoyable.

Remember what you have in common with each representative and casually hit those touch points during future meetings. It'll be harder for them to say no to someone they're friendly with than someone they see as just another vendor.

All of this is especially true for the one person in the pitch meeting who has clearly checked out before the meeting has even started—the one whose body language shows that he considers this meeting a waste of his time. Maybe he's already decided he likes another agency, or maybe he has a friend that he wants to give the business to. You won't be able to break those bonds if that's the case, but you can make it more difficult for the lone holdout to emphatically vote against you when the time comes.

MICHAEL HAND

THE CLIENT PERSPECTIVE

New business pitches can be painful on the client side. Nine out of 10 times you didn't ask for the pitch, and ten out of ten times you don't really have time in the day to hear it. The most important thing, then, is that the agency representative respects the client's time and has a point to deliver. The best new business pitches outline a problem the client may have and then provide a unique solution to making that problem go away.

In addition, the agency should make sure to get the right people in the room for the pitch. Too many times, the business pitch has little or nothing to do with the person with whom the meeting has been set up, so agencies should do their homework beforehand. They should be clear with their primary client contact (and new "best friend") on what they plan to discuss/present; this will enable the client contact to get all the right decision-makers in the room to hear the story—in a single meeting. It aggravates the hell out of me when I have to endure the same presentation twice because the right group had not been corralled for round one.

As part of the homework process, the agency should know something about the business they are going to talk with. On multiple occasions, I have been presented with concepts for brands that my company discontinued in prior years or, worse, shown concepts that could drive sales for brands manufactured by my biggest competitor. I mean, are you freakin' kidding me? Do agencies not have access to Google? If you know nothing about me and my business before you walk in with your canned presentation, I will show you the door rather quickly—even if your ideas have some merit. Do not—I repeat, do *not*—just drop my logo in the bottom-right corner of your standard sales deck and tell me this is a customized solution, especially if you've clearly forgotten to run a "find and replace" operation to remove the name of the company you visited yesterday from the presentation documents. Be prepared and pay attention to the details.

Q: HOW DO YOU PREPARE YOURSELF FOR THE RFP (REQUEST FOR PROPOSAL) PROCESS?

JASON MILETSKY

THE AGENCY PERSPECTIVE

RFPs can be both a dream and a nightmare. An RFP represents the agency's opportunity to break in with a new client and secure a new account. It also represents days or weeks of tirelessly writing, gathering data, capturing images, and crunching numbers to put together a novel that outlines who you are, what you can do, and how much you're willing to do it for. And quite possibly, all that work could end in a simple "Thanks, but no thanks."

For agencies, the most important part of answering an RFP is making sure no stone is left unturned. There's information we need the potential client to know about us, and it has to be in the RFP. We want to prove that we know who the client is, what they do, and what makes them special, so we sure as hell had better do our homework. And whether the end result is one page or one hundred, there shouldn't be a period out of place. One ugly typo can say more about the quality of our agency than ten pages of testimonials.

In my experience, responding to the RFP is a race against the clock from the moment it arrives. Deadlines are usually pretty tight, and the amount of information required can be immense. To get it done, the executive responsible for interfacing with the potential client should be ready to clear his or her schedule. He or she should anticipate questions that may come up and answer them before they can be asked. Every last detail needs to be put in place before the RFP can be called complete. And remember—we're in marketing. Yes, the RFP is primarily information, but that doesn't mean we can't try to sell ourselves and make our services stand out from the competition in the process. In the past, while I've closed my office door and typed furiously away at the RFP response, I've had our art directors and video editors produce short, one-minute videos, custom-made for the potential client, showing them that we get who they are, demonstrating our passion for our work, and providing a taste of the type of energy we'd bring to the account.

Michael Hand
The Client Perspective

⌐ From the client perspective, it is critical that much preparation be done before any request for proposal (RFP) goes out the door. The most important thing is making sure you have a clear vision of what you hope to accomplish before you start the process. In some cases, you may find out that your desired outcome is not realistic...and that is okay. You need to stay true to what you want; if the solution does not present itself in the form of an RFP, then look for an alternative method to obtain the desired results. I have been part of some very well-orchestrated RFPs, and I have been part of some that have not worked at all. With the ones that worked, you can't point to one single reason why; their success was really a sum of the parts. And the ones that failed never should have gotten off the ground. If you know your business well, you can narrow the potential candidates to a manageable number at the start before diving into formal meetings to make a selection.

Usually, you do an RFP for one of three reasons:

- To fill a void in the roster

- To drive consolidation across existing business practices

- To drive the incumbent a bit harder to perform better

Personally, I never want to do an RFP for the third reason, but it does happen. Regardless of the reason, if you are the incumbent agency partner, it is my opinion that any new RFP is yours to lose. Incumbents should already know the client's business model, the people working on the project team, how billing works, and how the internal approval process gets managed; the other guys will have no idea. I beg of you, Mr./Ms. Incumbent, step up and defend the business; because only then will I have no need to develop a transition plan, and my life will be a lot easier. Better yet, provide me with solutions from the onset that can help us avoid the RFP process altogether.

As I mentioned, however, there are times when an incumbent will not fit the bill. In such cases, an RFP is issued to bring in new ideas, to prompt a dramatic change in the organizational attitude, or to provide a brand with a needed burst of energy. This is an entirely different ballgame.

A big part of the RFP preparation process is having the right team in place from the start to make the optimal selection. The group needs to be cross-functional, and its members need to come prepared and committed to finding the right solution, however long it takes. (Notice that I said the "right solution"; you cannot simply focus on finding "a solution.") RFPs fail when team members on the client side come and go throughout the process. I have always mandated that in order to have a vote on the final partner, you must have sat through all presentation sessions that have led up to the selection. Too many times, you get a rotating group of decision-makers and you end up with folks comparing apples to oranges. Also, be clear up-front that this is not an election for your state senator; not all individual votes will be treated equally. I mentioned that the group should be cross-functional, but the folks who will be managing the agency and producing the work are the experts who drive the final choice. The procurement/purchasing team should be invited and needs to attend, as they can lend insight into how the process should work from an accounting perspective while also clearing tremendous amounts of red tape on the policy and procedure side. But let's face it: The marketing team is the one that will have to live with the selection. As such, that team's vote should count for more.

The team conducting the RFP needs to meet immediately after each part of the process wraps up. Don't withhold comments until the team regroups three weeks later. Even if you've diligently taken notes during the various meetings, odds are that three weeks later, you won't be able to read your handwriting or remember why a certain point you jotted down was relevant. Too often, individuals wait until the day an evaluation is due and can't remember if it was agency x that had the guy who kept telling stories about his brother Tom who loves Milk Duds or if it was agency y. After your meeting with the agency adjourns, take ten minutes and force the group to share first impressions and complete a rating sheet. Then, when you regroup in three weeks, you can recalibrate the scores if needed.

The rating sheet leads me to another very important part of RFP preparation: the period when a clear timeline emerges dictating when each step will take place. The details of this timeline should be clearly communicated both internally and to participating agencies. This communication is critical to the end-result, and allows agencies to be more mentally prepared throughout the process—not to mention reducing the number of phone calls and e-mails required. For agencies, responding to RFPs takes time and money; you need to respect that part of the process by being clear up-front on when you expect to have feedback.

A word for my agency friends: As you prepare your RFP, make every effort to avoid having everything feel too "new" to the client. A good business partner makes the client feel secure and promises in words and deeds that the transition will go smoothly. Agencies should be like a favorite pair of old slippers, giving clients just the right fit and enabling them to feel comfortable from the start. To do this, an agency must show its personal side. This keeps the client wanting to know more. The pitch is like a first date—and you want to get that call for date number two. The final decision will always come down in large part to gut feelings and the belief that a particular group can work well together.

Q: SHOULD AN AGENCY BE EXPECTED TO DO SPEC WORK OR PRESENT CREATIVE AS PART OF THE PITCH?

What's your perspective on this question?
Let us know at PerspectivesOnMarketing.com.

JASON MILETSKY

THE AGENCY PERSPECTIVE

This really depends on the size of the agency and the potential worth of the prospective client. In my experience, we've always done spec work or included creative as part of a pitch on a client-by-client basis. If it seems like the opportunity is there and the upside potential is worth the investment of time and resources, then absolutely. If not, then we'll take a pass on it.

Prospective clients who are reviewing agencies will always ask to see creative or have some spec work done before they make a decision on which agency to choose. That's their right. But it's also the agency's right to accept or decline. For example, when Hershey's Kisses was looking for an agency to handle their online marketing, my agency was one of three that was asked to pitch. As part of that pitch, we were expected to provide new designs for their Web site and a fully fleshed-out Internet marketing strategy. Of course we said yes, because the upside was worth the gamble: Aside from the potential revenue we could earn from this particular account, winning it would also provide an opportunity for our work to appear front and center for all other Hershey brands to see. Yes, there was always the possibility of losing the pitch (which we didn't), and no agency can expect to win them all, but the potential benefits made the choice to present creative in advance worth the risk.

Coincidentally, around the same time, a much smaller company asked us to handle their marketing. They were a solid company, dedicated to their cause, but by no means a household name. They had a respectable budget but nothing to get excited about, and the upside potential was limited: There'd be no media coverage of us getting the account, their budget wasn't going to go up, and, because they were small, it was very likely that they'd need a lot of hand-holding. Plus, we'd probably have to chase them down to get paid on time. After two meetings to discuss their needs and our services, they asked us to present creative in advance of signing a contract so that they could feel confident they were making the right choice with us. We politely declined, explaining that our record of success with other accounts would have to serve as a testimonial that we'd do a great job for them as well. Even though this request came only a few days after we had happily taken the opportunity to do spec work for Hershey's Kisses, the potential revenue and upside simply wasn't there. And in the end, standing our ground with this smaller client saved us more than just time and money. It showed backbone and established from the outset that our capabilities were worth something. By declining to work on spec, we made it clear that if they signed on with us (which they did), this wouldn't be a relationship where they could push us around just because they were the client and we were their agency. This would be a partnership of equals, or it wouldn't be a partnership at all.

Agencies are passionate by nature—we're hungry for the next account and for exciting new challenges. We hate to say no to new prospects. But it's also possible for an agency to break itself by doing too much work for free. Smart agencies understand that their work is valuable, and that in some cases you simply have to decline doing work for free—even at the risk of losing a potential new account.

MICHAEL HAND
THE CLIENT PERSPECTIVE

My writing partner will surely roll his eyes when he reads this, but as a client I not only think an agency should be expected to do creative work as part of the pitch, I demand it. Business pitches cost money—I get that—but the only way to truly assess an agency's capability is to see some of its work. I fully expect to put in time on my end by writing and delivering a brief and being open for questions throughout the process; an agency should likewise be prepared to deliver some potential solutions instead of relying on pseudo-related case studies. As a client, I see this as a true test of how a partner will operate when handed the keys to my brand's future. A client needs to see how the account and creative teams interact with each other, how ideas are generated, and who has the lead "voice" on the agency's team.

I am always anxious to see how a potential partner will take a brief and "break it down." Usually, the account team will rewrite your brief, translating it into the "preferred agency template"; I have no problem with this, but I do want to see the template so I can be certain nothing was left out. (We'll talk more about briefs later in the book; for now, I'll just say that we need to find a better way to make this part of the process run smoother.) I also want to see how they get the strategic planners and research team involved—this typically involves an overview of how they use a special process that only their agency incorporates to get you *the* big idea. They'll have dissected all kinds of information and showed you how Simmons data mixed with IRI data plotted on a map illustrates, say, where the most effective "Professional Rodeo" campaign will explode the marketplace with women aged 25–54. (Although I applaud the effort, and I am happy to observe the agency's fact-finding abilities, I *never* need to know that much index data on women rodeo fans in Ohio compared to the same demographic group in Idaho.)

When the client asks whether this level of research will be done for every assignment or if it's simply because the agency is in pitch mode, the agency had better answer with honesty. (This is typically when clients hear the standard "Every situation is different, and clients use these services many different ways. We do not ordinarily offer this depth, but we could add to the head count for a marginal fee....") Simply put, set clear expectations.

When the question shifts to actual creative output, you get a real sense of who wears the pants at the agency—and of the agency's ability to communicate with a client. To test them, I typically ask, for example, why a font treatment was selected or why a certain image was chosen—even if I clearly love the collective work and think these individual factors did not "make or break" the idea. Sometimes, the agency gets defensive about their choices; other times, they feel compelled to wax eloquent on why their choices demonstrate brilliant use of verbiage and the PMS color palette. If, however, they cannot articulate why they made the choices they made, if they cannot articulate their ideas on creative direction, how do you expect them to work with your organization on a shared creative idea? Put simply, I get worried when an agency cannot explain why they have done the work they have done. I lack the confidence that they can repeat it. Any success they've had starts to feel like a lucky shot rather than standard practice. Personally, I would prefer to work with the second-best creative shop on a given pitch over the number-one creative shop if the number-two group can offer really sound rationale for why they have made the choices they have made. To me, this is a better indicator of long-term success. To use a bad sports analogy, today's business model rewards companies that hit a single or double (with an occasional home run) every time they step up to the plate more than companies that hit a few more home runs but strike out every other at-bat.

Q: DOES IT MATTER WHETHER AN AGENCY HAS PREVIOUS EXPERIENCE IN A CLIENT'S INDUSTRY?

JASON MILETSKY
THE AGENCY PERSPECTIVE

Over the years, I've argued both sides of this coin many times over—and pretty convincingly, I think. In situations where we haven't had experience in an industry, we make the case that this enables us to bring fresh, new ideas to the table, while agencies *with* experience are locked into a set way of thinking and their ideas are tired and uncreative. On the flip side, when we're pitching an account in an industry where we do have depth of knowledge, we proudly display our experience and explain that our work in their field has given us a unique insight into their market—and with that insight, we'll be able to craft marketing messages that less-experienced agencies could never come up with.

But what do I actually believe? Well, at the risk of killing my chances with 50 percent of my future prospects, here's my answer: I do not believe that prior experience in an industry will make an agency more successful. What's more important is whether the agency has had experience with a specific *market*. With any market demographic, there will be subtleties in messaging, approach, design, and strategy that can make a campaign more or less successful, and prior experience with a market will give an agency insight into those nuances. The more experience an agency has with a particular market, the better they'll be able to drill into the minds of the audience, hitting touch points that the audience will likely respond to.

For example, suppose a national home goods retailer, like Pier One, is looking to reach married females between the ages of 30 and 45 with a household income over $100,000. (I'm just making these numbers up—I've never done any work for Pier One, but I can't imagine my demo assumptions are far off.) In their search for an agency, it will be less important for them to find a shop that has worked their specific vertical than to find a shop that really understands the affluent female market.

That doesn't mean an agency without experience in a particular market can't learn it on the fly—they can. But if a client decides to work with an agency that has no experience in the even most broad definition of the intended demographic, they must be willing to accept a potentially steep learning curve on the agency's part, that the agency may be slower to respond to necessary changes, and that the creative may not be on target in the early rounds of campaign development.

The other area of expertise that's more important than industry experience is the specific type of service required. This may seem pretty obvious, but agencies can sometimes sell a bill of goods that isn't always legit. Internet marketing, for example, is a complex and constantly changing field that requires specific skill sets. Left to an inexperienced agency, Internet campaigns can easily get botched, wasting time and money and potentially doing long-term damage to a brand. Similarly, a client wouldn't want to hire an agency to produce a national TV spot if the agency has no prior film or video experience. On-the-job training can work in some areas—and there are definitely areas in marketing where services can overlap, with the lines between them becoming blurry—but understanding how to execute and deliver is going to be a far bigger agency asset to a client than simply knowing their industry.

Michael Hand

The Client Perspective

 From the client perspective, this depends on two major factors:

- **The category in which your corporation competes and, by extension, the level of governmental regulation you face:** For example, if you are in the banking or insurance industry, it may make sense to find agencies (or agencies with key personnel) that have touched accounts similar to yours. Agencies will argue that "it is all the same," but let's be honest: It takes time to train somebody on the nuances of any new category—and if the government tightly restricts how you operate, you may be better off finding somebody who "gets it." That said, I personally believe that any *body* can do any *thing*. I also trust that passion and good ideas will win out in the end. If the client has strong people in place to aid in the training and development, you can make any base of industry exposure work to your advantage. In fact, I am of the opinion that too much industry experience can weigh down an agency with "the way things have always been." I want new ideas! I would rather adapt a concept/direction that worked in an entirely different category to make it work for me. I look at the end creative output as a solution to a problem that is targeted to a key consumer. If an agency really knows how to talk with young adult males in soft-drink marketing campaigns, why would they not be able to talk to those same people regarding their cellular phone service provider? You could argue they are better suited than the agency your arch rival recently fired.

- **The category in which your corporation competes and, by extension, the need for a strong Rolodex of industry contacts:** While every business faces a unique set of challenges, the potential agency partners in a given part of the marketing-mix model have a common environment and set of resources to function within. Putting that in English via an example, it takes a unique set of skills to conduct public-relations work within certain professional segments. The contact lists and the reporters who cover a particular trade are completely different in the automotive sector than they are in, say, the pharmaceutical industry. It certainly helps to bring a universal understanding of the important issues that will affect your business—as well as a reliable list of influential external partners situated to inspire that position.

For areas like promotional activation and interactive development, it will always help if the agency has some experience in the client's business segment—but again, the *idea* is king. If you have strong ideas that connect with consumers, you can find a way to understand the category nuances with a good client's assistance.

Q: WHAT ARE THE MOST IMPORTANT ISSUES TO CONSIDER WHEN NEGOTIATING THE CONTRACT?

JASON MILETSKY
THE AGENCY PERSPECTIVE

Simply stated, both parties need to feel like they're being treated fairly. Agencies need to feel like they're getting compensated properly for the work they're doing, and clients need to feel like they're getting real value for the price they're paying.

Okay, that was maybe a little too simply stated. For the most part, by the time the contract stage is reached, most of the important issues have been discussed and agreed upon in theory during the pitch process. But there are some specific points that I think agencies should consider when negotiating the contract:

- **Rounds of revisions:** Even though it's rare to stick to the letter of the law on this one, it's important to state how many rounds of revisions the client is allowed before the agency can start charging an hourly fee for more changes. At my agency, we typically cap this at two rounds, defining a "round" as each instance that a client provides feedback on art we've provided and requires us to make changes to it. With this definition, clients are encouraged to gather all their feedback and everything they want changed and tell us about it all at once, rather than call us dozens of times to make individual changes. Once again, it's rare that an hourly charge past the second round of revisions ever actually gets assessed, but it's good to have it in the contract as a reference for clients that drag the process out and refuse to pull the trigger.

- **Payment terms:** Just like any other company, agencies want to get paid as quickly as possible. Net 30 is pretty normal, and net 60 is becoming more common. Large companies pretty much never pay deposits, partially because their systems simply aren't set up that way, and partially because they just don't have to; there are plenty of agencies willing to work without requiring a deposit. Agencies should push for deposits from smaller clients, though, especially if there is any doubt as to their financial health. And except in cases where creative is presented as part of the pitch process, creative fees should *always* be paid in full before concepts are presented.

- **Client roles and responsibilities:** Clients hold agencies to any agreed-upon deadlines, and there's always the possibility of repercussions if those deadlines are missed. But just because a deadline isn't met doesn't mean it's the agency's fault. Clients need to be accessible and able to provide feedback on a timely basis, to provide necessary files, or to sign off when approval is required. A delay in any of these can cause the agency to fall off schedule, costing everyone time and money to get the project back on track. The contract should clearly state the client's roles and responsibilities in relation to the account.

The client/agency relationship should be a friendly one, so it's not surprising that negotiating the contract is often uncomfortable—there's an undeniably adversarial component to negotiating payment, terms, and issues. Depending on the size of the account, agencies often feel like they have to give more and take less in order to finalize the contract. But no matter how great a new account may be, it's important to look into the future and do what's necessary to protect the agency from potential harm.

MICHAEL HAND
THE CLIENT PERSPECTIVE

 Contract negotiations sound like big, scary endeavors, but they really aren't. In any contract negotiation between a client and an agency, there are two basic principles in play:

- The agency is always going to look to maximize revenue.

- The client is always going to look for efficiencies and ways to bring down total expenditures.

The most important issue when negotiating the contract, then, is ensuring that you remain fair. Also, you need to make sure it never gets personal. If the agency is run by a former colleague or college roommate, these lines can get blurred; in such cases, you must remove any and all personal connections from the process on day one.

Other things to consider include the following:

- Clients must closely examine the scope of work and honestly assess what expectations are built into the model. For example, should you assume that every program will go through only one round of creative revisions before the final art turnover? Or should you assume that two or three revisions will be needed and build in the hours accordingly? If you have a history of working with the agency— if this is a re-negotiation—look at hours spent on previous projects to build an accurate baseline. If this is a new agreement, share as much as you can from previous agency models (or, if on the agency side, share as much as you can on other clients from similar product categories or with similar work plans). Also, be sure to discuss how you plan to resolve any issues linked to "scope abuse" should it occur.

- Next, clients must look at the staffing plan—that is, what human resources will be required to get the job not just done, but done well. You will likely need to make some sacrifices, so start with having more people involved and providing deeper coverage (on the paper submission). This will allow you to really understand what is needed for success. (Indeed, I have engaged in negotiations that highlighted a broader need to shuffle workflow within my own team to provide more effective communication and results.) Enter the process with your eyes wide open, without the burden of trying to hit a budget number or to force current people into an antiquated staffing model.

- Clients must communicate the level of expertise required from agency personnel. You may well discover that the job can be done with three junior-level account people and one strong leader as opposed to one strong leader and two mid-level professionals. Ask yourself, is the goal to have more sets of arms and legs? Or is it to have folks with more work experience and leadership skills? The answers to these questions will affect the hourly rate per person for the full-time equivalents on the agency side, and they will affect the hours allocated to the task by the client's support team. Rates should also take into consideration the agency partners' office location—but the agency cannot get mad if the client is not willing to pay inflated overhead charges just because the agency has a higher rent payment than the client's other partners who are based in suburbia.

- Because we live in a world in which mergers and acquisitions happen all the time, any contract between a client and agency must include clearly outlined stipulations on termination rights and next steps should the fundamental business models of either partner change substantially.

As an aside, I try to remove myself from the final negotiation whenever possible. I work closely with the legal team up front to review the deal points and make sure that the business case is accurately reflected, but after that I step out—hopping back in only when questions arise on these areas or on issues that affect the team model. My removal from the process has nothing to do with title, grade level, or position; I simply think that you need to step out at a certain point and let the lawyers do what lawyers do. Getting out of the way allows you (as a marketer) to keep focus on the business issues and not hinder the future relationship by getting caught up in an argument over legal jurisdictions or confidentiality terms. If the folks involved in the deal are paying close attention to the everyday business with the agency, you will avoid surprises.

Q: Is It Better to Work Together on a Project Basis or on an Ongoing Retainer?

Jason Miletsky

The Agency Perspective

Selfishly, the agency will always be better off working on a retainer basis. There are three reasons why, and they all come down to issues related to billing:

- Retainers are usually set up for either six or 12 months at an agreed-upon monthly fee. For this fee, the agency promises to work on the client's account for a certain number of hours each month. Retainers allow agencies to calculate their revenue in advance for budgeting purposes and to allocate staff time, which in turn makes scheduling easier (and provides a clearer picture of when new employees are required).

- Although contracts usually have termination clauses, retainers give agencies the security of longevity with those clients.

- Retainers eliminate the potential for a final payment on an incomplete project to go unpaid. For example, suppose a client hires your agency to build a Web site for x dollars. The site should take about three months to build. The terms in the contract call for the first third of the fee to be paid when the project starts and the second third of the fee to be paid 30 days after the project starts, with the balance due when the project is complete. Sounds fair, except for one thing: Somewhere in the third month, the client drops the ball. They get caught up in an emergency and become tough to get hold of. Decisions aren't made quickly enough, and the completion of the Web site is pushed into the fourth, maybe fifth month—or beyond. The agency continues to work (chasing down the client for answers to questions can be time consuming), but they're not getting paid because that final payment isn't scheduled until the job is completed. This can create a strain on the agency's revenue and cash flow.

For many of the same billing-related reasons, I believe that retainers are better for clients, too. Plus—and I'm saying this because I actually believe it, not because I have an agenda as an agency guy—retainers draw both the agency and the client into a closer relationship. Retainers provide the client a set team of people to work with who will really come to understand what the brand is all about, and they give the agency time to think about the best way to achieve the client's goals as well as an opportunity to present new ideas without seeming like we're just trying to up-sell. The closer we feel to the client's brand, the better we'll be when we're working on it.

But while I'm clearly pro-retainer, I do make one exception. I think that new relationships should begin with a small project if possible so that both the client and the agency can get a feel for what it's like to work together. Usually, it only takes a quickie project to see if there's any synergy and to make sure that both sides can communicate and work well together; afterward, the client and agency can embark on a longer-term, retainer-based relationship.

MICHAEL HAND
THE CLIENT PERSPECTIVE

⤶ This is a hard question to answer, so let me take the easy way out by saying… it depends. From a client perspective, I would always prefer to work under a retainer-based agreement. This allows for stability in my month-to-month billing and eliminates those monthly peaks and valleys that my business model may otherwise support. Put another way, seasonality plays a very important role in most companies' sales cycles, and operating under a retainer removes that variable in my billing.

Moreover, retainers allow clients to enjoy continuity in agency personnel—an extremely important consideration for any business. In the last decade, every client has faced reduced head counts and the need to extract more efficiency from the business model, and having to retrain individuals from your agency every time a new project comes up is a contradictory solution. Besides, when was the last time you had a retainer in place and knew that people you had retained were simply sitting around waiting for a project to start working on? I can tell you when: *never*.

I also think agencies prefer this approach, for many of the same reasons. (Hopefully, my writing partner will have my back on this.) After all, agencies experience even more fluctuation when it comes to billing, so anytime they can count on a twelve-month revenue stream and staff accordingly, it's considered a big win. And just as retainers help to instill the sense of partnership I spoke about earlier for clients, so, too, do they enable agencies to feel connected. Yes, you can always terminate a contract, but a retainer is a commitment to stay together, to build a partnership rather than shop the street for a better deal.

On the opposite side of this argument, you can make a convincing case for the flexibility that project work allows the client. Assuming you can lock your agency partner into a pre-negotiated project rate, the cost of each individual assignment will take some mystery out of the equation for big clients for whom multiple needs frequently pop up. And small clients might want to "date other people" while they build their business such that a full-time partner is warranted. Project work removes the commitment, and may help ensure you do not force-fit an existing partner into a situation that falls outside their specialty. As an example, many companies today have their advertising agency develop the company Web site or provide public-relations support (or handle the pass-through) for a project if they don't have a functional expert in their existing partner roster. This may work just fine, but you will likely be better served by hiring a functional expert to lead for the scope of the project only.

In summary, a lot hinges on what area of services you are looking to source when making this decision. A retainer allows the agency and client to become a part of each other's business and truly get to know one another intimately. The ultimate goal is to create a seamless relationship, no matter what the structure of the working relationship is.

Q: WHAT'S THE BEST WAY TO DETERMINE A FAIR PROJECT PRICE OR RETAINER RATE? SHOULD LARGE CLIENTS BE "PUNISHED" WITH HIGHER PRICES FOR BEING LARGE?

JASON MILETSKY

THE AGENCY PERSPECTIVE

⤶ I'm going to tackle the second part of this first, and man, is this an ugly question—not because I don't know the answer but because I know that my response is going to sound cheesy, contrived, and totally self-serving. But here goes: Large clients do not get punished with higher prices for being large. Large clients pay higher prices because those prices are the right amount. They pay what the agency's service is worth because they understand the value that an insightful, creative, strategic, and organized agency can bring to the table. Small clients end up paying a lower price for equal service because they don't really get it and couldn't afford it even if they did.

Over the years, I've debated whether variable pricing based on client size is right or wrong with any number of people, have heard many different arguments both for and against it, and have determined that it all comes down to rationalization. The basic argument against it goes something like this: When you print a menu for a restaurant, you print the price next to each meal. You don't leave that part blank, expecting to charge a wealthy customer more for a steak than a poorer customer. It's the same steak for both parties, so they should both pay the same price.

The problem is, that's not really a fair analogy. For one thing, the service really isn't the same. An agency may be a single entity, but the people within the agency are still individuals who each have their own skill sets, some stronger than others. Chances are, smaller clients will be assigned the "B" team for their accounts, while larger clients will land the varsity squad. Further, the agency will most likely be forced to go through a far longer, more time-consuming, and expensive pitch process—usually lasting from six months to a year—with no assurances of actually landing the account. Smaller clients usually sign on far more quickly (between one to three months from the first contact), make the agency jump through fewer hoops, and provide the bread-and-butter revenue that's often needed while the agency pitches larger accounts.

Calculating how much to charge, especially for projects, can pose a tough challenge that involves knowing who your competitors are and what their rates are, how many hours will be involved, what the client is willing and able to pay, and how much (or, more precisely, how little) your agency can reasonably accept while still generating a profit. Typically, projects that are more design-based, such as Web sites or brochures, can be priced by multiplying the number of hours the agency expects to spend on the project by its hourly rate. For more concept-driven or creative projects, such as ad campaigns or re-branding efforts, agencies should expect to earn a creative fee—that is, a set fee for developing the concept (because an amazing idea will be worth far more than the time it may take to come up with it)—plus an hourly fee for production and execution.

Retainers, on the other hand, end up being relatively simple to calculate: You multiply the number of hours agreed upon per month by the hourly rate the agency charges (this can be a different rate for different people servicing the account or an average, blended rate). Agencies should be aware of their "level" (that is, the agencies they compete with and what they charge) when deriving their hourly rate. If, for example, large agencies in New York charge $300 to $400 or more per hour, then large agencies in New Jersey can get away with somewhere between $125 and $150 per hour, while smaller, less-established agencies may not be able to charge more than $75 or $80 per hour.

The truth is that pricing is always a mystery, and always will be. There is no set formula that can work for every agency and in every situation. We sell service and ideas—not commodities. What those ideas are worth really ends up being what we can get for them—somewhere between the most that a client is willing to pay and the least we're willing to accept.

MICHAEL HAND
THE CLIENT PERSPECTIVE

Pricing basically comes down to how long it will take to get a job done. Of course, reputations and agency/client size become factors, but pricing really needs to remain about the effort it takes to complete a task, not your zip code or size of your office building. The best way to determine a fair rate is to use history as your guide and establish clear baseline expectations. But let's be clear on this: In most cases, the reason you are getting a quote in the first place is because you don't yet know exactly what you need. So looking in the mirror should always be the first step in starting the pricing process and setting a benchmark. Additionally, clients must be willing to spend time up front when locking in rates (particularly for agency retainers) to make sure expectations are in line with the reality of their business model.

> Larger clients should not have a problem estimating the cost of a job from the start; if they are surprised by a quote from any agency, then most likely something has been communicated incorrectly with respect to the scope of work/job assignment.

This next part of my response is a bit difficult for me to admit, but I believe that large clients must view their size as both a blessing and a curse with respect to pricing. Having worked for many large international marketing organizations, I have come to expect agencies to be hungry to add my company to their client rosters—which, in my mind, should allow for a *better* rate. After all, not only do I provide them with clout in the marketplace, but more importantly, if they succeed, I have many more projects to offer them down the road. Now for the curse: Being at a large company can mean that everything takes longer. You tend to have more layers of feedback on a single creative execution, and the process might include brands, legal, marketing services, packaging teams, review committees, and senior management. This may not warrant a higher price directly, but it may warrant the use of a more seasoned member from the agency staff to shepherd the ideas—thereby indirectly raising the price.

This leads to another consideration to ponder as a client: Where do you need to be positioned (with regard to size and billing) within an agency's roster?

- Do you want to be a big corporate fish in a small agency pond? You'll command more attention, but resources and depth could be lacking. You must be certain that the selected firm can deliver on a daily basis and that it is stable enough to show continued growth. For a small shop, the shock of taking on a big client could force them to implode if they oversold their ability to handle the account. This selection is a major leap of faith, but one often worth taking.

- Do you want to be a small corporate fish in a large agency pond? This can be a concern if you want the undivided attention of senior leaders; they will almost certainly have other areas of focus. The benefit is that you may get exposure to broader opportunities for cross-partner interaction, and to ideas that would otherwise have passed by your company's door.

- Do you want an agency partner that is equal in size and stature to your marketplace position? A relationship built on mutual admiration can be one of strength, while avoiding the previously outlined pitfalls can allow for greater focus on the work. It can be very healthy for the agency/client relationship if both partners are on equal footing from the start.

Q: WHO SHOULD BE THE FACE OF THE AGENCY? DOES THE AGENCY EXECUTIVE WHO LANDED THE ACCOUNT NEED TO BE INVOLVED AFTER IT'S SIGNED?

JASON MILETSKY
THE AGENCY PERSPECTIVE

Clients—especially larger clients that have executed real marketing programs in the past—don't expect the executive who originally pitched them to be the face of the agency. It's understood that once the account is signed, the agency will put a team in place to handle that account, with an account manager assigned to assume day-to-day communication with the client, funnel work through the agency, and ensure that deadlines are met. In fact, if a key executive *did* stay on as the face of the account, it could make the agency look quite small—which would turn off many clients.

However, that doesn't mean the executive who landed the account should completely disappear, nor does it mean that the client will accept being lied to. As an agency, we make it clear throughout the pitch process who will be on the team, what their experience is, and what value they'll bring to the account. We make sure that the client is introduced to the individual who will be the face of the agency and responsible for daily communication. Through off-line discussions, we also make sure that the client is happy with this individual—and if they aren't, we make sure to either resolve any issues the client has or make a personnel change.

At the same time, it's important that the executive responsible for getting the account doesn't simply wash his or hands of all responsibility once the contract is signed. While clients don't expect key execs to be the face of the agency or to be in daily contact, they do expect them to be the brains behind the operation and to play a profound role in creative and strategic development. They also expect them to pick up the phone now and then (no, e-mail alone is not enough) or schedule face-to-face visits to make sure that everything is going well, to confirm that the client is happy with the team the agency has assigned, to discuss new strategic directions, to analyze results of previous efforts, and to brainstorm new ways of approaching the market.

For the agency, there needs to be a balance of time versus efficiency. Key execs who land accounts can't afford to spend their time managing those accounts. They also can't afford to be the customer-service rep on day-to-day issues; those are best left to project managers. They do, however, need to field general client concerns about the account and maintain an intimate understanding of how the account is progressing in order to keep the client moving forward. Project managers, even with daily client communication, can't be expected to increase sales or promote new marketing concepts. That is, and should always be, the executive's job.

MICHAEL HAND

THE CLIENT PERSPECTIVE

It happens all the time: A really strong creative team leaves a big agency and hangs their names, ampersands and all, on the wall of a new downtown office building. Then they hit the streets, looking to bring in new clients based on the reputation they established (and well deserved) through previous work experience. But I'd be willing to fly to Vegas right now and bet that this scenario will end badly; I simply don't like the odds for success. New clients will come on board—and they will drink the creative Kool-Aid when they sign on the dotted line—but there is no way that the people whose names are on the outside of the new office building can offer the same level of involvement to every client that walks through the door when things get started.

So, the short answer to part one of this question? The way I see it, no agency should rely on one or two faces to "be the agency." This model is flawed from the start. The best agencies don't have a single face; they have a single set of principles and ideals that dictate the actions of the collective group. These principles and ideals may originate from the founder's vision, but they must be instilled in every individual throughout the shop. When this happens, you achieve success, and the agency's reputation is built on more than one individual persona.

Part two of this question can also be answered in brief: The individual who landed the account does not need to stick around forever—but he or she had better be involved at the onset. Agency selection takes time, and it is a decision that is made based on a wide variety of factors—many rooted in personal relationships. What needs to happen is a transition over time from the "new business" guru who wooed the client into the relationship to the new primary point of contact who will manage the client's account. There is no set timetable for this transition, as each situation is somewhat unique. The critical point is that a timeline should be established early on for each individual's involvement; billing at 5 percent of an FTE for that person in year one is not the answer I am looking for after the contract is signed.

Creative and planning team members are a completely different story. This team should have more continuity within the group that the agency brought in to land the account. As a client, you never want to be the training ground for a group of new hires; you want folks who have been around the block, with a splash of new energy. These people on the pitch need to be around at the start; they can be phased out after the agency and client establish a common set of tactics/ideas that can be pooled and refreshed. The idea originator needs to foster that initial development and provide initial stability.

Q: HOW INVOLVED SHOULD SENIOR MANAGEMENT FROM THE AGENCY BE IN THE DAY-TO-DAY BUSINESS?

JASON MILETSKY

THE AGENCY PERSPECTIVE

They shouldn't. The key part of this question is "day-to-day"; any senior exec who is involved with the day-to-day happenings of any account is probably a micromanager to the nth degree.

Day-to-day operations are best left to the project managers who execute the strategy and make the magic happen. There are plenty of moving parts that need constant attention to get any marketing effort off the ground, and the one thing project managers *don't* need is a senior-level exec getting in their way—looking over their shoulders, making recommendations, or just being a general annoyance. A good project manager keeps everything under control and reports back to senior management so that they in turn can have more top-level conversations with the client and feel confident that things are getting done.

When senior management is too involved in the day-to-day operations, a few things happen, and none of them are good:

- The client is likely to start feeling that the agency is small—which isn't necessarily a bad thing unless they start thinking you're too small to handle the account.

- The senior managers spend time away from their real responsibilities: running the agency or bringing in new business. Chances are, they're commanding salaries that require more from them than doing day-to-day account work.

- The senior managers take partial control from the project manager but never fully do the job, leaving the *real* project manager out of the loop about what's going on. This will significantly increase the potential for mistakes.

It's easy for anyone to get wrapped up in day-to-day minutiae, but it's important for senior-level execs to know their place in the food chain. Clients don't expect or want them on day-to-day tasks. They want them sitting at the helm, developing new creative, coming up with innovative strategies, servicing the account, and keeping their home in order so that project managers can do their work expeditiously.

MICHAEL HAND

THE CLIENT PERSPECTIVE

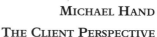 Earlier, I mentioned the importance of client interaction for senior leaders at the agency (see Question #1, "What Makes an Agency a Good Agency?")—but if you recall, I said *nothing* about "day-to-day" in that discussion. I stand by my belief that the best management teams find a way to get in and get out without the client feeling neglected. Continued contact day after day would be complete overkill—and frankly, the added pressure on agency account and creative staffs won't help them get the job done. These support teams need to feel empowered to keep the business flowing; they also need to establish themselves with the client as being able to "make the hard decisions" without needing constant supervision. A client will lose trust in the entire agency team when they appear unsure of their next steps. The client will start wanting senior agency leaders in every meeting to avoid the game of "telephone" for approvals. Even worse, the client may start to dial agency leadership after each meeting to confirm the presented work was an accurate reflection of management's thoughts. Bottom line, I don't want my account and creative team to feel that kind of daily pressure with their bosses circling above.

After the initial pitch, it is important for these individuals to stick around and make sure the onboarding process goes smoothly. This will involve a few meetings at the client's office and certainly a presence at the conference-room table when the client makes some initial visits to the agency. This isn't just "ceremonial"; it actually does serve a purpose. New business wins are important, to both the client and the agency. The value to the agency is somewhat obvious, increased revenue stream and a more diverse client portfolio likely top the list. The value to the client is not always as clear—but is usually even more important. Clients usually look at a major agency change as a way of moving in a new direction and bringing in a new level of energy to the business unit.

Remember, a change is being made for a reason. Having senior staff from the agency involved during the beginning stages of the business relationship serves as a symbol, validating the client's decision to move in a new direction. It also illustrates to the legions at the corporate office that their account is important to somebody outside their hallowed halls. But after an account is up and running, the need for the senior leaders' daily involvement is diminished. At some point, the relationships developed through regular interaction with the permanent staff take precedence over the "once in a while pop ins" from above.

That said, senior leaders do need to keep tabs on things and should be present for certain touch points throughout the relationship. These include the annual agency review meeting (at year end and mid-year if you are doing things right or quarterly if you are exceeding the expectations of Relationship Management 101). These individuals may also want to be present for critical meetings that involve any major changes taking place on the account. For example, if the agency is about to recommend a departure from a corporate tagline that has stood for a decade, then senior leaders should pull up a chair. Otherwise, as a client, I just want to know that they have been informed of the ins and outs of my business. If I see them at a corporate function, they should be familiar with who is leading my account and how my business is currently tracking. I want to know that they take pride in working on my business, and that they take it personally if the business is not performing well.

The exception is if I (the client) have hired a small boutique agency to manage a critical area of my business. If this happens, I damned well *do* expect senior management to be around my account on a regular basis. Often, I choose a small shop based on the leader's vision, and he or she needs to be active for me to see that vision come to life—and the fact is, most small shops don't have as deep a bench to tap into. Creative depth is usually the first shortfall, and the same thing goes on the account/planning side of the business: I have no problem assigning a junior person to the team to handle project management, but don't have the only seasoned veterans on the agency team walk away from my business as soon as the projects get rolling.

One final point on this: Senior leaders and agency teams as a whole need to make sure they use my products publicly. Nothing will piss off a client (and jeopardize the account) more than seeing the agency team using a competitor's brand. For example, if you run my Miller High Life account and I see you

Q: HOW INVOLVED SHOULD SENIOR MANAGEMENT FROM THE CLIENT BE IN THE DAY-TO-DAY BUSINESS? DOES THIS SLOW DOWN OR SPEED UP THE CREATIVE PROCESS?

JASON MILETSKY
THE AGENCY PERSPECTIVE

drinking Budweiser at a social function, start packing your bags.

At the risk of repeating myself, this depends on the size of the client. Some larger companies have a pretty complex hierarchy of titles and responsibilities, and the most senior people understandably simply don't have time to deal with the day-to-day business of marketing. But not every client is Hershey, Miller, or General Motors. There are far more small- to medium-sized clients in the world, which feed work to an uncountable number of hungry small- to medium-sized agencies. These agencies know that the smaller the client, the more likely it is they'll have to deal with their clients' top management, presidents, or company owners on a day-to-day level.

With smaller clients, this just goes with the territory. They have a greater personal investment, and every dollar really matters, so they'll play a more active role. This doesn't slow things down or speed them up, necessarily—small companies are notorious for working at an odd pace regardless, insisting on getting everything done in record time and then waiting weeks before finally pulling the trigger on any major decisions.

When, however, top-level management in larger companies get involved in creative, strategic, or day-to-day processes—and sometimes they do—it only causes problems and slowdowns, usually due in part to internal friction (at least, that's been the case in my experience). Inevitably, the client's marketing manager, whose job it is to work with the agency, feels annoyed that his boss is honing in on his turf, getting involved where he shouldn't, and becomes belligerent, basing his opinions and decisions not on what is best for the brand, but what is more likely to piss off his boss. The boss then flexes his muscles, making decisions on his own without consulting the marketing manager. And the agency is left in the middle, quietly trying to take everyone's side and to draw as little attention to themselves as possible. For the agency, this is one of the few instances where we really have no voice—and whether or not top management gets involved is up to them. All we can do is watch and pray.

MICHAEL HAND
THE CLIENT PERSPECTIVE

⤷ In broad terms, the senior management of every corporate client needs to be "involved" in the day-to-day business if that company wants to be successful. How you define the word "involved" is the bigger issue.

Senior leaders need to know what is going on with their people, and they need to know how the agency is performing across a variety of functions. But let's face it: Senior leaders who have time to be involved in every meeting and every decision are likely not doing a good job of leading. The major responsibility of leaders is to *lead*—they need to focus on bigger strategic imperatives and trust the fact that they have hired competent people to lead their brands/business on a daily basis. Corporate bigwigs must possess the ability to drive stronger business results and keep all members of the team motivated (at both the corporate office and within the agency team). This can be reinforced for the agency partner by simply acknowledging the role they play in getting great work out the door and into the hands of consumers. Unfortunately, too many senior leaders miss this point completely. Day-to-day leadership of the client-agency relationship belongs in the hands of the directors and managers; these are the folks who will spend countless hours in brainstorming meetings, photo shoots, conference calls, and talking with the legal staff. Simply put, the *best* leaders empower the client-agency team to take some calculated risks—and the *best* leaders support them if they fail.

That said, it is important to recognize that a chief marketing officer (CMO) has a vested interest in how the agency performs. A 2007 Spencer Stuart study covered in *Business Week* reported that tenures of CMOs across the United States were remarkably shorter than any other individual taking residence in the corporate suite—not shocking news considering every company and board of directors in America places an unbelievable amount of accountability on the corporation's marketing machine to drive stronger business results. The chief financial officer (CFO) cannot "show better numbers" if consumers are not pulling products off the shelf, and certainly the chief executive officer (CEO) isn't going to take the fall if the strategic plan has hit a few hurdles along the way. The CMO's job is packed with pressure to perform; it is no wonder that many individuals in this role get heavily involved in dealings with an agency.

The second part of the question—whether involvement on the part of the client's senior management slows down or speeds up the creative process—really depends on the individual leader. I have worked with some senior executives who brought the creative process to a standstill; I've worked with others who sped things up because they got folks energized to deliver the best possible end result.

Here's the way I see it: I don't sit in finance team meetings, voting on how the month-end close will work; why should the corporate finance director get a vote on my next TV campaign—especially when the extent of his marketing expertise is the Creative Writing class he took in college 27 years ago? The major problem is that often, these folks don't understand the impact of the decision or feedback they are providing. Simply changing the image, music bed, or font on the screen so "we can take a look at the other option" takes time and money. That said, many marketing VPs and chief marketers (and even CEOs) have a great eye for creative and really understand how the consumer thinks. I've worked with some extremely bright and gifted leaders whose involvement I valued greatly because they took themselves out of the desk chair in the corner office and put themselves in the seat of the consumer.

While working at the Miller Brewing Company, I spent as much time as I could with the then-vice president of Miller Lite marketing, Erv Frederick. It was not that Erv told you a bunch of things you didn't know or delivered amazing revelations every time you sat down; it was that he simply had a great eye for creative and copy. He was able to simplify a message to the consumer, and he never missed a thing. Of course, he always wanted to know what the research said and how the multiple focus groups reacted to the concepts, but he had good instincts, and he would throw away the "figures" if his gut knew it was the right thing to do. His involvement never slowed things down; it sped them up. The mission was clear: Deliver great work and stand behind it. That sense of empowerment and purpose brought the team alive and sparked a much quicker process.

Q: SHOULD THE AGENCY PRESENT CREATIVE THEY BELIEVE THE MARKET WANTS, OR CREATIVE THEY BELIEVE THE CLIENT WANTS?

JASON MILETSKY
THE AGENCY PERSPECTIVE

Before this question can be answered, one point has to be clear: Even though it is the agency's job to provide our expert opinion, consultation, and feedback, at the end of the day, it's the client that makes the final decisions and gives their approval on all strategies and creative concepts. There may be committees on both sides making their voices heard, but it's usually one individual on the client side who ultimately gives the go-ahead.

That being said, this is, unfortunately, a question that comes up all too often. In an ideal world, we'd always do work that we believe the market will respond to. But it's not an ideal world, and the truth is there's a lot more behind every decision than what might be right for the market. For one, there are individual tastes to consider. If the client doesn't like the color yellow, then no amount of marketing data proving it's the right color is going to change their mind.

Internal politics and self-preservation also play an important role in decision-making. Chances are, the person we're working with on the client side—and the person to whom that person reports—have families and car payments and mortgages to consider. They're not likely to take risks that could put their end-of-year bonus—or potentially their job—at risk. I once had a meeting with an automotive company where we pitched a viral campaign that would have been… let's just say risqué at best, borderline inappropriate at worst, but considering their target market of 18–24-year-old males, undoubtedly eye-catching. Sitting in a small, private room at a trade show in Vegas, the director of marketing and one of his associates sat in stunned silence after I finished presenting the campaign. Finally, the director of marketing drew a long breath and said, "This could be huge—we'd get a lot of attention with this." His associate gave a nervous laugh and said, "If we do this, we either end up on the cover of *AdWeek* or we get fired. There's no in-between." With a new baby on the way, the director of marketing ultimately decided that regardless of how the market might react, the conservative nature of his boss created too much of a personal risk. Self-preservation won out, and the campaign has since been shelved, locked away on some remote server, unlikely to ever get a chance to shine.

Agencies need to take all of this into consideration when making their recommendations to the client. In my experience, the best way to deal with this is to always give three options for every creative concept or marketing tool:

- One option that you think is perfect for the market you're trying to reach. If the stars are aligned, your client may go with it; they're not always at odds with what the market wants.

- Another option that you know the client will like. Find a way to do this so that if they choose this route, the market will still react positively.

- A third option that is deliberately okay, but not as good as the first two. This will make the first two options look better by comparison.

This method shows that the agency is being sensitive to all of the client's needs and concerns, and puts responsibility on the client for making the right decision.

MICHAEL HAND
THE CLIENT PERSPECTIVE

I can stand up and scream, "Don't just show me what you think I want to see" again and again, but the reality is that this dance will never change between clients and agencies. Clients (especially big ones) want to keep the lights on while not alienating anybody in their consumer base; this is true. But agencies will tell you that they always push the envelope and try to sell really compelling big ideas—and I'm not buying it.

This is not a shot at the agency world; we are all only human. Agencies have the same concerns and the same desire to keep their revenue streams in check as clients do. In fact, their concerns may be even more overarching, as they do not have a "product" to sell at retail, which can keep the dollars flowing in and the manufacturing lines at full production capacity. Creative capital is their currency, and when a client leaves the roster, it can be a bitter pill to swallow.

The truth is, what the market wants and what the client wants are hopefully the same thing. Where problems come up is when the creative idea for the market pushes the envelope, nudging people on the client outside of their comfort zone. In many cases, clients will know a change is needed before anybody else, but it still makes the process quite grueling and uneasy.

Simply put, agencies should *always* present work that the market wants, even if the market (or client) may not be ready for it yet. More importantly, clients should demand this. I believe that most agencies do deliver this over the term of a relationship, but let's face it—they always present three or four concepts for client review. We all know the exercise:

- One concept pushes the envelope too far, making everybody uncomfortable but allowing the next concept to appear not as shocking.

- Second, you get the idea that the agency actually wants to develop or produce. It might stretch things a bit, but it allows the brand purist to see his or her own reflection in the idea.

- Next, you get the 100-percent safe option—one that even your mother understands, and often a basic derivative of the existing architecture. This proves the agency knows your business and that you can count on them to deliver every time.

- Finally, you will get another safe bet—or, as I call it, the "wounded gazelle." This is the idea that is waiting to be devoured, once again propping up the other ideas for greatness.

These "designs" may get shuffled into a different order for the presentation, but let's face it—am I that far off?

We have also all been in the room when one concept board gets tucked in the back of the room; depending on the mood around the conference table, you might get the "We do have one other option we wanted to share" line. This always makes me laugh. These are always the concepts that can win the Super Bowl AdMeter in *USA Today* but scare the crap out of the client forced into making a decision. The bigger issue is whether that concept can drive sustainable growth for a client's brand over the long term. This is when you ask yourself if you have clearly established what the goal of the creative execution really is.

The truth is, developing creative is a risk. No two people will react exactly the same way. You need to be bold in your thinking and sell ideas with conviction. Taking risks can result in big gains, and watching consumers through a focus group window is not always the answer. Everybody in the process needs to realize that the marketplace is constantly changing, and that what worked last year may not be the solution for next year. As a client, I hire an agency to provide advice—not always to offer conclusions. Do not present me with what you *think* I want.

Q: • SHOULD CLIENTS BE IN ON • THE BRAINSTORMING PROCESS?

JASON MILETSKY

THE AGENCY PERSPECTIVE

↳ Initially, no. I totally get that brainstorming is the "fun" part of marketing, and there may be instances when the client wants to be part of it or thinks their input is absolutely necessary. But for the agency, brainstorming is rarely a structured event. It can happen spontaneously throughout the day, over lunch, during after-work drinks; like lightning, you never know when inspiration might strike. In my experience, the best ideas usually come when you're least expecting them. I've never believed you can order someone to "Be creative now!" and expect to end up with something useful.

More importantly, brainstorming is a process. Winning concepts usually aren't created in one shot, but rather are the result of a long evolution of creative contributions, one built on the next, until everyone collapses in a mixture of exhaustion and euphoria, knowing they've just nailed it. The funny thing is, the very first idea on which all the other ideas are based on is usually *horrible*—one of those concepts that someone just tosses out, after which the room goes silent, the record player coming to a screeching halt, while everyone tries to figure out if it was a serious contribution or just a badly told joke. Eventually, though, someone will say, "I don't think *that* will work, but what if we change the wording to…"—and the evolution begins.

The problem is, to get the ball rolling, everyone has to feel open enough to speak their minds and give their ideas, no matter how awful they are. The only way that's going to happen is if everyone is comfortable—completely at ease with the people they're brainstorming with. You have to feel like it's totally cool to say something ridiculous, to know that nobody's going to judge you—and, on the flip side, being completely okay with saying "Dude, that is *soooooo* not going to work" when someone else throws out a terrible idea.

And that, right there, is why clients shouldn't be in brainstorming meetings.

It's one thing to toss out a bad idea and look silly in front of your co-workers.

At the very worst, you'll all laugh about it over drinks later that night—or, if it was a *really* bad idea, you'll still laugh about it years later. But who's going to feel comfortable enough to offer a risky or bad idea when the client is in the room? Nobody. Nobody's going to want to say anything that will leave the client feeling like the agency creative is anything less than brilliant.

At the same time, when ideas are being tossed around the room like a beanbag and the client suddenly says, "I've got it! How about we...?" who's going to have the balls to tell them that it's a bad idea? It's their brand, after all, and they're the ones paying the bills. It's just an ugly situation—awkward, uncomfortable, and the complete opposite of the type of atmosphere needed for good brainstorming.

Agencies should always try to conduct their first round of brainstorming before the client gets involved. The best approach is to base all brainstorming on a creative brief written or approved by the client and prepare at least three to five concepts to present. If the client really wants to be part of the brainstorming process, then agency executives (not the entire creative team) can use those concepts as the foundation for new ideas. Although you can never underestimate a client's ability to take a great idea and make it worse, at least you're limiting the conversation to specific concepts rather than giving the client a blank canvas.

MICHAEL HAND
THE CLIENT PERSPECTIVE

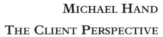 In my opinion, you need to include the client in the brainstorming process for big ideas—and *only* big ideas. If you are simply gathering the creatives and copywriters into a room to discuss some copy lines, then leave the client out. Involving the client in that level of the process will slow things down tremendously—not to mention cause you to overanalyze every thought. But allowing the client to participate in more "macro" brainstorming sessions can yield very positive results.

Brainstorming offers a number of benefits to the agency-client relationship:

■ The more the agency makes the client part of the creative process, the faster things will get through the approval and development matrix. Bringing the client in during the earliest stages (and hearing what they have to say) will establish them as supporters of the next steps. They will have taken part in the idea's genesis and will feel a sense of co-ownership.

■ Early client involvement can help agencies avoid countless hours of chasing ideas that will never get approved at the corporate office. The client's participation can provide greater clarity on the assignment and can help ensure that some concepts get nixed before they go too far.

- Clients want to think creatively, and many have great ideas that just need a platform/voice. Indeed, they might just need a little help and creative support to get their ideas off the ground—or to realize that the idea is not a fit. Brainstorming gives them a forum to be heard without feeling like they have to have all the details already worked out.

- Brainstorming prevents both groups from feeling that they are the only ones providing any answers, and can change the tone of a conversation from one that is very serious to one that is light-hearted and inspirational.

- Very few brainstorming sessions take place at corporate HQ. Including the client in the agency's sessions can serve as a way to re-energize the client, making them feel like part of the team. The best agency-client relationships are the ones where clients look at agencies as extensions of themselves; brainstorms can help forge that relationship.

Before gathering the client and the creative team for brainstorming, you must have some sense how these groups will interact. If the process goes badly early, concepters will be reluctant to open up and unwilling to put all their thinking on the table as the relationship moves forward. It is human nature to hold back when you fear continuous rejection.

HOW TO SUCCESSFULLY BRAINSTORM

Many people look at brainstorming sessions as free-for-alls—meaning you spend most of the time trying to get everyone focused and control them from talking over one another. For this reason, it is critical to the success of any brainstorming session that it have structure. Following are some guidelines, inspired by an article by Chris Wesley that appears on www.uklifecoaching.org, to help keep things on track:

Ideally, include between five and ten people in the brainstorm session. Conduct the session in a closed room, and do it in the afternoon. Shut off all cell phones and confiscate all BlackBerry devices. Order in caffeinated drinks and plenty of snacks. You need to get people energized. These events must be fun; people should look forward to them!

Nominate a session leader or facilitator. This individual should be somebody respected by the group and forceful enough to punish poor behavior. His or her job is to set and maintain a positive mood during the activity and to serve as the "gatekeeper of the whiteboard."

The facilitator should spell out the following rules before you get started:

Speak only when it's your turn and respect the voices of others.

Any and every idea, as crazy as it may seem, is a valued one.

Do not criticize or discuss any of the ideas during the brainstorm; the time to analyze and develop additional tactics will come later.

The facilitator should request an idea from each person in the group before breaking into one-off conversations, writing down each incoming idea *without modification*. When the whiteboard is full, the facilitator should stick it up on the wall for all to review. The facilitator should keep the pace moving quickly and the mood light-hearted. You need to be non-critical on "new thinking."

When a person is invited to share an idea, he or she should provide just one, and quickly—five seconds, max—or else say "pass." Note, however, that participants should resist the urge to say "pass" too often. Instead, say something outlandish! Someone else may take that "crazy" idea and turn it into something incredibly powerful. Just make sure the suggestion is grounded in some link to the main idea.

If an idea occurs to a participant when it's not his or her turn to speak, he or she should jot it down to avoid losing it, saying nothing until invited to share.

No one should comment on anyone's ideas. There should be no negative attitudes, and positively *no discussion of the idea at that time*. Beginners often get this wrong—and if they fail to rectify it, the session simply won't be a brainstorm, it will be a disaster. You *must* establish the "no discussion" rule. The facilitator should do this positively—but firmly—until everyone learns the rules of the session. The goal of brainstorming is quantity not quality when you are starting off.

When the flow of new ideas slows to a trickle, the facilitator should announce that the session is moving on. Open the floor to any additional ideas and allow anyone to chime in. The facilitator should continue to write these ideas down without discussion.

The facilitator needs to push the idea generation portion past the realm of comfort. When things quiet down, get them re-energized and make one final push.

That's it. If you follow these guidelines, you will almost certainly end up with a long list of ideas. Some will be obvious; many will be entirely ridiculous. But in there should be at least a few that are immediately actionable—or that at the very least suggest a way forward. You'll unearth gems that you would not have found any other way. They may even change your your brand direction forever.

Q: THE CLIENT INSISTS ON MAKING A MOVE THE AGENCY KNOWS IS A MISTAKE. SHOULD THE AGENCY DO IT ANYWAY?

JASON MILETSKY
THE AGENCY PERSPECTIVE

This is always a tough situation. As the agency, it's our job to speak our minds and do our best to steer the client in the right direction—even if it may cause friction with a client that doesn't like to be disagreed with. As a business, it's our job to keep clients as happy as possible so they keep paying their bills and hire us to do more work. And as creative, strategic professionals, we don't like to spin our wheels doing work we know will fail.

Fortunately, there are ways to deal with this. I tend to stick to the following process:

1. **Speak your mind.** One thing every agency needs to know is that no matter how hard-headed the client is, we're not hired just to be yes-men. We're hired for our expertise and insight—so we have to give it. If the client wants to go in a direction that's clearly not the right way to go, speak your mind, but prepare your argument well. Pick your time—chances are, you're not going to change anyone's mind in the minutes after they tell you what they're thinking. They're too hopped up on their own brilliance, and you'll look like you're being reactionary. Instead, let the client know that you respect their thoughts and just want some time to consider them. Then go back to your office and put together a compelling rationale as to why their idea won't work. Use statistics or real-life examples, not just your own opinion, and never, *ever* put the client's idea down. Compliment it while pointing out why they should consider another direction. Say something like: "I think you're idea is great, and we should definitely keep it mind for later on down the road, but for right now, I think…."

2. **Go the extra mile.** Okay, you tried, but the client still wants to at least explore their idea. So you really don't have a choice—you have to present it. But that doesn't mean you can't present something else along with it. It'll take some extra time, but come up with your own idea that you think will be better and show them that one as well. Offering options is always the

best way to get people to make the right decision. That said, don't make the mistake of downplaying their idea, purposely trying to make it look ugly, as a means of dissuading them from that direction. Maybe that'll work, but if it doesn't, and they're still adamant about sticking with their idea, you'll be stuck with a concept that's not only bad, but poorly executed.

3. **Protect yourself.** After all that, it's pretty clear: The client wants to go with the idea they thought up. You know it won't work, but it's what you have to work with. The only thing left to do is to protect yourself before moving forward. Eventually, when the client's concept or strategy doesn't work, you're going to get blamed—no two ways about it. When the end of the year comes around, and Christmas bonuses hang in the balance, and your contact on the client side is getting reamed by his or her boss for wasting money on a failed campaign, "Blame the agency" is going to be the new rule. Passing the buck is human nature, and the agency is next in line. Know it's going to happen, and protect yourself in advance. You don't need anything formal; just make sure you have and keep an e-mail trail where your protests to their concept are clear and their determination to run with their ideas is obvious. If the failure was monumental enough, written proof may not be enough to save the account—but if you're not in the wrong, you should at least go down fighting.

MICHAEL HAND
THE CLIENT PERSPECTIVE

 Unfortunately, this is a no-win situation for the agency. Let's face it: In this scenario, one of four things will happen:

- You tell the client they are making a big mistake, and they take your advice. Inevitably, though, the client will wonder what "might have been" had they executed their original idea, comparing all your future ideas with the brainchild you talked them out of. This problem—potentially a long-term one—can strain a relationship.

- You tell the client they are making a big mistake, and they ignore your feedback, following their own path—to great success. This will become an ongoing game of "I told you so." Indeed, the end result may well be that the client will wonder why they're paying the agency to come up with the creative horsepower when they can develop the ideas themselves in-house. Even if the success of the idea is due ultimately to tweaking by the agency, the fact that the client's idea served as the foundation will be difficult for the client to overlook.

- You tell the client they are making a big mistake, and they can ignore your feedback, following their own path—to ultimate failure. In this scenario, the agency will be perceived as not having been behind the idea from the start, and potentially even sabotaging it to work their own agenda. I know it sounds dramatic, but very few individuals will stand up and accept blame should this situation play out; the agency will likely become the sacrificial lamb.

- You bite your tongue from the start and never voice your thoughts. This is the worst approach, because if the client begins to feel like they've hired an agency that has no opinions or thoughts, it will be the beginning of the end.

When you look at it this way, I guess there really is no correct answer. Let's face it, the agency is screwed. Even so, I do not think an agency should simply turn its head from a foreseeable problem and make a move they feel is a mistake. But if the client insists on making that move after the agency has voiced its opposition, there is little choice but to quickly move on and execute with excellence. Agency partners need to remember that it is the client's money, but both groups' reputations that are on the line. The agency needs to make every effort to have their voice heard, but when the "green light" is given, you need to focus on the task at hand.

Q: HOW IMPORTANT IS WINNING AWARDS?

JASON MILETSKY

THE AGENCY PERSPECTIVE

Years ago, I was asked to sit on a panel of judges for some awards program. I was sent boxes and boxes of submissions to review, most of them print ads, brochures, collateral material, etc. For each one, I had to read a veritable book about who the piece was meant for, the budget they had to work with, how successful it was, and on and on. From there, I had to fill out a page-long score card, grading everything from creative concept to design skill, to printing, to construction…and on and on and on. The process was as drawn out as filling out an eHarmony profile—and even less rewarding. It took *days*. But I did it, and as far as I was concerned, there were clear winners for first, second, and third prize.

A couple weeks later, I flew to Florida for the banquet, where I was to deliver a keynote speech on brand building and oversee the presentation of the awards. The banquet organizers greeted me cheerfully, and we sat down to review the judging. I showed them which pieces I determined to be the winners, and told them why. They nodded thoughtfully for awhile—until one of them said, "I understand why you chose *those*, but did you consider *this* one at all?" referring to a truly horrific piece I had cast aside almost immediately. I respectfully told them that I didn't think that piece should have been *judged*, much less given a prize.

It turned out the piece they wanted me to consider was submitted by one of the largest members in their organization—who, coincidentally, also gave them the most amount of money on an annual basis—so they thought it would be more appropriate if that company's entry won. It also turned out that my opinions on second and third place didn't matter much either, as those awards went to other large member companies with deep pockets. So basically, the time I had taken to review and judge everything was a total waste. The whole thing was a fix, and the awards were nothing but a staged PR opportunity for the more generous members.

Needless to say, I've been a bit put off by awards ever since, and am more than a little skeptical about how honestly they're judged. I've noticed, too, that although we've won our share of awards over the years, it seems like we always do better when the work we submit is for a larger company or well-known brand rather than a smaller, unknown client—regardless of the quality of the work. Award organizers want their PR, too, and clearly they'll get more when larger names are involved. My bet is that in nine out 10 cases, the ugliest menu design for Pizza Hut will win out over the most beautifully designed menu for Johnny's Pizzeria in Nowhere, Wisconsin.

Clients like to win awards, so agencies have to take part. But personally, I think the *real* award is generating a positive ROI on each and every campaign that we develop. Large trophies may look nice on the shelf, but I haven't seen one yet that can make a cash register ring.

MICHAEL HAND
THE CLIENT PERSPECTIVE

⌐ Between advertising, promotion, public relations, and interactive, there have to be more than 50 award shows in the marketing industry alone. You have the Clios and the Reggies, the Tellys and the Anvils, not to mention the Effies and the ADDYS. But the way I see it, winning awards is important only if the award is for successfully driving your business objectives. Otherwise, who cares? Sure, awards look good in the lobby and they make nice decorative elements in conference rooms, but the bottom line is, I need my creative agency to help me move my business.

Okay, who am I kidding? The truth is, they *do* matter on some level. Everybody wants to be part of a winning team; winning awards allows many individuals to feel a greater sense of accomplishment for the time they spend doing their job all day every day. Often, winning an award is the only true recognition a creative/production team will receive for a brand's success, despite having spent countless hours writing and editing to get the work "just right." Sure, creative teams love to hear that sales are up by double digits, but they would rather have their peers recognize their role in developing the campaign that (hopefully) drove the success.

> I'm all for people getting credit where credit is due. As a client, I only ask that you resist the temptation to spend too much time reliving memories of successful programs gone by and get focused on the next round of planning and creative development to exceed previous deliverables. And let's get one other thing clear: I do not want the entire world to know the intimate details of my programming results. Your telling my biggest competitor the exact elements that are driving my business by +20 percent on the Web means I've just lost my entire competitive advantage. Make the competitors play catch up through trial and error, not by reading next week's issue of *Brandweek* or *Ad Age*.

And of course, many clients like to win awards, too. Winning awards offers an excellent opportunity to flaunt in front of those folks who don't understand marketing at the corporate office. What better way is there for a brand director to defend his or her request for a 53-percent budget increase than to say, "We are looking to place more TRPs behind our *award-winning* television campaign"? This quiets those who think creative output can be generated by anybody with a drawing pad and an art degree.

> There are some who feel that awards actually *hurt* creative development. David Ogilvy, who some call the godfather of advertising, said it best: "Nowadays, you know, the creative departments and agencies are dominated by specialists in television. Their ambition is to win awards at festivals. They don't give a damn whether their commercials will sell, provided they entertain and win awards. They won't have anything to do with research if they can help it. These creative entertainers have done the advertising business appalling damage." (Source: Nick Werden, "Advertising Awards Hurt Advertising," *FusionBrand*, 4/14/2007.)

Recently, I attended a meeting at the offices of an agency I was considering using. When I arrived, I noticed that they had named each conference room in their newly renovated space after various awards—for example, one was called the Clio Room. "The room titles are a good reminder to the creatives on why they are here," explained an account services team member. "They are here to produce award-winning work." I got to thinking, is that *really* why you hire an agency? And should that be what you tell a potential client? Later, I asked one of the agency's creative team members for his opinion on the room titles.

In response, he walked me to a trophy case by the front door of the lobby and pointed to his favorite gold figurine on the top shelf. Amidst a few Clios and One Show awards (at least, I *think* that's what they were) was a trophy from last year's City Bowling League Championship. This, I decided, was a much better representation of the agency; the account people were simply feeding me the agency's scripted lines.

The bottom line? I'd rather have work that is created flawlessly and drives my business than overproduced ads that don't move the needle at retail but win on the award circuit. Wait—I take that back. Actually, what I *really* want is award-winning ads that *also* sell more of my product. Isn't that what all clients want?

Q: HOW DO YOU DEAL WITH THE PAYMENT PROCESS AND ISSUES SUCH AS SEVERELY OVERDUE PAYMENTS?

JASON MILETSKY

THE AGENCY PERSPECTIVE

It'd be nice to think that this could be simple: Invoices go out, they get processed, the agency gets paid. Nice and easy—and about as realistic as hopes for peace in the Middle East.

The reality is, smaller companies may have cash-flow problems; larger companies may have to navigate a tangle of red tape for each invoice. Invoices may not get processed until a week, two weeks, or even a month after they're submitted—and then it's still a 30 to 60 day wait after that.

For agencies (especially smaller ones, which often live hand-to-mouth), waiting a long time for payment can be uncomfortable—even frightening. Campaigns can be expensive, and agencies are usually expected to front the money (within reason) to get client work completed within tight deadlines. (And forget about asking large companies for deposits, because it's not going to happen—and asking only makes you look small.) When an agency is laying out money for multiple clients, and those vendors require deposits or payment upon completion, this can cause a strain on the agency side as salaries and other overhead still need to get paid. (Not every agency is a huge multinational with deep pockets; most of us don't have spare millions lying around.) Scarier still is the often-unspoken reality that if the client suddenly runs into a wall (no company is safe—think Bear Stearns and Lehman Brothers), the last bills that are getting paid are the ones for marketing.

Every agency must be prepared for clients to delay payment or for the mail to take its time. That means establishing lines of credit at their bank and tapping into them as needed until the money shows up. And whenever possible, make sure you have all the paperwork you need filled out in advance. Get a signed contract or, if work needs to start before the contract is signed, get a signed letter of intention summarizing the account, fees, and payment schedule while the contract is being drafted. Get a purchase order and ask for a contact in the client's AP department so your own accounting department has a direct line of communications.

All that being said, there will still be situations where a client is just disgustingly overdue on their bills—but still expect the work to continue. Obviously, this can cause friction, and there comes a point when something must be said. But unless it's absolutely necessary, the agency exec who is the client's main point of contact (not on a day-to-day basis, but on an overall account basis) should *not* be the one to confront the client about payment issues. It'll make for an uncomfortable relationship later on, after the bills have been paid. Instead, have somebody else on the agency side be the bad guy; let the exec in charge of the account feign ignorance on the subject so he or she can maintain a strong relationship.

The following chain of communication is usually the best way to go about trying to secure payment:

Agency AR dept. or bookkeeper ⇢ Client AP dept. or bookkeeper

Try this route at least three times. If nothing comes of it, then try the following:

Agency AR dept. or bookkeeper ⇢ Main client contact

Try this route until it's clear that that's going nowhere. Then try this:

Other high-ranking agency exec (president or CFO) ⇢ Main client contact

Try this route until it's clear that that's also going nowhere. Then try this:

Main agency contact ⇢ Main client contact

If all of these options fail, the agency has to make the tough decision to pull the plug. It's the last resort, and nobody ever wants to do it, but if a client is pushing 120 days on a net 30 contract, it's better to cut your losses and concentrate on recouping what you're owed than to let the client accumulate more debt that they may not pay.

MICHAEL HAND
THE CLIENT PERSPECTIVE

↳ Nothing frustrates me more than the calls from an agency partner communicating that they have not been paid; if they are calling me on this subject, it means they are not focused (at that moment) on doing great work. Besides, I try not to deal with the payment process and purchasing issues. Being a member of a larger organization, I let my disbursements group and procurement team handle these issues—that's one benefit of having larger head counts at the corporate office. If, however, these groups cannot resolve an issue, I will get involved.

That said, here are a few examples of when not to call the client for help with bills, spoken from personal experience:

- If the payment terms clearly state that my company pays in net 45 days from the day the bill is submitted, do not call me on day 33 looking for cash. You know the deal—or you should—so don't waste my time. You should realize that smart companies wait as long as they can to make payments to keep the cash in their own account for as long as possible.

- If a program ended more than a year ago, I beg of you, do not send me a bill. You cannot wait until it is convenient to catch up on your invoicing and send a bill to the client. After a certain period, many clients will either close the purchase order or shift remaining funds into another project—meaning the money budgeted for you is gone. Stay on top of your invoices to avoid surprises.

- *Never* send me a bill for something that benefited another client of your agency. I will pay my fair share of anything from which I receive a benefit, but sending me a bill to cover "training costs" on an area of the business we don't even conduct is taboo.

- When you decide to exceed the outlined expenditure limit on travel and hotel costs because you want to fly first class to Los Angeles and stay at Shutters on the Beach in Santa Monica, you should know my purchasing group is going to be pissed. Do us all a favor: Bill me at the cap limit and then eat the cost on your own dime.

I believe that you sign a scope of work at the onset of a program and you pay your bills when they are due. It's that simple. If my company is at fault, and we simply are delinquent in getting the payments made, I will work to get you paid—and quickly. But you need to be part of the solution from the start. Show clear documentation on the missing bills and provide wire-transfer data to help expedite the process.

Q: • IS A SINGLE SERIOUS MISTAKE
• THE END OF THE RELATIONSHIP?

JASON MILETSKY

THE AGENCY PERSPECTIVE

This is kind of an odd question for me to answer, because ultimately, it's not my decision. Whether a single mistake is serious enough to end a relationship is for the client to decide. My guess, though, is that it's not that cut and dry. Whether an agency/client relationship can withstand a serious error will depend on what the error was, how expensive it was, whether it did any lasting damage to the brand, the history of the relationship, the agency's prior record, and whether the agency accepted responsibility for the mistake and did anything to fix it.

One thing I can say, though—and I think this is true of any relationship, whether it's between two people on a personal level, between a client and an agency, or between a brand and its consumers—is that one bad mistake will be more glaring and memorable than a hundred successes. It may not be fair, but it's the truth. It's also true that we all make mistakes, and I believe that everyone understands that. But at the end of the day, the logical reaction that mistakes are bound to happen won't trump the emotional reaction everyone experiences when they do.

More unforgivable than a single mistake is when a pattern develops. A single mistake can probably be explained away, but it's unlikely that any client will stand for a number of mistakes being made on a regular basis. Do they always catch grammatical errors when you send them proofs? Have you sent the wrong file once too often? Are you consistently a day or two behind on every deadline and always coming up with new excuses why? These kind of ongoing behaviors will ultimately kill a relationship (sorry agency execs—there're only so many times you can blame the project manager).

In my time as CEO of PFS Marketwyse, I remember only one instance where we made a *really* bad mistake. We had submitted an ad to a publication for a client that we had worked with for about a decade. Pretty standard fare—submitting ads for this particular client had gotten to be as common as a morning shower. So when that issue of the mag arrived at our office the next month,

I didn't bother looking at it—until the account manager walked nervously into my office, handed me the publication, and said, "We fucked up. Look at the phone number." My heart sank. We had gotten the client's phone number wrong by one digit. I immediately took the magazine over to the project manager, put it on her desk, and asked, "See anything wrong with this ad?" She looked carefully, and then, with her eyes bulging out, said, "Oh *shit*! We screwed up their e-mail address!"

This was one ad in about two dozen, and in one publication that was pretty inconsequential. It was actually pretty unlikely that the client would even notice the mistake. But was it worth the risk to keep quiet about it? If they found it on their own, life would be a lot worse. So after a morning of nervous pacing, I made a very ugly phone call to the client, followed by two separate trips to their offices in Minneapolis, where they basically beat the crap out of me during a couple of all-day meetings. But we retained the account (after paying for the ad placement)—partially because we owned up to our mistake and had no history or pattern of errors.

Mistakes are going to happen, and it is ultimately up to the client to decide whether to see past a problem and maintain the relationship. But there are steps the agency can take to soften the blow, and they start with owning up to what you did wrong.

MICHAEL HAND
THE CLIENT PERSPECTIVE

Part of being human is making the occasional mistake. It's simply a part of life. How somebody reacts after that mistake is made is what really counts.

A major error that has legal implications or creates a negative impact on the financial situation of a company could warrant a firing—especially if the agency partner is reluctant to accept blame or makes excuses for the mishap. If the root cause of the mistake was an intentional disregard of the provided direction, the agency is done. It really comes down to a question of ethics: A client needs to believe that the agency always has the client's best interest at heart. But if the client believes the error was a one-time thing, they may well stay committed to the relationship. If the error was a minor one, clients should remember that little mistakes are a normal part of business; the key there is to make sure people don't make the same mistakes repeatedly.

Although the statement does not always hold true, I do believe that everybody should be given a second chance to learn from their mistakes. The client and agency should work together to turn the mistake into a lesson, using it as a way to identify and educate the broader organization as to what they need to do differently. The value of learning and moving forward should outweigh the fear to admit fault.

To increase the chances of turning mistakes into future successes, be sure everybody in your organization is operating under the same set of principles:

- **Be constructive in your work attitude.** Turn negative voices into constructive ones by coaching through problems. Many errors happen when team members are trying to do too much too fast and fear getting negative feedback.

- **Don't be overconfident:** When folks get cocky, they tend to overlook the obvious or start cutting corners. Strive for a sound balance of self-confidence and realistic expectations to maintain forward momentum.

- **The bigger the mistake, the more important the lesson:** It can be extremely difficult to look at errors as learning tools, but you need to. As painful as it is to examine a tough situation closely, you need to really get below the surface to find out what the lesson is.

- **Put the lessons learned immediately to work:** Implement the teaching and make the findings very public. People will respect the new approach and, more importantly, they will be more aware of previous missteps—which they will know to avoid.

While I was at the Miller Brewing Company, our CEO, a South African named Norman Adami, was someone people believed in and rallied around. In addition to having a tremendous presence whenever he entered a room, Norman had the uncanny ability to remember everything anyone ever said to him. I mention Norman because he frequently used a great phrase: "Fail forward." Norman felt it was okay to make mistakes (he didn't like them, but he understood them); the fact that you were taking big swings, trying to stimulate change, was what mattered. If you failed in the process, at least you were in a better place than when you started. This is a great motto—one I encourage clients and their agency partners to embrace.

Q: • Is Any Relationship • Ever *Really* Secure?

JASON MILETSKY

THE AGENCY PERSPECTIVE

One of the most interesting things I've learned while writing this book is that there is a difference between an *immediate* reaction to a question and the *right* answer to a question. My immediate answer to this question was to say that no relationship is secure—that an agency must constantly prove itself to maintain its clients. But while I do think that's the truth most of the time, it isn't in every case. There are some relationships an agency can rely on.

Quick note for anybody who takes life very literally: I'm assuming here that the agency is fulfilling their minimal contractual obligations, and not making errors of epic proportions.

My agency has a client that would *love* to get rid of us. We've held onto the account for seven years—and they've been itching to fire us for five. Not because we've done anything wrong, but because the CMO wants to work with one of the large Madison Avenue agencies in New York. He believes his brand is a premier brand that deserves the attention of one of the major players. Even though my agency is a good size with national (and global) clients, our New Jersey address just doesn't hold as much caché as an agency in New York. Fair enough—we all know the 'burbs aren't as glamorous as the city. But we're also not nearly as expensive—and the fact of the matter is, they don't have anywhere *near* the kind of budget they'd need to get a New York shop to take on their account. They couldn't even leave us for another New Jersey agency; and any agency our size or larger is going to charge them more than we do. (We've given them preferential pricing for years.) Making a lateral move would mean paying more per hour—not to mention going dark for at least six months while their new agency gets up to speed. Besides, nobody knows their industry as well or has the PR connections that we do. So every year we go through this silly charade where the marketing director calls us to tell us that the CMO wants him to find a bigger agency, and that we may not have their account much longer. We feign concern, take them all to lunch so we can bullshit about vacation spots and assure them that we have all the resources they need, and move on happily until the game gets played again a year later. We know the situation, and until we decide we no longer want to work with them, this is a secure relationship.

Client complexity plays a big part in relationship security. That is, the more difficult the client or the industry is to understand, the tougher it will be for the client to end the relationship. Investment in an agency isn't measured only in money; it's measured in time. Ending a relationship requires time to interview and find a new agency, and even more considerable time to train that new agency. The steeper the learning curve, the more time that training them will take—and time is a luxury most brands can't afford. Once an agency fully gets them and their industry, clients will have as much—if not more—interest in maintaining a strong relationship as the agency does.

For every other situation—i.e., less complex clients with larger budgets—there is *no* security in relationships. Agencies need to be on constant alert to maintain strong customer service and keep strategies and creative fresh. (On this note, check out my answer to Question #23, "When Does Complacency Set In?") One of the most dangerous traps an agency can fall into is being lulled into a false sense of security by a long-standing relationship and confusing history for security. Ask your client straight out how they feel about everything at regular intervals. Are they happy with the project manager you've assigned to their account? Are they satisfied with the day-to-day communications they're getting? Never assume that because they were happy last year, they're happy this year. Markets change—as do internal politics, bonus structures, and stock prices. Any one of these changes can have a profound effect on the client/agency relationship.

MICHAEL HAND
THE CLIENT PERSPECTIVE

⤶ I wish I could tell you that all agency-client relationships are secure—that it takes a major shift in the world to make things change—but that is truly not the case. The relationship really never is 100-percent locked down; there are just too many moving parts.

Here are a few major relationship enders:

- **New leadership, on the part of either the agency or the client:** When an organization experiences employee turnover at high levels, it's highly likely that organization will begin moving in a different direction. New leaders like to reevaluate things, and the best time to begin that process is the minute they start.

- **A client outgrows an agency partner (or vice versa):** All it really takes is one major success in the marketplace for a client to find a new niche or a breakthrough product line. When this happens, the small guy—the agency that helped the client get where it is—no longer feels like the right fit sometimes. When clients get bigger, they believe they can stretch into uncharted waters. Or the reverse can also happen: An agency can outgrow a client. Most agencies build their roster one client and category at a time. After mounting a few wins and building a strong reputation for business success, those first few clients might not be as attractive anymore. It may be time for the agency to consider a move to a bigger player in your category, using the same team that uncovered the marketplace insights to date. This is not an entirely ethical maneuver, but remember, they call the big stage "show business," not "show friends" for a reason.

- **Understaffing:** This can be an issue if a client outpaces the growth model projected by the agency. Clients don't just want bodies; they want qualified people to join their support team, and timing may not always allow for the gradual build. Agencies need to have bodies in place (clear succession planning) *before* expansion announcements are made.

- **The ongoing need for strong return on investment (ROI) models:** Regardless of length of service and performance, the corporate world is driven by ROI. In many cases, companies are faced with the mandate to consolidate agency rosters to save money and improve efficiency. For the agency, this often means re-pitching the business you have helped put on the map for years. Emotionally, this can wear on any team, but incumbent agencies need to realize that it's not personal; it's business.

- **Shift in creative direction:** These shifts can spell doom for some relationships. If, for example, a company decides to shift a high percentage of media funding from television to the Internet because they are seeing online sales growth that outpaces their brick-and-mortar counterparts, the current roster might need to re-shuffle. Also at issue is the creative arrogance that many creative teams develop over time. Even with two high-scoring ads in rotation and a third on the way, clients don't produce spots to simply build somebody's reel. Don't get cocky and start forcing a creative agenda with a brand that has a list of potential partners in their top desk drawer.

- **Change in agency personnel:** Agency teams often make changes, shifting talent to other business when they think an account is secure and moving in the right direction. For example, they may reassign a strategic planner who was instrumental in developing your approach to a new account. Suddenly, your strategy and creative points don't line up on the business. A great planner can make or break an account, but when the linkage from pen to paper is broken, it leads to early issues.

In 1984, the average tenure of an ad agency with a client was 7.2 years. Over the following 13 years, that time span was reduced to 5.3 years—and the number continues to fall (source: American Association of Advertising Agencies, 1997 Survey of Client-Agency Tenure). When asking yourself if the relationship is secure, the correct answer is to say no or never. Remember one very important piece of advice: Successful relationships do not sustain themselves.

Q: HOW IMPORTANT IS IT FOR THE CLIENT TO VERBALLY EXPRESS APPRECIATION FOR QUALITY WORK?

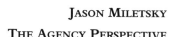

JASON MILETSKY
THE AGENCY PERSPECTIVE

Very! Money can buy you a lot of things, but as the Beatles said, it can't buy you love. Agencies need to hear it when we do a good job. Believe it or not, that's what really motivates us to do a great job on each and every project we work on for a client. We're kind of like puppies: We need that pat on the head now and then to let us know that all of our hard work has real value.

At my agency, we keep a "brag book"—a three-ring binder that we fill with e-mails we get from clients that thank us for doing a great job or that let us know how happy they are with our work. The funny thing is, we never even show the book to prospects as a sales tool. When we add a new entry to it, we pass it around to the project managers, writers, art directors, designers, bookkeepers— everyone internally who had a hand in making the client happy—so that they feel appreciated.

One client of ours has been known to arrange pizza parties at our offices as a way to thank the team for jobs well done. Another likes to call each team member personally to say "Great job." It's a good feeling for everybody! And although it's never a conscious decision, when I think about it, *those* are the clients we all work a little harder for—and they're the ones I'm more likely quote lower prices to when new service needs come up.

Our work as an agency gets better or worse based on our individual mental health and general enthusiasm level. And believe it or not, more money and more relaxed deadlines can't buy the same energy and motivation as a simple "Great job, guys!"

MICHAEL HAND

THE CLIENT PERSPECTIVE

A little thank you goes a very long way in my book. I am a big believer in showing appreciation for work that is done. The days of the intimate hand-written note have passed us by, but finding a way to show gratitude must live on. E-mails and voicemails are not as intimate, but "thank yous" are a very important task for all clients to master. It makes a world of difference when you need your partner to stay late and hit a deadline on your behalf.

Thank-you notes should not just be sent after the agency hits a deliverable. Tickets to a local game or a simple team happy hour at the nearby bar can be a great rapport-builder between partners. It is human nature to desire recognition and to seek approval from your peers. After countless hours on the job, people simply want to feel appreciated. The important thing is that the thank you must be genuine. It is also okay for the thank you to be private (as opposed to public) if the situation warrants it; you need to read each situation individually and act accordingly.

This is not just about client-to-agency thank yous—it works both ways. Agency management should not be afraid to reach out and say a few kind words to the client about the leadership and support they receive on occasion. Both groups are in this together. Not all clients are slave traders who crack the whip 24 hours a day. Clients go to bat for their partners more than most people realize. They fight for the creative integrity of programs, push for better clarity on work assignments, and insist on longer lead times for production. As a client, I can tell you that hearing somebody convey some thanks is a pleasant change of pace.

There is a famous Ralph Waldo Emerson quote: "The only way to have a friend is to be one." If you really want to be appreciated (regardless of which side of the business model you work on), show some appreciation to those around you—I call this the "reciprocation factor." Mutual admiration helps the health of any relationship.

Q: • Is the Agency a Partner or a Vendor?
• Is There a Difference?

JASON MILETSKY
THE AGENCY PERSPECTIVE

This is one of those questions that isn't up to me to decide. It's completely up to the client to determine how they see us, how they treat us, and how they want us to interact with them. What I *can* tell you is that clients who try to commoditize their agency's work and assume that we're all very easily replaceable are not only missing the point of having an agency, but I guarantee they're not getting anywhere near the kind of results or service that they could be getting.

Unlike a car manufacturer, which cranks out hundreds of the same cars every day, each identical to the next—every single agency is unique. Each one is different from every other agency in its own way. There may be more than one agency—hell, there may be hundreds or thousands—that can do a great job with any given client, but none of those agencies will do exactly the *same* job.

Clients hire us for our expertise, insight, and creativity, and because they believe they're going to enjoy working with us—that together we'll form a good partnership. And that's how they should treat us, as a partner, which means respecting our opinions and getting us involved in key campaign-related decisions. It means working through problems so that when we hit a speed bump, we can get back on track.

But while most clients hire an agency with the intention of forming a partnership, many don't see it through. Instead of working with us, they make it clear through words and deeds that we work for them—and we can be replaced at any time. Not very motivating. At that point, the client ceases to be a brand we care about and becomes just another invoice. I don't think any client—or agency, for that matter—will benefit in the long run from this kind of relationship.

MICHAEL HAND

THE CLIENT PERSPECTIVE

Before I discuss whether or not the agency is a vendor or a partner, I want to answer the second part of this question first. There is a *huge* difference between a partner and a vendor, and it is very clear which side of the equation an agency will want to find itself.

Vendors—which are very important to any corporate structure—are the folks who supply goods and/or services that the business needs to survive. Put another way, vendors sell you stuff and keep things running without interruption. With vendors, the job scope is usually clear-cut at the onset, and tasks are well-defined. Vendors show up when they are asked and do everything from deliver the bottled water to drop off the office paper for the printers and service the photo copiers and fax machines. The fact is, though, that vendors tend to be more like order takers than anything else, and most of these relationships have little impact on the strategic thinking process within a client's business. Do vendors have an important function? Absolutely. They are *very* important to the daily operations of corporate America. Without a strong vendor base, much of what we expect from the biggest companies in the world would not be possible. So I don't want to trivialize the role or diminish the value of the vendor. If you have ever been on the receiving end of a Vendor of the Year award, you can and should feel proud. But to be very clear, as an agency, you want to achieve partner status whenever possible.

Partners are in a much more desirable position than vendors. Partners need to feel an emotional connection with—really, a passion for—the relationship. When you are in a partnership scenario, you feed off of each other's success and share the pain of each other's setbacks. In more practical terms, partnerships have more balance with respect to risk and reward. Clients who think of an agency as a partner work harder to make sure that the business model is fair and provides economic stability to the agency. In return, they expect the agency to live and breathe their brands and provide that extra push come deadline time, never compromising on the quality of the deliverable.

Partners are critical to the long-term success of a company. Most large companies look at their primary advertising firm as a partner, but agencies in promotions, public relations, and interactive often fight an uphill battle to shake the "V word."

I strongly disagree with this philosophy. In many cases, these groups are actually *more* strategic in setting the path to consumer communication than the media group—likely the biggest line item on your budget. In this world of fragmented media viewership, engaging consumers is more difficult than ever; it can happen on the Web, at the point of purchase, or while opening up the day's mail. Partners are part of the "team" and that does not apply to only the advertising part of the house.

Partnerships are never easy; they take effort from both sides. They don't form immediately, and they can be a roller-coaster ride at times. But true partnerships withstand these trials and tribulations, and help provide longer-term viability for all involved.

Q: CAN ALL MEETINGS HAPPEN OVER THE PHONE? HOW IMPORTANT ARE FACE-TO-FACE MEETINGS?

JASON MILETSKY

THE AGENCY PERSPECTIVE

With e-mail, cell phones, FTP servers, and affordable overnight delivery, agencies and clients can work together regardless of their geographical location. Although my agency is located in New Jersey, we have clients in Minneapolis, Chicago, and as far west as California. In fact, I've long believed that savvy west-coast companies would be wise to hire east-coast agencies because of the time difference; by the time they get to their desks at 9:00 a.m., we've already been working for three hours. And since agency work never stops at 5:00 p.m., we'll probably keep going until they're almost ready to call it quits for the day—meaning they get our attention for a lot longer than they would from an agency in their own time zone. (That may sound convoluted, but trust me: In my mind, it makes sense.)

But while accounts can be serviced virtually, there's no question that face-to-face meetings are an absolute necessity. As I mentioned elsewhere, a general theme throughout my part of this book is that agencies don't sell creative and strategy as much as they sell service and relationships.

This isn't a mail-order–type business. Agencies need to shake hands, have dinners, and talk with their clients face to face about their needs, concerns, and vision. In-person meetings are the best way for agencies to show that they care about the brand they're marketing and respect the clients they're working for, and to map out everything that needs to get done. It's the only way to really forge a friendship with a client—to get to understand what they really want and will respond to.

From a more self-serving perspective, in-person meetings are also the best way to up-sell and stay in the clients mind so that they're less tempted to look elsewhere (don't forget—your client is constantly being approached by other agencies that want to steal away their business). There's something about looking someone in the eye that creates a more powerful connection than just hearing a voice on a phone or reading an e-mail could ever do.

Although it can't serve as a total replacement for in-person meetings, video-conferencing can be an effective way to have face-to-face meetings without having to travel too often. Today, all you need is a camera installed on your computer and a free instant-messaging program like AIM or Yahoo!, and you're off and running. I've actually found that for clients that are expensive to travel to (in-person meetings are on the agency's dime, by the way—billing them back to the client is a sure way to make them think that working with a more local agency would be a better idea), it's more cost-effective for us to buy them an inexpensive laptop with a camera built into the monitor and pre-install the necessary software for them so that we can have video-based meetings more often. It keeps you in touch, keeps things visual, and while I still believe it doesn't replace in-person meetings, it can help extend the amount of time between them.

MICHAEL HAND

THE CLIENT PERSPECTIVE

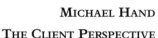

One of the biggest problems in corporate America is the fact that nobody meets face-to-face anymore. Instead, any time something goes wrong, we pick up the phone or, worse, draft an e-mail. Even after spending hours scrutinizing an agency—looking at its history, probing for hints on how everyone will interact, and poring through financials—in order to decide whether to hire them, it's all too easy to revert to a weekly phone conversation once the team is in place to check on the high-level status of various projects and discuss superficial issues. But in doing so, we lose the personal connection that keeps the relationship alive.

Let's face it: Conference calls can be a complete bust. Too many times, things go wrong:

- An employee calls from his or her car or the airport, resulting in non-stop static.

- Phantom beep-ins occur, seemingly signaling that somebody has joined the call, but nobody responds when you greet the new arrival.

- Someone calls in from home, subjecting all other participants to the crying baby or barking dog in the background.

- Everybody talks over everybody else, leaving you unsure as to whether anybody actually heard a word you said.

- Someone decides to multi-task for the entire call, meaning that all you hear from that extension is his or her computer keyboard clicking away.

- Some group calls in but accidentally stays on mute the whole time—meaning that although they have replied to every question throughout the conversation, nobody heard a word.

My biggest problem with conference calls, though, is that no one can see the facial expressions of the other participants. They don't know whether they are smiling at all the right times or shaking their heads in disgust. (And this, if I may digress, is why being able to read a room is becoming a lost art, and why eye contact is becoming extinct.)

That said, conference calls are not all negative. They're great for saving money and getting people together for spontaneous follow-ups, allowing you to reduce travel budgets and to meet more frequently. They simply must be done in a constructive fashion.

CONDUCTING AN EFFECTIVE CONFERENCE CALL

Here are some tips to ensure you have an effective meeting when you have no choice but to use the phone. (These are inspired by an article by Steve Kay, found on www.zeromillion.com.)

Keep things simple: Ideally, the meeting should run for no longer than 30 minutes. Go longer, and you'll find that people are unable to concentrate. Their attention will drift; they'll become distracted. Design your meeting to be short and to the point.

Establish a clear goal for the meeting: After you determine whether this goal truly represents the result you want to achieve, you must decide if a conference call is the best way to attain that goal. If the goal can be met using any other approach—say, sending a note, making a single phone call, or thinking through a solution by yourself—cancel the meeting.

Coordinate an agenda: A conference call without an agenda is like a journey without a map. Your agenda should include the desired outcome for the meeting and detailed information about the subject of each part of the meeting. It should also identify leaders/subject-matter experts to lead each portion. Agendas should be complete and specific so that someone else could use it to run your meeting if you were unable to attend.

Distribute the agenda at least a day before the meeting: This allows everyone to think about the issues and prepare for their role in the call. If appropriate, call key participants to confirm that they received the agenda and to check whether they have comments on how the meeting could be made more effective. Do not use this as an opportunity to work out an issue or argue with anybody; just confirm they received the agenda.

Distribute any materials related to the issues before the meeting: This includes PowerPoint slides, worksheets, and budget plans. The participants can use these tools to participate more effectively and focus the conversation. This will also help guide the call when you lack visual contact.

Invite only those who can directly contribute to the meeting: Ideally, conference calls should involve fewer than five people. Inviting more makes it very difficult to hold an effective meeting. With a larger group, some attendees try to dominate the conversation, which can derail the call. Others will become silent listeners, which is a waste of their time as well.

Q: WHEN DOES COMPLACENCY SET IN?

JASON MILETSKY

THE AGENCY PERSPECTIVE

I think it's interesting how this question was written. By asking "When *does*" complacency set in?" it assumes that it's a foregone conclusion that at some point the agency will, in fact, become complacent. It's true—the agency will always be at full attention, ready to go the extra mile, when they're pitching a new account—and they'll bring that same energy with them after the contract is signed and the work begins. But eventually, after a few successful projects and a couple of laugh-filled dinners with the client, the agency will start to relax, to not worry so much about deadlines (we can always buy a day someplace, right?), to cut a few corners, to place less importance on quickly returning the client's calls. We've gotten used to the regular monthly income, and we know what the client is going to respond to, so we don't have to work so hard. In other words, we become complacent.

Complacency can be a creativity killer—which can lead to the end of an account. Fortunately, complacency sets in slowly, and it comes with little warning signs that something bad is coming. It's kind of like the ridged patch of pavement on the side of the highway—the part that makes your car rattle if you fall asleep at the wheel and start to veer off. It wakes you up, snaps you back to full attention, and before you know it you're back on the road instead of wrapped around some tree. Of course, if you've ever been in that situation, you know that the part where you're at full alert doesn't last very long; before you know it, the smooth asphalt and familiar, rhythmic motion of the drive lull you back into a state of semi-consciousness. Once again you find your eyes closing—only to be woken up again moments later by the abrupt rumble of ridged road on the shoulder.

Complacency in the agency world works the same way. It's rare to go directly from brilliant creative strategist to useless idiot in one quick shot. Usually there are warning signs: sighs from the artists when the next project starts, indicating that they're growing bored with this particular account (artists like to have new creative challenges); an increase in typos and other errors before work makes it to the proofreader; and, of course, missed deadlines. Account execs need to be on the lookout for these and similar warning signs, and stop them before they escalate into something worse: mistakes that become visible or annoying to the client.

Sometimes it takes bringing the team together for a pep talk (or to read them the riot act, depending on what kind of boss or manager you are), or maybe even changing some team members just to get some new blood and fresh ideas flowing through the account. Personally, I've found that it works best to keep the energy level among the team as high as possible by celebrating wins and successful projects and by making sure they always have something creative to work on—even if it's fake. For example, if I know our creative team is starting to get stale and complacent with a certain account, I might throw them a curve ball and challenge them with a new creative project for that client that's radically different from what they usually work on—even if I have to make it up and the client will never see it. The excess hours they'll spend working (don't worry— these are non-billable hours!) will be worth it to keep their interest level high.

Complacency will undoubtedly settle in with any long-standing account, but it doesn't have to mean the end of the road. In fact, there is a positive aspect in the sense that when the comfort level rises, the agency will be better able to relate to the client in a relaxed fashion. As things get more friendly, though, it's critical that you watch for warning signs that the complacency has reached a more serious level, putting the account in jeopardy.

MICHAEL HAND

THE CLIENT PERSPECTIVE

You know that list of words that you aren't allowed to say on network TV, and that aren't allowed through your company's firewall if they appear in an e-mail message? Complacency should be put on that list of words. It's one of the biggest— if not *the* biggest—evils in an agency-partner relationship. It should never set in.

Think of this answer as a continuation of the one to Question #19, "Is Any Relationship Ever *Really* Secure?" These days, the business environment is ultra-competitive; anybody who gets too comfortable will lose in the marketplace. When complacency sets in, agencies stop producing their best work and clients start to lose market share. The agency model demands that you stay at the peak of your game all the time. You must constantly reinvent yourself and look for ways to create stronger consumer connections. Agencies should seek to add broader services to draw clients looking for a one-stop shop, and must do better creative work every time out of the box. For good or for bad, we have exposure to more data and research figures than ever before. Expectations are always going to exceed the previous deliverable. Given all that, how can you get complacent?

Clients must realize that just because they know their agency well and the members of their team have become like family doesn't mean the business world around them stops. There's simply no room for complacency on either side of the relationship. Besides, enjoying each other's company shouldn't diminish your ability to beat the crap out of your competitor.

One reason I enjoy working for companies that are positioned as #2 in the market is that complacency is simply not an option. When you are #1, even though there is always room to "increase your lead," the only direction you can truly go in the marketplace is down. When you are not the leader in a category, you can never relax. Your entire job revolves around playing catch-up. It consumes you. Resting is not an option, and neither is settling.

During my days at the Miller Brewing Company, we took pride in our brands and products—but we never felt good about being Robin to Anheuser-Busch's Batman. In response to this frustration, we adopted an "able challenger" mindset, inspired by the book *Eating the Big Fish* by Adam Morgan. For us, the approach was defined by the following principles:

- Fight it out for market share (survival)
- Focus on the short-term (immediate horizon)
- Fight for a just and noble cause with conviction
- Believe in yourself
- See your opponent's strengths as potential weaknesses
- Drive actions with a prejudice for speed and pragmatism

If you want to read some compelling case studies, I suggest you check out Morgan's book. His approach is designed to enable readers to redefine the game of business on their own terms—with an approach that emphasizes long-term focus.

Let's face it: This model does not work in all business genres and cultures, but that does not mean that you have to be complacent. You can avoid complacency by focusing on what can be improved. I am not suggesting that you become a "glass is half empty" guy—nobody will want to hang around with you and you'll be a big bore at cocktail parties. I'm simply saying it's okay to identify your areas for improvement and to work to get better. The phrase "Standing still is falling behind" comes to mind.

When CJ Fraleigh, current executive vice president and CEO of North American Retail and Foodservice at Sara Lee, became the general manager of Buick-Pontiac-GMC at General Motors, he pulled out a business-school tactic on our team and asked all of the division's employees to complete a simple homework assignment: creating a traditional S.W.O.T. chart. (For those who were not blessed with a Harvard MBA—myself included—and are still seeking the secret decoder ring for business acronyms, he wanted them to identify what they saw as our divisional strengths, weaknesses, opportunities, and threats.) I cannot speak to his exact motivation for issuing the assignment, but it has become something I ask my agency partners and staff to complete whenever I get to a new location. And while I am certainly curious to see how the strengths are viewed, my focus is really on the opportunities. If people identify an opportunity, it means they believe they can make it happen; when they call something a weakness, however, it means they have partially conceded that fight. The best companies and teams don't have weaknesses; they have a longer list of opportunities.

Whether he meant to or not, by insisting that his employees perform this exercise, CJ created a sense of ownership within the group. That simple chart enabled employees to self-identify the concerns and stimulated them to want to solve it. Similarly, you must make your employees part of the solution. These small steps will set you on the road to slow and steady improvement, which should be your goal. Don't get complacent; get better every day.

Q: DOES A NEW MARKETING DIRECTOR OR CMO ON THE CLIENT SIDE MEAN THE END OF THE RELATIONSHIP?

JASON MILETSKY

THE AGENCY PERSPECTIVE

Not always, but here's the deal: If the new guy coming in has his own agency that he's loyal to and wants to work with, it's pretty much a lost cause. You can try to be friendly with him, shower him with service, the whole nine yards, but if you understand branding at all, then you understand the power of loyalty—and know that no matter what you do, you're not going to change his mind.

The good news is, the change won't be immediate. There are always politics involved, and the new guy usually can't just come into his office on day one with a carving knife and start severing ties. That means you'll have a stay of execution, enabling you to squeak in a few more months of billing while you try to sign up another client to replace the revenue you'll soon be losing.

The way it typically works is that the new guy will want to meet you and the agency—maybe even go on a facility check and see what you're all about. Then he'll express some concerns he has with some of the creative you've done in the past and drop some hints that he'll be looking to change how the company markets itself. Then he'll place you under intense scrutiny so that when the time comes, any typo can be used to make a case against you. At the same time, he'll pass a small project on to another agency—the agency he really wants to work with. It'll be just enough work to get them some visibility at the company and onto the vendor list, but not enough to cause any waves. From there, it's usually a pretty quick descent into a sudden agency review—which you're guaranteed to lose. It is what it is, and there ain't nothin' you can do about it.

Now, that isn't always the scenario. Sometimes, a new marketing director or CMO comes in without having any prior allegiance to another agency. Great! You're not dead in the water! But you're not in the clear, either—and you definitely have an uphill battle to fight if you want to keep the business. In this case, the hurdle you'll be facing is that no matter how great your work is, the new guy is going to want his fingerprints on things. He's starting a new job to spearhead the marketing efforts. He's excited. He wants to make a name for himself, and who can blame him? Marketing is a passionate, creative, strategic challenge—it's a larger-than-life game of chess with a million moving pieces and clear opportunities to win.

Making his mark and bringing new creative strategies to the company often starts with bringing in a new agency that will reflect his own methods rather than the sensibilities of his predecessor—which is why it'll be an uphill battle to keep the account. But it's absolutely doable. It should go without saying that you'll have to ratchet up customer service a notch or two. The real trick, though, is to show flexibility—that you can adjust your thinking to align with his. Be an advocate for him and his new vision. If you can pull it off believably, hint that you're actually glad to have someone new on the scene since you had your doubts about the last CMO or marketing director. Show humility; let the new guy call the shots for awhile without contradicting him. His first few months on his new job is not the time to show off that you know more than he does. Marketing people (on the agency side as well) can have canyon-sized egos, and showing that you know more about the brand than they do (even if you do) is a sure-fire way to get the boot.

In either case, it's important to make as many connections at the client company as you can. Get to know their whole team and show respect for everyone's ideas. If the team likes you and your work, then you'll have some powerful advocates when it comes time for the new CMO or marketing director to make a decision about whether they should maintain your relationship or go elsewhere. If you've made deep inroads into the company, you may lose the main account, but you could still end up with departmental project work.

On the flip side, the best way to get new business is when an existing client's CMO or marketing director leaves his position and takes on a similar or higher role at another company. If he likes your work and believes in your agency, he's undoubtedly going to bring you along for the ride. Play your cards right, and you could end up keeping the original account *and* signing on a brand new one.

MICHAEL HAND
THE CLIENT PERSPECTIVE

⌐ Getting right to the point: It may not mean the end, but it does mean things are going to change. We've already discussed what constitutes senior-level involvement and have recognized the important role these leaders play in the agency-client relationship. As mentioned, the impact they have over the organization's DNA is more critical than anything they do on a day-to-day basis.

In some cases, the outgoing director or marketing chief may have alienated the masses with a particular creative direction or campaign; his or her departure may be deemed a good thing—meaning the support for the current agency team may leave with the individual. That's not to say this is the fault of the agency partner—they were likely following creative direction—but people in the corner offices remember only the most current work and recent sales results in market. So if the marketing director or CMO on the client side leaves and no love is lost, then the agency is likely not far behind.

Most of the time, when a new marketing director or CMO takes over, he or she will make it a priority to assess the current setup and direction. If he or she determines that this setup and direction are working and the existing relationships are strong, then nothing major will change. Just be sure to expect some new personal-level nuances in the daily style of doing business. These may present themselves as a new system for tracking progress on group projects or a renewed commitment to conducting constructive staff meetings. But if the incoming marketing director or CMO determines that business has *not* been booming, you can expect him or her to look toward the future and strongly consider making an immediate and sudden change.

Every agency needs to understand that they need to establish strong relationships. This is a relationship business. The agency must win support from all the corners of the client's office. It goes a long way when the procurement team says good things about how you handle billing and account reconciliation. It gets noticed when multiple brand teams ask for your agency to brainstorm on new ideas because of your strong collaborative style. And it doesn't hurt when the receptionist behind the front desk smiles from ear to ear when the agency team comes to the office for meetings. These things get noticed, and go a long way toward making the agency a mainstay regardless of leaders put in place.

Q: Is It Okay for Clients and Agency Partners to Be Friends Outside the Office? Or Does This Strain the Professional Relationship?

Jason Miletsky

The Agency Perspective

It's absolutely okay—but I don't think either the friendship or the professional relationship can be taken for granted, and you can't count on one just because you have the other. But let's break things down before we get into the mechanics of this balancing act. There are two ways that people can end up having both a friendship and a working relationship simultaneously, each with its own set of challenges.

Situation One: The Friendship Exists First

Classic story: Two old college buddies stay in touch after graduation. One finds himself in a marketing position with a large brand, the other is an account exec with an agency, and they end up working together. In this situation, it's important for there to be a clear separation of church and state.

I've known my co-author, Mike, since sixth grade. After college, we stayed in touch on and off, mostly touching base now and then to see what the other was up to, and sometimes getting together if we were both in town. But even though he was in marketing on the client side and I owned an agency, our friendship never really crossed over to a professional relationship until Mike took a job at Hershey.

When Mike finally landed at Hershey, and there was an opportunity for my agency to come in and pitch some work, Mike and I expressly discussed how we would keep our friendship separate from our working relationship. He was bringing us to the table based on our friendship, but we had to win any work we got by proving ourselves to be a creative and competent agency—and he wouldn't be the only one on his team to make the decision. Along with that, we don't mix conversations. If we need to discuss business, then that's what we discuss—period. We don't chat about the wife and kids and old high-school days when the real intent of the conversation is to deal with work issues. Those conversations are left for when we see each other more socially.

By keeping work relationship separate from social relationship, you reduce the danger that either will be harmed. It also diminishes the potential that the client will try to leverage the friendship to get lower pricing or that the agency will atempt to use it to get work they don't really deserve. Most importantly (because work and money aren't everything), keeping a separation will help protect the friendship in the event that anything goes wrong with the business side of things.

SITUATION TWO: THE WORKING RELATIONSHIP EXISTS FIRST

Suppose the client and agency have a solid working relationship. There hasn't been any turnover on the executive level for either company. Whether it happens quickly or slowly, the marketing director on the client side and the account exec on the agency side just start forging a friendship. No problem. But unlike the first situation, it probably won't be a *true* friendship—one that will survive if work problems end up severing the account—because work, contracts, and money formed the foundation of the relationship in the first place.

Because this situation usually happens over time (as opposed to the first situation, where a conscious decision to work together has been made), it can be harder to police. The lines will undoubtedly get blurry. The important thing for the agency to remember is to never let your guard down. Friends or not, work will always be present, even if it's not the topic of conversation.

My suggestion: If you've become friends with a client, great—have fun. But never get drunk around them, don't debate topics like politics or religion, don't confess anything you wouldn't want any other clients to know, and never have self-implicating conversations that you might ordinarily have with other friends (like how your agency is short staffed or how incompetent the creative director is). It's never quite as easy to separate work from play in this situation as it is in the first one, so always stay alert and keep your agency in mind.

Of course, there is a third situation that I guess I can't overlook:

SITUATION THREE: FORGET BEING FRIENDS—LET'S SLEEP TOGETHER!

Marketing is all about creativity, and creativity is all about passion. It's not too hard to imagine being in a closed office with your client, who's looking pretty cute. You start chatting it up about the account, which leads to a spontaneous brainstorming meeting. The excitement builds as you close in on a great idea, and then BAM! The idea you've been struggling with for weeks hits you both at the same time—and the next thing you know you're outside sharing an awkward cigarette. (For clarification, while my counterpart in this book is also a client, he is not someone I would have had this experience with. If Michael's name were Michelle, though, it might be a different story.)

We're all adults here, so I'm not going to comment on this much more than to acknowledge it's out there. But I think everyone already knows: This situation should be avoided at all costs.

So, basically, the answer is yes—you can be friends with a client, but never forget that work is still work. And no matter what the situation, precautions need to be taken to protect your friendship and your account.

MICHAEL HAND

THE CLIENT PERSPECTIVE

Like it or not, your team at work—including those members on the agency side—is really your second family. You spend so much time together, you know who is allergic to peanuts and who always orders their steak well done. You know people's political views and find out intimate details about their personal lives. You should not go through your career avoiding this level of human contact; people spend a lot of their life in the office or attending work functions, and they should enjoy being with the folks around them. I am a firm believer in the friendship factor—you just need to make sure the relationship is one of integrity, and does not cloud your judgment when it comes to the business side of getting things done and driving successful results.

The key to making these friendships work is to separate the work side from the personal side whenever possible. I have friendships with some agency partners where, although we've never explicitly made this rule, e-mails and phone calls never mix the "What are you doing this weekend" questions with the "Here are the research results from last week's focus group" replies. It's clear what is business and it's obvious what is personal. Both conversations have their place—but that place is not with each other.

On the flip side, I once had (notice the use of past tense) a friend who developed unrealistic expectations with respect to how I could help him professionally. Specifically, my friend used our relationship as an entreé for a business pitch for his new agency. I knew my buddy did great work personally, and his agency made the short list for final consideration. On paper, they were a strong match. But after the next round of meetings, his team was eliminated from contention. The fact was, the team he had assembled for the pitch lacked the understanding of our industry and strategic horsepower to match my buddy's creative skills, and it showed in the face-to-face session. Unfortunately, my friend took it as a personal insult. He felt it compromised his position with his new associates because he was counting on winning the business to make a strong first impression. As a result, we are no longer friends, and that is really too bad.

This experience has not dissuaded me from being friends with my agency partners, however. For one thing, I think this human factor makes me a better client; being friends outside the office enables me to see a different side of things. Friendships like these bring an understanding of how people think and react—a positive thing both personally and professionally. The experience did, though, open my eyes to where the line between friendship and business should be drawn. Misunderstandings like this one can (and should) be avoided by being very clear up front about the fact that friendships can get you in the door—but they offer no promise of closing the business deal.

Q: • WHAT ROLE WILL THE CLIENT'S LEGAL • DEPARTMENT PLAY IN THE RELATIONSHIP?

JASON MILETSKY

THE AGENCY PERSPECTIVE

It's late in the game, the clock is the running, and you have to get material out. That's usually about the time the client's legal department whips out their red pen and crosses out anything in your work that's remotely creative (although they did leave the word "of" untouched in one of the key sentences).

Actually, although it may *seem* like the legal department's role is to make life suck for everyone involved in even the most insignificant marketing effort, the truth is they do serve a valuable purpose. Yes, there are times when they can be a little too strict and stringent—sometimes you'll just wish they would lighten up—but they're there to protect the company they represent. Whether they're safeguarding the company's copyright and trademarks or making sure there's no language in the marketing copy that promotes unsubstantiated facts or promises, the work they do is to everyone's benefit—even if working with them feels like someone's throwing ice water in your face.

The bottom line is that sending work through legal is unavoidable, and as an agency, there's no point in whining about it. Just expect that they're going to review everything, be prepared for it to take at least two days (but probably more), accept in advance that they *will* make you make changes to anything you put in front of them, and work all this additional time into your project plan so they don't cause you to be late.

MICHAEL HAND

THE CLIENT PERSPECTIVE

The client's legal department should not seek to hinder the prospect of getting work done, but should nonetheless be omnipresent in any client-agency relationship. I realize that agency and client teams the world over will want to hang me from the nearest bridge by my toes for suggesting that legal remain involved for even one second past when the contract is signed, but I truly believe that legal can add ongoing value—and keep you out of trouble.

First, let's discuss that contract. I know we all just want to meet over a drink and sign the back of a napkin—after all, according to most corporate gurus, that is how marketers think—but let's agree that a solid agreement can be very valuable. From the client perspective, I like to have certain things clearly outlined, like exclusivity in my product category and how many hours I will have retained staff working against my scope. As an agency, I would assume you want spelled out with clarity the payment terms of our deal and what happens if my company merges with another major corporation (or worse, if my company goes out of business completely). The contract is a safeguard against surprises, and getting lawyers talking to lawyers on the terms and conditions allows you the freedom to get the "business deal" done—a benefit, from my point of view.

The legal team's ongoing role is extremely important to me when dealing with trademark issues and potential infringements. As a company, the most powerful thing you have is the power of your brand. Protecting the way it is used and making sure nobody else can take advantage of good ideas you develop is critical to sustaining growth. I recognize the value in using a ™ or ® when appropriate, and expect my agency to as well. So let the lawyers fill out the necessary forms and conduct the necessary legal searches to ensure compliance; just make sure you thank them when you are done, and that you inform everybody who touches your brand creatively of the findings.

Another area where the legal team adds value—which often goes unrecognized —is when you are on the receiving end of consumer complaints and countless unsolicited marketing ideas or proposals. Having a process in place to respond to these and to prevent from them escalating is crucial to ongoing success and to your ability to focus your time; nobody wants to end up in a courtroom over a frivolous claim. The issue of unsolicited ideas is more a matter of having an agreed-upon process in place to manage these submissions. Legal staff can provide marketing teams with "templated" responses to protect the corporation from somebody claiming years later that an idea was theirs. It is better to be prepared in advance and educate the entire staff, from administrative assistants to vice presidents, on how unsolicited work will be treated.

I think too many agency partners view the corporate legal department as their arch nemesis (okay, sometimes it is). But they need to embrace the value that legal can bring to the table. I recommend that my agency partners bring in their legal department early when exploring creative concepts, taglines, and ideas. I would rather know sooner than later if an idea is going to be rejected or will need to be reworked. I have worked for a few companies whose products are watched closely by regulators, and advertising/marketing messages must comply with governmental standards. In the beer category, for example, making it clear that all marketing communication was targeted to consumers over 21 years of age was not optional; we absolutely needed to be compliant, and we had to be able to prove it—down to media logs of viewing audiences by individual TV spot.

ADVICE TO LEGAL COUNSEL FROM A MARKETING GUY...

In addition to the openness discussed above, it can be helpful to provide your counsel with some pointers on how they can work better with you and your team:

Know the boundaries of your expertise: Marketers do not want your personal opinion on the individual creative executions; we just want to know if legally we can move forward.

Be approachable: Nobody likes to talk to lawyers because they feel like they've done something wrong before the conversation even starts. This is human nature.

Remain consistent in your point of view: Don't flip-flop on how you provide feedback for a given subject. For example, if the way we treated copy on one creative element gets re-sized per your instructions, you can't change your mind on round two.

Be clear on timelines: Often, legal is the final sign-off point before creative is turned over to the production department or cameras start rolling on a commercial shoot. If you need a week to reply, let us know up front. If you need two weeks, let us know who else we can talk to for legal advice/approval without making you angry. For the record: Yes, we know we wait until the last minute too often.

Be the expert: Don't leave marketing teams second-guessing your advice. We want to know that what you say from a legal point of view can be trusted and is to remain unquestioned.

Q: IS THE CLIENT ALWAYS RIGHT?

JASON MILETSKY
THE AGENCY PERSPECTIVE

"The customer is always right." It's one of those phrases we grew up with, right along with "It's all fun and games until somebody loses an eye" and "Wha'choo talkin' 'bout, Willis?" Out of curiosity, I Googled this phrase and found that while it dates back to 1908, when Swiss hotelier César Ritz used it in his advertising (actually, what he said was "Le client n'a jamais tort," or "The customer is never wrong"), it was popularized in America shortly thereafter by Gordon Selfridge, then employed by Marshall Field department store (and later the founder of Selfridge's in London).

Now, far be it from me to question the wisdom of Marshall Field, but either customers were far less demanding in the early 1900s, or Selfridge was simply a nut.

Clearly, customer service is the cornerstone of an agency's business. Clients can be tough at times, and there's nothing wrong with that. They have a brand to manage, a budget to consider, and their own internal goals to meet. But that doesn't make them "always right." Part of our job is to provide the outside perspective—to show them what they're not able to see. We all know that when you're too close to something, you can't see it properly, and may end up making assumptions and judgments based on limited or skewed information. The agency exists outside the boundaries, straddling the line between being close enough to the brand to effectively market it but far enough away to see it clearly. Because of this unique positioning, clients often find it's better to hire outside agencies than to build or use their own internal creative group (more often than not, when we pitch against a client's internal agency, we win). So when a client says something that we know is wrong, it's our job to speak our minds and steer them in the right direction. (For more on this, refer to my answer to Question #15, "The Client Insists on Making a Move the Agency Knows Is a Mistake. Should the Agency Do It Anyway?")

My guess is that when Selfridge used the phrase, he was referring to his store's desire to cater to their customers and do what they could to make them happy. Clearly, it didn't mean that if a customer walked into the store and argued that the world is flat, then all of the salespeople were expected to nod in agreement. In this more general definition, Mr. Selfridge may have had a point. It is our job to do what we can to make the client happy and satisfied with the relationship—with these conditions:

- They pay their bills on time (or are at least somewhere in the ballpark).

- They treat your team with at least a modicum of respect (see my response to Question #2, "What Makes a Client a Good Client?").

Making your clients happy means making them feel special. No client wants to feel like they're just another client; big or small, they want to feel like they're one of the most important clients you work with. That means you should do the following:

- **Go above and beyond:** Come up with new, fresh ideas to show you've been thinking about their brand. See an article in an industry pub that relates to their market? Send them a link to it. Show them that they're on your mind.

- **Be proactive:** Tackle problems or uncover opportunities before you're asked to.

- **Give them some face time:** Don't rely on e-mail for staying in touch, and don't get in touch only when you sense an opportunity for more work or higher billings. Even if it means hopping a flight out to their offices, make it a point to spend some time with your clients.

- **Listen to their ideas:** Seriously consider them, even if you don't agree with them.

- **Be respectful of their time:** As basic as it sounds, don't be late for meetings, and always be prepared.

Remember: Clients can always choose to work with other agencies. That doesn't make you an easily replaced commodity, but the fact is, they can probably replace you a little more quickly and easily than you can replace the revenue you generate from them. So do what's right, keep them happy, and remember: As Gordon Selfridge liked to say, the customer is always right.

Except, of course, when they're wrong.

MICHAEL HAND

THE CLIENT PERSPECTIVE

No, the client is not always right—but as an agency, you'd better know when you want to play that card. If the difference of opinion is not of major significance, then you might decide it's better to shut your mouth and live with the client's decision than risk losing the account over it. On the flip side, if you feel that something is *really* out of sorts, you need to assertively voice your concerns—with the realization that if the client does not take your advice, you may have to "get it off your chest" and move on.

> It's important to remember who pays the bills when decisions are being made in the client-agency relationship. He who wields the checkbook gets the final vote—even if that person doesn't quite understand the creative approach.

Many clients will make poor decisions when they don't have all the facts (or wrongly assume they do). But as an agency partner, you should try to avoid telling the client they are wrong. Instead, provide quantitative and/or qualitative data and illustrate your point/suggestion for improvement. Prepare a document that states your position and stand behind it without wavering. Generally, good clients will recognize their error when in possession of *all* the information—but until they have that data, they may head down an unfortunate path.

Remember, if your agency specializes in a particular area of the business, then *you* may be the expert—not the client. Indeed, many clients are not aware of the consequences of the decisions they are about to make when working in areas outside of the company's daily expertise. For example, the interactive space is constantly changing. If the client spends 10 percent of his/her time dealing with issues related to the online space and your agency team spends 100 percent of its time in this area, you have the right—indeed, the obligation—to point out any flaws in the client's decision-making process.

Often, creative teams have really strong feelings about and even emotional connections with their work—as they should. But that doesn't mean the client is "wrong" if they don't "get it" or if focus groups say they "don't understand." And at some point, every client will ask the agency to make the logo bigger or change the font. More often than not, this will not be the right call—but again, you need to decide if that's a battle worth fighting. After all, the client may not be *right*, but are they really *wrong*?

PART TWO

The Foundations

Q: WHAT IS THE BEST WAY TO DEFINE A "BRAND"?

MICHAEL HAND

THE CLIENT PERSPECTIVE

It has been said that "A brand is a brand is a brand"—a statement with which I completely disagree. Sure, the word brand is hard to define; everybody has some unique, "textbook" way of serving it up. To me, simply speaking, "brand" should be defined as "a product with a unique identity." Anybody can make a "product"—and some products are certainly better than others—but it is the company or individual that creates an emotional connection and establishes an identity for their product that ultimately wins with the consumer. This emotional connection is what separates a brand from an ordinary, "no name" product.

Take me, for example. I'm a huge sports fan, and I love to look at the athletic shoe category for inspiration—on a personal and professional level. When I was in middle school, I was a dedicated Nike kid. At the time, I had no idea what a special inner sole technology would do for me or how motion controlled sensors would stabilize my ankles; I simply loved the "Just Do It" campaign. The advertising and slogan spoke to me on a very personal level. Sure, Reebok made good products—I guess. Converse made good products—I guess. But those guys did not give me the emotional boost that Nike gave me. I trusted that Nike made great shoes not just because two-sport star Bo Jackson wore them, but because everywhere I looked, athletes on the streets and in the gym were wearing them. These users drove my desire to get more active and compete as well. I literally thought I could run faster, jump higher—whatever I needed—when those shoes were on my feet. (I even ran for Student Council President with "Just Do It" as my campaign slogan. Unfortunately, I lost by 17 votes; I guess the other kids were Reebok fans.)

Looking back, I know I was somewhat foolish. But as I begged my mom to save more money for the cool (but expensive) sneakers, it was clear that Nike had won me over with their brand. I know I wasn't the only kid in America watching

#23 on the Chicago Bulls dunk in his self-named Air Jordans or, in later years, watching Brandi Chastain tear off her Team USA jersey to reveal a Nike sports bra after the biggest USA Women's Soccer victory in history—not to mention watching Lance Armstrong overcome issues a lot more intense than those related to brand positioning—all supported by Nike.

The interesting thing about this branding example is that I am no longer a Nike guy. Now that I'm past my college-football–playing—and, most likely, my marathon-running—days, I've found that certain features I need can be found in other manufacturers' products. The emotional connection I felt for Nike when I was younger has given way to a more balanced approach in my shopping behavior. I still make very emotional decisions in the purchase process, but the functional need is something I think more about now that I am older (on my driver's license, at least). Running shoe brands like Asics, Mizuno, and Saucony have entered the purchase equation thanks to their stability and cushioning features. And while I still have a soft spot for the Nike brand and the attitude they convey, it is clear to me that brands like Under Armour (UA) are fast becoming the Nike of the next generation, delivering that emotional charge. UA has built a passionate fan base of testosterone-driven male jocks and strong-minded women athletes, and is fast becoming the choice of the next generation of athletes. At every high school in America, UA-clad future stars hit the turf for football games under the lights each Friday night and take to the practice fields throughout the week. They're the perfect Branding 1010 case study. Nike must keep an eye on this situation to avoid getting beaten by the very same tactics they used to build this market. I respect UA for taking on the Goliath that is Nike head-on, and I think it will be interesting to see what happens as they get deeper into the athletic-footwear category.

All this is to say that I believe a "brand" contributes to growth. Brands become symbols of a promise that you can trust the product to consistently deliver. Simply seeing a brand's trademark or logo can inspire consumers to purchase the brand again and again. It's also to say, though, that you must keep your brand fresh with consumers in order to sustain that growth. You can never forget that brands live in the hearts of individuals, not in a focus group and certainly not in a conference room; brand re-invention and relevance are critical focuses for success.

My advice? Get away from your office once in a while and try to look at your brand from an outsider's perspective. Try to see what they see and to understand why they see it that way. This fresh perspective—and, hopefully, the accompanying new set of ideas—will make you better and stronger when it comes to building your brand.

JASON MILETSKY

THE AGENCY PERSPECTIVE

↳ Understanding the brand, its importance, and how it is developed is vital to the success of any marketing campaign. In fact, the brand is the foundation upon which marketing programs are developed. But defining the word "brand" isn't always easy; I don't know for sure that there is a unified answer even within the marketing community. So in my opinion, the best way to come up with a comprehensive definition for marketing purposes is to break the word down, starting from the beginning.

Visit any cattle farm and you'll see herds of cows with letters or icons burnt into their butts with a branding iron. This practice of marking animals is at the very root of branding. Because cows pretty much all look alike (I've always wondered how a bull knows which cow is his wife...), farmers needed a way to tell which cows belonged to which farmer. To solve this problem, farmers started to burn a mark on their cattle to distinguish which cows belong to which farm should herds ever become intermingled. The mark (brand) helps to tell one cow (product) from another. Therefore, one definition of a brand is:

> **brand:** An icon or mark (logo) that helps distinguish one product from another.

But inevitably, the question "Is the brand a product?" is posed. By this definition, no—the brand *represents* the product. Pepsi Cola is carbonated water, sugar, and caramel flavoring. The brand is the red, white, and blue circle, the Pepsi name, and the distinctive lettering used. When you see it on the shelf, you immediately know it is different from the bright red and white Coca-Cola bottle on the shelf next to it.

But there is a slight disconnect with this definition. Let's revisit the farmer. The farmer brands his cows to prove ownership—not so that you, the consumer, can pick out his cows from those of another farmer. By the time his cow ends up on your plate, you are thinking far less about which farm it came from than you are about whether you will still have room for dessert afterward. That's a very different scenario from the one in which a consumer is choosing to drink Pepsi instead of Coke. For many people, that choice comes down to taste, which is more than just the basic ingredients. Taste is a feature of each product that makes it unique. That brings us to a different definition:

> **brand:** A specific characteristic or unique quality that distinguishes one product from another.

The Pepsi logo lets consumers know that inside a particular bottle is the specific taste they're looking for. What if every time you opened a bottle of Pepsi, it tasted different? What if sometimes it was bitter and other times it was sweet? Chances are you wouldn't buy it at all anymore. The red, white, and blue logo; the specific typeface; and the product name would no longer mean anything to you. What's important is that if you as a consumer see a bottle with the Pepsi logo on it, you know exactly how it's going to taste whether you are in New York, Boston, Los Angeles, or any one of a million other towns. You know what to expect. This brings us to the single most important definition of a brand:

> **brand:** The sum total of all user experiences with a particular product or service, building both reputation and future expectations of benefit.

From a marketer's standpoint, this is the definition that really matters (it should be noted, however, that the word "brand" can also be used interchangeably with the name of a company or product, as has been done throughout this book). Notice that in breaking down the word, the brand has gone from being tangible (an icon) to being intangible (a reputation). It's also gone from being a one-way communication (this icon tells the consumer what the brand is) to a two-way relationship (based on its reputation, the consumer expects something from the brand).

Q: WHAT MATTERS MOST TO CONSUMERS? BRAND, PRICE, AVAILABILITY, OR SOMETHING ELSE?

MICHAEL HAND

THE CLIENT PERSPECTIVE

If there was ever a question that could be answered 100 different ways, this is it. For most marketers, the answer will depend on what segment/category is being discussed, the demographic identified for the consumer, the occasion for which the person is shopping—indeed, this list of "it depends" factors can go on and on.

But despite all that, in my mind what matters most to consumers is the selection of the *brand*. Price plays an important role in narrowing the available options during the decision process; and certainly, if your product is not available, you will either lose the sale or force the consumer to seek you out at another location. Brand is the tiebreaker when a consumer is looking at two equally matched products. As marketers, we have one job and one job only: Create a point of difference that gives you a competitive advantage in the marketplace, and make sure the consumer's decision never comes down to price alone.

Personally, I am a brand-centric consumer (maybe that is why I feel it matters most). I buy Heinz ketchup, Brawny paper towels, and Froot Loops cereal, not the generic, store-label equivalent for 43 cents less. But although I don't go the grocery store with a mission to find only the best deals, many consumers do. They argue that the stuff inside those store-brand containers/packages tastes no different from the major labels. These are folks buying on price only (and many of them exist). If we as brand marketers allow this to happen, we will cut into all profitability projections and be forced to fight a battle over value.

Here's another example: When buying a car, everyone looks for a beautifully designed model that is sleek and rides smoothly while also offering great gas mileage. Nobody walks into a car dealership and says "I want to see the cheapest car you have on the lot" or "Can you show me the model you have the most of?" Prospective car buyers start the shopping process by determining what type of vehicle will meet their needs. Are they looking for a car, a mini-van, or a truck?

Two doors or four? Two-wheel drive, four-wheel drive, or all-wheel drive? What kind of options do they want? This part of the process, designed to narrow the field, is very fact-based.

Once these decisions have been made, the magical transformation—when the consumer goes from passive involvement to active engagement—occurs. They now look for brands that reflect how they see themselves. Is it Honda or Toyota—i.e., reliable? Is it BMW or Mercedes—i.e., performance and engineering? Is it Volvo or Saab—i.e., safety-conscious? Or is it, say, Hummer—i.e., just kind of ridiculous? These brands have successfully driven their images through consistent messaging that reinforces and supports their position. (This argument also holds true for Hummer being ridiculous, even though I thought their "Soap Box Derby" ad was very creative.) BMW's claim of being the "Ultimate Driving Machine" promises consumers that driving a BMW will be a life-altering experience (even if you never drive faster than 70 miles per hour on the highway). Even if consumers narrow their choices to more affordable options—for example, from the Chevy, Kia, Hyundai, or Pontiac product lines—they will ultimately make their decision based on the brand to which they feel most connected. The badge of the brand matters most.

JASON MILETSKY

THE AGENCY PERSPECTIVE

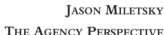 Consumers come in all shapes and sizes, each with their own touch points and sensibilities. What they respond to depends on the individual, product or service category, and the particular brand in question. Personally, I couldn't care less about paper towels; I'll just grab whatever brand is closest to the end of the grocery-store aisle regardless of color, price, number of sheets, absorbency, or whatever. In fact, the only factor I *do* care about is spending as little time in that aisle as possible. But offer me a Diet Coke for free or tell me I can drive five miles to buy Diet Pepsi at full retail price, and I'll thank you for the offer but be on my way to buy myself a Diet Pepsi every time. My affinity for particular brands is based first on how important the category is to me (paper towel products: not at all; cola products: extremely) and second on my tastes for and experience with individual brands within that category.

In considering the target market for any brand, consumers can be segmented into five distinct groups:

- **Brand loyal:** These consumers are committed to one brand—so much so that price is rarely a factor, and they'll go out of their way to get it. Very little will take them away from a brand they trust and are loyal to. These consumers are also typically eager to tell other people about their favorite brands.

- **Brand preferred:** These consumers prefer certain brands over others and will go a bit—but not far—out of their way to get them. Slight price differentials or reduced accessibility are not enough to make them change brands, but significant changes in either variable may cause them to research other options.

- **Brand aware:** These shoppers may like one brand over another—enough to recommend that brand to others if asked—but they're not that likely to go out of their way for it. Slight differentials in price or accessibility compared to competing brands might sway their purchasing decisions.

- **Brand conscious:** These shoppers do not have a preference of one brand over another, and they wouldn't go out of their way for a particular brand. Price and accessibility are often the determining factors in their decisions about which products to buy. These shoppers, however, do prefer to choose among brands that they know or about which they have formed an opinion (either through direct use or reputation). They stay away from brands they don't know and avoid generic, unbranded products.

- **Brand indifferent:** These are shoppers who base their decisions strictly on price and convenience. They are open to brands that they do not know and are also open to generic, unbranded products.

In maximizing their budgets, marketers should be looking to reach the "Sweet Center"—those people who make up the brand-preferred, brand-aware, and brand-conscious groups. These groups represent the most likely converts. Consumers who are already brand loyal don't need any further marketing; they're already convinced. As long as you don't forget them and you stay true to your brand, they'll be advocates. Consumers who are brand indifferent are also not worth spending money on. (Sorry, but no amount of money spent on marketing is going to get me to care about paper towels.) Marketers who want to increase their ROI need to target consumers who are sandwiched between these two extremes, starting with a heavy focus on those in the brand-preferred range and working down to those considered in the brand-conscious category.

Q: HOW FIRM IS THE BRAND GUIDE? WHEN, IF EVER, CAN THE AGENCY BREAK THE RULES?

MICHAEL HAND

THE CLIENT PERSPECTIVE

↳ While the mandate to use a brand guide will fluctuate slightly depending on the company you are working with, I am a firm believer that all brands need well-established guidelines and a set of rules that must be followed. The brand guide—a published document that should be shared with internal stakeholders and agency partners—should be held as sacred. All too many brands have no written brand guidelines; they live by a series of unwritten rules that have been instilled over time to maintain the brand's integrity. This is a dangerous and slippery slope rooted in blind faith, however, because it allows people to change their mind as often as they change their underwear—not a good thing when you are responsible for the brand's long-term health.

Can the rules in the brand guide be broken? Yes, but let me just say that you'd better have a damned good reason. As your most valuable assets, your brands should be treated like your children. They will evolve over time, but they must keep core values and imagery intact. Any changes or modifications should be seen as an evolution, not a revolution. You would not change your child's name or eye color just for the hell of it, would you?

A few things that must be addressed in every brand guide are the following:

- **Color palette:** Open a large box of Crayola crayons these days and you'll see 25 shades of blue. I promise you that when asked to pick their favorite, marketers at Lowe's, Pepsi, and Miller Lite are looking at different individual crayons in that same box. To each of these massive brands, a certain shade of the color is the unique expression they want to deliver. Color is a tremendous brand asset; just ask Home Depot about the color orange or Coca-Cola about the color red. Brands should never be afraid to leverage their color palette, but they must treat it with integrity, with every placement given equal importance. Pantones should not be compromised. Teams must be on press to ensure compliance for any activity ranging from POS production to packaging. Store managers should make sure signage color is correct and advertising teams need to lock down all creative elements within any given execution.

- **Logo usage:** No two logo placements will be used in exactly the same way, but they must deliver the same exact consumer takeaway for the brand. For example, if you are asked to provide a logo for a banner at your next corporate golf outing, that logo will be different from the one used on packages or on T-shirts offered as prizes for your next sweepstakes initiative. You must have multiple logo lockups prepared for these various uses: four color, two color, horizontal placement, vertical placement, embroidery, etc. You should also establish guidelines on how much clean space you need around the mark.

- **Typeface/fonts:** There are not many companies these days using a standard Helvetica or Times New Roman font for their brands; they have designed their own stylized look. And much like color, font says a lot about the identity of the brand. When Mountain Dew updated their font from the older, rounded, bubble-style font to their current look with sharper lines, it was to support the brand's new, edgier identity. Rounded and fun worked for the laid back and mellow attitude the brand used to convey, but it was not aggressive enough for what they wanted the brand to become. Font usage should be clearly outlined in the brand guide to avoid confusion.

- **Trademark usage:** As stated, brands are a company's most valuable asset. It is crucial that you go through the legal process to trademark your brand name and all associated slogans and taglines. It takes some time and effort to get this done and to build into your brand's identity, but that's what your legal staff is for. You need to protect your brands; they are your most valuable asset.

- **Additional brand images/characters:** For many companies, brand guides don't just define packaging and logo usage; they extend to characters that have become synonymous with the company. Take, for example, the M&M's characters or Ronald McDonald. These "spokespeople" have clearly defined characteristics, attitudes, and looks. M&M's in particular has been very successful creating personalities for each character. Consumers now define themselves as sarcastic and quick-witted like Red or confident and flirtatious like Green. These personalities need to remain consistent over time. You would never mistake one identity for the other. To protect that effort and make sure things remain consistent takes a lot of hard work. For starters, you must outline this information in the brand guide.

- **Tone:** This part of the guidelines is critical. Tone refers to the way consumers "hear" your brand voice and decide whether the personality fits their lifestyle. The images and words you choose (and how you show/say them) for your brand define who you are in their eyes. Do you want consumers to see you as approachable, funny, confident, or strong? Answering this question and then building your position will put you on the path to establishing your brand's tone. Geico's use of both a caveman and a gecko as "spokespeople" for the brand are good examples of using a light-hearted approach—in this case, to sell insurance. Geico's intention is to convey that they don't take themselves too seriously and to make you feel at ease when making what can be a very complicated choice. In contrast, Prudential takes a more serious tone, delivering a message of confidence and control. They want to be somebody you can trust when things go wrong. Of course, different demographics respond to different tones. For example, my dad would never call Geico for insurance coverage. Prudential's approach is more in line with what he needs to hear from his insurance carrier. His feeling is that if something goes wrong (for example, he is involved in a car accident or endures a hospital stay), he wants an insurance company that conveys strength and confidence—not a six-foot caveman who plays golf and drinks margaritas. I'm not saying that one approach is better than the other; I'm just illustrating that there are many ways to portray a brand and you need to choose carefully.

Brand guides are not meant to stifle creativity or limit opportunities for brands to evolve; but when used correctly, they can drive alignment throughout an organization.

JASON MILETSKY
THE AGENCY PERSPECTIVE

Brand guides are the bible upon which every strong brand is built. Within their pages lie all the details that marketing agencies, printers, publishers, Web developers, and everyone else remotely associated with promoting the brand would need to know. *What's the RGB breakdown of the logo?* Look in the brand guide. *Do we hyphenate the word "e-mail" in our corporate language?* Check the guide.

Whether it's 10 pages or 100—and I've seen both—it'd be unheard of for a brand of any real significance to embark on a marketing program without having a brand guide at the very center of its efforts. As a believer in and developer of brands, I have beaten the brand drum for many years, always emphasizing the importance of maintaining brand integrity and enforcing consistency. Consistency, after all, is one of the strongest weapons in the marketing arsenal for building immediate recognition over time—and one of the biggest benefits that comes with the development of a comprehensive brand guide.

But for all their value—not to mention the time, thought, and effort that goes into their creation—brand guides are often treated with contempt by marketing professionals on both the client and the agency side. That's because marketers are a creative species. Our imaginations seek out open canvases. The brand guide limits that canvas by providing strict procedures and rules for us to follow—and limits are like Kryptonite creativity.

This creates a chasm between the "brand police," whose job it is to ensure that the brand guide is followed, and creative marketers, who want to break free from their constraints. The important thing for everyone to remember is that the brand guide is exactly that—a guide. It provides information and direction, details when needed, and answers when questions arise. Brand managers must remember that the agency can't function in a police state. And while people on the production end of the food chain—printers, for example—may need to follow the guide by the letter, creative directors and key strategists should be given certain leeway when it comes to look, feel, and voice. The guide spells out what the brand should be conceptually, but in certain media—print advertising, for example—going outside the lines to promote a stronger message can benefit a brand.

At the same time, creatives on the agency side need to work within the general umbrella of the brand and absorb the guide on a conceptual level. The guide does more than break down colors and fonts; it defines the personality and promise of a brand. Creatives must work within those boundaries and remember that everything they do is reflection of the brand to the public—not an isolated canvas for them to paint upon.

Q: DOES THE PERSONALITY OF A BRAND NEED TO BE REFLECTED IN ALL MARKETING EFFORTS?

MICHAEL HAND

THE CLIENT PERSPECTIVE

A brand's personality is an extremely valuable asset. It is key to increasing customer connection, attachment, and loyalty; it's critical to building the long-lasting relationships that all companies seek with their customers. Just as people are drawn to individuals who they find engaging or interesting, so too are they drawn to brands. If you want your brand to resonate with its audience and to solidify its role in the lives of those who use it, then yes, the brand's personality needs to be reflected in all marketing efforts. The brand's personality is what brings the brand strategy to life. Consumers must see and hear who the brand is. The brand's personality must come through loud and clear. Without a clear personality, brands become just a series of words and images. They become empty promises stacked on grocery store shelves, in the pages of a magazine, or wherever else they place a message.

> Be careful about giving consumers too much to react to in the area of brand personality. Consumers will take only what they need and deflect the rest. Do not thrust too much upon them.

Realize, though, that brand personality works in conjunction with product quality. That is, you can build all the brand personality in the world and build it into all of your marketing messages, but if your product sucks, you are doomed. Likewise, even if your product is great, if customers don't connect with your brand personality, you will fail to secure their loyalty.

You need to look at the product experience as part of collective "marketing effort" and deliver consistency. This dynamic plays out in one of two ways:

- Consumers will start the relationship at the product level to fill a particular need, enjoy the experience, and then get to know the brand on a more intimate level. If they connect with the brand's personality that they are seeing in all your messages at that point, you just may win a customer for life. If, however, they don't share the brand's genetic makeup, they will either abandon ship or use the product on and off based solely on the functional delivery until they find a replacement. Again, if your brand personality is a strong reflection of the product and has been consistent across all layers of the marketing mix, you are in a better position to maintain a consumer's usage.

- Consumers will discover your personality before they discover your product. (Today, thanks to the Web, every wallflower and small business has a shot to be discovered.) If they like what they see/hear/feel, they will then try your product. If the product delivers on the perception conveyed by the brand's personality, you win. If the product falls short of the expectations that have been built up, however, then you have lost any shot of ever winning over that customer for the long haul.

The agency and client branding experts must find the brand traits that will persuade consumers to seek this bond with your brand. One way is to consider the five dimensions of a brand personality and supporting traits, which were developed by Jennifer L. Aaker from the University of California, Berkeley and featured in *Journal of Marketing Research* in August 1997. She highlights "sincerity, excitement, competence, sophistication and ruggedness" as the key dimensions to review and analyze. The scale in Aaker's study provides a systematic way of looking at these traits and seeing how a brand stacks up against other brands across categories.

The Virgin brand is a great example of keeping consistent in your brand personality regardless of the category where you place your products/services. Virgin, which operates in multiple sectors ranging from entertainment to travel to mobile communications, doesn't believe they need to be the cheapest on the market, but they *do* believe in providing honest pricing that is transparent to the end-user, and they go out of their way to provide the best customer service in all sectors. Virgin does not compromise on quality, and they always seek innovative solutions—even to challenges that seem mundane. In his 1998 book, *Losing My Virginity*, British billionaire and Virgin CEO Richard Branson notes that "A lot of chairmen of a lot of companies are terrified of the press. Our attitude is if CNN wants an interview you never say no, you always say yes, because we want to become the most respected brand in the world and we have to get out there and talk about what we are doing." Not surprisingly, the brand's personality strongly reflects Branson's attitude and this personality shines through in every marketing piece Virgin generates. It supports Virgin's commitment to providing a fair price while still having some fun. They deliver both humor and conviction in a very relaxed, yet professional way.

Don't get me wrong: I'm not saying you need a Richard Branson, a Phil Knight (Nike), or a Jack Welch (General Electric) at the top of your company to develop a brand personality—although it can help in some cases. The bottom line is that the brand personality must come to life through all aspects of the product line and through the interaction with all departments and employees of an organization. Consumers have more information than they could ever imagine about products on the market, but there simply aren't enough hours in the day for them to process it all. As a brand champion, you need to help them *feel* your personality (and then help them feel it again and again and again).

JASON MILETSKY
THE AGENCY PERSPECTIVE

In Question 42, "What Is the Difference Between a Project and a Campaign?" I talk about, well, the difference between a project and a campaign. One of the distinct differences that I point out is that in terms of advertising, a project usually has little to no creative concept or emphasis on brand personality. Examples of this can be seen on any cable channel where a low-budget commercial promotes a local jeweler or pizza place, or in a small-town newspaper that features an ad promoting a sale at the local hardware store. These ads don't usually express any particular personality because that's not what they're selling. They're sending a direct message to a local audience, where the consumer's decision to purchase relies less on brand and more on elements such as proximity and price.

But if you're a more serious brand looking to build market share and increase your exposure, reflecting the brand personality is how you connect emotionally to potential customers. It's what makes them feel like you get them, and it's how your target market can relate to you on a personal level.

I know this sounds like complete bullshit, but it's not. Granted, nobody walks around thinking, "Gee, maybe I'll buy a Macintosh computer today because they're such a hip company, and I really feel connected to that young guy in their TV commercials. That brand really understands me!" But that's not the point. The emotional connection exists on a subconscious level. Even if it sounds like a load of marketing crap, it's not—it's real. The brand promise gives you access to your target market's mind, but it's the brand personality that gives you access to their hearts. This powerful one-two punch can dramatically affect consumers' buying decisions.

The trick is to remain consistent, to make sure that the personality is reflected in absolutely everything the market will see—and to do so in a way that doesn't seem heavy handed. Somebody who's really funny doesn't introduce himself by saying, "Hi! Nice to meet you. Just to let you know, I'm really funny!" If he's genuinely funny, you'll figure it out for yourself—you don't need him to point it out to you. Brands are no different. A brand with an edgy personality loses its edge the minute it admits to having one. Whatever the brand's personality, take care to use it as a subtle support that underscores who the brand is rather than in an overt way that could potentially undermine its very reason for being.

Q: SHOULD THE BRAND PERSONALITY REFLECT WHAT THE MARKET WANTS, THE COMPANY HISTORY, OR THE PERSONALITY OF THE KEY EXECUTIVES?

MICHAEL HAND
THE CLIENT PERSPECTIVE

This answer might be completely different from one company to the next —meaning every company needs to find this answer on their own. To guide you, I've laid out a few examples where each of these scenarios works—and where, in my opinion, they don't.

WHAT THE MARKET WANTS: GOOD

You see this approach in every political campaign—and the 2008 presidential election was no different. Barack Obama found a way, through his campaign messages, to tap into the public's desire for change. His team of supporters focused on what the market wanted after years of bad economic times and international conflict and then used simple, one-word directions, such as Hope, Change, and Progress, on campaign posters. Regardless of your political stripes, you have to admit it was impressive to see the Obama marketing machine spring into action to apply this market-centric tactic. As a politician, he achieved the ultimate "be all things to all people" message—and won the election as a result.

Another great example of a brand personality centered around giving the market what they want is Apple. With a strong focus on fresh design principles and innovative products, Apple lives their mantra to "Think Different"—and consumers will line up for hours to get the next product from the company portfolio the minute it's released. Through their branding strategy, Apple has achieved iconic status with today's youth, who clamor for the next iPhone or iPod derivative.

What the Market Wants: Bad

Oldsmobile enjoyed a loyal following for decades, but when the brand entered the 1990s, "new thinking" and "fresh design" were not phrases that consumers associated with the brand. General Motors knew that new car buyers wanted fresh sheet metal and better designed cars—hence the Oldsmobile campaign "It's Not your Father's Oldsmobile Anymore." There was only one problem: It *was* your father's Oldsmobile—at least it was when you walked into the dealership. The campaign broke on television before the necessary modifications to the product line were complete. Although the campaign did draw new people into the dealerships to check things out, they left pissed because the available inventory didn't match the brand's new promise. Meanwhile, turned off by the campaign concept, the older generation stopped buying Oldsmobiles, finding what they needed elsewhere. All this is to say you can build a brand personality to reflect what the market wants—but you have to back it up with the product to match.

Company History: Good

Having a brand personality that is rooted in the company history can work only when the story is truly authentic. Trust me: Consumers can see through the fabricated crap and they will call bullshit every time. Consumers want honesty; and in return, they will give you trust. An example of a brand personality rooted in company history that works is Jack Daniels. A brand of whiskey, Jack has always remained true to their founder, the state of Tennessee, and the white oak barrels in which the whiskey is made. They have done very little to modify their square bottle design, black labels, and award-winning taste; all serve as constant reminders of the brand's well-known history and its connection to its heritage.

Company History: Bad

The Ford Motor Company has tried numerous times to play the company-history angle—talking about the good old days and how they are reinventing themselves on the same principles and values as their founding fathers. But the company continues to falter in finding the best way to deliver on their foundation as a manufacturer who created the modern automotive industry. For one, they've attempted to use this approach during times when the market viewed the product as being outdated, or when safety recalls were more on people's minds than the need to redesign the Mustang. And it didn't help that, after seeing the ads they ran with the relatively youthful Bill Ford, Jr., consumers couldn't help thinking that he didn't come across like the public figure needed to lead such a "historical" company. The result was less Norman Rockwell painting that reminded folks of the good ol' days and more a disconnect between the past and present generations set to rock 'n' roll music.

PERSONALITY OF CHIEF EXECS: GOOD

In my opinion, this approach has more successful examples than the others for one simple reason: When the chief executive makes his or her image the focal point of the brand, you better believe people within the walls of the corporate office will support it. And when the founder gets involved, taking a personal interest in the results, the level of support—and the chances of flawless execution—intensify. Nike *is* Phil Knight. Under Armour *is* Kevin Plank. These guys started out by selling products that they deeply believed in out of the trunks of their cars—and if you don't support the same mission, with the same rigor, you can find the door.

Starbucks is a great example of a brand built to match their founder—but lost their way. Howard Schultz's personal experiences spending time at little corner cafes in Italy led him to build his Starbucks empire. Because of his personality, the brand focused on intimacy and small gatherings with an emphasis on delivering unique, high-quality products in a casual setting. But when the brand started to grow rapidly, Schultz stepped aside—and that's when things spiraled out of control. With Schultz gone, the company's emphasis became expansion—but placing a store on every corner meant that the brand suddenly lost the intimate factor. And the unique, customized experience became a thing of the past with the advent of cookie-cutter goods and products that diverged from the backbone coffee fare. But when Shultz returned to the leadership position, the impact from his personality was felt immediately. Stores were closed, menu offerings were reduced, and even the smell of coffee was increased at the retail level. The end result remains to be seen, but with Howard at the helm, I am betting on them turning the corner and getting things right again. His personality will be at the center of their success.

PERSONALITY OF CHIEF EXECS: BAD

The diet industry has always been one for which consumers show high levels of skepticism. When promises are made about losing 40 pounds or dropping three dress sizes in a month, people will inevitably question the tactics and messaging. This was never truer than when the famous diet-book author and founder of the Atkins Diet, Dr. Robert Atkins, died from serious head injuries after a fall at the age of 72. The issue was not the cause of his death; the issue was that, at the time of his death, Atkins was declared to be clinically obese. The same man who told us to cut carbs but eat all the bacon and eggs that we wanted had himself suffered from heart trouble and hypertension for years. His family has fought hard to defend the credibility of the diet, declaring that his health concerns were completely unrelated. But whether the diet was what caused his health problems is actually irrelevant; the fact is, now consumers will think twice about the merits of his plan because of its association with the founder.

JASON MILETSKY

THE AGENCY PERSPECTIVE

This answer isn't clear-cut. This issue can be tricky, because the truth is that the brand personality needs to take many variables into consideration. On the one hand, because the personality of a brand is the key to creating an emotional connection with the audience, it would be reasonable to conclude that the personality should reflect the market. On the other hand, however, a brand needs to be comfortable in its own skin in order to consistently maintain its personality—and very often, there can be a conflict between what the market wants and what the brand can actually maintain.

It's too easy to say that the personality of the brand need not reflect the personalities of the company's founders or executives. I think their personalities will absolutely play at least some role in how the brand's personality is developed. I can't say for sure, but I have to think that the key executives behind the popular video-game developer EA, for example, are at least a little edgy and fun. I'd be shocked to find out they all wear three-piece suits to work every day, where they smoke cigars while discussing the moral decline of modern society. But how influential the personalities of key execs are to the brand may be somewhat minimal, and may instead depend more on the product being sold and the market being reached. That is, it's pretty safe to assume that the key execs behind Barbie aren't eight-year-old girls.

The real answer is that the personality of the brand isn't reflective of any one entity in particular, but a balance of all of them. There's no point in the brand personality for a gaming company being stuffy and serious simply because that's the personality of the key execs, because it'll turn off the market they're trying to reach. At the same time, there's no point in that same gaming company presenting itself as wild, crazy, and edgy simply because that's what the market wants. If the decision-makers aren't comfortable in that skin, they won't be able to sustain that brand personality. Every brand needs to find a balance between what the market will respond to and what it can reasonably be expected to consistently present. The point where these two needs meet is the starting point for developing the brand's personality.

Q: DOES A CLIENT'S MISSION STATEMENT PLAY A ROLE IN MARKETING THE BRAND? OR ARE MISSION STATEMENTS JUST MEANINGLESS CRAP?

MICHAEL HAND

THE CLIENT PERSPECTIVE

⌐↳ This is one of those answers you could argue both ways. Some companies really do live and breathe their mission statement; others hang it on a wall in the lobby and then do the exact opposite. I can tell you that very rarely does a company with multiple brands use the "corporate" mission statement in actions for the individual brands. The statement tends to break down when it gets spread across multiple brands; if this is forced, the brands will lose their unique identities. Companies that do not worry about sub-brands, but instead hold up the company name as the brand, tend to do a better job of living and breathing the mission statement through marketing efforts.

Target is one of those corporations that puts the ideals articulated in their mission statement into practice. According to the company's Web site, Target's mission statement reads as follows:

> *Our mission is to make Target the preferred shopping destination for our guests by delivering outstanding value, continuous innovation and an exceptional guest experience by consistently fulfilling our Expect More. Pay Less. brand promise.*

Target delivers on the value equation via everyday price points but also by bringing world-class designers like Michael Graves and Liz Lange into their family to create high-end designs that are affordable. Value is purposely not linked to being cheap. They also maintain a strong community connection by giving back 5 percent of funds from all purchases to community programs for the arts, education, and social services. And when it comes to assisting in environmental protection, they again act as true leaders. In 2008, Target ran print ads in *People* magazine that invited consumers to mail in five Target plastic bags and, in return, get a voucher for a free re-usable bag made from the recycled materials. It's innovations like these—coupled with clean stores and strong customer service—that will ensure Target remains a leader in the retail sector for decades to come.

On the opposite side of the spectrum, companies like Enron create mission statements and then act in the exact opposite manner. The collapse of Enron—at one time the seventh-largest U.S.-based company—will be noted in history as one of the most dishonorable abuses of power in the past 100 years. Unethical practices to hide debt and inflate earnings were not what you signed up for if you read the company motto (albeit not quite a mission statement): "Respect, Integrity, Communication and Excellence." Do you think the employees who lost all their retirement savings and could no longer pay their kid's college tuition wish the company had acted on these principles and had had a Board of Directors that actively pursued these ideals? Damn right they do.

JASON MILETSKY
THE AGENCY PERSPECTIVE

Personally, I think mission statements are pure crap. At least, I've never seen one that makes sense to me or rings even remotely true. Most of them don't say anything meaningful at all, and just use standard marketing buzzwords that could just as easily relate to any company.

Take this charmer from Aflac:

> To combine aggressive strategic marketing with quality products and services at competitive prices to provide the best insurance value for consumers.

What? Are they serious? What's the point of that? All they did was take a bunch of the most important words in marketing—"quality," "products," "services," "prices," "best," and "value"—and string them together in a sentence. It doesn't say anything useful to anybody, doesn't make any bit of difference to how they do business, and if the word "insurance" were removed could just as easily apply to any other company regardless of size or industry. Plus—and I don't want to argue semantics, but I will—that's not really their mission anyway. Corporations aren't that altruistic. Their mission is to make money. Look at this mission statement for AGCO, a leading agricultural equipment manufacturer:

> Profitable growth through superior customer service, innovation, quality and commitment.

At least that's honest! Their mission is to achieve profitable growth. Everything after the word "growth" simply states the means by which they plan to generate that growth.

But I still don't really see the point in having the mission statement. The AGCO mission statement might be honest, but does it say anything? Okay, they want to generate profitable growth. What company doesn't? And, okay, they'll do it by providing superior customer service, innovation, quality, and commitment. Does any legitimate company go into business with the intention of providing sub-par customer service, out-of-date ideas, useless crap, and indifference? Not likely.

So no, I don't think the mission statement does squat to help define the brand. I don't think it helps to promote the brand, direct the brand—I don't think it has anything to do with the brand. Now, the brand promise, on the other hand, is a different story. Where the mission statement is some ambiguous line meant more for internal purposes (I guess), the brand promise is the stated or implied benefit that the brand will provide to its customers—and it's one of the most important elements of the brand. So let's leave the silly world of mission statements for a minute and talk about the brand promise (it's a little off topic, but important enough that I think it's worth it).

Simply stated, the brand promise is the benefit the brand will deliver to consumers—and keeping that promise is one of the most important things a company can do. The brand promise can be expressed directly, made crystal clear, or it can be subtle and unspoken; either way, a promise is a promise and needs to be kept.

Suppose you're planning a vacation. You visit a Web site that promises to provide more comprehensive information on remote destinations than any other travel site on the Internet. While using the site for research, you notice that it speaks highly of the island of St. Maarten in the Caribbean, detailing an exciting night life, a championship golf course, and award-winning restaurants. You're sold! You book your flight, pack your bags, and head out, anxious to play a round of golf and dance the night away. There's only one problem: The Web site neglected to mention that a hurricane that hit the island a few years back destroyed the golf course, which was never rebuilt. It also left out the fact that the night life consists of bars and clubs that are open only during specific months of the year—read: not when you're there. So much for "comprehensive information!" The bottom line: The site did not deliver what it promised. It promised comprehensive information, but the information it actually provided was old and incomplete. The next time you are planning a trip, it's highly doubtful you'll return to the site for information.

While trust can be difficult to build, losing it can be a much quicker process. Keeping the brand promise is key to building trust in a brand. Initially, the consumer can only go by what the brand promises and assume that that promise will be kept. If the promise is kept, then the brand is strengthened. A positive reputation has been maintained and the expectation of positive future experiences with the brand is increased, making it more likely that the consumer will use that brand again. If the promise is broken, the brand is breached, raising doubt and diminishing trust—and regaining trust is often impossible.

Do consumers really give a brand only one chance to fail? It depends on the brand. How much leeway a company has in breaking its promise will largely depend on its longevity and history—or, put another way, how much trust equity the brand has built up. The more trust consumers have in a brand, the more likely they'll be to forgive broken promises—to a point.

Take Nike, for example. Nike makes sneakers—the sneakers are their product. Their brand reputation is delivering high-quality, stylish products that will enhance athletic performance. When a consumer purchases a pair of Nikes, the expectation is that the shoes will be comfortable and last a long time, even after aggressive use. For decades, Nike has kept that brand promise and met consumer expectations, even though (to my best recollection) that promise has never been expressly stated. Now suppose a consumer purchases a new pair of Nikes and they fall apart in the middle of a basketball game just two days later. That consumer will be annoyed, but his or her confidence in the Nike brand won't have taken too much of a hit. Because Nike has built enough trust equity to overcome a single bad experience, chances are the customer will assume it was just one bad pair of sneakers off the assembly line, and will obtain a new pair. But now suppose that a few days later, the consumer's ankles start to hurt during his or her weekly tennis game because the sneakers aren't providing the proper support. Will this consumer buy *another* pair of Nikes? Maybe, but his trust in the brand will have been shaken—and he just may look at a pair of Reeboks the next time around. Sure, after enough time has passed, the consumer might write off these negative experiences and buy the Nike brand again, but there is no question that on some level, damage will have been done. And of course, most brands don't have the time, money, or exposure that Nike has to overcome isolated negative experiences. Brands must take care to keep their promises each and every time in order to develop the trust necessary for gaining and retaining consumer loyalty.

While the brand promise often has to do with the quality of a product or service, that's not always the case. McDonald's does not claim that eating there is akin to dining in a five-star restaurant. Their promise is to provide you a quick meal that is inexpensive and tastes good. Women don't buy sweatshirts from Juicy Couture because of their promised high quality. The subtle promise is that if you own Juicy products, you will be part of an elite, fashionable crowd. The promise in this case involves lifestyle factors rather than product-related factors, such as speed or quality.

As brand-builders, marketers must manage how the promise is expressed and how consumers understand it to make sure they're not inadvertently promising something they can't deliver.

Q: HOW MUCH RESEARCH SHOULD BE DONE PRIOR TO DEVELOPMENT OF A NEW CAMPAIGN?

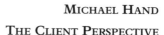

MICHAEL HAND

THE CLIENT PERSPECTIVE

I'm a big fan of going with your gut feeling, but that doesn't erase the need to conduct some research to validate your approach or see if your gut is simply way off. My issue with research, though, is that data can in many cases be manipulated to say just about anything that you want it to say. Research is helpful only if you're really willing to let it change your direction. As for how much research should be conducted, let your research team help to be the judge. As a rule, though, make sure you get a good balance of feedback to help you construct your final ideas.

First, you should conduct some qualitative research (i.e., focus groups) to determine which of the preliminary creative executions warrants further development. During this phase, you need to make sure that the consumer appeal and breakthrough value of the creative concept is registering with these important end users. Be aware, though, that in focus groups, you often wind up with a dominant individual who can persuade the group to think differently or make them feel uncomfortable voicing a differing opinion. For this reason, you may also want to consider one-on-one dialogue with target customers through interviews during this stage. This can be more expensive, but it will likely trigger deeper insights that a group setting simply cannot capture.

Be careful during this stage when using benchmarks set in previous campaigns as criteria for success. Too many companies go forward with the "next" campaign solely because the testing results exceeded those for the previous campaign. That's great—but it doesn't take into consideration where your previous campaign stood against the rest of the category. If your old work was weak, simply clearing the lowest hurdle may not be enough to win in the marketplace. This step should be used more for refinement of ideas than as the sole judge and jury for what you should put on air.

After some good qualitative reads, most organizations require that some quantitative work be done (although I personally think this can be an excellent way to kill good ideas). This research should provide the necessary feedback on consumers' understanding of the campaign's main idea and, most importantly, their recall of your ads when shown in a block with other work. They should also score on likeability and purchase intent after viewing. If you proceed with quantitative assessments of television ads, you must make sure that any animatics that are created give a true depiction of the end vision. It can be difficult to articulate the vision of ads that use special effects or post-production tools to create a particular look and feel. Likewise, if you plan to test print or radio work, you should make sure that you are using pieces that are very close to final in order to get a true assessment. But remember: These steps should be used to make refinements only—*not* to make the final creative decision for you.

JASON MILETSKY

THE AGENCY PERSPECTIVE

I tend to like to do at least some research before launching a new campaign, but the problem is that most clients don't want to spend the time or money. I don't mean the Fortune 500, multinational type of clients; I mean the small- to medium-sized companies, especially in the B2B world. These companies almost always want to forgo the research process and skip right on over to development—and from there boogie on into execution and call it a day. If absolute speed is the thing, then chances are research won't be part of the mix, which is kind of too bad. I like going to market quickly, but I'm not a big believer that common sense is enough to base a campaign on. There needs to be at least a modicum of research done prior to launch.

Research doesn't always have to be official. In an ideal world, a large campaign would be put in front of an independent focus group or be subject to surveys prior to going live (the more expensive and more potentially visible a campaign is likely to be, the more important these efforts are). But life's not always ideal. If official research isn't in the budget, try gauging reaction more informally by asking people in another department of the company or people within the agency who aren't connected to the account for their feedback. At the very least, you'll be able to find out the following:

- Does the campaign get its message across?
- Is it eye catching? Will it stand out from other competing marketing efforts so that the audience will notice it?

- Does it leave the audience with a positive impression of the brand?

- Would it make the consumer more or less likely to interact with the brand in the future?

Keep in mind, though—and this is more for readers on the client side, since all agencies already know this (and I expect plenty of fan mail from agency people for spelling this out)—that when I say "informal reaction," I am *not* talking about your barber, mailman, sister-in-law, or anybody else you happen to come across and feel like asking for their opinion, regardless of whether they understand marketing or are part of the market you're trying to reach. Those people's opinions *do not* matter, and it's a waste of time and money to make changes or judgments based on their feedback.

Q: • HOW DO YOU DETERMINE
• THE TARGET AUDIENCE?

MICHAEL HAND
THE CLIENT PERSPECTIVE

As a brand, you cannot be all things to all people. You must know who your target audience is so you can market accordingly. There is no exact science to identifying the target audience for your brand. Essentially, the target can typically be split into two unique groups: the targeted user for your product and the targeted buyer of your product. Much of this conversation will focus on the targeted user, but be aware that plenty of moms are in the store buying for their kids, and numerous "significant others" are in the stores seeking products for their loved ones.

The target user audience consists of the people you want seen holding, eating, driving, drinking, lathering, scrubbing, or [insert other action word here] with your product. To get in touch with them, you have to combine everything you know about them from both a demographical and psychographical perspective. You must use consumer research to move beyond demographics into the consumer's lifestyle, mindset, emotional makeup, and values, and you must understand what these people aspire to, dream about, and worry over. The targeted buyer is slightly different. As I mentioned, these are often moms in the store buying for their kids and/or "significant others," trolling the aisles for products they've been told to buy. You need to closely examine the target groups' relationship with the entire category in which you compete, not just the relationship with your individual brand.

Also, be aware that your target user is not necessarily the same person you see as your current user right now. While these groups may be the same, in many cases they aren't—and reaching them will likely require different tactics than what you have done to date in order to create a change.

Once you've defined the target market, it's critical that you match your message to the group/groups you want to reach. The mistake many companies make is that they find two or three opportunity areas for their brands with consumers, but they do not modify their message for the various groups. Instead, they stick with an undifferentiated model that treats all consumers the same. While this "one size fits all" approach can save money in production (important when you have limited funds to invest in marketing support) and allow for a singular focus on one or two specific brand attribute(s), you must proceed with caution, making sure you execute against the ideas that truly resonate. For years, companies in the overnight-delivery category have used this undifferentiated approach; until recently, Federal Express and UPS broadcast generic messages that talked to everybody in the marketplace the same way—treating the small business owner the same as the mom trying to get cookies to her son for his birthday on campus. The model worked on the surface, but did it really illustrate a functional value for each of the variety of end users? No. These ads relegated the end users and companies to sameness and pushed neither brand to an emotional space.

Of course, using a differentiated strategy means you are using differentiated insights—but it does not mean you use differentiated brand values. The messages directed to each segment of your target market must be tied together in a cohesive manner so people know what you stand for as a brand in totality. The trick is to find the correct emotional levers within each core target group and make sure the benefits of using your brand (although possibly the same in each scenario) are illustrated differently. For example, if you are splitting your audience by gender or race, a simple fix may simply be to change the casting in the spot or the music selected for background. Again, however, you must make sure that changing creative expression of your brand does not change the audience's interpretation of your brand. Be aware, too, that segmenting by numerous niche markets can be costly; think twice before you start to split the atom, running different messages in 74 ZIP codes or copy-splitting your print message for 12 different retailers. Yes, you *can* break down your message to that level of granularity, but it does not necessarily mean that you *should*.

When a brand connects with a wide variety of end users—like, for example, Reese's Peanut Butter Cups—the scope can be pretty wide with respect to who the target user audience is. Well-constructed media plans allow the brand to drive "emotional" messages (for example, "Stop Global Warming before All the Peanut Butter Cups Melt!") toward one particular audience, perhaps through sports, late-night, or reality programming, and then shift to a more "rational" message ("Fill your Candy Bowl!") for daytime TV, cable, or grocery in-store executions. Neither message would scare the other group away, but hopefully the message focus will increase brand perception and relevance with the core users.

JASON MILETSKY

THE AGENCY PERSPECTIVE

⌐↳⌐ Once in awhile, in the course of answering these questions, I've flipped through some other marketing books to see how different experts approached this topic. For the most part, it seems that the crux of the matter, the *how* part, has been largely ignored in favor of long ramblings about the *why* part—that is, why determining the target audience is important. I don't know who's reading these books, but I'd like to assume that *Perspectives* readers are smarter than that, so I'll limit the "why" portion of this answer to simply saying that figuring out who your audience is allows you to better focus your sales and marketing efforts, thereby increasing your chances of generating a positive return. (One of the marketing books I read needed about two and a half pages to say that.)

So how do you go about it? The truth is, I don't think you should think about this issue as though you're starting from square one. I'm guessing you haven't developed your product or service with no concept of a target market in mind; I mean, nobody opens a store that sells crazy expensive watches and thinks putting up billboards in low-income neighborhoods is a good idea. They open the store knowing their target market is people with high expendable incomes, who are over 30, and who are predominantly college-educated (or better). That's why they've opened the store in or around a wealthy neighborhood, not next door to a road-side White Castle. The target market comes already built into the business offering.

So the basics are there from the outset. It's getting a little deeper that can be the tricky part. Continuing on with the expensive watch store example, while they might have a good general idea of who their market is, they might not necessarily know whether more of their customers will be men or women (common sense would probably peg men, but common sense can't always be relied upon), whether more customers will buy watches for themselves or as gifts for someone else, what age groups the customers fall into (if their assumption of being over 30 is correct, and what, in fact, the average age actually is), and other such information.

For the operators of the watch store, the first step in finding this information is by simply keeping their eyes open and observing. Who's coming into the store, looking around, and leaving? Who's coming in and actually making a purchase? How often do the same people visit the store before buying something? How old are they? What's the percentage breakdown of single men, single women, or couples shopping together? Early marketing efforts, which may have been educated shots in the dark, can slowly evolve into more targeted strategies as information is collected and analyzed.

Simple observation really is the first and most important step. Even major-label brands with national or global distribution of products hire agencies to observe consumers at the retail level and make notes on who's buying what, where, and when. The larger brands, of course, have bigger budgets that open up other research options, including focus groups or purchasing information from research companies such as Nielson. But no matter how you go about it, it comes down to the collection of data. Most brands aren't going to have the money to simply pawn off their research to a data-collection agency; they'll need to take it upon themselves to gather information. Work from the base that's already built when you launch your brand. Keep your eyes open, and make sure salespeople, distributors, and customer-service reps make it part of their job to get to know the consumers interested in your products or service. Most people automatically associate marketing with creative, but marketing is really about analytics—and you can never have too much information.

One last thing I'd like to add, even if it's slightly off-topic: Never rely on what I call a "focus group of one." I see this all the time: A bunch of marketing people (the agency, the client, or all together) are talking about the target market and one person says something like, "You know, personally, I really like this product. I would totally buy it for myself!" Then, everyone in the room decides that because that one person claims he would buy it, he must represent the target market—and they base all subsequent strategic planning on any demographics he represents. Even worse is the "focus group of one, twice removed," which is when someone in the meeting says something along the lines of, "I was talking to my brother's wife about this, and she said that the women in her Wednesday night book club would definitely be into buying this brand." Wonderful. That information isn't just completely pointless, it's dangerous; for reasons I cannot comprehend, people actually give it weight when they set their marketing strategies. Please, for the sake of the brand and your budget, when someone offers these types of quippy pieces of information, simply smile, nod, thank them, and move on to real data.

Q: Is There Value in Focus Groups?

Michael Hand
The Client Perspective

I do find some value in focus groups for getting preliminary responses on brand direction. Real consumers are passionate about all the things that affect their brands; if done correctly, focus groups can provide some great feedback early in the development cycle. That said, focus groups should not be your sole guide when making creative decisions.

Although marketers tend to focus only on advertising when they discuss focus groups, these groups can be just as valuable for feedback on promotions, logo development, and/or packaging design work. I've used focus groups to test potential sponsorship opportunities and their possible promotional elements with great results. In these cases, I was able to gather the consumers' thoughts about the resulting brand association, which enabled my team to better evaluate which area of the particular sport we should harness in communication efforts. For example, should the focus be on the league, the individual teams within the league, or the top players? Or on better understanding how valuable it would be to have an endorsement from a star player in conveying the brand's message? Most importantly, did the consumer perceive that the league was riding our corporate coattails or was the perception that we were equal partners, with both sides having something to gain in the relationship? Even worse, were we seen as a nobody trying to use the property just to get on the map? As it moved into the promotional support area, we were able to probe on methods for contest or sweepstakes entries and the use of packaging elements to tell the promotional story and engage the fan. By using a focus group, we were able to better understand how far the average fan would go to get involved with our program elements and how far the passionate fan needed to see us go to justify his or her involvement.

Before you even walk into the room with a focus group, make sure you have a really good moderator to lead the conversation. The moderator is in charge of getting the answers from everybody beyond the glass, from the token jackass, who wants to make everyone laugh, to the focus-group bully, who convinces everybody in the room that his opinion is the only right one. (It's particularly critical to weed out the bully right at the start to ensure he doesn't make the other participants cave. When faced with such a person, many group members decide it's not worth fighting with a guy they'll never see again.) The moderator will control the end result of the focus group, *not* the consumers in the group. Spend some time with this person in advance to make sure he or she knows exactly what you want to find out and which areas you want to dig into more deeply. It's also a good idea to take breaks during each session and have the moderator come behind the glass to check in and make sure the brand team is getting what they need. Focus groups sometimes become redundant, melding into one similar storyline; touching base with the moderator enables you to discuss other key areas worth probing and alternate directions to take the dialogue.

A final point on focus groups: Focus groups aren't a contest to see how many bowls of pretzels you, as an observer, can eat or how many backed-up e-mails you can cut through in a session. It's critical that you pay close attention. Don't just rely on the moderator's final report to tell you what you saw; be observant from the minute you walk into the room. Really *look* at the people in the group—their clothes and shoes, their makeup and jewelry. Get to know your consumer on a more intimate level through observation. This may be the closest you'll get to them; use it to your advantage. And make sure the moderator encourages the group to *never* filter their thoughts. You need a candid critique and commentary to get better; encourage this.

JASON MILETSKY
THE AGENCY PERSPECTIVE

In 1985, in response to a growing threat from Pepsi and a generally flat soft-drink market, Coca-Cola made a bold move: They changed their formula. While surveys and other testing mechanisms showed a highly favorable response to the new formula, focus groups revealed a picture that was more reflective of the final outcome. Most consumers in the focus groups liked the new formula and said they would buy it. A small faction of the group, however, was angered by the suggestion that Coca-Cola would change at all, and emphatically declared that if the original formula were changed, they would no longer buy the product. Apparently this small faction was quite loud, and their negativity infected others in the group, who then began to express their *own* negative feelings about the product. Likewise, when the new formula was introduced, many consumers reportedly liked the new taste—but outrage from a small minority became so strong that *not* liking New Coke became fashionable. Consumers jumped on the growing bandwagon and trashed the updated formula.

With a relatively limited means of measuring audience reaction, opinion, or sentiment, focus groups can be an effective way to get inside the minds of consumers. With every focus group I've been a part of, I've learned something valuable. Sometimes what I learn is surprising, and other times it's just a confirmation of what I already know, but there's always something.

At the time same time, marketers on both the agency and the client side must remember that although focus groups can provide a look at what's going on inside the consumer's mind, they don't exactly represent the entire market. Even if they're from all walks of life—socio-economic classes, races, religions, and ages—they still represent the segment of the market that is willing to spend an hour or two giving opinions for as much as $100 or as little as a $5 Starbucks gift card. They can't possibly represent the far greater number of people who can't be enticed to sit in a focus group—not because they're apathetic, but because they may not feel like they want to share their opinions or may want to spend their time doing other things instead. Focus groups also don't represent the general public that may not express an opinion simply because there's no real opinion to express. In other words, in my experience, people who take part in focus groups tend to be the types who want to make a little noise and have their voices heard. (I can't back this up with hard statistics; it's just my own observation.) They're more likely to manufacture an issue or express an opinion they might not have under different circumstances just to feel like they've contributed something. That doesn't mean that the thoughts expressed during focus groups shouldn't be taken seriously, only that the marketers involved should be aware of these issues.

Similarly, both the agency and the marketer must to be conscious that when all is said and done, the numbers are crunched in such a way that they present a clear and unbiased analysis of the focus-group results. (This is usually best done by a third party with little invested in the outcome.) Although focus groups are often run with a thesis in mind—even if this thesis isn't obvious or expressly stated—it's important that both the agency and the client approach focus groups with open minds. They must avoid asking leading questions, and analyze the results for what they are rather than try to manipulate the numbers to support pre-suppositions.

Q: IS A LONG-TERM STRATEGY A NECESSITY?

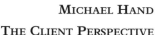

MICHAEL HAND
THE CLIENT PERSPECTIVE

Yes, yes, and yes. All too often, we focus all our efforts on immediate gratification and think very little on the long-term consequences of our actions. But failure to formulate a long-term strategy is one of the biggest mistakes that any client (or agency) can make. It's simply not an option to operate with only the short term in mind—but that doesn't mean you should focus solely on saving for a rainy day. You need a balance of short-term and long-term tactics.

I believe that *every* company—client and agency alike—needs to be able to articulate a one-year, three-year, and five-year plan. These plans should not get locked in a desk drawer, but they shouldn't become corporate gospel either. Rather, these living, breathing documents must outline what all employees and agency partners are chasing to ensure business health.

ONE YEAR PLAN

The one-year plan needs to capture the immediate deliverables and tactics. It's about driving results right now. It needs to illustrate the game plan for the next battle, not how you will win the actual war. It needs to describe how you will deliver a short-term boost in sales and profitability. The focus here is on tactics. This plan should include new product launches and should clearly address issues related to product manufacturing, commodity cost pressures, the competitive situation in the market, retail-related factors, and planned budgets—issues that can fluctuate over time but that need to be solid within the one-year horizon. Marketing plays a critical role in this portion of the plan. You need a detailed roadmap to follow; elements of the plan should be locked for execution 12 to 18 months in advance, depending on your category.

THREE YEAR PLAN

The three-year plan is the happy medium. It should be steeped in realistic assumptions, but it should include a bit in the way of stretch goals and marketplace projections. This can be the toughest of all plans to write because of the variables that are in play. You shouldn't play guessing games on whether you will add new line extensions or products to the market, but don't expect to have total clarity on the competitive environment or the retail landscape either. From a marketing perspective, most elements of the plan will be fuzzy, but you should have a clear point of view on where you see the trends taking you and what it will take to respond to this direction. Issues like global or market expansion must be included because they take time to prepare for and build toward.

FIVE YEAR PLAN

The five-year plan is critical to long-term corporate health and overall success. You must have a vision of where you want to take things and how you will maintain a steady stream of consumers. This is similar to the "Where do you see yourself in five years?" question you get asked on job interviews. When somebody asks that question, they don't expect you to tell them your future title, new office location, and projected annual salary. They want to get a sense of what your vision for success looks like and to understand what motivates you. Is it more money, a bigger title, corner office, or something else? How a person answers this question can be very telling about the individual; so, too, can a company's five-year strategy document. It indicates how poised an organization is for growth and if they truly believe they can achieve it. It should outline the areas of opportunity that will be the foundation of the future and should include some ideas on how current marketplace opportunities will be realized. It needs to consider how current organizational gaps will be closed over time and to show a commitment to remain profitable and take care of employees. Marketing involvement is likely less present in this document beyond broader corporate vision and mission statements as well as brand health indicators.

JASON MILETSKY

THE AGENCY PERSPECTIVE

The obvious answer is, duh, of course you always have to have a long-term strategy. But as I started typing that, I realized that the reason that answer seemed so obvious was that my instinct was to think in terms of marketing campaigns. With any kind of marketing campaign, there absolutely needs to be a long-term strategy. Without it, managing the campaign is equivalent to playing darts in the dark.

Sure, every campaign will have twists and turns, and although you'll be evolving strategies on the fly as new results and measurements are taken, there must be a baseline long-term strategy to start from. This strategy must take into consideration goals and expected results, and choreograph the wide variety of media that may be included in a single campaign, like print, TV, or roadside billboards.

Even if only a single media outlet is used, increased Web traffic can be expected. How the site gets tied into the more broadly based campaign creative, how your audience will experience the site, and how visitors who want to take a desired action will be funneled to the right pages all require long-term strategies and planning, set against hard, numeric goals.

Developing a long-term strategy involves looking at least one quarter into the future and deciding which avenues are going to be the most effective for capturing consumers' attention. Outside of some really crazy PR stunt, it's rare that a marketing campaign will get its biggest bang right out of the gate. Most campaigns will work on some variation of the standard bell curve, where market interest will gain over time as your campaign continues to promote your message until it finally reaches a peak before fading past the point of diminishing returns. But the bell curve will work only if the campaign is executed properly—which means determining in advance when new creative should be added and new media introduced. Much like in a war, in which the generals consider all variables—including terrain, weather, and enemy reaction to movements—wise marketers must consider as many twists and turns as possible before launching a campaign. Not only does this make marketing efforts as effective as possible, it also helps in the budgeting process, since any given part of a campaign can be expensive and dollars for execution are usually limited.

So here's where my dilemma came in: Campaigns are only one part of what agencies do. In addition to campaigns are some less sexy—but still vital—services such as marketing collateral, standard Web site design, PowerPoint presentation templates…the list goes on. These tend to be the more project-based, everyday services that all companies require but that aren't necessarily tied into any established campaign. In fact, for many agencies, the lion's share of revenue will come from these types of services, with full, extensive campaigns being the cherry on top. So if these pieces aren't tied to a campaign, do they require long-term strategies?

I'd like to think the answer is yes, and certainly other agencies will disagree with me because to say otherwise casts out necessity into doubt, but my honest feeling is no, these type of services don't really require long-term strategy. They require consistency with the brand, and they definitely require pre-planning and project coordination, but not always a long-term strategy. Sometimes a brochure is just a brochure—something salespeople will have to show when they talk to new prospects. They're simple, clear-cut, and project-based, and that's all there is to it. Allow projects like these to be just that—projects. Put your creative hats on and go crazy designing brochures that will dazzle clients and walk home with awards. But don't kill yourself developing long-term strategy for material that doesn't need it. Save your long-term strategic planning for your more visible, external-facing marketing campaigns.

Q: SHOULD INTERNET MARKETING STRATEGIES BE PART OF THE GENERAL STRATEGY, OR KEPT SEPARATE?

MICHAEL HAND

THE CLIENT PERSPECTIVE

I am going to be short and sweet on this one (hold your applause), as I will assume my writing partner will take this opportunity to spew about the virtues of Internet marketing strategy. The fact that this question even still gets asked concerns me. Internet marketing is no longer some random outside influence. The early 1990s, when people were still wondering what e-mail was all about and why it was being used, are long gone. Wake up people!! It's imperative that every company's general marketing strategy includes an Internet marketing component, regardless of the size of the company or agency. An Internet marketing plan that exists by itself cannot be successful; it must be linked in with the larger strategic vision.

As you fold your Internet strategy into the larger plan, you need to keep these points in mind:

- You must have a strong focus on the products and brands that your company brings to market. A strong product is the foundation of any great marketing strategy. A key aspect of any great product is that it's something that nobody can replicate; the point of difference could be a taste profile, an odor, or the results that it delivers. The bottom line: Your product must be unique, and you should leverage the Internet to communicate that uniqueness.

- You must know your target market and how they will use the Internet to build on their connection with your brand. If your brand is youth- or young-adult–oriented and leverages social networking or virtual tactics to build on your brand experience, it should be spelled out in detail in the interactive strategy how this can be accomplished and what is expected to be gained. If your demographical targets push a bit older and they are only using the Web experience to get facts and information, then you need these elements available and called out in your plan.

- The Internet takes your product global with a click of the mouse; can your organization deliver against that wide of an audience? Can you control that via the message on your Web site? Do you need multiple translations or other international tools?

JASON MILETSKY

THE AGENCY PERSPECTIVE

For the life of me, I cannot understand why clients continue to keep Internet marketing strategies separate from more traditional, general strategies. I get why this was the case in the '90s and the Web was brand new; clients didn't yet see the true value of Internet marketing, and the older, established agencies had no clue how the Web worked. The general fear of the Internet during that period made sense. But even though we're rounding out the first decade of the 2000s, not much has changed in the way some clients handle their Web marketing. Yes, they all get that they need a site, and that that site has to be a serious reflection of their brand. Most even understand that they need to have an Internet strategy in place, whether that means planning out how to build and evolve their site, adding streaming-video components, blogging, including CPC advertising, implementing e-mail marketing, or something else. But it still seems like most clients insist on separating these efforts from more traditional strategies the way a kid tries to keep the peas on his plate from touching the mashed potatoes.

I'm not saying a single agency needs to the at the helm of each and every effort. Clearly, different agencies have different strengths, and these should be leveraged properly. But as hard as it might be, I think agencies must force themselves to play nice and develop strategies together. There's no longer any question about the magnitude of the Internet's importance to marketing (which I'll review in greater detail in the next question); what seems to remain in question by many brands is how many new avenues the Internet opens for finding and capturing new audiences. It's not just about building a great site; it's about driving the right traffic to it, keeping them there, encouraging them to take the desired action, and enticing them to return.

The danger is in the potential for a disconnect. Not everything will just automatically work together. Like trying to retrofit a turntable to play CDs, getting a site or entire Internet strategy to work in sync with a traditional marketing strategy could be potentially inefficient and seemingly forced or, worse, simply not possible. Setting the general strategy first and then forcing the Internet strategy to comply underscores the naiveté of brands that have yet to grasp the Net's complexities.

In an ideal world, brands would develop a single strategy that simultaneously considered both traditional and Internet efforts in a somewhat layered fashion, sharing concepts in the online and offline space so that there's consistency in creative, design, and messaging. Brands should also consider the potential actions of consumers as they are exposed to various marketing efforts, the likelihood that they will (encouraged or on their own) visit the brand's site for more information, and how that reaction will be managed. By doing this, brands can fully exploit the power of all media outlets rather than concentrating on the strengths of traditional strategies and potentially weakening their Internet strategy.

Q: HOW IMPORTANT IS THE WEB
• TO ANY MARKETING EFFORT?

MICHAEL HAND

THE CLIENT PERSPECTIVE

The Web has become a critical part of the marketing effort for every brand that exists in America today, and should be given more than just passing consideration for every product or service that goes to market. Interactive elements must be called out in all marketing plans, and they must play a prominent role in building awareness and keeping brands contemporary.

The Web works on a variety of levels to do everything from engaging prospective buyers, persuading them to purchase your products, or simply entertaining everyday consumers through your messages and brand-centric activities. The Web should be utilized on two primary levels:

- **The awareness-driving level:** i.e., advertising via Web banners, streaming video components, engaging in viral efforts, leveraging social media, seeding a video on YouTube, etc.

- **The information-gathering level:** i.e., corporate Web sites, online product reviews, corporate information/history, media updates, leadership contact details, etc.

In the past decade, this second level has become critical to corporate success as most consumers now go to the Web to gather information before making any meaningful (and even not-so-meaningful) purchases. Whether leasing a car, buying a home, obtaining medical insurance, shelling out $8 for a movie ticket, or procuring a new book, consumers go to the Web to gather information before they buy. Indeed, the average consumer spends countless hours sifting through data points and online customer (and expert) reviews before making a major purchase. For example, if a consumer is in the market for a new flat-screen TV, that individual will no longer walk into his or her local electronics store and ask the manager of the TV department, "What do you think?" Instead, that consumer will gather data on the Internet. He or she will check out multiple reviews (at the time of this writing, a basic Google search on the phrase "flat screen TV reviews" yielded more than 540,000 hits), visit multiple manufacturer Web sites, and maybe even e-mail friends and family to ask for their opinions. After this stage, the person *might* walk into a store to buy a TV—but could just as easily make the purchase online. Simply put: All roads will drive consumers to the Internet at some point along the journey.

I want to acknowledge the Internet's evolving role because it illustrates the importance of keeping Internet marketing activities in the same conversation as traditional TV and print advertising. It also makes it very clear that you no longer can control 100 percent of your company's or brand's message and image in the marketplace. Third parties now greatly influence people's buying decisions. The Web is never turned off. It's a 24-hour-a-day, seven-days-a-week, 365-days-a-year information source that can give any time-pressured individual access to products and services (as well as customer feedback on these products and services) worldwide with a simple click of the mouse. Where other media forums are a one-way dialogue, the Web is equally strong in getting messages out as it is in taking them in. The Web's ability to update in real time as comments are shared is also something no other form of media in the marketing mix can deliver.

JASON MILETSKY

THE AGENCY PERSPECTIVE

According to a report by the Pew Internet and American Life Project, a leading research organization, more than 80 percent of all Internet users use the Web to research products and services before they make an offline purchase. This staggering statistic highlights exactly how important the Web has become to marketers.

But rather than making my entire point by quoting numbers (even though those numbers alone could easily make the case for the Web's importance), I'd rather use this section to deconstruct the Web a bit and examine what makes it different and why it's become such a huge deal. Part of it is that the Web is a hybrid entity, in that it's both an advertising medium and the object being advertised. Other factors include how messages are delivered, the potential for increased markets, particular reinforcement of the brand, and heightened consumer interaction. Let's take a look at each of these individually.

THE WEB AND ITS HYBRID STATUS

Advertising, for example, is used to promote a product or service or increase awareness of a brand. Its a single-effect communication requiring the audience to take action on their own. A reader of a print ad, for example, can't make a purchase directly from that print ad. He or she must take some sort of action such as making a phone call or visiting a store in order to make a purchase. The ad promotes the brand, and the company or the store sells the product.

The Web, however, falls somewhere between the promotion and sales processes. A Web site can act in exactly the same way as an ad in a magazine: by promoting the brand and pushing consumers toward a product. In this sense, both the print ad and the Web site exist for the purpose of driving consumers to make a purchase (take action). They each work to advertise a brand. The Web is different from other marketing tools, though, in that visiting a Web site is often the very action that other marketing tools attempt to persuade consumers to take. Rather than making the case to consumers to visit a store and purchase a product, a print ad may instead make the case to consumers to visit the brand's Web site and gather more information or make a purchase from there. In this sense, the Web is not only a means of advertising, it is also the thing being advertised. So in this scenario, one marketing tool—i.e., a print ad—is, in a way, marketing another marketing tool—i.e., the Web.

The Web offers infinite space to provide information, promote the brand personality, and offer e-commerce capabilities, while social-media tools enable the brand to interact with its market, delivering a far richer experience than a 30-second commercial or one-page print ad ever could.

INDIVIDUAL MESSAGE DELIVERY

Traditional mass marketing tools and branding efforts address the audience as a single entity, regardless of how many people that audience might include. This approach offers no way to speak to individual members of a target market. Instead, it sends messages to large demographics, which are targeted based primarily on assumptions made about the shows being watched, the magazine being read, or what have you. For example, the investment firm Charles Schwab can reasonably assume that they are more likely to reach people interested in their services by running ads during *The Suze Orman Show* on CNBC than by advertising on *Rock of Love* on VH1. While individual shows can provide a more narrow audience demographic, the message is still sent to the audience as a whole; the commercial has no way of reaching out to a particular member of the audience and saying, "Hi, John. We noticed you've been looking around for a high-yield IRA. You might be interested in one we offer…."

In contrast, thanks to social-media tools, the Web can speak to each member of a given audience on an individual basis through personalization. Sites like Amazon.com have perfected the art of promotion based on intuitive, one-to-one marketing. When you first get there, the site features items that it's trying to push most aggressively because at this point it doesn't know who you are or what you are interested in. After you've tooled around on the site a bit, however, this changes. Do a few searches and then check out Amazon's home page the next time you visit—the featured products will now reflect what the site thinks you'll be interested in based on your previous search and/or purchasing history. Face it, no retail outlet in any industry can suddenly change its window display based on my previous shopping habits in their store!

The ability to market to individuals based on previous buying behavior increases the potential for sales by making brands accessible to the people most likely to buy them. From a brand perspective, this creates significant opportunities for increased revenue and brand recognition from key markets.

INCREASED MARKETS

Traditional marketing can be expensive. One full-page print ad can cost anywhere from a few thousand dollars to a few *hundred* thousand dollars, depending on the publication. Television spots can be even more pricey. Thirty seconds of air time can range from a few hundred dollars (for example, to air in a single county on a relatively unpopular cable show) to nearly three million dollars (for example, to air during the Super Bowl). This can add up quickly, limiting reach and exposure.

Technically, the Web's exposure is limitless and easily accessible to anyone, regardless of demographic or geographic boundaries. This doesn't mean everyone *will* see your site, just that everyone *can* see it. This creates opportunities for marketers to increase the reach of their brands by concentrating efforts on driving people to their sites through traditional marketing, word-of-mouth, and links shared between sites. By opening themselves up to new audiences, brands can generate increased exposure and sales.

REINFORCEMENT OF THE BRAND MESSAGE

Because the Web is so dynamic, marketers can use it to reinforce their brand image and promise without the consumer even making a purchase. Pampers.com, for example, has developed their Web site specifically to enhance their promise of being a brand that cares about babies and toddlers. For decades, Pampers has earned the trust of parents all over the world by consistently marketing safe, reliable, and high-quality products specifically for babies—an area in which gaining trust can be particularly difficult. To reinforce this trust in their products, Pampers uses its site as a marketing tool by providing a true informational resource for parents, presenting helpful insights, expert advice, and information for parents about child development, growth, activities, and more. Much of this information has little or nothing to do with the products they sell.

Why would Pampers bother? After all, the company is in business to sell a product, not to provide advice. The reason is the difference between the product (what Pampers *sells*) and the brand (what Pampers *promises*). The site shows that although Pampers manufactures diapers, they in fact care about kids before caring about profit. This is what builds trust, which in turn builds loyalty—which, eventually, translates to increased sales.

When translating their brand onto the Web, marketers should ask themselves (or, better yet, their customers) what information they can provide beyond standard product information that can improve the lives of their customers. The Web offers brands increased opportunities to provide value-added services over and above their product offerings and engage their market in far more personal ways, thereby increasing trust and reinforcing their brand.

Heightened Consumer Interaction

In addition to enable brands to market on a one-to-one basis, the Web also provides the ability to create a community of customers. Indeed, through blogs, Wikis, social networking, and other tools, brands can interact with consumers more closely than ever before. The Web lets brands learn from customers. With the Web, brands can gather opinions, run more effective marketing and promotional campaigns, and give consumers the opportunity to interact with each other. These efforts help to build trust and strengthen the emotional connection between brand and consumer, providing increased opportunities for the brand to more closely connect itself to its market.

Q: WHAT ARE THE BEST OBJECTIVES BASED ON? WHO ULTIMATELY DETERMINES SPECIFIC GOALS?

MICHAEL HAND

THE CLIENT PERSPECTIVE

When I think about goal setting, I get a little textbook-centric, so I apologize to readers in advance for regurgitating college theory. In my mind, the best objectives are based on realistic targets and are best determined jointly between employee and supervisor or client and agency. When setting objectives and establishing goals (be they departmental or individual), I use a method called the S.M.A.R.T. approach, espoused by author Peter F. Drucker in his 1954 book *The Practice of Management*. S.M.A.R.T. is an acronym for the five characteristics of successful goals:

- Specific

- Measurable

- Attainable

- Relevant

- Time-based

Using this simple approach moves you from hypothetical direction to actionable plans that can drive results. Let's take a moment to recap these principles that define what objectives should be based on.

SPECIFIC

Well-written goals are very clear and focused. By being specific, you remove any existing ambiguity. You cannot be vague, leaving things open for arbitrary interpretation across levels of any organization, when setting your goals. This step is often connected to "how much" and "how often" measures. Having a mathematical factor determine how you judge the final result drives concrete deliverables with a greater level of precision. Goals should not be written simply as "Increase sales" or "Provide several rounds of creative concepts"; they should have a percentage or exact number attached to make them clear. "Increase sales in the Boston market by 17 percent" or "provide five rounds of creative concepts for each unique campaign" are much more meaningful and provide better direction. Making goals specific won't necessarily reduce the potential for failure, but it will make people aware of the desired results and allow for clearer expectations.

MEASURABLE

Let's be clear: This is business. Even if you enjoy what you do for a living, people are keeping score. Performance is being measured. After all, would you watch NFL games every Sunday if they decided to stop keeping score? Probably not.

Goals need to be measured and results need to be defined. If they cannot be quantified, then something is likely missing. Numbers are critical to business, and being able to measure your progress on your goals is the only way you'll know if the business is staying on track. Building from the previous point, telling an employee "The business must grow" is not enough; you must assign a percentage or dollar figure to measure against. This can be calculated, maintained and monitored with greater ease, enabling you to link individual accountability/progress reports directly to the task at hand.

ACHIEVABLE

It doesn't do you any good to set outlandish goals. Yes, it's great to be ambitious and to set stretch goals for yourself and your group, but you need to be realistic. Your goals must have a chance to succeed. If average sales growth in your industry during the past five years has been 5 percent, don't make it your goal to achieve 25 percent sales growth. Otherwise, you're just setting yourself up for failure, which is *never* good. Not only does the goal become useless within the first month, it reduces motivation. The same argument can be made for goals on the other end of that spectrum. Never set goals that are extremely easy to achieve, or you will not maximize effort. Goals at both extremes of the achievable scale become meaningless.

RELEVANT

Objectives are relevant to an individual only if he or she can do something to achieve them. When goals are developed, they should link to results for which the people assigned the deliverable are accountable. It is not relevant for the marketing team to worry about the computer system's efficiency levels; go see the guys in IT for that. And it's not the accounting department's objective to drive more impressions from the public-relations efforts; that's up to the communications team. You must also ensure that the selected objectives really affect the business. Every measure you can think of does not need to end up on the final annual mission list.

Time-Based

If you want to drive results in your business, you need to set definitive deadlines for getting things done. Unlimited time requirements make it impossible to measure whether an objective has been hit. You need clear start and end dates to hold people accountable. An objective of growing 5 percent by the end of the year is good; but do not get caught celebrating the fact that after three months, sales are up 7 percent. You need to maintain that position for nine more months. This works in tandem with the aforementioned "measurable" principle.

Setting objectives is not the most complicated thing in the world, but doing so is critical to both the short- and long-term success of your business. They are the default direction during times of turmoil and they drive both lower-level employees and management alike. It is human nature to be driven to succeed, and using the S.M.A.R.T. approach when developing goals will ensure better end results. The best goals are written in unison with the client (or senior manager) and agency (or employee) sharing in the final determination of how the goals read.

Jason Miletsky
The Agency Perspective

First of all, let me just get it out there: Specific goals are an absolute necessity for any marketing campaign. The key word is "specific"—numeric whenever possible. General or vague goals that have no pre-established definition of success—for example, "To increase traffic to our Web site"—are pointless. They don't provide any real guidelines. Increase traffic...compared to what? Does a single-user increase render the campaign a success? Without firm numerics, there's no way to know whether any effort has been worthwhile.

What goals should be based upon, how they should be measured, and what they should be measured against are three different issues. Whenever possible, goals should be based upon ensuring a positive ROI. All marketing campaigns are costly, so goals must be based on ensuring that for every dollar spent, more than that dollar comes back. Otherwise, what's the point? How that formula is derived depends on the client, the agency, and the type of campaign (public relations, for example, can be particularly difficult to equate into revenue generation). But however it's done—even if it's initially through trial and error—all measurement devices must somehow be capable of conveying to people that the money on a campaign has been well spent.

> I always think it's funny when agencies' Web sites say things like, "We work to ensure our clients receive an ROI on their marketing investment." ROI stands for Return On Investment, so ensuring an ROI isn't a big deal—returns can be negative! What you're shooting for there, champ, is a *positive* ROI).

Measurement devices can be numerous and varied. Which of these devices are used depends on the type of campaign. They can include, in part:

■ Web traffic

■ Sales

■ Leads generated

■ Open and/or click-through rates

■ Column inches or broadcast minutes

Except for new brands that are going through the marketing process for the first time, companies can also reference past performance to help in setting new goals and objectives. Generating a positive ROI needs to be the basis for the goals, but how much is enough to make the effort worthwhile? Rather than establishing this number arbitrarily, marketers should look to their past. For example, if Web traffic is being used to measure goals and last year was a successful year, a realistic goal for an upcoming campaign (assuming there are similar budgets and market conditions from one year to the next) could be 10 percent over traffic rates for the same quarter last year. Again, such things as market conditions, available budgets, and competitive movements need to factored in, but however the math is done, setting goals against past results is a strong way of measuring success.

Finally, goals have to make sense. We once had a client that wanted us to run a print ad for a $10,000 home theater they were manufacturing. No question about it, it was a beautiful piece of electronics. The plan was to run a print campaign in upscale publications like *Robb Report* and *Millionaire Magazine*. As we were talking about the concept behind the campaign, the client revealed their goal: to sell 300 units of the home theater each month. And they wanted the print ad to be the vehicle behind those sales. (I should mention that this was before the Web had become such a primary source of consumer information.) After a moment of stunned silence, I told them flatly, no. If that was the goal, I could guarantee that we'd fail. There was no way a print ad could drive the sale of 300 units of a $10,000 home theater each month. I doubted we could sell even *one* unit. Why would I want to get involved in a marketing effort destined to crash and burn? Clearly, price wasn't the issue—our target demo was afflu-ent individuals who could afford to spend $10,000 on what was pretty much a really fancy TV. But nobody was going to buy it so they could watch Seinfeld by themselves; they were buying it so they could have their friends over for Monday Night Football. For our demographic, the ultimate purpose of this $10,000 home theater, which would undoubtedly end up being the centerpiece of a $50,000 room, would be to show off a little now that their trophy wives had stopped drawing as much attention as they used to. So with so much at stake, there was no way these guys were going to buy the home theater sight unseen. So, I explained, instead of selling 300 units, the goal of the ad should be to encourage 1,000 people to call a local distributor for a demonstration. (Along with creating and placing the ad, we also had to alert distributors about our plans, train them on the best way to present and sell the product, and make sure we developed and sent them all the brochures and materials they'd need to close the sale.)

The point is, goals in marketing are an absolute necessity for determining which efforts have been successful and which need to be fine-tuned or scrapped alto-gether. But you have to make sure that you're judging your work based on the right goals in order to get a clear understanding of the results.

Q: THE CREATIVE BRIEF: WHO WRITES IT, AND WHAT'S NEEDED TO MAKE IT USEFUL?

MICHAEL HAND

THE CLIENT PERSPECTIVE

One of the biggest mistakes made by marketers at companies across the country is allowing advertising/media/consumer promotion/interactive agencies to write their own creative briefs. This practice must stop ASAP. Clients will never truly take ownership of the end product unless they play a strategic role in the development of the concepts and plans involved—and writing the creative brief is the best way for the client to do that.

What should a creative brief contain to make sure it is useful? Every good brief will consist of the following information, regardless of what marketing discipline is developing the work:

- **Business situation:** What's happening in the marketplace that has required this work to be produced? This is the section to share information on usage behavior, brand perceptions (both internally and externally), category dynamics, and competitive threats. It's also where you should include any charts or graphs that convey important data points as well as research findings to date and current brand health measures. The strategic planning team will refer to this section of the brief more than any other area.

- **Marketing/communication objectives:** What is this project looking to achieve? What exact action do you want the consumer to take? How will success be measured upon completion? This is the section to lay out share gain and volume goals, key competitive measures, and marketing challenges with both customers and consumers. Leave no room for ambiguity. This is the section to which the client's senior management will refer during the creative selection. They will probe to confirm whether the measures can realistically be achieved by the recommended action. As an agency, do not try to "re-interpret" these objectives. You can seek clarity, but do not look to rephrase for your purposes. Objectives must be lifted verbatim from the brief.

Use the S.M.A.R.T. approach outlined in the answer to Question #40, "What Are the Best Objectives Based On? Who Ultimately Determines Specific Goals?" to establish both how success will be measured and strong criteria for making the creative selection.

- **Assignment description:** To help you avoid overdeveloping a concept, this section of the brief should clearly define what tactics are required and establish what the final creative review will (or will not) include. The "will not" portion is equally important here; if you have an agency that specializes in interactive work on retainer and you are briefing for a consumer promotions concept with your CP agency, be clear that you do not expect to see Web extensions in their final presentation. This level of clarity will save everybody time and effort, while also forcing a more focused deliverable. This section is also where you should specify exactly what the client expects to be presented and which products/line extensions/models are to be included. I beg the agency: During the review of the brief document, spend extra time on this section and ask as many clarifying questions as you need.

- **Target audience profile:** Who are you trying to reach? Is the program focused on the end user or on the person actually making the purchase at retail? This section should include as much demographic and psychographic/attitudinal information that is available on the audience you want to reach with your message. It should also include any insights not shared in the "Business Situation" section that relate to the user's lifestyle and behavior. It may also include a primary and secondary target for the program at hand. (You should be clear on how big a priority these alternative audiences are.)

- **Positioning statement:** This section serves to ensure that nothing created falls outside of the brand character. It provides a frame of reference for the brand in general, and should highlight the brand's unique point of difference that will need to be reinforced in the development process.

- **Geographic/seasonal/class-of-trade priorities:** Not every brief will need this, but if you work in a business or with a brand that skews more heavily based on a particular factor, it must be added. Geographic skews come into play when you compete in a segment that includes many small regional players or if you want to tailor your message to a particular retail location. Seasonal considerations must be articulated for products that see big fluctuations in consumption or purchase behavior depending on the time of year. For example, the auto industry often sees lower sales volume in January and February, and the beer business typically experiences big spikes during the summer (from Memorial Day to Labor Day). Class of trade is of great interest for brands with different shoppers who may be in the market at the same time. Creative teams need to know if they need to alter a message going to young adult males at the convenience store for the 35–44-year-old female who is the primary grocery-store shopper for her family. Some program overlay may occur, but you need to be careful to avoid alienating the user base. In the confection arena, I personally faced the issue of whether to select a spring movie property that worked very well for young adult males and promised great revenue gains at convenience stores but could also be deemed too violent for mom in the grocery store. The brief should help you choose the correct path on tough issues like that.

■ **Budget:** How much do you really have to spend? As the client, you must be realistic. I myself have been guilty of writing a brief that requests $2–3 million ideas when I knew full well going into the project that my budget was $1.5 million. Yes, it's always exciting to see what more money can get you, and it's tempting to hold onto the idea that if the idea is big enough, you'll find the money. But the reality is that funding is usually hard to come by, and too many ideas fall apart when you start stripping elements to hit your lower (read: more reasonable) dollar figure. Be realistic from the start and manage expectations. Ask the agency to bring some ideas for what they might change/add if more money were to become available—not the other way around.

■ **Timing/critical path:** When will you sit down to review the concepts, and when will the program be executed in market? Be very direct about when you need to see the first round of ideas and lock the date on your calendar from the start. Things may change a bit along the way, but two dates should never move: the first review date and the in-market execution date. Make sure the timeline includes enough time for approvals, legal reviews, and contract negotiations if third parties are involved. This can be more complicated than you ever imagined. Dealing with multiple members of a band or an entire cast on a film extends the time needed to get things signed off. Plan accordingly to avoid surprises and rush charges.

To establish the timeline, look at the end date and work backward.

■ **Creative Mandatories:** Is there anything that absolutely *must* be included in the final work? This is the section where you should include your trademark guidelines, talent requirements, color palette demands, POS specifications, etc. If you have specific tactical or executional considerations, they should be listed here.

- **Signatures:** After the briefing process is complete, make sure you have an agreed-upon document to work from, signed by the individual(s) who will be driving the selection process. If a VP gets the final vote, that person should sign the brief so he or she knows what to expect and does not change the direction at the eleventh hour. I would like to avoid going up the chain of command on the brief development process, but I can swear by the fact it will save you time in the end. Creating ownership and a commitment by agreeing to the brief will only help you down the road.

The creative brief should be altered to reflect any changes made during the review. This document needs to be 100-percent accurate before you commit to the assignment. A major stretch, I know, but you cannot change the brief after the work gets started.

I mentioned that clients should write the brief—and I believe they should. That said, if the agency *does* take the lead in writing the brief—perhaps due to time factors or a shortage of human resources on the client side—the document must be approved by the client before the creative juices start flowing. More so than any other file you exchange between parties, you *must* have agreement on this document. The brief-review process also requires solid conversation; it can't be a simple "We e-mailed the brief for your review." Take time to get on the phone or, better yet, get in a room together and discuss the deliverables.

JASON MILETSKY
THE AGENCY PERSPECTIVE

I've worked on some accounts where the client writes the brief and others where we write it. I've even worked with clients that couldn't have cared less whether or not there *was* a creative brief—but that really should never be the case, so I'm not going to spend time discussing that.

It's an interesting situation: Creative briefs can be a pain in the ass to write, so it's always a relief when the client takes on that responsibility. (Plus, it gives them the opportunity to put their thoughts and needs into writing.) But even though it can be a chore, I honestly believe that creative briefs should be written by the agency, because that way the agency can prove to the client that the agency understands their needs. Typically, we have one or two meetings with the client to discuss the purpose of an upcoming project or campaign, what it should entail, who we're trying to reach, etc. Then we'll put together the creative brief as a detailed review of these meetings. We submit the creative brief to the client to ensure that we're all on the same page and that we took from the meetings the directives they were giving; their sign-off on the brief is their seal of approval—acknowledgment that we did, in fact, understand everything correctly.

I don't know that there is a single best way to write a brief; I think every brief will be a little different depending on the client, their brand, and their needs. But there are some elements that every brief should include in order to be effective:

- **Contact names and account information:** After the first brief for a client, this can usually be copied and pasted from one brief to another, but should still be present. Just standard info like the main contact names on both the client and agency side, phone numbers, e-mail addresses, project or account numbers (usually assigned by the agency for organizational purposes), and who prepared the brief.

- **The project or campaign and its primary objectives:** Obviously, there needs to be a review of the project or campaign in question, what's being worked on, and what the deliverables will be. These should be accompanied by the objectives of the effort—not necessarily numeric goals (although you can use 'em if you've got 'em) but at the very least a more general statement like "To build awareness of XYZ's west coast capabilities" or "To increase weekday traffic in ABC's retail outlets."

- **Competition:** A list of potential competitors that the brand is up against. Agencies should be aware of what these competitors are doing and saying in the market to make sure that similar efforts being undertaken are both starkly different and markedly better.

- **Target market and audience insights:** The specific demo you'll be trying to reach and any insights (statistical or otherwise) that might be helpful to keep in mind during development.

- **Desired message:** A description of what you'll be trying to get across. This is the most likely point of disagreement between agency and client, and should be reviewed by both sides to guard against subtle differences that might change the scope of the project or affect the outcome.

- **Communication tone:** The tone of the messaging as it'll be related through copy, image, script, design, or something else. This is usually already determined by the brand guidelines, most likely in reference to the brand personality.

- **The brand promise:** Another brand guideline issue. It's helpful to reiterate what the brand promise is, even if it won't specifically be referenced in the campaign or project in question.

- **The brand's USP and support for the USP:** Specifics about what makes the brand unique among it competitors and evidence that supports these claims. Again, these may not be specifically mentioned in a given effort, but they should be included in the creative brief for any subtle references they might inspire.

- **Specifications:** Depending on the effort, there may be specifications that need to be considered such as the size of a print ad or how long a commercial or other video should be.

- **Mandatories:** Unless these are standard and can be copied and pasted from one brief to the other, this section is one that almost always needs to be completed by the client. It includes information such as which phone number or URL to promote, any legal language that should be included (like copyright or trademark info), etc.

Like I said, each client will have a different setup and might require information I haven't listed here, but you'll never go wrong having at least this information included in every brief.

One more thing: At the start of this answer, I mentioned that some clients couldn't care less about creative briefs. On the other extreme are clients who are brief-happy, requiring one for every single project—even simple sales sheets or PowerPoint decks. My personal theory is that if the creative brief is going to take at least half as long as the project will take to complete, then you shouldn't bother writing it. The creative brief should be helpful in getting the project done right, not an exercise in how to waste time.

Q: • What Is the Difference Between • a Project and a Campaign?

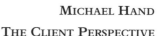

Michael Hand

The Client Perspective

My high-level answer is that a "campaign" has more staying power than a "project." Campaigns show a deeper commitment to a creative direction by the client. Campaigns are intended to be a model for all future work to flow from and thought to be the root of all new ideas. In contrast, the world of projects is a tangled web of one-off ideas and executional tactics that, initially, do not have staying power (although that's not to say that a project can't evolve into a longer-term effort). But while the common misconception is that projects have no real deliverables or expectations for results and analysis, the truth is that projects must also have a clear, identifiable end goal—albeit with a shorter time horizon for getting results—and must rigorously follow the same guidelines.

The creative brief for a project assignment must be very tight. To avoid brand schizophrenia, it is critical that all projects ladder back up to a broader brand/company positioning statement and reinforce the brand personality. If a one-off project lacks this strategic linkage, all too often it will end up being detrimental to the long-term health of the brand. Companies screw this up all the time, trying to be "cool" and doing things that simply don't fit. When working on a project, you must keep the brand voice, tone, and manner in check. Projects tend to allow more freedom for creative thinking and breaking from the norms of the brand, and are often a fantastic way to build some real excitement around a brand, product, or service. They can open numerous doors for future exploration.

For an agency, project work often provides an entreé into a longer-term relationship.

Perhaps the biggest difference between a project and a campaign is that most folks enter into campaign discussions looking for longer-term success right from the start and focus on instilling a new/revised brand identity. Very few new campaigns are an overnight success; they take time to build a following and garner support. They must be managed and built with the brand's personality at the epicenter.

So those are some of the differences between campaigns and projects. There are, however, many ways in which campaigns and projects are similar:

- Projects and long-term campaigns must both talk to the appropriate target audience. Otherwise, you simply waste money while fragmenting your brand to non-users.

- You must make sure you bring in the right people for the job. Just as you wouldn't hire a chef to fix your car, you shouldn't bring in your ad agency to develop a Web site just because you have their phone number programmed into your speed dial. Do not treat projects with lesser importance than long-term campaigns.

- Your team should be disciplined with the details. Just because you're working on a project does not mean you can cut corners.

- Both projects and long-term campaigns must honor trademarks, taglines, and brand values, and must add to the value of the brand.

- You must stick to your budget, and be very clear up front about what you want to accomplish. Whether campaign or project approach, set objectives at the start and track your results.

JASON MILETSKY
THE AGENCY PERSPECTIVE

⤶ About $100,000. Ba-dum-bum! Thank you! Thank you very much. I'll be here 'til Thursday. Try the veal!

Seriously, the main difference isn't actually cost; it's time and concept. Projects are meant to be relatively quick—or at least finite with a pre-determined deadline—and very often involve the development of tools. Building a Web site is a project. So is developing a series of brochures or flyers or a video for a sales meeting. Broad-based consumer advertising can also be project-based, usually with direct-message marketing such as a newspaper ad announcing an upcoming sale at a local retail store or even a one-off "this is who we are" kind of ad for local cable or a B2B publication. These types of ads typically involve very little strategy. They dial down the brand personality and all but eliminate any creative concept, and instead feature straight-up information.

Campaigns are less about tools and more about marketing. Strategy is key in campaign development, and often involves multiple media outlets as part of a well-choreographed plan to reach the market through various channels. While campaigns may have benchmarks and completion dates, there's always the potential that they can go on as long as they continue to connect well with the audience. (How long has that Energizer bunny been going? And MasterCard continues to be "priceless," so many years later.) Rather than concentrating strictly on information, these efforts deliver their message through creative concepts that play up the brand personality while speaking to their audience, with the concept often playing a prominent role in the project-based tools that are developed around it.

As for pricing, projects tend to be invoiced at the start of the project, with a final invoice at completion of the project and other invoices during the life of the project depending on how long it lasts. Campaigns are typically more retainer-based.

Q: IS A RISKY CONCEPT WORTH TRYING IF FAILURE MEANS POTENTIALLY LOSING THE ACCOUNT (OR, FOR A MARKETING DIRECTOR, LOSING YOUR JOB)?

What's your perspective on this question? Let us know at PerspectivesOnMarketing.com.

MICHAEL HAND
THE CLIENT PERSPECTIVE

Risk-taking is a major part of life and can bring tremendous rewards. It's important to remember, however, that risk-taking can be extremely dangerous if the risk involves tampering with something that is currently working and if done without careful thought. Then again, risk-taking may also result in a huge win by driving incremental sales growth. So how do you assess whether a risk is "worth it"? Before anyone can answer that, they need to ask themselves a few questions: How badly do they need the account and/or how badly do they need this particular job? Is the upside for the business really there? Are you the only one who sees it? Answer these questions, and then you can discuss whether the risky concept is truly worth pursuing.

While I'm all for taking creative risks and pushing the envelope, any campaign concept that is so risky it could actually jeopardize your livelihood or alienate your current user base might be pushing things too far. Some risks are just bad ideas that should be put back in the creative drawer, never to be seen or heard from again. The number of people who might be attracted to the idea could be totally eclipsed by the number of those who will be turned off. Some risks will result in only marginal impact, creating a minimal swing—but that doesn't mean they aren't worthwhile. The only real downsides in such cases are the loss of time and productivity from pursuing the effort; if more consumer insight was gained, then it was worthwhile. On the other hand, if the risk has the potential to drive large sales gains and increased consumer awareness with your only concern some potential media backlash, that's not a risk at all. Go for it!

If you believe an idea is extremely strong and has major upside potential, you might propose a market test to see how things go. But realize that within hours of the test, your biggest competition in the segment will be fully aware of it—thus removing the element of surprise and allowing your rival to prepare for any potential national rollout in the near future. Your idea will instantly become public knowledge, making the concept ripe for the taking.

The bottom line? Be willing to make a mistake and go after big opportunities. Too many companies are mired in short-term thinking and are foolishly risk averse. Go change your corner of the world—just don't act carelessly with your brand equity.

JASON MILETSKY

THE AGENCY PERSPECTIVE

Absolutely. But that's easy for me to say; I represent the agency perspective. No smart agency (no smart company in any industry, really) is going to let a single client account for more than 15 percent of their overall revenue. So while we never want to lose an account, the truth is it's going to happen sooner or later. Eventually, clients move on. And when that happens, like any good business, we'll make some internal adjustments, scramble to replace lost revenue with new business or by increasing billing to existing clients, and carry on.

That's a completely different scenario than the one facing a CMO or marketing director on the client side who could potentially lose his or her job. That job isn't 15 percent of that person's income; it's pretty close to 100 percent—and losing it can be pretty damned scary, especially considering that there aren't a lot of CMO job openings out there. When you factor in families and mortgages and other bills, I don't blame clients for not always wanting to take chances with their marketing. It can be frustrating from the agency perspective because there are times when we want to be "out there," but I get it.

Years ago, soon after winning a big new account, we presented what I felt was some of our best advertising work for any client to that point. But it was out there—a completely different direction than they had ever taken before, and something that would have really raised some eyebrows in their industry. Our client looked at it carefully, nodded, and remarked that he thought it was "Outstanding"—that was the word he used—before putting it aside and saying it was too bad they couldn't use it. "Why?" I asked. He said, "Jay, I'm three years away from retiring with a full pension. You think I want to rock the boat? Give me something that's safe and I'm a happy guy." So basically, because of his personal situation, he dumbed down our work, steered his brand along the straight and narrow, and happily worked to keep the company right where they were—with no more or no less market share than they had the day before. And the thing is, I understand that. Self-preservation will always come before company loyalty, and it comes *way* before market happiness.

What I would urge, though, is for both parties to change their thinking just a little. Agencies need to present ideas that are out there and risky when it's called for and could prove beneficial to the brand. But unfortunately, when agencies present wacked-out ideas, it's usually just because they want to be noticed. They want to see how much dust they can stir up. Those kind of ideas aren't always what the client is looking for, and *really* "out there" ideas aren't always in line with the brand's personality or message. On the client side, I'd say loosen up a bit. If the agency has a risky idea but it makes sense and could potentially reach your brand's target audience, give it some real consideration. Playing it safe might not get you fired, but it's not going to land you on the cover of *AdWeek* anytime soon either. Yes, you have to protect your income—but you have to take some risks of you're ever going to reap the reward.

Q: WHO HAS BETTER "OBJECTIVE" INSIGHT AND OPINIONS INTO THE BRAND AND THE MARKETING NEEDS?

MICHAEL HAND

THE CLIENT PERSPECTIVE

This question was clearly written by an agency guy, what with the word "objective" being placed in quotes for emphasis. Yeah, Mr. Jason "Agency Perspective" Miletsky, I'm talkin' to you. No doubt the idea here is to get me to say that clients are too close to the brand and marketing process to be open in their thinking; sorry, I can't do that. I'll leave it to my counterpart to wax poetic on the virtues of agency insight that is always "objective."

Okay, I will admit that it can be more difficult at times for the client to avoid getting emotionally attached to a program, process, or perceived need. But the best marketers find a way to look beyond this and provide great insight. They use an abundance of data to try to deliver the best thinking with respect to the brand deliverables. As an added benefit, the client has the day-to-day experience of walking through the hallways at his or her corporate office. Unless the agency can also hear the rumblings about proposed budget reductions or potential production capacity issues at the manufacturing plant, and unless the agency can witness with their own eyes the verbal exchanges in corporate strategy meetings and monthly financial reviews, they cannot have more "insight" than the client. Agency folks shouldn't perceive this as a dig against them; it's a simple fact. Does this mean the client always has an "objective" perspective? Maybe not—but it certainly puts them in a position to root their opinions in fact.

When it comes to the "opinions" part of the question, however, I do believe the agency is stronger here. For all the same reasons that I think the client has more objective insight, the agency has more objective opinions. Too much common or shared information can breed sameness in thinking and execution across an organization. Because agency personnel often bounce from account to account, they can bring new perspectives to a client from other product categories and suggest valid new ways of looking at problems and issues, much like leadership changes in an organization can drive new thinking within a corporate structure.

JASON MILETSKY

THE AGENCY PERSPECTIVE

There's no question that the client knows their brand better. They live it and breathe it every day. They get the ins and outs, the politics and the problems. They know when to expect sales spikes and when to prepare for shortfalls. I don't think I could ever know a brand that my agency represents as well or better than they know it themselves.

But knowing a brand and knowing what's *good* for the brand are two different things. As I've mentioned, agencies are hired in part to provide a third-party perspective and to give recommendations based on their vantage point, which naturally differs from that of the brand execs simply because they're too close to it. We don't live the brand full time, so we can better see the whole picture and get a truer sense of market sentiment. A good agency can tell the client what they *need* to hear, not just what they *want* to hear. (An agency that simply yeses the client on all points is a waste of money. Clients can yes themselves. They don't need to pay agency rates for verification.)

Where this gets more complicated, though, is knowing at what point during the agency's relationship with the brand their insight can *really* be trusted. Some might argue that the agency has the absolute best insight into the market and what the brand needs to do to reach it is on day one of the account, and that the insight lessens every day after that. The rationale behind this argument is that the longer the agency works for the brand, the closer the agency gets to the brand—eventually getting too close to it, much like the brand execs. It makes logical sense, but personally I don't buy it. No matter how long an agency holds an account, they understand their place as the provider of the outside perspective, and therefore never cross that invisible line in their collective consciousness that separates the way an agency thinks from the way the client thinks. So I tend to believe the opposite: The longer an agency works with an account, the more insight we can offer them—not just because we've gotten to know the brand better, but because as we feel more secure with the relationship, we feel more comfortable expressing contradictory opinions or presenting information the client may not want to hear.

The tricky part of this question is the word "objective." The truth is, objectivity in the agency/client relationship is about as common as unbiased journalism during a presidential campaign. It just doesn't exist. As soon as money is involved, it becomes impossible for anybody to be completely objective. Sure, agencies want to do what's right for the brand—but they also want to protect their account. Likewise, the CMO or marketing director on the client side wants to do what's right for the brand—but they also want to protect their job and end-of-year bonus. There's always an element of self-preservation in every consultation, recommendation, and decision, which in turn diminishes everyone's ability to be completely objective. But even considering all this, I believe the agency is more likely to be objective. We have many accounts and can handle losing one of them if it comes to that; the marketing director, however, has only one job.

Q: IS THERE TRUE VALUE IN A CAMPAIGN THAT BUILDS THE BRAND RATHER THAN PROMOTE A SPECIFIC CALL TO ACTION? CAN A POSITIVE ROI BE MEASURED ON A BRANDING CAMPAIGN?

MICHAEL HAND

THE CLIENT PERSPECTIVE

In my days working in the auto industry, navigating the "build a brand" campaign approach versus the "call to action" campaign philosophy always proved to be a delicate balance (and at times prompted spirited debate). But I have always been and will always be first and foremost a brand ambassador, so I will say yes, there is value in a campaign designed to build the brand rather than promote a specific call to action. What I have found, however, is that you simply cannot try to make your message do too much.

When I worked for Buick, we established a long-term strategic relationship with professional athlete and all-around sports god Tiger Woods. The choice was puzzling for some; many people could not understand why we paid him so much money to represent us, and even more people wondered why Tiger had agreed to be associated with our brands. After all, he was the hot 20-something with endorsement deals with Nike and EA Sports, which solidified a youthful and cool image—but the median age of customers who purchased a Buick four-door sedan was 70. The belief among many was that Buick would be better off with somebody the existing owners could relate to (hence the brand's relationship with veteran golfer Ben Crenshaw prior to the Tiger deal), and clearly Mr. Woods would be better off with a hotter performance/design-driven car company like Mercedes or Lexus. Naysayers around the globe mocked the deal and asked if anybody really believed he would be caught dead driving a Buick.

The key to ensuring success (and a positive ROI) was in how we would use him. First, we needed to be clear that Tiger was serving as the new and evolving face of Buick; this was a move for the future. He was not being used to lure more septuagenarians into the market; he was helping to put a new face on the brand—while (and this is extremely important) not alienating the current user base. So we placed Tiger in all ads that focused on new product introductions, starting with the first-ever truck entries from Buick. The message in these ads was very brand-centric—they simply encouraged consumers to find out more about the "New Buick" and reconsider it when shopping for a car. And even though there was no price-centric, offer-laden "call to action," the response was overwhelming. These vehicles sold and, more importantly, the average age of buyers of these new models was 20 to 30 years younger. Finally! A group that would be able to buy more than one more car in their remaining life span! This had tremendous impact on the ROI, because Buick has always enjoyed very strong customer loyalty; when you own one, it is very likely you will come back to the dealership to get another.

Of course, challenges would sneak up at month-end close, when we would inevitably receive a mandate to hit a specific number of retail sales units. Boom—next thing you knew, we were dropping finance charges and adding cash incentives. But we held firm that Tiger would not hop around on a pogo stick in a dealer's parking lot while wearing his green jacket from the Masters yelling, "Tent sale! Everything must go!" We ran ads with distinct calls to action that offered specific deals by region with timelines for delivery, but never tied in our brand-building icon. So all this is to say that we found value in building the brand without a mandatory sales-oriented call to action. Moreover, if we had not done so—if we hadn't built up the image and increased brand relevance—Buick would have likely have gone the way of Oldsmobile and disappeared. So before you run your mouth about how ridiculous this relationship was, you need to do a little homework and get the facts. Tiger Woods, in many ways, saved Buick.

Experience in the confection category has shown me that the theory of running brand-building advertising to drive sales holds true in other categories as well. During my tenure at The Hershey Company, brand leaders have found ways to grow the company's largest brands (Reese's and Hershey's Milk Chocolate) simply by getting advertising in front of users and reminding them of the choices they have. The sales data backs this up.

Actually *measuring* the ROI on a campaign like this is tough. The best way, in my view, would be to set up a control group where no media is planned for a comparably sized market with similar market demos and market conditions. You can compare the sales trend in advertised weeks against the trend in non-advertised weeks to see what kind of incremental lift you are driving that is attributable to your brand-building ad campaign.This isn't rocket science, and there are clearly numerous additional considerations that must be taken into account, but on the surface, it can help you develop a number to extrapolate incremental units against your total investment.

JASON MILETSKY

THE AGENCY PERSPECTIVE

↳ Yes, there is true value in a campaign that builds the brand rather than promoting a specific call to action. But realizing that value takes time—and there aren't a lot of companies that are willing or able to invest in it. Here's the ultra-basic three-step process behind how it works:

- **Step 1:** Brands market themselves and get their names, logos, and messages inside consumers' heads.

- **Step 2:** The more consumers are exposed to the brand (repetition is key to advertising), and the more the brand fulfills its promise (promise fulfillment is the brand's job; marketing their success and their message is the agency's job), the more trust is built in the market.

- **Step 3:** The more trust is built, the more likely consumers will be to purchase a particular brand.

Pretty simple, and it only took a few minutes to write! The problem is, what took minutes to write can take months or years to execute. Building a brand is as much about time as it is money—in some cases, more so. But with aggressive quotas, internal incentive programs, and the increasing need to show returns quickly, it's less common for companies to engage in campaigns that just build the brand. I'm not talking about Fortune 500, multinational companies with deep enough pockets to really invest in continuously building their brands. I'm talking about the far larger number of small- to mid-sized companies that could seriously benefit from brand campaigns to foster solid, long-term growth but, due to time pressures, must opt for the shorter-term success brought by call-to-action campaigns.

So yes, there absolutely is value, and yes, ROI can definitely be measured. The ultimate measuring stick is always going to be sales and revenue—specifically, whether they have increased over time or compared to specific periods in the past. But this isn't always the best way to measure ROI because brand-building campaigns are slower builds over longer periods of time, often underscored by separate, shorter-term efforts. (The same holds true for measuring traffic to a brand's Web site.) One of the better ways to measure the effectiveness of a branding campaign is to research the market prior to the campaign being launched to understand what percentage of your target audience is familiar with your brand, what their feelings are toward the brand, and how likely it is they'd purchase it. Similar studies should then be conducted at pre-determined periods during the campaign as well as immediately after to gauge improvement in brand exposure and consumer sentiment.

Q: WHO SHOULD PRESENT THE CREATIVE WORK OUTPUTS TO FINAL DECISION MAKER?

MICHAEL HAND

THE CLIENT PERSPECTIVE

I am a firm believer in joint ownership of the creative process. I prefer to be involved during every step of the development and review progression. I like to hear feedback first-hand, and I like to examine the room when creative is unveiled. You can learn a lot by simply observing people's facial expressions and other reactions as the agency reveals an image or copy line. So naturally, I like to be present when creative is presented to decision-makers. But while I support the "joint with client" approach, I do think you need to outline the roles and responsibilities of client and agency representatives before this very important meeting.

At the actual meeting, the client representative should set the stage by providing for the decision-makers a recap of the assignment, program objectives, and business case. This demonstrates to management your conviction, your belief in your team, and the fact that you know your shit. Passing this duty off on the agency does not reinforce your leadership role in the eyes of senior management. The agency may reinforce these points as they kick off their presentation, but it should come from the client lead first.

The client representative should never, however, present the creative ideas. This is something the agency should own to the end. The agency team needs to deliver their vision and articulate how it will come to life to deliver against the objectives set forth in the brief. They need to "sell it" on their own. The agency needs to keep the meeting entertaining and on track; the long, awkward silence should be avoided at all costs. They need to get the client involved in lively discussion from the onset.

When the time comes to share feedback, the agency and client representatives should then join forces. The agency must get every ounce of feedback they can to make the program better and also (selfishly) to make their own life a bit better by avoiding rework and lack of clarity on direction. The client partner can drive the conversation around importance of next steps and also provide a point of view to steer the conversation.

There's nothing worse than a client who provides advice and counsel after delivering the brief but, when the time comes to stand up behind the direction in front of senior management, shows utter disregard for the agency's efforts.

JASON MILETSKY

THE AGENCY PERSPECTIVE

Usually, the way it works is that we'll work closely with someone pretty high up on the marketing food chain—on the manager, director, or VP level. In turn, they'll have someone they report to who needs to give his or her blessing to all campaign concepts before we can move forward into development. (Clearly, I'm talking about larger scale initiatives like campaigns, not smaller collateral-based projects. I'm also talking about mid- to large-sized clients, not small companies where the CEO or owner takes a more active role in marketing.) Our job, after the creative brief has been signed off on, is initially to develop a few options that comply with the creative direction on which everyone has agreed. Our contact will select a direction from those options, and we'll go through a round or two of revisions before we're all comfortable and confident with the final creative.

Now we're ready to present what we've come up with to the main decision-maker. The head honcho. The big cheese. The top tamale. The guy who will be able to tear all our hard work apart with a sneer and a simple "I don't like it." Doing this meeting the right way should be considered supremely critical; if it doesn't go well, you're either sent back to the drawing board or given the boot. You have three options here—I'll leave it to you to figure out which one is best:

- **You can present alone:** Bad idea. You don't know this guy. You don't know what he likes or what he doesn't like. You don't know if he's going to be in agreement with the creative brief you worked from or if he even saw it (which he probably didn't and will first learn about during your presentation). If the shit comes down, you've got no cover. You can't throw your main contact under the bus, so you have no choice but to take any heat yourself. Like I said, bad idea.

- **Your client can make the presentation without you:** Even worse idea. Sure, your contact may have been in on the early creative meetings and given you his or her feedback for each new round of creative you showed, but it's still *your* creative. Nobody will be able to explain or present your ideas as well as you can. There will be subtleties that you'll want to mention, questions you'll want to field yourself, and explanations you'll want to give. Plus, if you're not there, your contact may not defend your creative properly, letting it all fall apart, or possibly even commit something you can't or wouldn't want to do.

- **You can present creative in a joint effort with your contact:** This is the way to go. By going in with your contact, you're presenting to the decision-maker with an advocate from his own team, so there's some trust built-in. If questions are asked that seem to put you in a bad light (regarding the creative brief, for example), your client can come to your aid. You're creating a united front. It will appear that his or her own team advocate has already bought into your vision and, by extension, that you're not just showing ideas with your own best interests at heart.

PART THREE

Getting to Work

Q: • Do You Need TV Advertising
• to Build a Brand?

Jason Miletsky
The Agency Perspective

↳ Of course not. Television is a great way to get a brand noticed by a lot of people over a large geographic area in a highly targeted way. And there's no denying that not only can TV spots help get the brand name and message ingrained in the minds of the market, but they probably have more power to establish a brand personality than any other marketing medium. With TV, a brand can send a message, raise awareness, create an emotional connection, start a buzz, and drive people to take action—all within a single 30-second spot (well, a really well-done 30-second spot, anyway...).

But to use TV as the single distinguishing factor between what is a brand and what is not a brand, or whether or not a brand can be successful, is to both underestimate the usefulness of other media and misinterpret what a brand actually is. TV advertising is only one element that can be used to determine whether or not a company, product, or service can be considered a brand. The truth is, there are brands all around us all the time, and only a small percentage have the budget or need to advertise on television.

Consider companies that strictly market their products or services to other companies. B2B brands spend serious amounts of money to reach their audiences— companies such as AmerisourceBergen and Dendrite, which market their distribution services to pharmaceutical companies, and ADP and Ceridian, which market their payroll services to accountants and any company with employees. For most companies like these, television would be a waste of their budget. They're trying to reach a highly targeted audience of specific decision makers, not the general public, most of whom would have no connection to their brand or ability to sign off on a purchase. For these companies, online and print advertising, direct mail, trade-show marketing, and public relations are more efficient and cost-effective ways of building their brand.

The same goes for B2C brands—while many rely on television advertising to support the national distribution of their products (such as major-label apparel, home goods, or food or beverage brands), television isn't the only way to reach large audiences. Nobody can deny that rock bands like Kiss, Aerosmith, or Metallica are brands in their own right, having built a worldwide market hungry for anything new they produce—and none of these would point to television as the main reason for their growth and popularity. Radio, live public performances, in-store promotions, and great PR were clearly the main factors behind their success. Smaller brands that rely more on a local market might also avoid television as well, as may brands that rely strictly on an online audience. Amazon, MySpace, Wikipedia, and Google have all built amazing brands without having to rely much—if at all—on television.

The trick to building a brand through marketing is not to get caught up in the allure and romance of television advertising, and simply run TV spots for the sake of running TV spots (read: for the sake of stroking your ego). The best way to build a brand is to be realistic about who your audience is and where they can be found, and to determine the best media mix to reach them given your available budget.

MICHAEL HAND

THE CLIENT PERSPECTIVE

Building a brand can be quite complicated. Along with making a great product, having strong packaging, and providing reliable service, one of the major factors that goes into the brand building effort is sheer awareness of who you are. I do not believe that you must have a tremendous television advertising budget to build a brand, but it certainly plays a major role in accumulating broad awareness quickly. TV is a great tool for creating interest in a brand that the consumer masses may not be very familiar with or informing them about a brand they may not have been introduced to yet.

The 30-second TV spot has become a panacea for the marketer at major corporations launching a new item/product/service because TV still provides the fastest way to create extensive reach through media. Every February, you read about the company that buys a 30-second commercial in the Super Bowl and instantly gets over 95 million viewers to see their brand. Does this alone build a brand? No, but it can certainly get you on the radar screen in a hurry (more to follow on Super Bowl spots later).

Building a brand is the hard work that happens after folks click through to your Web site, visit your store, or seek more information about you from friends and family members. When you can afford to keep your message on air for an extended period of time (creating frequency), television ads can prove to be effective in brand building. Every reminder of your product/service in the public eye is another chance to create a potential buyer/user. The world of TV advertising will remain an important marketing tool for the foreseeable future, even with the shift in technology and use of digital video recorders (DVRs) that allow consumers to time shift their favorite programs and fast forward through the ad units. The ads that are created must become more interactive and get the consumer involved; they need to have more stopping power. TV commercials need to shift away from passive entertainment and move more to creating an active consumer engagement.

As consumers continue to become more tech-savvy, they will be online more while they are watching television; unlike me, the next generation is very adept at multi-tasking. This multimedia experience will be critical in adding to the power of television for brand building as we move to the future. More than ever before, advertising efforts will need to be cross-platform, with TV and Internet working together to create stronger brand perceptions. Research from the Internet Advertising Bureau and Thinkbox show that consumers who own a digital television and use broadband Internet had a 47 percent increase in positive brand perceptions when combining TV and online viewing together compared to using either in isolation.

One of the first major successful efforts in this area was Nickelodeon's interactive chats during the 1999 Kid's Choice Awards. It got kids engaged through the entire programming process, from the original voting to in-telecast commentary. Giving consumers a voice in the outcome of your brand always assists in building the relationship. Work from marquee brands like Doritos and Chevrolet that have allowed consumer-generated ads to run in the Super Bowl are clear-cut examples of building a two-way conversation that gives consumers a dynamic voice. Plus, the resulting ads can be pretty good—the user-generated spot in 2009's Super Bowl from Doritos won the *USA Today* Ad Meter, and the ad's developers took home a $1,000,000 prize. Consumers define themselves by the brands they use, and this type of emotional connection creates a potent bond.

Q:
HOW DOES THE FRAGMENTATION OF TELEVISION CHANGE HOW BRANDS REACH THEIR AUDIENCES? WHAT ROLE DOES STREAMING MEDIA PLAY IN THIS?

JASON MILETSKY
THE AGENCY PERSPECTIVE

↳ Not long ago, I had a debate with a friend about what we each thought was the most important consumer invention since the late 1800s. My buddy went with the telephone (which I thought was a pretty standard, if not boring, answer). His rationale was that the telephone opened up communication networks, allowed businesses to expand, enabled news to travel faster, etc. I can buy that, and I don't think there's any question about the importance the telephone has played in the shaping of the world. But even so, I stuck by my answer: the remote control.

That might sound silly, but hear me out: A long while back, people watched TV on sets that had dials and had—at most—five or six channels to choose from (along with some grainy programming on a dial called UHF). To change the channel, people had to get up—yes, actually rise from a seated position—go to the set, and manually turn the dial. Obviously this was a pain in the ass, so people were more likely to find a channel they liked and stay with it for the duration. There was no such thing as "channel surfing"—even though there were only five or six options to choose from. Imagine if they had the hundred or more channels back then that we enjoy today! There's no way anybody would get up off the couch and stand in front of the set to change the dial a couple of hundred times to find what they like before sitting back down again—only to do it again after each show. The remote control is the tool that's allowed for the expansion of stations and programming, in turn influencing everything from pop culture to news consumption. MTV built new legions of music fans, simultaneously affecting the record, fashion, and other industries. CNN changed the way we look at news, eventually giving people access to more and deeper information from across the globe. Further segmentation such as ESPN for sports and Disney Channel and Nickelodeon for kids have all contributed to fragmenting audiences into distinct demographics that are easier for marketers to locate. And all of this, thanks to the simple remote control.

Overall, this segmentation has made life a considerable challenge for media buyers, who have a veritable mountain of possibilities to choose from when deciding which shows, channels, and times of day to run their ads, as well as how to best segment budgets between online and offline media. It's no longer only about ratings; the fragmentation of audiences has created new opportunities for marketers to reach a smaller number of eyeballs—but with far less waste than they would have had in the past, allowing every media dollar to count. As more video-sharing sites come online and television continues to segment itself in search of new viewers, marketers should see the fragmentation as an opportunity to better build their brands.

Of course, the remote control doesn't have as much to do with streaming media, which has helped to further segment audiences as more people develop an appetite for online video. Aside from user-created amateur video uploads, which have driven YouTube to greatness (and continue to increase as more people buy cell phones with built-in video cameras), online clips and full episodes of TV shows have helped to pinpoint specific demographics, and the ability to stream TV commercials within these presentations has helped marketers reach their audiences in new ways.

MICHAEL HAND
THE CLIENT PERSPECTIVE

The fragmentation of the television world has a tremendous impact on how brands connect with their consumers via media today; in fact, the impact goes far beyond media as corporations continue to look for alternative ways of getting eyeballs on their brands. I hate to date myself, but I can still remember the days when you grabbed the "TV book" out of the Sunday newspaper and it became the bible that you kept on the coffee table in the living room to see what might be on during the week. Of course, we only had 12 channels then and Al Gore had not yet invented the Internet; you actually had to get up and walk to the TV set to change your channel manually by spinning a dial. For those who think I am making this up: Screw you. I'm not *that* old; this was just real life in the early '80s.

Even when we first got cable television (and HBO) in my childhood home, the channel box was either a long slider numbered from 1 to 100 or it was a clicker unit that was numbered 2 to 13 and had letters A to Z underneath—still no remote though. Flash forward to today when I review all my programming choices via the on-screen "Guide," and the days of my extra 50 steps a day to change the channel have been replaced by a remote control (the true cause of childhood obesity in America, if you ask me). The real WOW factor here is that I now have more than 250 channels to choose from across my standard network offerings, basic and extended cable packages, sports package, and premium channel add-ons. With this many options to choose from, a brand's message clearly gets diluted. If watching a TV show live (another practice that happens infrequently with my DVR in non-stop action), I bounce over to ESPN (or ESPN2, ESPN News, etc.) and watch two minutes of a bad college basketball game or World Series of Poker repeat to simply catch the "ticker" and get up to speed on the happenings within the world of sports. Personally, I have no time for commercials in my life. The scary part of this commentary…I am a guy who helps make commercials (talk about a sad state of affairs).

The big new addition to this dynamic is the fact that you can now watch your preferred television programs whenever you want via the online world of streaming media portals. Sites such as Joost and Hulu.com have formed strong alliances to get content from the likes of CBS, FOX, and NBC to stream it within moments of the televised airing in real time. This can be looked at as a new avenue to reach dedicated viewers who are truly "seeking the complete viewing experience," or you can look at this as the next step in TV's slow death. Time-shifting of viewers is not going away anytime soon.

The good news is that most viewers in the online world know that nothing in life is really free and their favorite show did not magically appear before them, thus they anticipate the single ad that appears before a show starts and they accept its placement—no ad skipping allowed here against marketers. Not to mention, this expansion of television into the online world could actually be adding new viewers to select programs and maybe even driving some viewership back to the networks for important moments (season premieres and finales during sweeps week). Think about it: You can commit 20 minutes of your life online to watch a sitcom that you heard the guys at work talking about, laugh hysterically while watching it, and suddenly become a fan of the show who will now seek it in real time. You could also see how the dedicated fans of some TV shows would seek out the online version to watch repeats while travelling for business (or dare we say during a quiet moment at the office). Apple's iTunes has proven this model is applicable to consumers by actually charging fees to download shows that consumers can get for free in other places; the simple premise of watching it anywhere and at anytime has strong appeal to the time-pressed society in which we live.

The trend to keep an eye on is the shift of sports fans to the Web to watch streaming video while tracking their fantasy line-ups or keeping tabs on their NCAA hoops tournament brackets. Sports have always been seen as programming you have to watch in real time on TV to capture the full experience; this online shift could have tremendous impact on the television revenue model and fan engagement.

To me, all of these facts illustrate the fact that television viewing has become fragmented beyond belief and streaming media is here to stay; we need to embrace it as marketers or risk losing a robust platform to reach our consumers.

Q: THE DIRTIEST FOUR-LETTER WORD: TiVO. WHAT DOES IT MEAN TO MARKETERS, AND HOW CAN YOU PLAN AROUND IT?

JASON MILETSKY

THE AGENCY PERSPECTIVE

Nothing. I'm sorry, but I'm just not one of those people that buys into the idea that TiVo is going to the be the "commercial killer." It's not now, and it's never going to be.

For those of you who aren't sure why it's even an issue, the fear is that with TiVo, viewers have the opportunity to easily skip over the ads instead of watching them. But according to their own annual report, TiVo only had 3.46 million subscribers as of October 2008—down by almost a million from their peak of 4.36 million subscribers in January 2006. Compare that to the more-than 300 million people in the U.S., and consider the fact that 99 percent of all homes in the U.S. have at least one TV, and TiVo isn't exactly the great dragon-slayer advertisers feared it would be. (I suppose I should note that DVR provided through cable providers is growing, but none of the numbers that I've seen so far have made me feel like TV commercials are in any real trouble.)

If it ever happened that a significant percentage of people began to adopt TiVo or one of their competitors (like Verizon) into their homes, and subsequently began to skip watching TV commercials, then one of three things would happen:

- After persuasive lobbying from the advertising and TV-production industries, the government would pass some kind law that forced TiVo (and others) to stop allowing users to skip over ads.

- After persuasive lobbying from the advertising and TV-production industries, TiVo (and others) would self-regulate and stop allowing users to skip over ads.

- The standard ad model would change. Instead of running 30-second spots, marketers would figure something else out, like maybe sponsoring segments of shows and having their bug onscreen at all times during those segments and showing a short 10-second intro and exit from those segments.

But it doesn't matter—it'll never come to that. TiVo isn't going to change TV advertising in any way that'll matter to anybody. The real hurdle for television is the Internet, but that's another question entirely.

MICHAEL HAND

THE CLIENT PERSPECTIVE

⌐ Similar to the previous answer regarding streaming video, marketers need to stop complaining about TiVo and the role it is playing in diluting media messages. Consumers will continue to time shift their favorite shows and fast forward through commercial interruptions. Can you blame them for loving the ability to watch a one-hour drama in 40 minutes? Digital Video Recorders (DVRs) were in more than 28 million homes at the end of 2008, and that number is expected to reach more than 52 million homes by 2014, an increase in penetration from 25 percent to 44 percent of all TV households according to Magna On-Demand Quarterly, December 2008 data. This increase is directly linked to the fact that the majority of in-home cable boxes entering the market today are being distributed with DVR capability already built in.

The way to beat this phenomenon is a topic of great debate in marketing conference rooms across America. One of the solutions major television networks are using to get around this and show "value" to advertisers is the excessive use of product placement in telecasts. Reality shows have always been great at working brand-name products into the program, such as a competition to win a Chevy truck on *Survivor* or kitchen staff using equipment from General Electric on *Top Chef*, but the trend has really taken off in scripted programs where lead characters now drive specific models of cars or eat specific brands of cereal in the program. As it is part of the content of the programming, viewers cannot escape the constant brand reminders, marketers just need to hope that the message and use of the product in telecast remains positive and in line with brand strategies. Savvy marketers are shifting their investment from straight advertising plans into this model of integrating products and buying adjacent commercial spots where brand personalities align.

Also worth mentioning as TiVo/DVR impact is analyzed are the added capabilities of Video on Demand that the major cable operators are adding to their services. These offerings are fast becoming a major revenue stream to the cable company as consumers watch recent blockbuster movies no longer in the cinema at a moderate cost and catch a range of "free" programs from music videos to children's shows—all offer marketers a commercial before the program starts as a way to combat the lack of in-program ads.

The other consideration to beat this movement as a marketer is to shift more funds into "live" viewing occasions like sporting events and awards shows. These programs tend to require people to watch in real time or risk not taking part in the office banter the next day about what actress wore a "too revealing" dress on the red carpet or which wide receiver made an amazing over the shoulder, game-winning catch with only seconds left on the clock. Costs tend to be higher for placement of these spots, but the return on investment could be much stronger in the long run.

The fact remains: According to TiVo vice president Davina Kent, when customers watch recorded programs, they skip 70 percent of the commercials (source: *New York Times*, May 2006). As marketers, we need to roll up our sleeves and find a solution to this problem.

Q: FIVE MINUTES OF FAME: HOW IS OBSESSION WITH "REALITY" CHANGING THE FACE OF TELEVISION?

JASON MILETSKY

THE AGENCY PERSPECTIVE

I'm not a reality TV fan. I'm not even sure I know what "reality TV" is anymore because so many different types of shows seem to fall under that category. The one show I do kind of like is *Project Runway*—I don't know much about fashion, but the show's well done and I think it's interesting to watch people be creative. But I don't know that I would really consider that "reality" in the same way MTV's *Real World* was considered "reality."

One night, when I was aimlessly flipping through the channels in the minutes before 11:00 p.m. (when *Family Guy* comes on), I caught a scene of *High School Reunion* on TV Land, where they put a bunch of people who had graduated high school together 20 years earlier in a house for a couple of weeks in Hawaii. The scene I caught told me everything I need to know about reality television: The class geek, who had grown up to be a pretty good-looking guy, was lying on a blanket on the beach behind the house with the woman who was the most popular girl in class. As he gently pushed her hair from her eyes, the geek said, "I always had a crush on you in high school. I never dreamed I'd have a chance to be alone with you like this." *Alone?* What about the guy holding the camera— you know, the one kneeling in sand about five feet from you? And there's probably at least one other camera guy around, not to mention a guy holding a boom mic to capture every romantic word, a director, at least one (if not two) lighting guys, a make-up artist, and a couple of interns. And does anybody think that the geek's line was delivered that cleanly the very first time? People stammer and stutter through sentences even when they're *not* on national television—and believe me, those cameras don't make things any easier.

The point is, reality TV is anything but. But however it's defined, it's here to stay. Reality TV shows are cheaper and easier to produce than sitcoms or dramas, and they've found a concrete audience. But reality on TV caught fire not too long before YouTube grew to its enormous size, underscoring the fact that people are clearly eager and ready to share in the Hollywood elite's celebrity status, even if only for a short while.

In terms of how reality has changed the face of TV, I don't believe reality has done much more than help TV keep an audience during what used to be the traditional re-run season and through the years that sitcoms dwindled in popularity. It has also helped to capture the imagination and attention of very specific demographics that have made reality TV a part of their lives, helping marketers better reach specific audiences. So as much as I may not like it personally, and as far from reality as reality TV is, I believe it's helped TV as a medium when the medium needed it, and it's helped marketers better find the people they're looking to reach.

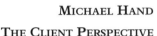

MICHAEL HAND

THE CLIENT PERSPECTIVE

The impact that reality television has on our society continues to shock me. I will admit that I am a closet fan of most reality-based programs, but I cannot believe the influence these shows actually have over people's lives. On a personal level, I am simply a sucker for any type of competition that produces a winner and some drama (and I am clearly not alone). Reality fans typically are drawn in for a variety of reasons and each of these reasons is satisfied with multiple programs to cover that craving. Here are a few of the things you can overhear viewers saying and the shows they have set up on those dreaded DVRs for weekly recordings to help with their *reality* needs:

- **"I love to root for the underdog and think everybody should get a shot at stardom."** These celebrity lovers enjoy watching shows that promise fame and fortune for the guy who was bagging your groceries last week or the girl who was taking your order at the local Starbucks on Tuesday. Viewers like to think "that could be me" or believe that they know a person who deserves that same chance at fame. No show is bigger in this category than *American Idol*. They have turned a simple musical tryout into the most watched show on television, one of the highest grossing summer concert tours, and they sell more merchandise at retail (ranging from dolls to video games) than any other property in the market. Wannabe shows in this category are too many to count, using everybody from P-Diddy to Tyra Banks and the Pussycat Dolls as "celebrity" names to create a draw. This genre of reality has extended from music and dancing competitions to modeling (*America's Next Top Model*) and clothing design contests (*Project Runway*).

- **"They make it look so easy; I wanna learn how to cook like that."** The Food Network is a dedicated resource geared to help these viewers facilitate their obsession of all things food. This television channel launched the careers of Emeril Lagasse, Alton Brown, and others, turning them from simple chefs into instant celebrities and product endorsers. They basically took a five-minute segment from the Today Show and turned it into a weekly/daily series. From their somewhat noble beginnings rose the competitive side of food preparation in shows like *Iron Chef* and *Top Chef.* Offshoots on major networks took it one step further and created behind-the-scenes looks at restaurant life in shows like *Hell's Kitchen.* Let's face it: People are obsessed with food. This genre has changed the face of television from a single dedicated network on the subject to programs scattered throughout the primetime lineup.

■ **"I know I can still find Mr. Right; true love does exist."** This category gets broken into two sub-parts. First you have the desire for real-life romance in shows like *The Bachelor.* Do these people really expect it to last when proposing after three dates and one visit to your future partner's hometown? Next you have the completely obnoxious in shows like *Blind Date* and *Shot at Love.* Watch MTV after 11 p.m. on a week night and you will find shows linking every washed up rock star and rapper to a stable of women who find it okay to be denigrated on television. I don't know who's watching (or editing) this stuff, but the "real life" versions of eHarmony and Match.com it ain't.

■ **"I love to watch celebrities make a mess of their life (or try to clean up their life)."** Where do you start on this one? *The Osbournes* gave us the first "real" peek into the insanity of celebrity life and even made a star out of Ozzy's talentless daughter (and his wife got her own talk show to boot—are you kidding?). Nick Lachey and Jessica Simpson put their life on display and saw their marriage implode in the process (*Newlyweds*); as did Hulk Hogan, who found his wife wanted a divorce through a news reporter (*Hogan Knows Best*). Please tell me this madness will stop.

■ **"These people are idiots; I could last longer in that challenge and win the grand prize."** The competitive spirit of reality starts with *Survivor* and the mantra of "Outwit, Outplay, Outlast," and the godfather of reality competition programming illustrates that you can find a way to reinvent a premise every year in some new exotic locale with some new outlandish physical challenges. The show is as much about crowning a winner as it is seeing everyday people struggling to get along. My personal favorite, *The Amazing Race*, takes you around the world and shows various types of human relationships under the microscope. What better test of your future together as a couple than racing around the world with a million dollars on the line when you have never shared more than a bowl of Frosted Flakes together back in Cleveland. Viewers can see their own reflection when they watch these shows and in a bizarre way use them for advice when dealing with their own complex issues—saving money on psych bills in the process.

The fact remains that people like to live their lives vicariously through what they see in others. It brings to mind the car accident adage; you want to look away but find yourself drawn to it. Sometimes the celebrity angle is needed, but many times you just need to see two parents fighting with their kids at bedtime on *Super Nanny* to know you are not alone in the world. Reality television can take the edge off a bit and lets people know that "real world" others out there may actually be worse off than them.

The face of TV has changed tremendously as a result. When in need of new programming as the scripted slate of fall premieres fail or midseason re-runs have lost their sizzle in January, reality provides a lower-cost production alternative to fill the gaps, and network executives know that every concept has an audience in waiting. Reality offers a little something for everybody, even the folks who never admit they watch it. Reality has changed the face of television, and we need to comprehend that it is here to stay.

Q: WITH SATELLITE AND HD RADIO SEGMENTING AUDIENCES, WHAT'S THE FUTURE OF RADIO, AND HOW WILL IT AFFECT MARKETING STRATEGIES?

JASON MILETSKY
THE AGENCY PERSPECTIVE

Rather than repeat myself needlessly, I'll ask you to please go back and re-read my answer to Question #48, "How Does the Fragmentation of Television Change How Brands Reach Their Audiences? What Role Does Streaming Media Play in This?" but this time, insert the word "radio" every time you see the words "TV" or "television."

MICHAEL HAND
THE CLIENT PERSPECTIVE

Let's face it: The future of AM/FM radio is not looking very positive right now either. The onset of satellite and online streaming radio, which offers music in every genre and enough talk radio to cover anybody's range in topics, provides little need for the existing model with everyday users. The only thing that traditional radio still has working in its favor is the local news angle. Those individuals who commute to work via car will still want to know about the local traffic jams and they will be curious about the local weather patterns, but they will likely be unsatisfied with the balance of commercials and poor music selections to stick with one particular station for long.

The proposed merger of XM Radio and Sirius will basically offer the best of the best in musical variety with the highest quality of sound. How many times have you been in the car for more than 10 minutes and your local signal starts to fade? In the town where I grew up, you can't drive more than five blocks before static sets in. Cost has been the major hurdle that has prevented the mass exodus to satellite, but you have to believe that the pricing structure will change and local radio will not be as desired just because it is "free." Even those without satellite are spending more time hooking up their iPods and listening to their own music mix.

When not in the car, Internet music services have also become more popular. Why would you want to hear countless used car commercials when you can type in your favorite artist's name at Pandora and stream countless songs that have the same profile—free! This is the equivalent of having a DJ at your beck and call playing "your request list" 24 hours a day, and you can just skip to the next track (or mark your new favorites) while you listen from anywhere you get an Internet connection. Who wouldn't want that?

As a marketer what all of this means is that traditional radio will not be a medium on the radar screen forever. If you pride your business on being local, look to integrate your radio messages into meaningful content that demands locals to listen (news, local sports and game broadcasts, weather, and traffic). If you have a national message that is currently being run across local radio networks, consider the options of satellite. Commercial time may be limited on key stations, but you can sponsor segments and create destination listening platforms that tie directly to your brand and the genre of your targeted consumers.

Q: Is Print Advertising Dead?

What's your perspective on this question?
Let us know at PerspectivesOnMarketing.com.

JASON MILETSKY

THE AGENCY PERSPECTIVE

From what I can tell, print has been a dying medium for most of my adult life. I've been reading articles about the impending demise of the print industry since the early days of Web commercialization (of course, the irony seems to escape the journalists whose articles appeared in paper magazines). I can't figure out why people seem to be in such a rush to kill off the entire industry.

Yes newspapers have been on the decline, and it's harder for magazines to get advertising than in the past. Numbers don't lie, and there's no denying that as a marketing medium, print has some serious challenges ahead of it. I predict there will be some significant shake-outs in the industry that may leave even some of the most well-known print names in the dust. But I also guarantee that 20 years from now, people will still be proclaiming that print advertising is dead—minutes after executing their last insertion order.

The problem with print is that it's pretty much left out of the innovation loop. TV changes constantly, the Internet regularly comes out with new ways of sending messages—even radio has found ways to renew itself through satellite and HD radio. But where else can print go? Paper is paper, and not everything has the potential for innovation.

Is it possible that paper could evolve to such drastic extents that it could one day be replaced by wireless electronic readers, such as those developed by Amazon or Sony? It's possible, but it's not going to happen anytime soon. In order for that transformation to take place, two things would have to occur:

- The price for book readers would have to drop considerably. Most readers still cost somewhere between $200 and $400, and that doesn't include any books. That's way too much—especially in a tough economy—for people to spend in such droves that it would threaten the print industry.

- A new generation of kids not yet born will have to grow up with so much access to the Internet, video games, and electronic readers that they would simply never develop a feel for print. (As much as I hate to inject ambiguous emotion into my rationale, I'm going to in this case: There's something about holding onto a newspaper or a magazine that you don't get from reading content on a computer monitor or any other type of screen. It's the rustling of the pages, the ability to read without clicking buttons or worrying about batteries.)

As with any industry suffering through tough times, there will be a rebalancing of supply and demand (assuming, of course, that the government doesn't bail out the entire industry). Some publications will fold, and surviving publications will lower their ad rates until prices and available space is such that it makes sense for marketers to continue including print advertising as part of their media mix.

Print advertising works as a powerful tool for brand building, even if it's only for the two seconds that readers see an ad before turning the page. (Sorry everyone, but the truth is nobody reads body copy.) Repeated placements help increase brand awareness, if only through the personality and creativity of design and the message sent in the headline. Similarly, print can work for direct advertising, especially in local newspapers or circulars, where readers may go to find out about upcoming sales or look for bargains. No matter what the reason for the ads, as long as print is alive and has an audience (and it *is* alive, and *does* have an audience), marketers who commit to the medium can enjoy positive results.

MICHAEL HAND

THE CLIENT PERSPECTIVE

⤶ It pains me to say it, but the days of print advertising are definitely on life support these days. As much as I love the ritual of running outside to get the newspaper on a cold morning and then sitting down for breakfast with the local sports section in tow, it appears that few people have my sense of nostalgia. The ability to never leave the house, pop open the laptop, make three clicks, and get the same information (including any last minute updates on a story) has much more appeal to the general public. In almost every major city, including Boston and San Francisco, the readership at America's biggest news dailies is sinking fast and ad revenue is sinking even faster.

The Web has taken over the distribution of the physical news, but more important to the folks looking at circulation audits and financials, insertions to spark car sales and real estate offerings are now shifting almost entirely to the digital world as well. When you want to buy a new car, the first place you go for data is the Web, and you continue through the process until you actually select a local dealer to talk to. Even the calculations on monthly lease payments can be done online, so you have very few surprises at the dealership level and can avoid the dreaded encounter until the last minute. In regard to real estate, most shoppers are going directly to sites like realtor.com where they can take a look at the full listings of every house on the market and pre-sort by any category of interest. The newspaper listing cannot weed out houses with less than two bathrooms or pre-select houses in a certain price range; once again the advantage goes to the Web. Today's buyers feel like they have less time to conduct these kind of searches and thus spend most of their time looking online for photos of every room and virtual tours; these tools give them a better sense of what to really expect. Real estate agents who relied on the local paper to build a clientele are now creating their own Web presence with links from these composite sites. They are becoming marketers as much as they are reinforcing their skills as home sellers.

According to the 2007 National Association of Realtors Profile of Home Buyers and Sellers:

- 84 percent of recent home buyers used the Internet in their search, up from 80 percent in 2006. Those statistics indicate that of the 84 percent of buyers who used the Internet, 99 percent of them found it to be a useful resource.

- Of the 51 percent of people who looked in newspaper ads, about half of them found the ads a useful tool.

In my mind, these drastic shifts in the print news model spell doom for the nation's smaller papers and put a major strain on the larger players. I suggest the powers at each of these parent companies look for ways to reinvent themselves in the online space, right down to providing the show times at the local movie theater and covering the area high school conference tournaments.

Magazine print advertising also faces some tough sledding ahead; layoffs have been deep and widespread as the financial model and ad revenue are also drying up here. Again, the presence of online media sources makes it difficult for news magazines like *Time* or *Newsweek* to break new "news." Even in the world of gossip, *Us Weekly* and *Star* are beat to the punch by sources on the Web. The major difference in this genre is that people think of magazines in a different way than they think of newspapers. Magazines are not about the "read it right now and throw it away" approach; to many individuals, they are about the "read at my leisure" approach. Magazines become a trusted friend who can provide everything from in-depth stories and how-to tips for Mom to a profile on a remarkable athlete and added statistical analysis for the sports fan of the house. With more than 10,000 unique titles in print, you would be hard pressed to find a subject that does not have a dedicated resource at the bookstore or newsstand. How many people have sat in a doctor's office and checked the table for something to read or while waiting for a haircut checked the wall rack for something to pass the time? My guess is 99 percent of us have done this and that half of this group swiped the magazine to take home and finish perusing something that they had started. That is a powerful statement and something that every magazine ownership group and magazine advertiser wants to hear/see. My suggestion to the magazine world is to keep yourself up-to-date on emerging trends and be ready to adjust your subscription plans. You too may need a less traditional print approach and foster the move to online in your own terms. The number of titles will certainly be in sharp decline, but the traditional favorites will carry on.

The death of print will be long and drawn out, which is painful for the "believers" to sit back and watch unfold. The reality is that the future will look very different and it will likely feel a bit less personal. Sure the content will be customized, but nothing can replace the way my dad would take the daily newspaper and fold the pages back and then fold it in half again so that he had a manageable way to still wield his coffee mug and read at the same time. Those memories will not exist for my kids; they will be replaced by our collective online search for baseball box scores and a review of the latest animated film to hit theaters while texting to get start times.

Q: • WHAT ROLE DOES PROMOTION
• PLAY IN EFFECTIVE MARKETING?

JASON MILETSKY
THE AGENCY PERSPECTIVE

There are so many words in the marketing vernacular whose meanings overlap with other words that it can sometimes be a struggle to know exactly what people are talking about. "Promotion" is one of those words. Most people tend to lump any number of exercises under this category. A quick read of Wikipedia lists the following as "promotional content": advertising/branding, direct marketing/personal sales, product placement/public relations, publicity/sales promotion, and underwriting. There is also a note on the top of the Wikipedia page that says, "It has been suggested that this article or section be merged into 'Advertising.'"

I have to be honest, I've never thought of promotion in any of these ways. Indeed, I'm a little baffled by how haphazardly people seem to lump marketing elements together. To me, promotion typically refers to non-advertising efforts taken to generate short-term results and otherwise create a shift in consumer behavior. (By the way, when I say "non-advertising," I mean that the ads themselves are not the driving force in causing the behavioral shift. Promotions, however, can be advertised.) More specifically, promotions tend to be limited-time events in which a specific incentive is introduced. For example, a company might run a limited-time promotion in which they'll give consumers one item free if they buy two or more of some other item. Other types of promotions come in the form of sweepstakes or contests, in which people are moved to take certain actions in the hopes of winning some sort of prize.

Sweepstakes and contests have especially grown in popularity with the rise of Web 2.0, with many companies running Web-based promotions to keep people coming back to their site and becoming more intimately engaged in their brand. For example, a brand might ask entrants to upload a video of themselves using their products. Other site visitors would then be allowed to rate and comment on each uploaded video, with the winner being the entrant whose video scores the highest rating. These types of efforts compel people to interact more closely with their brand and can attract entrants and viewers for increased awareness.

Obviously, promotions aren't going to work for all brands, but there is no question that they hold significant weight in terms of reaching out to consumers. In truth, while companies clearly want to generate profits from their promotions, the biggest benefit lies in their ability to compel consumers to experience the brand, increasing the chances of more regular use in the future.

MICHAEL HAND

THE CLIENT PERSPECTIVE

When people think of the "Four Ps," (Product, Price, Place, and Promotion) they tend to lump a variety of disciplines under "Promotion," including direct marketing, public relations, premium items, and even advertising. For this answer I will focus on traditional consumer promotions and events, with an occasional reference to tactics for trade relationships. As a guy who has spent the better part of his career working in promotional marketing, you'd better damned well believe I'm going to say that the role of promotion is of the utmost importance.

Advertising work tends to focus on driving changes in opinion about your brands and building greater awareness. In contrast, promotional activities—whose primary objectives are to increase merchandising, excite retail partners, improve brand awareness at the point of purchase and trial, increase brand loyalty, and grow market share—are used mainly to create a short-term spike in activity or to get your product on the floor at a retail location. Promotions are a great way to engage with your existing loyal consumer base while bringing in promiscuous shoppers looking to explore other brands in the short term.

The main idea behind promotions is actually quite simple: The more consumers see your product on the floor at the point of purchase, the more likely they are to purchase it. A promotion always gives the end user an incentive to act. This incentive could range from a potential sweepstakes prize to a better price point to a special gift with purchase to a better value/bonus pack.

The role of consumer promotions has increased in recent memory based on a number of marketplace realities. First, we have seen an unprecedented shift in the power of retailers. (I'll talk more about the "Wal-Mart Effect" later in this book—although Wal-Mart is hardly the only establishment flexing their retail muscles.) Promotions can enable brands to draw greater customization at the retail level. You can customize a message on point-of-sale material or offer a retail partner exclusive pass-through rights for a select property or event. This need to be unique has elevated consumer promotions to a critical channel role; they allow a more turnkey solution to separating a 7-11 from a Kroger or a Rite Aid from a Costco.

In addition to creating distinctions between classes of trade, promotional efforts can also differentiate within a class of trade. For example, brands associated with the sport of auto-racing can create a multi-pronged approach across retail partners and split an existing team sponsorship across multiple players. They might provide unique sweeps ticket packages by geography, create on-car impressions via special paint graphics when the race is in the local market, leverage local hospitality and/or tickets, and leverage team-owner or driver appearances at the retail or corporate office level. Each of these tactics not only provides individual retail points of engagement, they can ladder back up to a national level as part of a greater overlay.

In a marketplace cluttered by a number of brands all trying to say a similar thing or benefit a similar consumer, or when product formulas or distribution tactics are fairly identical, you can use consumer promotions to amplify your brand's unique point of difference. Promotions that drive individual brand equity by playing off the brand's color palette, attitude, taste profile, or advertising message will separate the brand from competitors in stores and demand incremental floor space to get the point across.

> You should stay abreast of what your competitors are doing with respect to retail promotions, but avoid basing your path to market solely on their direction. You need to utilize promotional efforts to provide differentiation among brands, not sameness.

An example of a brand that has used promotions with great results is the M&M's brand. This brand has been highly successful in the chocolate candy category playing up their biggest brand equity: the use of color and the hand-to-mouth nature of their product. Movie partnerships and brand-led sweeps events have consistently focused on color, and to further solidify their position as a leading brand in NASCAR, they conducted a "Most Colorful Fan" program in 2008 and 2009 in support of their team and league sponsorship that clearly linked the brand's color position into a sport with consumers who passionately "wear their colors" every race weekend. It elevated M&M's promotional efforts in the racing sector beyond simply slapping graphics on a car, touching a deeper aspect of what the sport is about and relating to fans who may (or may not) even root for their car/driver each weekend.

Broadly speaking, promotions feed off the idea of driving consumers to "come see," "come get," or "come experience." Tactics range from instant-win programs to self-liquidating mail-in offers and bonus-size bags. To succeed in the sweepstakes/contest arena, you must make sure you find the right balance between believability and cautious optimism. You cannot make the odds so ridiculous that somebody will never win; this will piss consumers off. On the flip side, you can't make things so easy that everybody wins; this will break your budget.

"Evergreen" programs are also important. Evergreen programs revolve around the idea of creating an ownable and repeatable program—one that can be refreshed every year and maintain its place on a promotional calendar. These evergreen events are hard to do successfully, but when you have one that works, it can be a gold mine. For one thing, you need to set up the infrastructure for the promotion only once, saving you money in the years that follow. And if the first year or two are successful, the future sell-in will be much easier to duplicate. For example, McDonald's has been very successful in making their "Monopoly" promotion a regular program at their franchise locations over the past decade; consumers have come to look for their "peel and reveal" labels on drinks and food packages every summer. All McDonald's has to do to refresh the promotion is simply add fresh prizes and/or increase the odds of winning. They just need to be cautious to avoid oversimplifying the idea and risking consumers becoming bored with the approach.

Another evergreen concept that many companies love to use is to provide "bonus" sizes of products or to discount products at the same time every year. This, too, can be effective, but does have one significant pitfall—namely that in many cases, the retailer (and, in turn, the consumer) become trained to wait for the product to go on sale or provide this added value. If consumers stock up on your product only at that time, it will kill your overall margins by taking these consumers out of market at regular-price time frames. Retailers are also getting smarter and have begun to "over order" the value pack, placing it in their everyday shelf set to provide ongoing value to their shoppers (and compete with Wal-Mart). Proceed with caution on the discount front.

As the use of promotions increases, deeper findings on sales results and consumer impact will be needed to assess their effectiveness. Stronger ROI models for promotions must be developed, as must a better understanding of shopper marketing dynamics. And of course, promotions are no different from other line items in the marketing mix budget: they must reinforce your brand identity, and they must deliver results to justify their spend.

When developing these programs, ask yourself (and your agency/client) three questions:

- What's in it for the brand?
- What's in it for the retailer?
- What's in it for the consumer?

If you can answer all three—and feel good about the answers—you just may have a great promotional concept right in front of you.

Q: HOW CAN A MARKETER BEST LEVERAGE THE ONLINE SPACE?

JASON MILETSKY

THE AGENCY PERSPECTIVE

I don't think many marketers really understand the power of the Internet and everything it can do to help both build a market and bring that market closer to their brand. So the best answer I can give to this question is, *learn*. Learning about the online space is the best way to leverage it. And by "learn," I don't mean watch the evening news on TV or eavesdrop on co-workers when they talk about who they've reconnected with on Facebook. I mean really get to know the Net. Read up on it. Surf. See how other brands handle their online campaigns. Talk to an agency that gets it and see what they know. Whatever it takes, marketers who really expect to make an impact with new or existing audiences can't just skate by with the bare minimum of Net know-how; they need to really get it to get the most out of it.

But I'm sure you want something tangible. Nothing sucks more than a book that only talks in generalities. So even though there's no one way for every brand to take advantage of the Internet—how you work into your overall marketing strategy will depend on your unique needs, budget, audience, and situation— I can do a run-though of some important specifics.

THE SITE

Clearly, if there's one element that deserves significant attention, it's the brand's Web site—the home base for any marketing effort and the first place consumers will turn when they want to find information about your brand. The trick is to create a site that reflects the brand while maximizing retention and encouraging return visits. That said, sites may be visited by large numbers of people and it'll be impossible to please every one of them—which is why it is especially important for marketers to understand who their audience is. Marketers must make certain that the retention techniques they put in place speak directly to their core demographic to ensure that the highest possible number of people within their target market come back regularly. There are many ways to do this, but the real keys to increasing brand loyalty on the Web are the same online as they are offline: striking the best balance of quality customer service, value, and product selection.

Encouraging users to return to a site begins with strong design that both reflects of the brand and is organized in a way that makes content easy to locate. An attractive design gives users a sense that the site is established and professional, and that a solid, legitimate company is behind it. At the same time, quality design specifically geared toward the target audience will help to establish the brand personality through images, color, and general layout. Successful site layout will accomplish the following:

- Make the purposes of the site clear, letting the visitor know what they can expect to find there.

- Promote the brand.

- Provide easy access to information.

- Lead the user to specific areas of interest or areas that the site owner wants them to see.

- Provide an attractive, aesthetically pleasing environment for the user.

Similarly, navigation requires careful consideration during site development; content on the Web is presented in a manner unlike any other media. Most media tend to be fairly linear. Sunday newspapers have different sections, and news is found by turning from one page to the next. Television is similar—a show is selected, and the viewer watches, scene by scene, in the order that those scenes are presented. Web sites are quite different. Aside from the interactivity that the Web provides, Web sites allow visitors to review information in a non-linear fashion, jumping from one page to another in any order they wish to find the information in which they are most interested. Unfortunately, though, the information that visitors are most interested in isn't always the information you want them to see, which is information related to sales. Because of the non-linear nature of the Web, marketers have a dual responsibility when it comes to site organization:

- Creating a navigation and hierarchy of content that makes finding information easy for site visitors

- Serving information in such a way that visitors are led to pages that the site's owners most want them to view

Finally, marketers must take advantage of social-media tools—such as blogs, ratings, reviews, polls, comments, avatars, Wikis, social networks, and more—to keep users engaged. The Web is no longer a brand-to-consumer one-way street when it comes to information. Using these social media tools, marketers can create an online environment in which the market becomes more interactive with the brand and in which consumers can even become more interactive with each other—all of which facilitates a more secure community of users and heightened brand loyalty.

USING THE NET TO BUILD AND KNOW YOUR AUDIENCE

With the popularization of social media, the Net has transformed from an advertising medium into a global conversation—a platform for exchanging ideas. It's energized people across practically every demographic boundary to interact with each other and with the brands they're in contact with. Marketers can use these tools to better understand consumers' frame of mind, keeping a pulse on how the market perceives their brand and what new buzzwords are gaining popularity.

The blogosphere is a particularly valuable resource for gaining these insights, as are product reviews on retail sites. Consumers are eager to discuss their feelings and experiences with particular brands. Indeed, various research firms claim that as much as 30 percent of all consumers don't feel that the shopping process is complete until they have left a review on a Web site. Marketers should stay constantly aware of online market sentiments as they relate to their brand, making changes in product strategy based on new information they uncover.

At the same time that the Web acts as global forum, intermingling demographic categories, it also gives marketers a powerful vehicle to pinpoint particular audiences with measurable precision. The word "measurable" is key—one of the most valuable aspects of the Internet is how easily almost any marketing campaign can be tracked and measured for cost-efficiency. It's impossible in this limited space to review all the opportunities for driving measurable traffic that the Web offers, but marketers should consider at least some of the following:

- **E-mail blast campaigns:** Whether it's company news or information your customers can use, e-mail blasts speak to each user directly and can play a big role in building brand awareness and pushing new and returning visitors to your site, with open rates and click-through rates easily measured. Personally, I haven't found a good list provider yet, so I'd recommend either growing a list organically or working through consumer-based print publications, which usually offer blast services to the subscriber base.

- **Pay-per-click advertising:** Google may not have invented this, but they sure as hell did perfect it. Offering one of the best arguments for abandoning print advertising, PPC ads allow marketers to target specific Web users by placing ads on specific sites or by having them appear when surfers search for particular keywords. Best of all, you only pay for the clicks you get, so budgets are controlled and waste is minimized.

- **Streaming video:** Did someone say TV? Who needs television when users can get video content on demand through any one of a million sites? Video can capture attention more powerfully than any other medium, and while streaming Web video hasn't replaced television yet, it's starting to show signs that it could soon reign as the new king. One of my favorite statistics from eMarketer is that among viewers who already had a favorable opinion of a brand, consideration to purchase rose by 61 percent after viewing an online video of the brand in question. Even more amazing is that consideration also rose by 21 percent among viewers who had pre-existing unfavorable opinions about the brand. 'Nuff said!

Lastly, while I've really only skimmed the tip of the proverbial iceberg, I don't think any discussion about the best ways to leverage the online space would be complete without talking about measuring traffic. Analytics tools like Google Analytics track and measure site usage, including the average length of time people spend on your site, how many people come back regularly, which pages are the least and most popular, the average number of pages people see per visit, geographic locations of all visitors, and so on. If the saying is true that a little knowledge can be a dangerous thing, then with the right tracking program and a real understanding of how to use the information it collects, marketers can be downright lethal.

Michael Hand

The Client Perspective

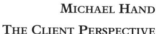 Technology has become a major part of the American household. According to Internetworldstats.com, as of June 2008, almost 74 percent of the North American population was using the Internet—more than 221 million people in the United States—an increase of 130 percent since 2000. And according to the Nielsen Online Home Panel, those users average more than 35 hours a month surfing more than 60 unique domains (sites). It goes without saying that the scope of the online world's impact is significant.

In my answer to Question #39, "How Important Is the Web to Any Marketing Effort?" I discussed the importance of the Web and highlighted a number of areas for companies to consider in their efforts. To build on those points, I would like to add a few more thoughts about leveraging the online arena to ponder:

- **Get feedback:** Use the 24/7 nature of the Web to spark conversation and find out how you are doing in the marketplace. This learning tool can make your products better and can make you smarter as a marketer. Be willing to listen and be prepared to make changes.

- **Build a community:** Get people to bond over one common entity: your brand. Whether through blogs or the simple joy of sharing recent photos, social networking tools offer a great way for your brand to stay on your customers' minds. People like to feel like they are a part of something big; give them a reason to keep coming back.

- **You are not alone:** Don't fool yourself into thinking you're the only game in town. Consumers are shameless. They won't stick around if you don't have anything important for them to see or do online. Check out the competition on a regular basis and never stop looking for innovative ways to connect.

- **Don't take yourself too seriously online:** Companies and categories that in the past have been perceived as boring or stoic have driven some amazing transformations using the Web as a catalyst. For example, in the winter of 2007, office-products retailer OfficeMax broke the mold of simply selling paper and pens on the Web by creating a fun viral campaign aimed at the office workers who could use their services. Their "Elf Yourself" campaign spread like wildfire, driving nearly 200 million site visits worldwide—many of which would never have occurred otherwise. The Internet can be a source of great enjoyment, and people love to share the hidden gems they find.

Q: HOW POWERFUL IS VIRAL MARKETING? CAN VIRAL MARKETING BE A PLANNED EFFORT, GIVEN THAT IT RELIES SO HEAVILY ON CONSUMER INVOLVEMENT?

JASON MILETSKY

THE AGENCY PERSPECTIVE

With e-mail making communication between friends, family, and associates as quick and easy as clicking the Forward button, viral campaigns have become a hot topic in marketing circles due to their potential for high visibility rates and their relatively low cost (when compared to other forms of mass-media advertising).

In short, a viral campaign is one in which the marketer deliberately creates aspects of the campaign in such a way that the audience will be compelled to pass the message on to others. This is typically done in one of two ways:

- The marketer can offer an incentive to a consumer to pass a message on to others (often called a "refer-a-friend" program). Marketers who use this tactic offer existing customers anything from a free T-shirt to reduced rates to cash if they refer someone to a site and that person then signs on and becomes a paying customer. The consumer who passes the word along is happy because he or she stands to profit from passing on the name of a brand with which he or she already feels comfortable; the person who receives the information is comfortable that the recommendation is coming from a trusted, reliable source and not directly from the brand itself; and the brand is happy because they have set the referral price at a reasonable cost per each new client acquisition.

- The marketer will try to create a marketing piece that can capture people's attention—so much so that they feel compelled to pass it on if for no other reason than to show it to other people. Typically, these tend to be videos that are either heavily comedic, extraordinarily shocking, or both.

According to Jupiter Research, more than 60 percent of all Internet users have passed along an e-mail to a friend or colleague that they found interesting or funny.

With new content infiltrating the Web every day, however, marketers are finding it more difficult to capture consumers' interest and are increasingly pressed to push the envelope to attract attention.

While the term "viral campaign" refers to any portion of a campaign that gets passed from one person to another, savvy marketers seek to create campaigns that are more complex than single, outrageous videos. Truly effective campaigns that can maintain audience interest for longer periods of time need to tie back to a single creative concept that helps to reinforce the brand message.

My favorite viral campaign launched in 2004. Initially, only 20 people were told about the SubservientChicken.com Web site—friends of the ad agency that created it. Before long, however, 20 million people had registered with the site (according to the *Wall Street Journal*). The site shows a video of a man in a chicken suit standing in a rather unassuming living room. Visitors who log on can tell him what to do. A command of "Do three pushups" results in the guy in the chicken suit doing three pushups. Although otherwise pointless, people found the site fascinating, spending an average of six minutes with each visit. Throughout the campaign, rumors swirled as people tried to find out who was behind the site. (Although the site today has a brand logo clearly visible, it was not as obvious when the site first launched.) Ultimately, it was revealed, to much publicity, that the site was part of Burger King's marketing effort, underscoring its long-held "Have it your way" brand promise.

Viral campaigns can be less expensive than mass-media–centered efforts and may be seen by far more people, but they can also be uncontrollable and unpredictable. It is practically impossible to target any one demographic with a viral campaign, and there is no guarantee that any viral effort is going to work. Simply igniting the viral flame will not necessarily produce a raging fire.

MICHAEL HAND

THE CLIENT PERSPECTIVE

The world of viral marketing is growing in strength and stature with each passing day. Despite the obvious links some make between the words virus (very negative connotations) and viral, it has fast become a universally accepted, low-cost method to spread the word on your brand to consumers using the Internet. It capitalizes on the aspect of human nature that drives people to share what they perceive as good/bad information with friends and family members, ranging from a "free" offer on a product or service to an uncomplicated tool for communication and keeping connected. This connection can be something as straightforward as a video that makes you laugh and brings a smile to your face.

Creating a positive online experience for consumers has become one of the fastest ways to build a brand (and generate sales) through a loyal customer base. On the flip side, creating a bad online experience can destroy all brand building efforts almost instantly.

Traditional thinking has always been that the average consumer who has a positive experience with a product/service will turn around and tell six to eight additional people about his/her occurrence; a consumer who has a negative encounter, however, will tell twice as many folks about the bad result (this according to "The Profitable Art of Service Recovery" by Hart, Heskett, and Sasser, published in *Harvard Business Review*). That said, more recent data from the Austin, Texas–based company Bazaarvoice has surfaced that shows online consumers provide more positive reviews than negative by a margin of 8 to 1 in the online environment. Companies clearly need to invest in this area for positive growth.

Many viral efforts are not planned far in advance; they just "kind of happen." Everybody has the friend who is the king of the e-mail forward. Yes, he is annoying but you have to admit that he definitely passes on a few hidden gems that make you click through on whatever he passes your way. This alone has become one of the leading drivers to YouTube: the desire for humor or off-beat human experiences captured on video that you "simply have to see." When this phenomenon was started, I am pretty sure that it was not of the intention to create millions of page views. Site users just liked the ability to post bad wedding clips or funny moments captured on video that fell short of reality TV standards—it was basically a place to post *America's Funniest Home Videos* rejects. It was the resting place for the too perverse and off-color but sometimes hilarious. Now YouTube has become a place to seed video clips from films, launch music videos, and post "behind the scenes" looks at the mainstream entertainment world; no longer is this a place for only the obscure family memories.

Despite the randomness aspect of viral marketing, these efforts can be (and should be) planned to be most effective. The launch of Hotmail is a great example of this planned pattern of behavior. When Hotmail launched, they placed a strong emphasis on the "you can also get a free Hotmail account by clicking here" message at the bottom of every outbound note—that was their entire marketing campaign. It was 100 percent viral, and it was an implied endorsement that the sender believed in the service and so should you. It was a simple text format built into the bottom of the everyday note, and it required no additional effort by the user or recipient to view. Simply click on the link and you too could have this "great service" for free. This was not a random pop-up ad placed across the Web while you were surfing for information; it was text at the bottom of a note in your e-mail from a trusted friend. This basic strategy has clearly paid off, with Hotmail now available in 36 languages and having over 280 million users worldwide. The beauty of planning for the effort in advance is the ability to control the dialogue with consumers and to have the back-end support in place from the start.

Delivering a positive online experience will pay strong dividends for any viral effort, in particular when using an online service. Entities like Evite are now the leaders in capitalizing on this "free" endorsement from current users. After you get invited to a party through Evite and see how they track responses and allow you to customize your invitation, it is hard not to consider it the next time you throw a party yourself. Every outbound message they serve to a guest starts the viral process and gives them another chance to increase their future user base. Key takeaway: provide value and keep it simple. You just need to make it easy for the next participant to get involved—the simpler, the better.

The world of humor, as mentioned earlier, is also an area to not overlook in the viral space. The ability to bring a little smile to someone's face at the click of a mouse can drive an entire viral campaign. Burger King's "Subservient Chicken" campaign kicked off in April 2004 and had people buzzing for years as BK reinvented the interactive landscape through agency partners Crispin Porter + Bogusky and The Barbarian Group with a chicken that acted out over 300 unique commands. It was "quite possibly the most successful marketing Web site of all time. Over a billion hits. One hundred million unique visitors. Sales of Burger King's chicken sandwiches doubled in a matter of weeks. It was the One Club's campaign of the year (source: www.barbariangroup.com/portfolio).

You can now also expect each season to bring along viral executions like "Elf Yourself" from Office Depot at Christmas or work from companies like JibJab and Will Ferrell's "Funny or Die" to carve a niche in e-mail comedy. The association of your brand with a positive attitude and smile can be just enough of a boost to put the brand on somebody's radar screen for purchase consideration. It can also be an extremely strong marketing tool to drive site traffic quickly.

As a side note, I beg you not to simply add a "tell a friend" button to your Web site and start passing it off as a viral marketing effort. I think this is a great functional tool to include in your design, but this is not how you start a viral effort. People will tell a friend about good and bad experiences regardless of whether or not you prompt them. Reviews will be written and feedback will be posted; viral efforts need to be about more unique experiences and have a reason to exist.

Q: WHAT WILL THE ONLINE SPACE LOOK LIKE IN FIVE YEARS? HOW ABOUT 20 YEARS?

JASON MILETSKY

THE AGENCY PERSPECTIVE

Here it is: the dreaded prediction question, where we set ourselves up to look like geniuses or idiots. As with any prediction question, there are two ways it can be answered: safely or truthfully. Well, nobody's ever accused me of being too safe, so at the risk of being laughed at by my peers, ridiculed by reviewers, and shunned by my business partner (who will probably not like or agree with most of my predictions), here are my honest thoughts on the future of the Internet:

■ Truly creepy innovations that have already been introduced will start to become commonplace. These range from "smart" appliances that know when you're running low on OJ and either alert you or just add it to a digital shopping list to Net-based grocery-store shopping carts, which will take that same list and map out the best route through the store—leading you past specific products and alerting you to savings, specials, and recipes along the way. With these and other innovations, the Internet will officially evolve from something we "go on" to something we "live in."

■ Facebook will officially replace MySpace as the market leader in social networking (and it'll stay that way). They'll do so, however, with a much smaller U.S. population than the two sites compete for now. We're not a society known for having long attention spans, and people can only participate in so many Facebook snowball fights, vampire bites, and mafia wars before they start to get bored. Plus, the excitement of reconnecting with people you've lost touch with will start to disappear as old high-school cliques reform online more 20 years after the popular kids gave you your last wedgie. At some point, the hype over these types of social networks will cool down, audiences will fall off, and growth will end, with the most easily bored audiences falling off until a solid plateau is formed among steady, regular users. This same falling-off will cause the collapse of tons of small, niche social networks that simply can't afford to stay in business based on a few cents per click from their Google AdSense account.

- With the exception of Facebook status updates, microblogs will join Chevy Chase's late night talk show in the category of "Gee, it sure seemed like a good idea at the time" after hordes of Twitter users simultaneously realize that they don't care if someone they've never met before got a ketchup stain on their new sweater during a particularly raucous lunch.

- Scores of smaller video-sharing sites will disappear as their investors conclude they just aren't pulling large enough audiences to generate the ad revenue they need to turn a profit, leaving YouTube and a handful of others to compete for the entire market. However, while independent video-sharing upstarts will slowly wither and die, Hulu will draw in more TV network support and become an increasingly large threat to YouTube with a legitimate chance of dethroning the king—not in number of viewers, but in generated revenue. Marketers, more eager to find audiences watching well-produced shows over audiences entertained by cell-phone video of a cat flushing a toilet, will move their marketing to Hulu. As a reaction (and remember, you read it here first), Google will buy one of the major TV networks—my guess being the CW because of their continued focus on young adult programming. This will give them greater control of professional content, and YouTube will begin to shift its focus away from primarily offering amateur videos.

- There will be a sharp spike in the number of companies that look to market themselves through streaming video as the cost of production drops and more brands start to see positive returns with this form of marketing.

- Thanks to Apple and HP, there will be a new surge in popularity for touch-screen monitors, followed by new Web languages that make sites more touch-screen friendly. (The AJAX programming language could provide the foundation for new code.) The new way of interacting with sites will run parallel with an increase of original television programming streaming over the Web as networks start to accept the Web as a necessary part of their future rather than an enemy that threatens to bring them down. Ultimately, this combination will lead to the next major step toward the integration of TV and the Net that was originally promised with the short-lived WebTV in the '90s and will bring with it a shift in mass-media marketing. The standard 30-second–commercial format will fade away, replaced by show sponsorship based on 15-second streaming clips and show-surrounding display ads as well as a sharp increase in product-placement opportunities, with viewers able to simply touch a product within a show to download coupons, leave a review, or just get more information.

- SecondLife will die, a victim of the sex industry, MLM proprietors, and a management team that didn't do enough to keep these scavengers out. This will leave a black hole in the metaverse (nobody will notice), which will eventually be filled by the people who created the Sims empire—and these guys will do it right. Family friendly, more creative for the medium (virtual worlds should be more than just 3D re-creations of the real world; SecondLife never seemed to realize that there's no need for things like, say, chairs in a virtual world, because avatars don't typically get tired), and faster to download, a new virtual world will finally give marketers a new platform for reaching their audiences.

MICHAEL HAND

THE CLIENT PERSPECTIVE

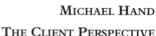 This is a really tough one to answer, considering that the Internet as we know it is has only been around for slightly more than a decade. This fact alone makes it difficult to predict the 20-year horizon because things are evolving so rapidly. In the early days, consumers were reluctant to share personal information on the Web; now it's a dumping ground for people's most intimate thoughts. Each year a new record is broken as it relates to e-commerce, and in the world of holiday shopping, "Cyber Monday" now mirrors "Black Friday" as the biggest shopping day of the year. It is hard to imagine that the next generation of Internet users will not take the level of online engagement to even greater levels. So I'll be holding off on the 20-year response; hopefully, my writing partner has some wonderful insights he can bestow upon you.

I will take a stab, however, at talking about the shorter-term horizon through the eyes of the client. The next five years promise to be an interesting transition period. My parents don't even know how to turn a computer on, let alone make business transactions on one. Yet my three kids, who are all under the age of 10, are already showing me how things work in this space. Between games on Club Penguin, worlds in Webkinz, and all sorts of activities from Nickelodeon and Disney, they are well-versed in the online space and its connective powers. With some basic supervision, we allow them to play games with their cousins from across the country while sitting at home.

As I previously mentioned, the digital revolution has taken hold and things are moving fast. A few key areas to keep an eye on:

- **E-commerce.** One simple word will drive e-commerce: comfort. The current e-spenders (and certainly the next generation of online users) think very little about the risks involved in purchasing things online. The identity theft scares have done little to stop folks from sharing credit-card information and handling all their banking online. The days of stopping into the local bank branch to make a transaction and check on an account balance are long gone. Keep an eye on sites like eBay, who helped to create the online financial model and put brands like PayPal on the map, as they look to evolve the transactional space. Whether the economy is struggling or not, people will always look for better deals, and the online world is rich with such offers. Let's face it: People simply like to shop from the couch in their pajamas—and there is something comforting (and convenient) about avoiding the mall and getting what you need delivered to your door. They also like to think/know that they got a good deal, so expect the use of comparison sites to increase in the next five years. (These are sites where consumers can get all the details and specifications on consumer products and offerings.) The ability of consumers to share their own reviews will also increase, and sites that allow open dialog on likes and dislikes will continue to see growth. Finally, as the presidential campaign of Barack Obama proved through its results, you can expect many non-profit organizations to shift greater efforts into the online space for fundraising. Obama attracted more than 1.7 million contributors online, with 93 percent of his $2.9 million in online donations coming through in increments of less than $100 (source: *Mediaweek*, 12/08). Consumers will be willing to share their personal information, and even though they are pressed for time, they still want to find ways to give a little something back in the community or to a good cause. Making the transaction process easy (and fast) will encourage people to consider online giving.

- **Social networking**. Facebook, Twitter, MySpace, YouTube, LinkedIn, and more blogs than you can imagine—these days, the online space is used by many as a way to "overshare." One thing is for sure: We don't have a shortage of ways to get our opinion out in the public and to tell our friends and family (or even total strangers) everything that is going on in our life! Online users can share what they want, whenever they want. This power shift in the marketing world from "talking *to* consumers" to "talking *with* consumers" will continue in the foreseeable future. It will require smart marketers to stop the "We can post it on our corporate Web site and consumers will find it" attitude, and will force corporate staffs to uncover new places where their consumers mingle and to integrate their companies/brands/services into the existing conversation streams. Brands will need to become part of the actual story, woven into the experience and not disrupting the established flow of dialog. Services that promote sharing and connecting will continue to evolve and replace the mainstream communication patterns of today. Facebook surpassed 130 million users worldwide in 2008; clearly this "social networking thing" is not a fad (source: *Mediaweek*, 12/08).

- **Search.** Ahhhh, remember the good old days of cracking open that set of *World Book Encyclopedia* (every house in America seemed to have one) to write your middle-school research paper for social studies class? No Google searches to get the most current articles and Web sites; no online access to databases full of research documents and journal entries. It really is hard to imagine a world without Google, but remember—it only launched in 1998.

The next five years promise to deliver even more detailed ways of getting information—and frankly, getting a lot more (perhaps too much) information. The online world helps to save the environment by limiting mass production of periodicals (a convenient way for printing companies to save money and chalk it up to environmental diligence) and it saves people the time and effort it would take to search through an actual library (the bricks and mortar kind) for information in hard-copy form. But search is bigger than just term papers and book reports; it has become a way to find out about everything that is happening in the world. For example, go to your favorite local bar with a group of good friends, and eventually a debate will be sparked about some nonsense issue that keeps you up at night. It can range from where your favorite NFL quarterback went to college to more "serious" issues like an actor/actress and the great/horrible films that person has made. As the debate gets more heated (and the bar tab increases), you will inevitably get the over-served friend who is convinced that Angelina Jolie first hooked up with Brad Pitt while they filmed *Ocean's Eleven* together in the days "before she was super hot" (or maybe something more/less eloquent after seven cocktails). The only way to solve it on the spot is to use your BlackBerry and search IMDb.com to get the real scoop. (Side note for you movie aficionados: They hooked up while filming *Mr. & Mrs. Smith*.) Once again: the power of search, helping to solve the world's biggest and most complex problems. While I don't mean to trivialize the role of search by comparing it to drunken nights and movie facts, the importance of having your Web site surface at the top spot on any given search can be critical to business success. The days of using the *Yellow Pages* near the phone are over, and smart Web designers are now embedding words within their domain to guarantee top billing and increase streams of site traffic.

- **Online advertising.** The days of basic banner ads are already passing us by, and click-through rates for these standard units are clearly on the decline. You now have streaming video, unique approaches using site takeovers, aggressive use of pop-up ads, and road blocking across sites. The game has changed. In addition, marketers are getting a bit savvier on the payment model, and I expect to see a greater move toward the pay-per-click model that rewards the host site for driving actual traffic back to the advertiser, not just serving an ad to an empty room. With this pay structure in the works, you should also expect to see tighter guidelines and policing of the design. Hiring people to sit in a room all day and click into advertisers' sites in order to drive the numbers is fraud. This is not added consumer impressions, and the results need to reflect the actual engagement.

- **E-mail marketing.** Even though folks are getting more comfortable in the online space, they still want to avoid spam at all costs. Because I once registered to get e-mail from a popular sports site or registered my fantasy football team online does not make me a leading candidate for future "penis enlargement solutions" or in great need of "avoid bankruptcy now" services. (Hey Judy69 and SonjaXOXO, consider yourself informed; please stop filling up the spam folder on my Yahoo! account with your messages.) It has gotten to the point that I refuse to open e-mails unless I recognize the name in the "from" column as someone I actually know. E-mail marketing has become the replacement for the "bad direct mail" of days gone by—just a cheaper and wider-reaching version. I believe the future will see more strict control in this area and make it harder for the spam world to live on as it currently does. E-mail efforts will still be great tools to communicate with brand loyalists, but the expectation that you have something meaningful to say will be even stronger. Look for this type of communication to shift to cell phones and play an increased role in the form of mobile texting via SMS; let's hope we can expect it to be tighter to brand messaging. This is an opportunity for the marketers with passionate user bases to make a big difference. Loyal users want to hear from the brands they love; if you can provide updated news for them to make their life easier, it will pay off in the end. This will need to evolve from monthly e-mail newsletters to more custom solutions, but the stage is set.

- **Tighter metrics.** Currently, data points are somewhat flawed when measuring figures like online conversion rates. People like to shop around; it is human nature to look at more than one source before making a purchase. They will likely visit your site, but they will look around the Web at the competition as well. So what happens if they eventually come back and purchase the item they originally found on your site? Conversion rates need to be calculated off the total of unique visitors in a given period of time, not off every individual visit that is made. Marketers need to remember that every encounter with a potential customer counts, not just the most recent one. Also, look for deeper data on Web viewership in the next five years as the universe of users gets harnessed for marketers in a more readable and reliable data source. We are already seeing the world of television viewership and ratings expand to include "online viewership" trackers with the goal of securing a true audience count. These findings will continue to evolve and gain in stature with marketers.

All of these changes are seismic in their own right, but when put together, they form an extremely important face in the future of marketing. No area of the marketing mix is as under-developed and open to modification as the online space.

Q: TAKING THE SHOW ON THE ROAD: HOW VALUABLE ARE MOBILE UNITS IN CREATING A BRAND EXPERIENCE?

JASON MILETSKY

THE AGENCY PERSPECTIVE

I'm not going to spend a lot of time on this question, because I just don't feel that it warrants a lot of detail. Mobile units are mobile units, and an ROI analysis should be done on their anticipated value before launch, just like a smart marketer would do before launching any other initiative.

The plusses behind mobile units, of course, include the fact that they are constantly on the go and can spread a message over wide areas (unlike a roadside billboard, on the other hand, which plays only to the audience directly in front of it). Additionally, mobile units are generally such that they are goofy or bold enough to catch some people's eyes. I don't know, though. I guess I'm just kind of ambivalent to the whole mobile-unit thing. There's not a lot out there that's shocking anymore. Marketing is everywhere, and between reality TV, YouTube, video games, and everything else that barrages our senses, I'm just not sure that a truck in the shape of a hot dog is going to do the trick. It's cute, and maybe a decade or two ago it raised some eyebrows. But now I really can't see it doing much more than making people take an almost bored second look before turning away and saying, "It's nothing—just a truck shaped like a hot dog." So in that sense, mobile units become simply one more method of brand-building that may or may not be a good addition to an overall strategy, depending (like any other effort) on its cost versus how you expect people will see it.

MICHAEL HAND

THE CLIENT PERSPECTIVE

⌐ Much like ambush marketing in the previous question, mobile marketing is not for everybody. Mobile efforts can be a costly endeavor, and they take a strong organizational commitment to execute with success. Many companies like to create a mobile unit, announce its existence to the sales organization, and send it out on the road having no real plan for where it fits into their brand plans and what the expected return will be. Before committing to a mobile unit, you need a plan. First, make sure it aligns with your overarching brand story and make sure all the communication via the unit matches your other national efforts. If you find inconsistent points, so will your potential consumers. Second, make sure you have a usage plan. The worst thing you could do would be to invest millions of dollars in building the unit and then have it sit for weeks at a time in an agency warehouse while you pay insurance and storage fees. Create a full calendar by seeking placements through the sales team, key accounts, trade shows, and anywhere else that people convene, such as music and sporting events. Also, do not underestimate the value it can bring with people from your own organization. Having your exhibit trailer or race team's "show car" on display at the manufacturing plant can deliver a sense of company pride to the people not tarnished and jaded by marketing messages all day. You cannot put a return on investment on this type of visit, but take it from me: It works to increase employee morale. You will get letters weeks after the visit inquiring when it will be back and thanking you for breaking up their daily grind with something "cool."

Consumers of your brands are a moving target, and you need to find them rather than waiting for them to find you. A branded experience can have a tremendous impact and create a stronger brand memory than a simple TV ad. It can also be the best way to get your potential target to "touch and feel" your products. While at General Motors, we utilized mobile efforts through our golf relationship at Buick to get potential car buyers behind the wheel without ever entering a dealership. Using Tiger Woods and golf as a backdrop was a great way to demonstrate car features and interact with consumers at PGA events. Green screen photos and virtual test drives brought in a younger demo, and free golf balls for answering product-specific questions made sure that on-site participants walked away with better knowledge of the new models. It was also very important to local dealers who used the trailer and exhibits outside their own showrooms on days prior to the tournament or along the tour route at local auto shows and car club activities. Tracking participants against our sales database allowed us to see what kind of impact we had with actual sales volume over a short- and long-term horizon. When dealing with high ticket items like cars, it does not take a lot of sales to start building an impressive return.

Brands like Oscar Mayer and Hershey's Kisses have taken the visual experience one step further by building units in the same forms of their iconic brands. When you see the Kissmobile outside a local drug store or the Weinermobile in a crowded stadium parking lot before a big game, the image stays with you for some time. This backdrop for delivering product samples is quite powerful and creates the pass along story/picture that gets people excited and builds an emotional connection.

Johnsonville Bratwurst has also done a fantastic job with their Big Taste Grill in generating consumer interest about their products at fairs, festivals, and sporting events, while creating an impactful footprint on-site and on the road. The tour has existed for more than 10 years and still draws attention when it shows up at an event. Bottom line, mobile marketing can be a high-visibility asset that reinforces your product's point of difference and enhances your brand identity to your consumer—that is a value.

Q: WHAT ROLE DOES PUBLIC RELATIONS PLAY IN A MARKETING STRATEGY? HOW CONNECTED SHOULD PR EFFORTS BE TO MARKETING EFFORTS?

JASON MILETSKY
THE AGENCY PERSPECTIVE

I've read a lot of books on marketing and branding. Some of them I like quite a bit. They definitely have some interesting things to say. But I've noticed that many of these books end up being little more than 300+ page advertisements for the author who's trying to sell creative or consulting services. I really don't want to do that here. You bought this book to learn something, not to give me business. So while I've mentioned my agency now and then, I've really tried to keep it low-key, bringing it up only when it closely related to a story I'm telling.

But I'm going to break my own rule now and be a little self-promotional. My agency, PFS Marketwyse, is a full-service agency. I oversee the branding and advertising departments, and my partner, Deirdre Breakenridge, oversees our PR/communications department. One of the main reasons why PFS has grown as quickly as it has is because when it comes to PR, Deirdre is really about the best there is. She has an amazing eye for strategy, and she's a leading voice in her industry. (Although it's for a competing publisher, you really should check out her books *PR 2.0: New Media, New Tools, New Audiences* and *Putting the Public Back in Public Relations*. Both are required reading for anybody looking to understand the intricacies and subtleties of today's PR landscape. Also check out her blog at www.deirdrebreakenridge.com.) With such a brilliant resource at my disposal, it seemed silly for me to answer this question myself, so I've asked Deirdre to provide a guest perspective on PR's role in establishing and promoting a brand.

PR serves many functions for brands that want to increase awareness, manage their reputation, and build relationships with key stakeholders. Although companies have valued PR for years, they do more so today because PR is one of the most powerful weapons in their interactive marketing arsenals. Communication professionals have learned that the new PR 2.0 landscape allows a brand to interact one-on-one through social-media tools including RSS, podcasting, streaming video, blogging, and social networking, to name a few. These 2.0 resources enable brands to talk directly with customers, prospects, media, and of course new influencers or bloggers.

PR 2.0 is not a new principle. As a matter of fact, it's been around for over a decade. It's only recently that a tremendous focus on enhanced Web 2.0 collaborative applications allows professionals to fully take advantage of the communications resources available in Web communities. Pre–Web 2.0, brands used PR to go through the media and other important groups as credible third-party endorsers. Today, not only can professionals develop those relationships—for example, using 2.0 sharing tools to help journalists build their stories with social-media releases (SMRs)—they can also interact with new influencers or bloggers in ways that were never possible and with more reach and impact.

However, bloggers, like other influencers, have expectations too. Similar to media relations and a PR person's approach to media outreach, there are rules of engagement with new influencers. Brands can engage with bloggers to increase brand awareness and build relationships that lead to endorsements, but you can't just jump right into their conversations. It's very important to listen first, to hear what your influencers are talking about, and to discover what interests them—and *then* provide meaningful information or communication that they can then share with their followers or members of their communities. In many cases, these very influencers are the people who buy a brand's products/services. Because social media allows sharing in communities, brands are reaching people directly and can listen, learn, interact with, or engage in new ways to build awareness and brand loyalty through a great experience.

New PR provides a direct experience with key stakeholders in addition to the traditional endorsement approach of the past. For instance, brands can use a social media release, which is becoming a popular new social-media communications tool, to reach the media, the blogosphere, customers, prospects, etc. This doesn't necessarily mean you abandon the traditional news release to your media outlets. On the contrary, you can still have a traditional-style release that is distributed via a wire service—but with a PR 2.0 enhancement that allows you to give new influencers/bloggers, customers, prospects, and other groups in communities the ability to take parts of your release and share them. The SMR is a viral PR tool. The body of the release houses links, MP3 downloads, video, and sharing tools, including the ability to pass the release virally to members of different communities through Twitter, Facebook, Redit, Delicious, Digg, Technorati, and Newsvine, to name a few examples.

The PR landscape has changed dramatically, allowing PR professionals to promote and enhance their brands' reputations through social media. Engagement and conversations with the media, bloggers, and people in Web communities provide real-time, direct communication that builds loyalty and trust. Brands, through PR 2.0 and social media, have a voice. They are no longer hiding behind their monikers, but can actively engage and show their human sides to the people that want to hear from them directly. Brands will continue to build awareness and loyal brand followers through PR 2.0.

MICHAEL HAND

THE CLIENT PERSPECTIVE

Public relations can be a very powerful tool in an integrated marketing plan for any client; it can add millions of dollars of value through free publicity that reaches potential consumers via all forms of communication. In today's media-centric world that is filled with skeptical consumers, PR plays an increasingly critical role. When used effectively, it serves the primary function of spreading the word and creating added positive awareness for your marketing campaigns. It must be mandated that any public relations effort is tightly linked to marketing and reinforces the "story" that you want to tell throughout your campaign; connectivity is critical. In many organizations, PR is designated as a sheer support role that is designed to share corporate announcements to Wall Street and get the latest company news to employees. In addition, some companies will add the role of "defense specialist" to the PR team in times of crisis, acting as the first line of defense for issues related to negative business results, lawsuits, and/or product recalls. When public relations is limited to these areas, overall market impact is sacrificed. Marketing teams at any size of company need to realize that public relations professionals do more than just write press releases.

Public relations work needs to be incorporated at the first step of your planning process; the foundational communication of the story can help set the tone and control of any third-party dialogue of your overarching direction. The PR team's primary function is to ensure that everything the press sees or hears is controlled and consistent with the overall image plan. The public relations leader on any team will quickly become the "face of the brand" to the press if this effort is done correctly. But remember, the press will not just wake up one day and suddenly decide they endorse your product line or want to share news on your brands—it takes a commitment to this part of the marketing mix to get press coverage and strong reviews. Some of the best PR efforts are conducted by the major movie studios, creating excitement and anticipation for the next Academy Award winner one day and then creating the same excitement and anticipation for the summer's biggest flop the next. They have mastered the ability to generate interest in films and control the press, regardless of how good the actual product is.

Do you want press coverage for your campaign/event/product/service? Try the following public relations tactics to create buzz and maintain/increase your awareness level within your key user base:

- **National news release:** Get broad reach and general placement.

- **Targeted lifestyle/geographic news release(s):** This will get you localized and/or key user awareness that could incorporate an exclusive angle to the story that is most relevant.

- **Trade press coverage:** Let your own industry start the buzz for your activity and let your competitors know you are an industry leader.

- **Behind-the-scenes looks and exclusive content/exposure/sneak previews:** Everybody wants to feel like they are getting something exclusive before the rest of the world takes notice.

- **Photos/press kits:** Don't force them to simply imagine how the event/item looks, show it to them; people tend to be very visual, and a photo can help tell the story.

- **Online blogs/user forums:** Go to the places where passionate people talk and let them help spread the word.

- **Satellite media tours:** These are a great way to create national exposure and never leave your hometown.

- **Celebrity spokesperson:** Adding a celebrity that has name recognition can be the boost you need to get additional coverage and create an identity (just be careful they do not overshadow your brand).

- **Community outreach/cause related efforts:** People tend to support the people who support them, so consider staying closer to home and provide a helping hand.

In everything that you do through public relations, you need to remember that outside media outlets are not looking for quantity of stories, they are looking for quality. They have countless items they can choose from to fill print space and/or Web sites; you need to make sure that what you provide is worthy of excitement and a reaction. You need to have a hook that makes it newsworthy and interesting, while connecting to your overarching marketing strategy. Great agencies will bring you ideas that have PR value built in from the start (as well as a plan to get the word out); they understand the value in creating greater impact and recognize that a company's reputation is necessary to its success. The average American consumer can be quite skeptical in today's era of corporate shenanigans, thus the role of public relations today is more vital than ever before. You need to decide what you strategically want to communicate and then go after it with a newsworthy message, making sure the plan reinforces your brand personality.

Q: ON THE RETAIL LEVEL, WHAT DO EFFECTIVE IN-STORE CAMPAIGNS LOOK LIKE?

JASON MILETSKY

THE AGENCY PERSPECTIVE

The retail level is the marketer's last best chance to pry money from consumers' pockets—not necessarily an easy task. Consumers often don't know the particular brand they want to buy when they go into a store, and even when they do, it can be fairly easy for them to get sidetracked and purchase a competing brand. This is also the marketer's opportunity to catch a consumer's eye and get that person to buy something they didn't even know they were shopping for.

Like anything else, in-store campaigns are a function of budget, space availability, the market, and the type of store in question. Clearly, not every store will provide the same opportunities, and marketers may be faced with certain obstacles that make in-store campaigns unique, but if I may speak in generalities, there are some points that should be considered for all in-store efforts:

- **Simplicity:** Retail outlets are a smorgasbord of sights and sounds, overwhelming consumers from every direction. Numerous brands are fighting for attention as shoppers try to focus on what they want and where to find it. So complex messages are going to get lost and overlooked. Simple, direct, and to the point is what marketers should be shooting for to get noticed in-store.

- **Creativity:** Simplicity shouldn't be an excuse for easing up on creativity. Creativity is still required to get people's attention. Whether you're dealing with a display, signage or something else entirely, you must be creative in how you go about catching people's eye. And if you can somehow tie the in-store creative in with external campaign concepts, even better. Creativity can be harnessed particularly well in stores where technology plays a more prominent role—for example, where LCD monitors can be placed on shopping carriages or in key locations throughout a store.

- **Position/location**: So this is a fairly obvious point, but one that should be made: In-store campaigns should be up-front and highly visible. Smart marketers will know the route people will take around the store and to reach their product, and will try to reach consumers along that path. Endcaps, for example, can help to highlight your product and encourage spontaneous interest—but the endcap has to be where your market is likely to pass it in the store. (These books, for example, probably wouldn't sell very well on an endcap in the pets section of the bookstore.)

- **Encourage immediate action:** Time-sensitive coupons offered at the point of sale or on the shelf directly next to your brand can be the encouragement needed to make the sale. Before long, it'll be commonplace for products to beam coupons directly to shoppers' iPhones or to a carriage-based computer.

- **Current relevance:** In-store campaigns can leverage specific events that are happening throughout the year to draw attention to their brands. These events don't need to be limited to holidays like Valentine's Day, Mother's Day, or Halloween. There's always something going on throughout the year that can be tapped into, such as back to school, football or baseball season (you can have a sports theme without referencing the specific major-league associations or their franchises), or summer fun and vacation seasons. Staying topical is a good way of staying top of mind.

- **Multi-sensory:** Visual elements like signage and displays aren't the only ways of reaching consumers in-store. Messages can be played over loudspeakers, and product sampling can reach people through taste and smell. Consider sparking people's curiosity and desire to buy through multiple senses as part of a smart, effective in-store campaign.

MICHAEL HAND
THE CLIENT PERSPECTIVE

Effective in-store campaigns have one major common thread: They stop you in your tracks and make you take notice. In-store campaigns really serve only one purpose: get shoppers to pick up the product and put it in their carts. According to research performed by OgilvyAction in 2008, nearly 40 percent of shoppers in the United States wait until they are in the store to decide what they are going to buy. This reason alone is why all the major consumer package companies are creating shopper marketing teams and looking for an edge at retail.

OgilvyAction's work also stated that 29 percent of consumers will switch brands at the point of purchase, while another 20 percent leave the store without even getting what they walked in for on the trip. These facts alone demand that you focus resources against in-store activation. The "moment of truth," as Proctor and Gamble first hailed it, has become the last chance to sway a purchase decision and possibly build some extra brand equity with your target.

To build an effective in-store campaign, you need to know what the shopper mindset is on the path to purchase and you need to recognize that not all classes of trade have the same driving principles. Based on consumer demographics and who your brand needs to reach (both user and purchaser), you can devise plans that work best and stand out among the thousands of messages fighting for in-store attention. For example, the young adult male convenience store shopper likes to get in and get out with a very focused path through the store—he is on a mission. If you want to disrupt his behavior, you need to be in that purchase path and have a relevant message that he cannot miss. While working in the beer category, our team would start at the front door if possible (push/pull signs), drop product displays with warm product in the snacks' area to create added awareness, and then work to own the cooler space. This might include signage above the door that is visible from the minute you walk in (custom neon signs always broke through) and then everything from static clings on the actual door to branded pricing markers on the shelf strips. In addition, we would hit you again on the way out the door with reminders at the register (placemats and "give a penny, take a penny" trays). All of this was an effort to make sure our brand was top of mind and forced a path into the consideration set for that guy who is making up his mind four out of 10 times after he enters into the store (as referenced earlier).

In larger outlets, the objective is to create "retail theater" that demands the shopper to take notice of your presence. The tactics to create this disruption are getting more advanced; winning displays in the POPAI Awards show each year are getting more multi-sensory through the added use of disruptive sight and sound elements. These facets of the displays are designed to help overcome the mundane aspect of an ordinary shopping experience and create a true interruption from the norm.

The most critical building block to include in anything that is placed at retail is clear and concise, consumer-centric messaging. Make it obvious to consumers what you want them to remember about your product; build off of the brand equity that you work so hard to establish and help move them from being passive shoppers to active buyers. You will have four to six seconds to get your point across; be direct and have something to say. Too many words will get passed over no matter what they say; shoppers are in the store to buy what they need, not to read the Gettysburg Address off a header card.

In-store execution that is truly groundbreaking only comes around once in a while; many of the practices marketers currently use feel repeated and not extremely innovative. The work from Campbell's Soup and Leo Burnett in Canada to support a local food bank, however, was outstanding. They used 4,820 cans of Campbell's Soup to build a massive display piece that spelled "HUNGER" in the store's high-traffic area.

Signage beside the piece encouraged shoppers to buy one can of Campbell's Soup and donate it to their local food bank. Naturally, as shoppers bought cans from the display, the word "HUNGER" slowly disappeared; this allowed people to see how their individual effort could help bring an end to the problem of hunger.

It created an amazing visual at retail to engage consumers to help a very important cause. It is something that can be held up as truly best in class. (To see images of the display, try Googling "Campbell's Soup Hunger Display." When you do, ask yourself how anyone could walk past that display and not buy a can of soup!)

Q: WITH RETAILERS DEMANDING "CLEAN STORES," HOW CAN YOU BREAK THROUGH AT THE POINT OF PURCHASE?

JASON MILETSKY

THE AGENCY PERSPECTIVE

For marketers, the hope is that the "clean store" movement is just a fad—that this particular interior-design style will go away sooner rather than later. Much like graphic-design styles change regularly, so too do interior-design styles, and stores regularly make alterations to remain trendy and modern. But it's unlikely that the pendulum will swing back the other way anytime soon. Because unlike the latest fashion trends or hairstyles, there's an actual—and viable—reason for stores to "go clean." The movement toward clean stores is retailers' push toward promoting their own brand over the brands they are selling, keeping aisles less cluttered and signage to a minimum by reducing the number of displays and in-store marketing campaigns. It's their way of driving traffic by creating a unique and (supposedly) improved shopping experience that helps separate their stores from competing outlets.

To be clear, though, the shift toward "clean stores" doesn't mean the wholesale elimination of all in-store marketing efforts, with large, gaudy displays being carted away and leaving nothing but stark, open aisles in their wake. It just means that retailers are looking to have *fewer* large, gaudy displays. So there are still plenty of opportunities for marketers to take advantage of reaching consumers once they've got their hands on their shopping carts.

But even a slight reduction of these opportunities could cause brands to consider new ways of reaching consumers in-store. The key here, as with any marketing effort that has certain variables working against it, is to find creative ways to bypass the problems and reach a goal. The first thing brands need to do is take a good hard look at themselves. I don't mean that in a philosophical, student-out-of-college-trying-to-find-himself-by-going-to-Europe-instead-of-getting-a-job kind of way. I mean, make sure your packaging really stands out. With fewer displays and signs, your products are going to really need to jump off the shelf and grab passers-by. (For more, check out the answers to Question #67: "What Does Packaging Say About a Brand?" and Question 68: "When Is a Packaging Change Needed?")

Marketers should also look for innovative ways to make their products more of a "must-have" rather than an "if I happen to think about it" kind of purchase. Brands like Oreos and Hershey's Kisses have done a great job of not only marketing their products as stand-alone items, but also as ingredients in recipes for any number of cakes, brownies, and other desserts. Kraft has a pretty cool app for the iPhone that gives users recipes that require Kraft products. By making their products part of something larger, they create an inherent demand that can help to compensate for fewer in-store marketing opportunities.

In-store marketing still exists and will continue to exist, even if the amount of space allotted to it is shrinking. Brands need to do what they can to ensure strong campaign creative for those in-store efforts that they are able to run (see the answers to Question #59, "On the Retail Level, What Do Effective In-Store Campaigns Look Like?"), but supplement these efforts with other creative ways to compel consumers to buy.

MICHAEL HAND

THE CLIENT PERSPECTIVE

Breaking through at the point of purchase can be a matter of life or death at the retail level for any client. As more national retailers begin to reduce the sheer number of manufacturers' displays they will allow, it has become even more critical to find creative ways to deal with this issue. Depending on who you talk to, the size of the reduction on allowable in-store displays has been somewhere between 10 and 25 percent from 2006 to 2008. Retailers cite their desires to create cleaner shopping environments and the need to eliminate clutter from the aisles for this aggressive action. The retailers are also much more focused on branding their own name and driving private label sales, while creating their own unique store design and characteristics to stand out from their competition. For example, having the same Super Bowl display for a manufacturer as every other retailer in the area does not create differentiation; yet building their own equity for this time period can drive better perceptions of the store's own brand and way of thinking.

The work at Wal-Mart around the "Game Time" theme in August 2008 is a good example of taking a store-centric approach to a retail time window. While many retailers were talking up the Back to School time window or running generic football season "kick off" programs, Wal-Mart transformed more than 1,700 of its Garden Centers around the country into tailgating headquarters. Key competitors may have been running similar creative themes around football (as mentioned), but the Wal-Mart effort had unique branding supported by the great prices that consumers expect to find at their stores. The program also included a desktop widget that football fans could load onto their computer and create party invitations, shopping lists, and more—all with Wal-Mart's name attached. This is a great example of a retailer finding a way to "break through." While not having a "clean store" approach per se, they were 100-percent focused on an ownable store-centric theme.

To build on the original question, how to break through, here are a few thought-starters for consideration:

- **Make sure that your packaging stands out on shelf.** Package design is still the one thing you can completely control with your corporate voice. Make this the beacon of how you want the world to see your product and control your real estate in the store. If using on-pack promotional offers, make sure they do not encumber your design or diminish the impact of your trademarks. Marketers make this mistake all the time, giving top billing to a prize partner over their own brand. Promos should be secondary in communication; the brand should always lead.

- **Find ways to create a bigger footprint inside the store, and when possible, outside of your own aisle.** Look to forge relationships with other manufactures and develop cross merchandising initiatives. Retailers will always be receptive to bundled offers that give the shopper more value and show potential to increase the overall "basket ring." The soda guy needs to join with the chips guy, and the beer guy needs to connect with the salsa guy; these connections can create two joint displays for the "big game" instead of your one shot at a shelf in your own space.

- **Get creative with other store assets; everything can be had for a price.** Consider things like floor graphics, shopping cart ads, in-aisle coupon dispensing, and in-store radio/kiosk advertising. These vehicles can give an additional brand reminder during the shopping experience and keep your products top of mind. When exclusive to a retailer for a limited time, you would be amazed how the "clean store" demand takes a back seat in the conversation.

- **Provide design solutions to the retailer that add value for them and insert your branding into the actual fixtures.** Budweiser has seen success in select Hispanic accounts across Texas by painting murals that reinforce the environment the retailer wants to depict near the produce and meat departments; the brand logo and packages are incorporated into the art, and the shopper gets a subtle reminder from the brand while shopping other areas of the store. You can also be the partner who provides retail solutions on things like food and wine pairings, quick meal solutions for folks on the go, or suggestions on ice cream toppings via wire racks in the freezer area.

■ **Provide retailers the ability to customize your existing displays with their store name and logo.** As previously mentioned, the concern retailers have in placing their brand behind yours is very important to recognize. If you create a flexible POS development process that allows you to customize header cards or merchandising vehicles with the retailer's name incorporated into the design, you are assured of display penetration. Smart marketers are now creating numerous account-specific programs that build off of a national program to create additional lift for the retailer and brand across multiple classes of trade, while laddering back up to a bigger national message.

You can look at the clean store approach as a major hurdle to overcome, or you can embrace the challenge and look to create more relevant, customized displays that enhance the retail environment and get consumers thinking about your brand in a different way. Just make sure that whatever you decide to pursue is welcomed by the shopper and puts more products into the shopping basket for the retail partner.

Q: HOW MUCH POWER DOES WAL-MART HAVE IN THE DEVELOPMENT OF IDEAS/MARKETING PLANS?

JASON MILETSKY
THE AGENCY PERSPECTIVE

Did you ever see that HBO show *Oz*? If not, it was a pretty gritty and sometimes disturbing show set in a prison. There's no real need to go into details, except to say that some of the more alarming scenes, regular occurrences on the show, depicted one of the smaller guys basically bending over and becoming a bitch for one of the bigger guys.

I'll bet the producers of *Oz* never dreamed these scenes would one day be used as a metaphor for the relationship between Wal-Mart and major brands, but here is it, and I think it's appropriate. Wal-Mart has become an absolute behemoth and leverages its size, strength, and influence to force the hand of their vendors in ways that benefit their own needs. I'm not going to bother going into all the numbers as far as annual sales, customers, etc. There's no need to bog you down with constantly changing statistics that are easily found on the Web. Besides, they all ultimately add up to one thing: Wal-Mart is like no other retailer, and brands need to bend over backward (or forward, as the case may be) in order to make them an ally.

Wal-Mart's entire brand (although it's gotten reamed for any number of issues, including how it treats its employees) is based on the company's ability to provide the largest assortment of goods at the lowest prices. To meet Wal-Mart's pricing demands, companies often have to make severe adjustments, including sending manufacturing work overseas, using lesser-quality raw materials, or completely changing shipping routes to accommodate Wal-Mart's 4,000-plus stores. With this kind of power, brands need to ensure that Wal-Mart will not only carry new and existing products, but that they can do so and still eke out a profit. These considerations will play a major role in whether new ideas ever reach the development stage or how aggressively a product gets marketed. Wal-Mart has transformed itself from a retail outlet into a primary business concern.

MICHAEL HAND

THE CLIENT PERSPECTIVE

⌐ The easy answer to this question, coming from the consumer packaged goods side of life, is that they have more power than any other retailer in America when it comes to affecting brands' decisions. According to *The Morning News of Northwest Arkansas* (in an article updated in September 2008), about 176 million customers visit a Wal-Mart retail location each week, and they are the world's largest public corporation by revenue as declared in the 2008 *Fortune* Global 500. To put it in perspective, *The Morning News* added the following interesting facts in their report:

■ During a recent one year period (June 2007 to June 2008), Wal-Mart shoppers spent $4.2 billion on pet food and an additional $1.6 billion on pet care products.

■ Computers and electronics generated an equally impressive $4.8 billion in the same period, led by DVD and flat panel TV sales.

■ Wal-Mart shoppers spent $2.5 billion on candy, while also spending $316 million on diet aids.

■ Approximately $1.1 billion was exchanged on car care products.

■ Even "staple" products for the pantry and refrigerator have seen tremendous recent growth, with sales of eggs up 55 percent, flour up 31 percent, and pasta up 38 percent.

There really is no other way to say it: Wal-Mart is huge, and in order to have sales success in most any product category, you need them on your side, and you need to consider them in your calendar planning and development stages. You simply cannot grow your financial bottom line without finding a way to be successful at Wal-Mart first.

When ideas are being hatched for promotional efforts, new products, or SKU rationalization, the Wal-Mart name always comes up first in the conversation. You can never run the risk of having Wal-Mart not take one of your products because of a conflict with their planned efforts; this loss of volume alone (after eliminating the products that would ship through Bentonville) will hinder any chances to create a return on your investment. In some instances, you will stick with your original plans even if Wal-Mart rejects your program (because you have a pipeline to fill and have likely been on the street selling your program for four months already to other retailers before they rejected it), but you always need to have a "Bentonville alternative" up your sleeve to placate them and adjust for the volume blow. To put all of this in perspective, when discussing the various classes of trade, Wal-Mart tends to get listed as a standalone "class" before even mentioning grocery, convenience store, drug, warehouse club, etc.

In my research for this particular project, I came across a legendary story about how Wal-Mart changed the world of pickles (yeah, I said pickles) by forcing a major manufacturer to sell a "value-sized" jar that basically made profitable sales impossible at any other retail outlet in America. Once the value equation was set at Wal-Mart, no other retailer would touch their item because it was priced three times as high on a per-ounce measure. How much of the story is fact and how much is fiction I do not know; the bottom line is they can make or break your sales projections and have a major impact on your balance sheet. Major U.S. brands like Huffy bicycles and Levi's jeans have also found that providing the low-cost solution one needs to compete in Wal-Mart's 4,250+ U.S. stores can force a dramatic shift in the manufacturing process and the cost structure to produce their goods. In many cases, production and operations are being moved outside the country to deliver on the required price points. I find it amazing how the mantra of "Wal-Mart providing hard working people with items for less" is at the same time costing those hard working people their jobs.

As we move to the future, Wal-Mart is certainly not sitting back and remaining complacent with their leadership position. *Adweek* recognized their in-store digital network as one of the top innovations of 2008. The "Wal-Mart Smart Network" is the result of $10 million in research and aims to offer a new level of in-store targeting when it comes to purchase behavior. You can only imagine the expectations they will have of manufacturers to leverage the asset (and offset the development cost) as we move into the next decade.

Wal-Mart strikes a very emotional chord with consumers, some with very positive remarks and others with very ill feelings. Wal-Mart is clearly both America's most admired and most hated company. The staff in Bentonville will continue to wield power over marketers' plans as they systematically drive home everyday low costs with more shoppers in their stores than anybody else.

Q: MANY COMPANIES HAVE STARTED CREATING THEIR OWN RETAIL OUTLETS OR BUILDING "POP-UP" OUTLETS FOR THREE TO FOUR WEEKS. IS THIS EFFECTIVE?

JASON MILETSKY

THE AGENCY PERSPECTIVE

My book *Perspectives on Branding* included a question about whether it's possible to make customers into brand advocates. A large part of my answer to that question was centered on Apple and the amazing work they've done to create and maintain an almost cult-like fanaticism within their market for their brand. To illustrate the point that brands can, under the right circumstances and with appropriate brand-building measures, turn consumers into advocates, I offered the following closing paragraph:

> Want proof that brand advocacy exists and can be effective? Go to the Garden State Plaza in Paramus, New Jersey, on any Saturday afternoon. Check out the Apple Store on the upstairs floor. See how long it takes you to get from the entrance to the cash registers—make sure you have some free time, because the store will be packed. Next, go downstairs and check out the Sony Style outlet—a far roomier store selling far less expensive computers—but try to be quiet. You don't want to wake the salespeople up. Brand advocacy at its best.

This example also works as a good illustration of the viability of brand-specific retail outlets. Can it work? Absolutely. Apple is living proof of it. But Apple also had the absolute perfect landscape to take this kind of bold step:

- They had a consumer base that was wildly into their brand.
- Their new line of computers was a huge hit.
- They had revolutionized the music industry.

- Their computers are far more expensive than PCs and therefore stood to benefit from being presented on shelves away from competing brands.

- Their ad campaigns were highly visible and routinely touted as brilliant.

- Retailers such as the now–nearly defunct CompUSA never quite gave Apple the spotlight it deserved, almost treating them like annoying second cousins.

As a brand, Apple has a style and reputation for innovation that makes them more than just a company; it makes going to their stores an event. Not every brand is going to have those same favorable conditions, however. In the paragraph I quoted from my other book, the Sony Style outlets are a great example of a brand not being able to pull off the standalone format. (Apparently, Sony doesn't release their numbers on store traffic, so I don't know anything for sure, but it doesn't take more than a few trips to one of their near-empty stores to get the sense that it's just not working.) Ironically, launched the same year Gateway shuttered its retail stores, Sony has always been viewed as a safe choice for consumers, but they've never stirred the emotions of their market. Yeah, the stores are sleek and nice to look at, but Sony has never been the must-have brand that Apple's become, and they haven't given consumers a compelling reason to buy products from the Style outlets when it's more convenient to just head on over to Best Buy or, hell, even Wal-Mart.

Running a retail store or chain requires different considerations than manufacturing a product, including the high cost of rent, interior design, retail-sales training, inventory-control issues, etc. For a brand-specific retail outlet to work, then, there needs to be

- A reason your brand will do better on its own than on the shelves at a mass merchandiser

- A firmly established brand and product that the market will specifically seek out due to some measure of loyalty

- A strong brand personality that has already created an emotional connection with consumers

In my opinion, that last point is the reason why the Sony Style outlets are so lonely. Where's the brand personality? Where is the emotional connection? They don't exist. That's why Apple can succeed where Sony can't. Self-contained retail outlets aren't going to be successful based on being the low-cost provider; they're going to be successful based on consumers' love of the brand.

MICHAEL HAND

THE CLIENT PERSPECTIVE

⌐ The creation of one's own retail outlet or "pop-up" outlet has been met with mixed reviews from consumers across the globe. This tactic can prove to be a very effective marketing tool where you can control the entire environment with your brand experience; you just need to make sure you have a brand/product/service that is worthy of so much direct attention.

From my perspective, the two leaders in the standalone retail outlet space have proven to be Nike, via the Nike Town locations they have opened in major markets around the world, and Apple, who has been successful opening Apple Stores within major shopping malls around the United States. The reason they are both lucrative is that the retail space works to capture the essence of their brands, and they deliver a very unique experience to the consumer to take away. Nike has always been known for their stable of endorsed athletes and teams, a relationship that comes to life within Nike Town. The Nike mission of giving athletes the best tools to provide a dominating performance—and capturing their hearts and minds in the process—are on full display in these locations. As you travel from floor to floor in these Nike-controlled universes, you get a sense that you contain within yourself the same greatness these athletes exude. The actual sneakers and clothing come to life and take on a value that gets lost in your local Foot Locker or Dick's Sporting Goods. You also get a better feel for the role Nike is playing in your local community by learning about area running events and philanthropic or recycling efforts that Nike is directly linked to. Overall, Nike Town feels like the next best thing to being on the campus of Nike HQ outside of Portland. The dedicated retail extension works for them on many emotional and functional levels.

Apple has also been successful in making their stores a "must stop in" location. They use the store to reinforce their image of being on the cutting edge of technology, and as they pop up in upscale malls across America, they always appear to be crowded with "Apple-heads" looking for what is "next." The fact that they offer youth workshops, group training programs, and on-site, hands-on technical expertise helps to extend the brand image in positive ways for all types of consumers. The Apple Store has also become the first place to buy the hottest new products and/or give them a test run for yourself. The design of the stores is sharp and clean with brand imagery oozing from the walls. Apple has certainly taken retail to a whole new level for their products and accessories. If that wasn't enough, you can even be assigned a "personal shopper" to get exactly what you need without the pushy sales pitch. Apple has a great model, and backs it up with even better execution.

The use of a pop-up outlet needs to be looked at through a different lens. The fact that these outlets are typically in the market for a short time period and are intended to increase brand stature as much as they are to sell goods make them a very different business model. The success and failure can hinge purely on location, but it really comes down to having a story to tell and disrupting the status quo of the surrounding retail area. The promise of exclusive items and unique experiences are always a traffic driver. Let's face it, consumers want things that appear to be limited in supply.

Target has done a great job of using these outlets in New York to pre-launch products and remind city dwellers that they have great values to offer every day. Their use of big name designers and pricing for any budget creates a major buzz and then, before you know it, the store is gone. This leaves the consumer hungry for more and invites them to seek out the product line at their suburban locales, and Target has certainly mastered this approach. Back in December 2002, Target actually created a floating store on the Hudson River and followed it up in subsequent years with stores in small grocery store-like spaces and 1,500 square foot locations dedicated to their "celebrity" designers. They even traveled out to the "exclusive" Hamptons on Long Island in New York and created a five-week high-end experience called the Bullseye Inn during the summer of 2004 to focus on beach and patio ware. They leave the shopper always wondering where (and when) they will "pop up" next.

Non-retail brands continue to push the envelope in the space of pop-up every year. These efforts range from Crown Royal, who opened barber shops aimed at African American males to drive trial and brand awareness through a highly targeted approach, to Charmin, who utilize their toilet paper and clean bathrooms around the holiday rush each year to get city shoppers using their product in New York. Finally, even brands like Meow Mix have created "cafés" for cat lovers to get more folks experiencing their array of food and treats. According to *Promo Magazine*, Meow Mix generated 100 million media mentions and distributed 14,000 wet food pouch samples. The café was scheduled to be open for five days, but it was extended an additional seven days after getting 3,000 people to check it out per day in the first week alone. In addition, Meow Mix raised and donated more than $20,000 to the ASPCA in the 12-day period from the sale of toys and accessories. This was a major success for a brand that does not exactly exude charisma and exhilaration.

"Pop up" is a trend that bears watching, as it is likely to stick around for the long haul and continue to expand around the globe.

Q: HOW VALUABLE ARE LOYALTY PROGRAMS? WHAT'S NEEDED TO MAKE ONE A SUCCESS?

JASON MILETSKY

THE AGENCY PERSPECTIVE

Most loyalty programs are consumer-oriented points-based efforts (although there are other types, as discussed momentarily). The concept is pretty simple: People take an action, like making a purchase, and somehow that action is translated into points. Over time, as more purchases are made, points get accumulated; users can then redeem them for rewards, such as free merchandise, discounts on future purchases, free travel, gift certificates, or whatever the company allows.

It's not going anywhere, and I doubt I'll be able to do much to change it, but I don't really like the term "loyalty program." I think it's a misnomer. Rather than inspiring true loyalty—where consumers find the brand appealing because it delivers on its promise, because it has sparked an emotional connection, or whatever—these programs encourage increased and repeat purchases (or other actions valuable to a company) by offering something of value in return. Sure, these programs can play a huge role in increasing sales, but it's not through loyalty. Take me, for example: I tend to fly Continental Airlines because, as a member of the company's OnePass program, I can earn instant upgrades and free travel—not because I'm a huge fan of the brand per se. (They're not bad, but I always find the cabins to be too cold, and I'd rather fly an airline that serves Pepsi products instead of Coke. Just a preference.) But regardless of whether the term "loyalty program" is appropriate, one thing is certain: These programs do hold value if they can bring people back to make purchases again in the future.

To get a quick idea of how popular these programs are, look at online shopping, which was tailor-made for points programs. According to a recent report by DoubleClick, 70 percent of all frequent online shoppers (defined as those shoppers who spend at least $500 online annually) belong to two or more points-based loyalty programs. Moreover, while prices are an important factor for online shoppers, those consumers who belong to two or more loyalty programs are less concerned about price and are less likely to comparison shop than shoppers who do not belong to these programs, choosing instead to shop at the online stores that enable them to earn points. Not bad.

But simply offering a points-based loyalty program won't be enough to encourage consumers to take future action. For this kind of thing to work, companies need to consider a few important issues:

- **Ease of use:** Points-based programs are notoriously difficult to understand, and they often have fine print that severely limits how users spend their points. The more difficult a program is to understand and use, the less likely users will be to participate.

- **Realism:** Earning points needs to be an attainable endeavor. Stringent programs that severely limit when points can be redeemed—"You can only cash in your points in conjunction with a stampede of wild elephants in your own living room on the fourth of July between 3:55 and 4:00 p.m. during a hail storm" (God bless Daffy Duck)—or include too many other restrictions.

- **Value:** Before enrolling in any points-based loyalty program, consumers want to know what rewards are available and how many points they'll need to accumulate before being able to redeem them for something of value. If furnishing their entire home at a single store earns consumers only enough points for a free set of plastic coasters, not many shoppers will find that all too valuable.

I know I've already written a good amount on this topic, but I have a really great resource who knows about as much about loyalty programs as anybody: Jack Benrubi, VP of Business Development at Advertising Checking Bureau (ACB). One of the powerhouses of trade marketing, ACB specializes in consumer-rebate, incentive, and consumer-loyalty programs, serving more than 40 percent of all Fortune 500 companies. I think he's the perfect person to answer this question, insofar as he knows his stuff but doesn't come off sounding remarkably smarter than me.

GUEST PERSPECTIVE: JACK BENRUBI

A points program is only one type of loyalty program. Another very popular program involves the distribution of reloadable debit cards. These offer an advantage to marketers, as their logo appears on the card with a possible theme or illustration of the product. Gift cards from select retailers are also popular with loyalty programs because they can be used to purchase anything at a given specialty retailer. These debit and gift cards can usually be spent on merchandise in traditional retail outlets or online.

Also, loyalty programs aren't just for consumers. Often, loyalty programs encourage loyalty from the retailer in an effort to increase sales. For example, a "spiff" program offers rewards to retail salespeople for products sold. The more they sell, the more rewards they get, typically in the form of cash, dollars loaded onto an existing debit card, or gift cards from their favorite retail outlet.

The most successful loyalty programs incorporate a theme—for example, a NASCAR theme. In this scenario, you might have retail salespeople competing with, or "racing," each other to sell the most products, with the winner receiving cash or a debit card as well as a bonus prize and being heralded on the company Web site for all participants to view. Speaking of Web sites, we've successfully created Web tools that enable participants to register themselves on a Web site with the look and feel of the manufacturer's site, entering encrypted Social Security numbers and other pertinent data about themselves and the retailer where they work. Web sites such as these also list the products that are eligible to be sold under the loyalty program and include details on the program such as sales data, eligibility requirements, eligible retailers, etc.

Loyalty programs have proven very successful for manufacturers, helping to bolster sales in both good and bad economies, but especially in bad ones, when companies refuse to accept status quo and watch their sales further decrease. Case in point: Our incentive division has increased by more than 50 percent over the last five years, a clear indication that companies have been successful in running these types of programs.

There are a number of keys to building and maintaining a successful loyalty program:

- The claiming process must be kept simple.

- The Web site associated with the program must to be easy to navigate and must make data entry simple—for example, enabling visitors to enter information using drop-down boxes. Anything less, and the loyalty program will be a guaranteed failure.

- If the total value of the loyalty-program reward is less than $20, participation will normally be very low. Rewards of $20 or more will generate high participation and excitement.

- The loyalty program's communication piece or theme is critical. If the program is not adequately communicated, it will not succeed no matter how high the dollar amount. Programs are usually communicated at the retail level, via the brand's Web site, through local and national advertising campaigns in traditional advertising media, etc.

MICHAEL HAND

THE CLIENT PERSPECTIVE

⤶ Loyalty programs have become one of the strongest ways to keep a consumer connected to your brand/service in the marketplace. Frequent shopper cards exist at almost every grocery store in the United States; they offer bonus values, local school donations, gas discounts, and free turkeys during the holidays. Every business traveler you meet belongs to multiple frequent flier/travel programs and seeks incremental miles for every task on their journey (including car rental and hotel stays). It does not stop there: Your credit card is likely tied to a purchase frequency incentive for cheaper gas or inexpensive trips to Disney for the entire family. Even buying tickets to see your favorite Major League Baseball team comes with a loyalty kicker these days: Buy a 20 game package and get opening day tickets free. Bottom line, loyalty initiatives are woven into the fabric of how we live (and play) throughout our life. We have become infatuated with loyalty offers.

These offers all appear to be adding value to the companies and retail outlets who are offering them. They are gaining valuable data on their shoppers with each transaction and, in many cases, leveraging rewards that show their appreciation while also encouraging them to use more of their products/services. Increased retention rates can directly lead to increased revenue in these situations. In the grocery store industry, they also give major retailers leverage with outside consumer packaged goods (CPG) partners as they can now offer a way to target core users at each linked transaction. The question is not really how to make them an overnight success; the question is, are they really good for the long-term health of your business?

I know it sounds silly to ask that after showing all the glowing examples of loyalty in practice and highlighting the benefits of repeat purchase, but has this new "expectation" of added value forced companies to offer more things for free? The ill effects of "giving it away" is killing the travel industry and driving up the average flight price for everyone (including an increased airline mile total to redeem for a free flight). And CPG companies are feeling the pressure of reduced profit margins at the same time they are seeing increased cost on the commodities that help them produce these goods. Clearly customers like to get "free stuff," but you need to decide if it is enough to keep them coming back in the door. Most loyalty club folks would switch allegiances in a heartbeat if the offer got better down the street, and if you ever cancel your loyalty program, be on the lookout for some angry shoppers. It is not enough to simply have a loyalty program; this alone does not ensure loyalty. You need to break through with these customers by offering superior service and solid products.

So how do you make your loyalty program a success?

- **Make it easy to sign up.** Don't overdo it by asking for too much personal information because it will scare off potential users.

- **Show customers their progress.** Business travelers tend to have multiple mileage cards. How many times have you asked yourself if you had enough miles for a free flight only to wonder where you placed your last statement? Make all status checks easy to keep tabs on.

- **Ensure that rewards are attainable.** You can certainly offer high level rewards, but give everybody a chance at something for their effort through lower level deals.

- **Value and variety.** Keep it fresh by bringing in new partners and provide users flexible options on how to redeem. This can be a great way to provide added value.

- **Customize the offer.** As people get more involved and express greater loyalty, look for patterns in their behavior and make offers that suit their particular needs. People like to feel special, use the data.

- **Get feedback.** Periodically check with your members to see how you are doing. Ask what they would like to see more of (or less of). Give those who respond something extra. If somebody has become inactive, find out why and address the concerns.

- **Be patient and commit to long-term success.** Loyalty does not happen with a single purchase; make sure your users know you intend to stick around for a while. The longer the program runs, the greater the future return.

Q: IS SAMPLING THE BEST WAY TO DRIVE TRIAL OF A NEW PRODUCT?

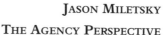

JASON MILETSKY

THE AGENCY PERSPECTIVE

Every time I try to think of ways to drive trial of a new product that are better than sampling, I come up blank. There are other ways, of course—coupons, limited-time sales—but with each argument I can make for alternative approaches, I feel like for many categories of consumer goods, I can make a stronger argument in favor of sampling.

Sampling, after all, isn't limited to the blue-haired lady in the grocery store tempting passers-by with a paper plate stacked with free bite-sized pieces of cheese (although variations of that are definitely a part of it). When you really think about it, sampling happens with each new song we hear on the radio—we listen to a single before deciding to buy the full album. It happens when we test-drive new cars before buying one. We're sampling a product every time we watch a preview before the featured movie starts, sit in one of those crazy massage chairs at Brookstone, try on clothes in a dressing room, or walk around the shoe store trying to decide if a certain pair of boots is comfortable.

Sampling is all around us, and we're involved in it more regularly than we might realize. I don't believe it can replace other forms of marketing when it comes to piquing curiosity, sending specific messages, or building a brand, but sampling definitely plays a pivotal role in new product trials and even in helping push consumers to the point of making a purchase.

MICHAEL HAND

THE CLIENT PERSPECTIVE

⌐ Sampling has certainly become more sophisticated in recent years and plays a valuable role in driving trial on new products. It remains one of the best ways to get your products into a consumer's hands for their first product experience. However, the reality is that sampling alone will not guarantee you success during your launch activation window. The product or brand that is being introduced will have very little appeal to consumers emotionally through a detached sampling effort, but it can deliver strong on the functional essence. You need a balance of these messages at introduction, and that often means you will need to get the word out to the masses and start to provide relevant context for your product to the future user. This is typically done via media extensions and in-store activation. Marketers need to do a better job of setting up the desired usage occasion in a consumer's mind before they jump directly to solving a problem.

It is estimated that more than half of all product introductions stumble out of the gate and never see the shelf in year two; one product sample alone will not solve that problem. Bigger companies have the advantage of "scale" with major retailers and can typically get themselves shelf placement upon launch, thus increasing their chances of success. However, outside the top 25 companies, it is a dogfight for space on the shelf (and on the floor via display); only folks with integrated plans will succeed.

The following is a "hot list" of things to help any company, regardless of size, avoid a doomed product introduction:

- **Plan ahead.** Most retailers are locking down plans 12 months in advance, and shelf sets are only done one to two times a year, so make sure you are in the pipeline with key buyers at the retail level.

- **Have a strategy, but be flexible**. Assuming you get the placement upon launch, what is planned for year number two? Make sure your target market is clearly defined and develop volume expectations. Expect success, prepare for success, and you will achieve success. Also know that everything will not go exactly as planned, so be ready for Plan B.

- **Make sure you are ready.** Certainly you are excited to get things moving, but make sure everything is ready before you commit. Many times brands push go before checking to see that everything is ready. This includes knowing that you have marketing team support and the budget to back it up.

- **Be realistic and set goals.** Everybody wants to achieve dominant market positions overnight, but it does not happen. Have stretch goals and reach for them, but set realistic expectations. Falling short of an overblown target should not feel like a failure; set realistic goals and deliver on them.

When sampling is part of the trial development plan, make sure your samples are not being wasted. You can target your distribution in very finite ways if you are on a budget. Handing out samples in an NFL parking lot during pre-game may be a way to get large quantities of samples into consumer hands, but I am not sure that would be defined as a quality distribution point for most companies. When doing mass distribution efforts, walk the grounds and check in garbage cans to see if you find opened packages (they used the product) or actual sample items tossed out (they took it and dropped in trash). You also need to consider putting some level of a tracking mechanism in place for sampling during launches. I am a big fan of providing a low value coupon for the first purchase of the item. You can create a unique coupon code for each site that will allow you to track sell-through based on samples in each unique location. This will help gauge the return on investment for your efforts. Also, when sampling at retail, make sure you have the product available to buy on the spot. More than one-third of all customers who like the sample will throw it in their shopping cart that day, and you have no guarantee they will pick it up (or remember you) next time through the store. People love free stuff; just remember you want to get them to pay for it next time around.

Q: WHAT ROLE CAN MARKETERS PLAY IN PRICING, AND HOW DOES THE PRODUCT PRICE AFFECT THE MARKETING PLAN?

JASON MILETSKY
THE AGENCY PERSPECTIVE

Ah, finally a break! I don't think a lot of people realize it, but writing a book can be hard work. So I'm going to consider this question a much needed break and let Mike have the spotlight to himself, because while I'm sure there's room to have a spirited debate between who has more say in pricing between marketing, sales, and biz dev, the one thing I know for sure is nobody has ever asked the agency for an opinion on it.

MICHAEL HAND
THE CLIENT PERSPECTIVE

Marketers can (and should) play a role in the pricing strategy for the brands and products they oversee, as this strategy will dramatically affect marketing messages and product positioning. The fact is, consumers' overall perception of a product is based largely on the final price point. When a product is priced as "cheap," many consumers link it to words and phrases like "unreliable" and "bad materials" rather than to the word "value." Many will seek ways to distance themselves from this perception among their peers. Hyundai has fought for years to overcome the "we are cheap" image that is the only point of reference some consumers have of the company/brand. Despite major gains in product reliability and tremendous shifts in styling and design, Hyundai continues to struggle to shake off the negative stigma. Most consumers don't mind being tagged as "budget conscious" or "value seekers," but "cheap" is not considered a term of endearment.

When developing your pricing strategy, you'll want to ask the following questions (or at least make sure the pricing department at your company is asking them):

- **Where is the competition currently priced?** Do you want to price at the same point to create parity on the shelf or in the market? If your product is one of a kind, then you need to decide where to establish the benchmark for later entries. You can either overprice because you are unique or you can initially price down to spur broader trial and, hopefully, universal acceptance. In many instances, fostering strong market penetration from the start will prevent any competition from ever threatening your leadership position.

- **What kind of profit margins do you need to make so this product is viable for the long term?** Look at the overall cost of goods (ingredients, packaging, etc.) and calculate the cost of marketing the product over time. What type of volume do you need to sell at the defined price point to make money and operate efficiently?

- **Where do you want to position your product in the market?** Do you want to be a "value" player or do you want to be a player in the "premium" category? Airlines often grapple with this in their retail sector. Some, like Southwest, provide no-frills travel and focus on volume; others, like Jet Blue, provide premium service, relying on their exclusive reputation and premium services to drive business.

- **Is price your only avenue to getting a spot on the shelf?** Many companies have stories about trying to secure placement in Wal-Mart and the need to price aggressively for consumers. Companies must decide whether they can afford to tighten profit margins under the optimistic assumption that volume will be the success factor and that competition will be held out of the market.

- **What role will price discounts play in your strategic plan?** If you train the consumer to buy your product only when it is on sale (or to wait for the next sale), it will kill your sales velocity when everyday pricing is in effect. A great example of this is when General Motors launched the "Keep America Rolling" promotion after 9/11. The company was given a lot of credit at the time; the promotion provided shoppers with a sense of pride in the U.S. auto industry and in their role in supporting democracy and the "American Dream." The only problem was that the 0-percent financing offered during the promotion became the expectation, the new benchmark for automotive leases. Moving forward, car dealers would find that they couldn't sell without great lease or loan rates and piles of cash back on the hood. (Is it better to launch a new model at a retail price of $35,000 or to launch it at $39,500 with $4,500 cash back for new buyers? You can probably argue both sides, but the point is that pricing becomes an identifier with consumers. Cash back could signal that a company is having a hard time selling the model or that the reviews aren't good so they are discounting already.) Cars aside, other markets face similar problems. One way to counteract this is to offer volume discounts. That way, you can keep the price of a single unit in a place that maintains your image, but lower that price if the consumer buys more than one. Value-conscious shoppers who want to get the discount may load up on your product, buying more than they actually need in the short term—which is a win for them and for you. Consumers who shop for instant gratification, just buying what they want when they want it, also win; they paid what they expected to pay and still deemed it a fair price.

Q: WHAT'S THE BEST MEASURE OF A GOOD MEDIA PLAN: REACH, FREQUENCY, OR SOMETHING ELSE?

JASON MILETSKY

THE AGENCY PERSPECTIVE

Although I have worked on and with media plans in my career, I can't say it's my area of expertise. So rather than do a disservice to this question, which I think is an important one, I'd like to hand the reins over to Sheila Cohen, an independent advertising consultant I've worked with many times on media plan development. I've always considered her a very talented and insightful marketer, and I'm excited that she's agreed to lend own expert perspective on this topic.

GUEST PERSPECTIVE: SHEILA COHEN

Media planning is a four-step process that consists of the following:

1. Setting media objectives in light of marketing and advertising objectives

2. Developing a media strategy for implementing media objectives

3. Designing media tactics for realizing media strategy

4. Proposing procedures for evaluating the effectiveness of the media plan

There are two basic objectives of every good media plan. Simply put, the first objective is to reach your target audience with pinpoint accuracy or as closely as possible. The second one is to deliver enough frequency against your target audience to achieve real results, from branding and image (which will maintain and grow your customer base) to product and service advertising (producing increased sales).

Let's define each term briefly:

- **Reach:** Reach is the number of individuals (or homes) you want to expose your product to through specific media scheduled over a given period of time. Reach is usually expressed as a percentage.

- **Frequency:** Frequency is the average number of times the individuals in your target audience need to be exposed to your advertising message. It takes an average of three or more exposures to an advertising message before consumers take action. Frequency is important because it takes a while to build up awareness and break through the consumer's selection process.

Both reach and frequency play an important part in the development and execution of a successful media plan. But which is most important in evaluating the effectiveness? The real answer is that sales results are always the ultimate measure of the effectiveness of any ad campaign. Since sales results are affected by many factors such as price, distribution, and competition, which are often out of the scope of the advertising campaign, media planners must include other measures to help evaluate the effectiveness of the overall strategy. For example, did the ads appear in the media as ordered? Media buyers use "tear-sheets"— copies of the ads as they have appeared in print media—for verification purposes. For electronic media, the ratings of the programs during which commercials ran are examined to make sure the programs delivered the promised ratings.

The most direct measure of the effectiveness of media planning is the media vehicle exposure. Media planners ask, how many of the target audience were exposed to the media vehicles and to ads in those vehicles during a given period of time? If the measured level of exposure is near to or exceeds the planned reach and frequency, then the media plan is considered to be effective.

The measurement of the effectiveness of a media plan can be conducted by an advertising agency or by independent research services, using the following methods:

- **Surveys:** Surveys can be conducted in a number of ways, generally among a sampling of the target audience. Feedback devices include reply cards, toll-free numbers, coupons, and Web addresses that can help to tally the responses or redemptions to estimate the impact of advertising media. Advertisers often use a different code in direct-response ads to identify different media vehicles and more accurately assess the response rate of each.

- **Tracking:** Media buyers use this measurement method to track the effectiveness of online ads. When a user visits a Web site or clicks on a banner ad, Web servers automatically log that action in real time. The logs of these visits and actions are very useful for media buyers, because the buyers can use them to estimate the actual interaction of audience members with the interactive media.

- **Observation:** In the physical world, media buyers can use observation to collect audience reaction information at the points of purchase or during marketing events.

MICHAEL HAND

THE CLIENT PERSPECTIVE

This is another one of those questions that you can't answer with a blanket response. For every individual media plan, you need to develop your own unique goals to deliver the required results that work with your target. The goals should be both realistic and measurable, and consideration should be given to the existing base level of awareness (potentially accumulated from previous media efforts), competitive noise in the marketplace, and other elements you have working in the marketing mix. You need to define your target market in terms of demographics (gender, education level, age, income, etc.), psychographics (lifestyle, attitudes, values, aspirations, etc.), and geography (BDI, CDI, etc.) when creating your plan; these definitions will be the most important factors in selecting which type of media to use. You need to understand not just where your target consumes media, but what type of shopping behavior each form of media results in. This will help to drive the final plan of where to place your ads and for what duration of time.

First let's define the terms reach and frequency to make sure we are all speaking from the same starting point, and then we can look at the abilities of each individual form of media to deliver these results. For the media novice, *reach* is the number of different people or households that are exposed to your message during a specified time period; *frequency* is the sheer number of times that your target prospects are exposed to your message. When your target is extremely broad and you want to "talk to all people," then an approach that drives wide reach is your best option. Reach focus will command a larger variety of broadcast television and print magazines in the final plan. When you have tightly defined who you want to talk to and you know where they are most likely to react positively to your message, then you should drive the frequency strategy at this group. The final piece of the puzzle in this initial stage is looking at the ability to establish continuity with your message. I am of the belief that you do not need to reach everybody on the planet with your ads, and you do not need to wear out every ad that you place on the air—you need a balance. You need to develop a continuity schedule to create bursts of activity and "noise" in the marketplace to draw attention to your products/services when prospects are most likely to be receptive to your message. These flights should correspond with the seasonality of your offering (don't push tax preparation services in mid-summer) and capitalize on the cyclical nature of your buyer's behavior. Use good judgment to establish minimum thresholds on spending and look to maximize both your weeks on air and weekly reach. Your overall budget will drive the final plan you can deliver and the impact you can create. Let's face it; advertising is not a cheap date.

Here are some of the pros and cons of different media placement opportunities to consider, particularly as consumers are users of more than one medium. It is up to you to exploit the advantages of each form of media to provide efficiency and extend your reach.

TELEVISION

- Pros: Best way to generate immediate reach at national or local level, can be very targeted with message (via channel and/or time of delivery during day), best form of media for image/brand building

- Cons: Expensive to produce and place ads, very fragmented market structure with thousands of potential channels, use of DVR or TiVo is creating more "ad skipping," may require longer lead time for purchase (not placement) based on limited inventory

RADIO (LOCAL)

- Pros: Cost-effective way to create local/community connections, wide variety of genres to create stronger brand linkage, message delivery can be timed to fit your business needs (such as morning drive or during lunch break), ads can deliver more "personality" or "attitude" than print, strong for sales efforts

- Cons: Very small geographic reach, no ability to "rewind" or re-read for pertinent information, typically radio is a secondary activity at time of media consumption (that is, the consumer is doing something else, such as driving, working, or what have you, that requires focus), ads do not always get full attention

PRINT/MAGAZINE

- Pros: Consumers are very passionate about the magazines they read, high level of reader involvement, strong pass-along value creates multiple impressions, image quality is high, can be very targeted, long shelf life for your ad (e.g., old magazines stay around for a while in places like doctor's office and other waiting areas), can be good tool for brand building

- Cons: Long lead times for creative development, very niche market for each publication, placement can be expensive on cost-per-thousand basis, readership is not time bound, and your ad may not be seen immediately, not good in driving immediate sales/consumer involvement

PRINT/NEWSPAPER

- Pros: Very locally driven, daily aspect allows for short-term messaging needs and focus on current events in market (such as local election or holiday sale/offer), space is unlimited (can add more pages or size ad to page as needed), good for sales-focused efforts

- Cons: Consumer shifting to Internet for local news (market penetration is in decline), very broad readership (untargeted), quality of message can vary as news print does not always reproduce well, can be expensive, lots of clutter (everything from grocery stores to car dealers has an advertisement), not good for brand building, limited pass-along before tossed in trash

INTERNET

- Pros: Ads can be updated and edited with very short lead time, very topical message delivery (down to the actual hour of the day), can be very targeted based on site content, available metrics to track performance (ad click through), e-mail efforts can be personalized to user, directly drives traffic to Web site, extends campaign reach and visibility

- Cons: Lots of ads to compete with creates a concern over clutter, less history related to direct sales impact, not strong in brand building, requires more than just an ad (need Web site or other back-end landing space)

The best media plans are not just about reach or frequency; they are about finding the custom model that works for your needs; no two companies are exactly alike. You will need to evaluate your plans based on your own definition of "quality."

Q: • WHAT DOES PACKAGING
   • SAY ABOUT A BRAND?

JASON MILETSKY
THE AGENCY PERSPECTIVE

↳ First, I want to make one thing clear, because I don't want anybody to get confused: Brands are not limited to packaged goods. In my book *Perspectives on Branding*, there are a number of questions dealing with the best ways to define a brand, what constitutes a brand, etc.; and from my own experience, I know there is often some confusion on this point. So just because we're discussing what packaging says about your brand, we are not implying that only packaged consumer products can be defined as "brands."

Packaging says it all. This is your product's canvas for showing off its personality, and for showing consumers who you are. It's the area where you can promote your promise and what you're all about as bluntly as you'd like. Think of your home, and what it says about who you are. I mean everything—the exterior design and the colors you've chosen for the base and the trim. The lawn and the landscape. The interior design, including your selection of furniture, paint, flooring, and wall art. How clean or messy it is. None of this is done or chosen at random. All of it reflects your personality (or, if you're a married guy, your wife's personality…), and all of it together tells a story about who you are, what you're like, and what people can expect when they get involved with you.

That's exactly what your package says about your brand. Is it bold? Brash? Refined? Clean and stark? Busy and colorful? Does it have energy and generate excitement? Is it toned down, providing a more relaxed feeling? When everything is put together—the logo, colors, fonts, copy points, images—it tells a story and helps attract and gain the attention of a specific audience. It's the reason why kids go straight for the box of Lucky Charms, with the bright colors, constant motion, and cartoon leprechaun, while their moms go for the box of Special K. Looking at the big box of Tide, with the brilliant orange and yellow bullseye, consumers would immediately expect that its job is to get colors brighter.

There's nothing about the box of Dove soap that screams "This is the soap you should use when you're in a hurry!" Instead, the package design tells you (without saying it) that this is the soap to use when you want to relax and lose yourself in a nice, hot bath.

In the eyes of the consumer, package design is the foundation upon which everything else is built, including the Web site, print ads, TV spots, and all other marketing efforts. It's the final and most important step: After all the commercials and radio spots and print ads that have bombarded your demo, the last thing they'll see before making the decision as to whether or not to make a purchase will be your package design. Whether the package says what it needs to say about your brand will make all the difference.

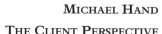

MICHAEL HAND
THE CLIENT PERSPECTIVE

I am no designer, but I am a firm believer in the power of packaging. To answer this question directly, I feel that packaging says everything about your brand. It is the first line of interaction that a consumer has with your product and the one that has the most staying power after the initial purchase. Packaging is the only element of the marketing mix that stays with your consumer through the entire product experience. Let me give you two exaggerated examples to prove my point on the power of branding through package design:

- Customer is new to this country and walks into their new "local" grocery store (Kroger, Safeway, Shop Rite, etc.). In the "local" store in their home country (Europe, Latin America, Australia), they had two to three choices of shampoo brands they could purchase with 10–15 total SKUs. Today, they turn the corner of aisle number three and look at the shelf of shampoo and conditioner to find more than 30 brands and 200 SKUs to choose from. How do they make a decision?

- Customer is a new (and nervous) father and he just brought home his first child from the hospital with his wife. He needs to pick up diapers and baby wipes for the first time. Two leading brands jump off the shelf as dominant players, but among the 10 total brands on the shelf, each comes in seven different sizes and offers a variety of extras (comfort, leak resistance, easy opening for quicker changes, etc.). What does he pick to spare himself the humiliation of calling his wife on the spot?

Both of these examples show how the impact of packaging can be felt at retail. They illustrate the power of this consumer touchpoint in the shopping process, the importance of breaking through the cluttered retail landscape with clarity of message, and the need to help consumers through the decision-making experience. In the cluttered world of marketing "speak," packaging is the last (and many times the first and only) line of communication in getting your product into the consumer's hands to generate trial. Shoppers have more choices than ever before, and packaging is what makes the brands people buy feel more "real." Good packaging design connects with your corporate image through the use of colors, graphics, and text. It delivers the brand's assets quickly and effectively when done correctly, sparking an emotional reaction and leaving the "right" impression with your potential buyer. Well-designed packaging can bounce off the shelf and take over a category, making a consumer pause in the aisle or stop to see more. The iconic brand Coca-Cola has mastered (even with a few missteps) the use of the color red, unique bottle design, and their script font to stand out on the shelf and create consistency. It can feel nostalgic (yet contemporary) and even remind you of a story that links your life to the brand, all the while never straying too far from its signature brand identity. Start-up brands can also use design to engage consumers by promising enjoyment and helping to tell a story. Don't just slap on a bunch of facts, nutritional information, and ingredients on the package; deliver it with a purpose and style. As my mother always told me, you never get a second chance to make a first impression.

As much as Coke has worked to keep their consistency over the years, Pepsi finds ways to reinvent itself via design and stay true to the mantra of being "the choice of the new generation." They prefer to reinvent themselves regularly and use packaging as an iconic callout of that change. They may tweak a logo lock up, slightly modify the color palette, or use celebrity designs to create buzz, but each of these changes stays true to their brand equity and comes across as expected—not disruptive. Blue, red, and white still play a strong role, but they believe in the energy of design change to drive the brand's creative direction.

Even retail brands can use things like shopping bags and boxes to create their brand presence. The big red star of Macy's and the script font of Neiman Marcus provide a certain feeling to shoppers and deliver a sense of pride when walking the mall with that particular bag in hand. The best example in this arena would be Tiffany & Company. Look in the eye of anybody who receives the little blue box as a gift, and you will see what I mean. This emotional response has undeniable value and allows Tiffany to charge a premium for the same luxury item you could get at any other jeweler in the world.

It is only a matter of time before we start using packaging to distribute added information for our brands and link consumers into our brand family through online and mobile resources. We will start to create feedback groups and consumer forums for product commentary. Getting customer involvement while sitting at the breakfast table and building a dialogue through loyal brand stewards is a logical next step. It will be the evolution of the cereal box on the crowded kitchen table next to the gallon of milk; you will want to read it, not peruse it "just because it's there."

Packaging must be simple, clean, and direct to drive memorable connections that spark emotions in your consumer's mind. This is extremely difficult to accomplish, but it illustrates the importance of the packaging element in building your brand story.

Q: WHEN IS A PACKAGING CHANGE NEEDED?

JASON MILETSKY

THE AGENCY PERSPECTIVE

Packaging changes come with their fair share of headaches, expenses, and risk, so it goes without saying that these decisions are never taken lightly. If done right, they can spark new life into a product, catch people's eye, and send a message that yours is an active, not stagnant, brand. If it's *not* done right, new packaging can confuse or even repel consumers—and possibly even make them question whether a product they prefer has been altered in some way that they're not going to like. Case in point: In the back end of 2008, the packaging on the Diet Pepsi bottle changed from light blue with a dynamic design to a supremely boring metallic silver with no design on it at all. The first two times I saw it, I assumed it was a new flavor, and that the store was out of Diet Pepsi. Eventually I figured it out, and I'm still loyal to the brand, but I think the packaging change was a huge misstep on their part.

Brands do need to evolve over time. I typically advocate doing some sort of major update to a brand every three to five years in order to keep up with the times and to continue to catch consumers' attention. Design styles change, competition moves forward, tastes change, and so the brand has to evolve accordingly. But there are other times when packaging needs to be updated, such as when external forces or current issues affect how consumers view the brands they buy. Depending on the seriousness of these issues, brands often have to react quickly to make sure they don't alienate their market—and one of the best ways to do this is to change the packaging.

For example, a while back, there was a big issue about dolphins being killed by the nets used to catch tuna fish. In reaction, the major tuna brands introduced new packaging that visibly declared them to be "dolphin-safe." Today, as the public now largely assumes that store-bought canned tuna is dolphin-safe, the packaging no longer announces it quite so powerfully. Instead, most have adjusted their packaging to reflect the health benefits associated with their product, with extra space provided for promoting themselves as a good source of Omega-3, another hot-button issue on the minds of consumers today. Another example is the "going green" fad (for lack of a better word), which has become so intense that many products have changed their packaging to let consumers know that their company is doing its part to help save the environment. (I expand on the green movement in marketing considerably in my answer to Question #73, "Is 'Going Green' for Real? Or Is It Just a Fad?")

Packaging is a brand's last chance to seal the deal when the consumer is making a decision about what to buy. If a company is going to score points, this is where they need to do it. Anytime a new message can help maintain current sales or increase the customer base in a way that the return is worth the investment will ultimately be a good time to change the packaging.

MICHAEL HAND

THE CLIENT PERSPECTIVE

 "Change" is the word that throws me off a bit in this question. Packaging changes for any brand should be few and far between; you want to build an identity on the shelf and keep it stable for as long as possible so that people identify with you at all times. I think slight design tweaks and modifications are needed every few years to simply make sure your logo and design remain contemporary, but wholesale change is never a good thing unless it is a last resort or a major functional need has evolved in the marketplace that must be recognized. Think *evolution*, not *revolution*. Packaging change is an area where you need to be very careful; you should never just screw around with your package for the sake of change. The design objective should be to maintain core equity, yet evolve with the rapidly changing retail landscape in which we live. Changes should really only be made to create better function for the end user, keep up with the category in terms of materials, and reemphasize leadership in design. This last point is critical: You never want to be stuck in a position where you are forced to react with your creative execution. Be on the forefront of changes and modifications and do not wait for the category to dictate them for you.

Great packaging does not come easy, and it is the most important statement you make with your brand's equity every day. Many companies spend unlimited resources on copy testing television ads and producing animatics for research on new television campaigns, but they commit little to no financial resources on their packaging upgrades and brand health tracking each year. Smart marketing organizations should be fielding opinions on their packages regularly and making sure that they are benchmarking success beyond just their current product category.

The existing category is certainly the place to start with your assessment, but you need to think bigger and consider all the brands that are sold in the same retail establishment when a consumer is participating in the purchase process. Staying in a vacuum can detract from greater success and cause your brand to lose broader relevance with your target market. Whatever you do with the packaging, you have to keep the loyal user base intact. These loyalists will likely comprise the greater portion of your sales volume and provide greater value. However, you also must be sure to appeal to any new customers who are coming to the category and considering your brand for the first time. It is critical that any changes need to be looked at outside the walls of a corporate conference room, and they need to be assessed by people who are not getting a paycheck from either your company or the design agency. When you have all the "knowledge" and data on your brand, it is easy to overlook the obvious and form an unrealistic perspective on your own self image. You need an honest feedback session with consumers who have nothing to lose (or gain) from making their comments. When considering any type of package modifications, you need candor, but you also need to realize that consumers are reluctant to change. Change is uncomfortable and feedback provided could point you in the direction of maintaining your current look.

You need to make sure that you cast a wide net when having design teams look at your brands. A diverse set of eyes with a diverse set of experiences can make a major difference in getting better results. Each of the potential designers will benefit greatly form both a strong brief and a history lesson. Looking through a company's archives can trigger many ideas that bring instant equity connections. Passionate and loyal consumers love to hear the back-story and know that it has influenced who your brand is today. Small notations on your package that celebrate origins or founding dates give products a sense of being grounded when done correctly. When done poorly, they can simply date your product and make it feel past its prime. Nostalgic looks are a very slippery slope, however, whether used for a longer-term design play or short-term promotional effort. They can overpower any "modern" or "forward thinking" efforts you are making to spark new interest. Designers will benefit from the history lesson more than anybody; it could spark an entirely new area for exploration.

Generally speaking, change is really only needed when your consumers determine that your brand needs to be refreshed due to lack of badge value or social cache or if the category is evolving without you.

Q: WHAT'S THE BEST WAY TO APPROACH GROWTH MARKETS, SUCH AS THE HISPANIC AUDIENCE?

JASON MILETSKY
THE AGENCY PERSPECTIVE

⤶ Earlier in the book, we talked about whether it's important for agencies to be familiar with a clients' industry in order to be effective. Here's what I wrote:

> "I do not believe that prior experience in an industry will make an agency more successful. What's more important is whether the agency has had experience with a specific *market*."

I think that sentence applies just as easily to this question. Hispanics, to pull from the example in the question, are not an industry—they're a market. And growth markets, particularly ethnic markets, require a deeper understanding than you're going to be able to acquire by reading this book or any book like it. Each culture has different values and beliefs and places different levels of importance on a variety of issues. For example, while most white Americans love their extended family, for the most part we're happy enough seeing Uncle Herb at Thanksgiving, Christmas, and the once-every-other-summer barbeque. Hispanics, on the other hand (and forgive me for generalizing, but sometimes that's necessary in marketing), are much more family oriented. They often center their plans and activities around their family. But just understanding this doesn't necessarily mean you'll be able to market to this point effectively. There are often too many subtleties that can't be understood if you're only academically familiar with a certain culture. Rather, you must live within the culture to understand.

I doubt that a white guy with Irish ancestry could have written the movie *My Big Fat Greek Wedding*. But having grown up in a Greek family myself, I could see the subtle additions that only someone with that background could have thought to include—and it was these small cultural details that made the movie so great. This same principle applies to marketing. Growth markets can be exciting opportunities for brands. Very often, these markets haven't formed a lot of brand loyalties yet; they're still looking to make those connections. And not to sound opportunistic, but let's face it: We're all in this to generate a profit. Growth markets are often the focus of strategies because they have an increasing amount of money to spend. So it's important that brands understand who they're dealing with—that they really live and breathe the details.

So what's the best way to approach a growth market? My answer is simple: The first step for any brand looking to expand their exposure into a growth market is to hire a specialty agency that really gets it. As much as I believe that my own agency does great work in setting strategy, developing creative, and executing campaigns, I have no problem admitting that we're the wrong choice if you're looking for effective insights into reaching the Hispanic markets. Yes, my conversations with taxi drivers in Cancun when I was 17 years old gave me some wonderful insights into their culture, but I'm not sure it was enough to warrant paying us a bundle of cash to throw darts in dark. For any growth markets worth setting separate strategies for, especially those markets defined by their ethnicity, there's an agency out there that lives in that world and truly understands how to speak to that audience. Brands need to let their lead agency do what's best for the brand overall, but spend their money more wisely by hiring specialty agencies to reach out to specific growth markets.

MICHAEL HAND

THE CLIENT PERSPECTIVE

For every organization, the approach to growth markets will vary. So many factors come into play—individual priorities, unique market dynamics, and so on. In my mind, you should keep a few basic considerations in mind when developing your approach. To illustrate these, I've used the booming growth of the Hispanic population as an example:

- **You need research and facts to get started.** You must understand where the growth is coming from and how this new group interacts with your company or brand. For example, according to the Pew Hispanic Center report, released in October 2008, Hispanics accounted for 15.1 percent of the total U.S. population in mid-2007. Using census data, experts project that by 2025, that number will be 16.8 percent, and by 2050 it will be 22.5 percent—meaning this "highly targeted market" is fast becoming the "general market." The majority of this growth has occurred in Texas, California, and Florida; this is where the next generation of the Hispanic population is being born every day. Marketers must realize that this population growth is not entirely due to increased immigration from Mexico and that not all parts of the country have the same Hispanic composition when you break down country of origin—and assess how this will affect them. Is your company already a strong player in Mexico with strong brand recognition? If so, then a strategy that leverages California and Texas for phase one could make sense. Does your brand perform well with Puerto Ricans and Caribbean-rooted Hispanics? Then maybe a Florida or New York expansion plan is a logical first step. Organizations should conduct research groups with Hispanics in multiple markets (across various levels of acculturation) to find the right business opportunity and to see where they will be most likely to enjoy a positive response.

- **Determine how important it is to create new products and messages to reach the growth market.** Every individual company will need to look at their manufacturing capabilities and decide what they can do to create line extensions that could better relate to the selected population (Hispanics). They must look at their overall marketing expenditures and decide whether they want to take a dedicated approach with unique new offerings or if they want to utilize existing products that have potential to form a deeper connection. Will they dedicate mass communication vehicles to reach this user? If so, what percentage of your spend should go there? Will your message be best conveyed in a bi-lingual, Spanish-only, or English-only format? Lots of questions need to be asked and evaluated. You need to show insight and connect with Hispanics emotionally. Avoid the two major mistakes that are often made: developing very stereotypical messages featuring Cinco de Mayo, an old grandmother, or a family meal with 35 guests; or just translating the voiceover or copy into Spanish but leaving everything else in the communication exactly the same as it appears in the white-centric general market. Is that really how a population this big thinks and reacts? Do your homework.

- **Establish realistic expectations**. Don't assume you'll drive a large amount of business overnight. You need to do more than just show up to get Hispanics (or other growth markets) connected and engaged; a push into the Hispanic market needs to be a plan within your plan. You must develop short-term, medium-term, and long-term goals if you want to stay relevant with this market for generations to come. Have a phased roll-out process, and make sure that the timing is realistic to build on your learnings along the way.

Hispanics and the 2008 Election

Much continues to be said about the role of Hispanics in the changing face of America and the evolution of the "general market" in the United States. Never was this evolution more evident than in the 2008 United States Presidential election. According to an analysis conducted by the Pew Hispanic Center and CNN, Hispanic voters supported the Democratic ticket of Barack Obama and Joe Biden by a margin of more than two to one (67 percent) over their Republican counterparts, John McCain and Sarah Palin (31 percent). Although Hispanics represent only 9 percent of the total voting population—a seemingly small number—the Hispanic vote in key battleground states like Florida, New Jersey, and California, where Hispanic support ranged from 57 percent to 78 percent, set the tone for a seismic shift in political opinions and values. This impact will be felt in even more avenues as key Hispanic politicians fill critical roles in the Obama cabinet and potentially set the stage for a future Latino Presidential candidate.

Q: HOW AGGRESSIVE SHOULD YOU BE IN MARKETING TACTICS THAT MENTION OR AMBUSH A COMPETITOR?

JASON MILETSKY
THE AGENCY PERSPECTIVE

⬐ This really depends on the personality of the brand, the industry, the type of audience they're trying to reach, and other factors. The "cola wars" of the '70s, '80s, and '90s represent the classic example of two industry titans, Pepsi and Coke, battling it out on a stage that had all the props necessary for the combatants to put on a great show:

- The beverage industry is one of the most visible and lucrative industries in the world.

- The cola category is dominated primarily by two players that publicly dislike each other and are fiercely competitive in securing the number-one spot.

- Their core demo tends to be active and sports-oriented, so they're used to a certain level of aggression and competition.

- They've got the marketing dollars to play out their ongoing grudge match on a number of fronts in a variety of media.

And neither opponent was afraid to name names, starting with the campaign that kicked off the wars, 1975's Pepsi Challenge, in which consumers were given a blind taste test to determine their preference between the two brands.

The competitors, industry, and market are much more fertile ground for cola-war combatants to publicly go for the jugular. In fact, throwing a few public punches could only jack up their credibility with their male-dominated target market. It's completely different, though, from the far more benign (though also highly competitive) laundry-detergent industry. Tide, Downy, and others often run ads showing how their product gets clothes whiter than competing brands, usually by showing one really bright white sock or T-shirt next to a far more gray-looking sock or T-shirt. But ordinarily, they associate the white article with their brand and the gray article with a "leading competitor." They don't name names, and they don't need to. They have numerous large competitors, it's not a purchasing decision people make every single day, and their target market isn't going to think any more highly of them for attacking another company by name.

Attack ads can work if done well and under the right circumstances. Apple's ongoing "I'm a Mac" campaign has struck the heart of Microsoft and has infinitely upped Apple's credibility while actually doing some damage to Goliath's image. What did Apple have to lose? They're already seen as ultra innovative, they're a pretty distant second in terms of market share with no other significant player behind them, so what the hell. They attacked PC in a smart, creative way, and it worked. But when Microsoft played into it with their "I'm a PC," campaign, they suddenly found themselves a player in a war where they weren't throwing a direct punch and with a campaign that made them look silly while heightening Apple's legitimacy.

If you are going to start attacking a competitor and name names, you should consider a few things first:

- You'll be painted as an aggressive brand. For a time, you may even be seen as a villain for throwing the first punch. How will your market feel about that? It could backfire, especially if you're a big brand picking on a smaller one.

- Can you back up whatever claims you're making about your own brand and your competitors? This is the age of social media, and if you make a big deal out of a claim that's not true, you *will* be found out.

- How will the competitor respond? They may very well attack back. Are you ready for that, and creatively capable of continuing the fight?

- If a war is waged and your competitor swings back, do you have deep enough pockets to keep it going? Because it can get expensive.

- Are you prepared to lose? It is possible.

Personally, I prefer more subtle blows and references. They just seem smarter. For example, the Avis car-rental company gained market share despite the dominance of number-one rival Hertz not by pointing out all of Hertz's flaws, but by embracing their number-two status in their iconic "We Try Harder" campaign. The war was referenced, but it was subtle and smart. That's just a personal preference, though—it's not to say that there isn't a need for direct fire at times.

MICHAEL HAND

THE CLIENT PERSPECTIVE

This truly is a two-part question, and I will need to split them apart to provide my personal view on the subject. First, let me tackle the broader question regarding marketing tactics that mention a competitor. When you are the industry leader you never—in any way, shape, or form—bring your competition into your tactics by name. Never, never, never! The leader needs to remain above the fray and continue to drive self-brand image and awareness only. The minute you introduce your nearest competition to the conversation, you are telling your loyalists that it is okay to consider the other guy also—after all, you did. You need to hold a steady course and continue to reinforce your own identity not build their awareness.

On the flip side, if you are the second or third leading brand in a particular category, then I strongly encourage you to take shots at the leader in a public forum once in a while. You need to make sure people know what you stand for first, but it never hurts to get the "leader" a little upset. When trailing behind, you simply want to be in the consideration set with the select few. By comparing yourself head to head, you are showing the world that you are confident enough in your own product to share the main stage. More and more brands are using this tactic to reframe the conversation and take on the competition directly. One of the most famous uses of the head-to-head approach was Pepsi's challenge against Coke in taste comparisons of the early 1980s. Positioned as the "choice of the next generation," Pepsi made consumers question their own selection criteria and urged them to try new things after taking a single sip. The campaign worked as trial takers began to perceive Coke as an "old person's drink" and for individuals who simply stuck with the status quo. Coca-Cola got caught up in the battle and actually introduced "New Coke" to mirror the taste profile of Pepsi before realizing the error in their ways and getting back on track. The folks from Atlanta maintained their leadership position, but the landscape was clearly changed and the positioning of both brands has been impacted ever since.

One of the most successful marketing platforms I ever worked on was rooted in this exact case study; it was when I worked on the Miller Lite team, and we decided to take on the market leader (Bud Light) in a toe-to-toe battle for taste supremacy. We firmly believed our product was far superior (and we had data points to back it up), so we built a program that would get samples in the hands of consumers at bars across America and at the biggest events in the country so that they could experience it firsthand. We urged consumers to drink a sample of Bud Light and a sample of Miller Lite back to back, judging it on the "see it, smell it, taste it" mantra. We knew the color of Miller Lite was richer, the smell of Miller Lite was crisper, and we were confident that the taste was much better as well. We had so much balls (excuse my language), we even offered to take the challenge live on TV with news anchors and entertainment reporters. The insight we had was that consumers had become like sheep following the herd and just lived by the "I'll have what he's having mantra." Beer drinkers were making beer selections simply on public perception or to meet the goal of fitting in—we wanted it to be about taste and healthier choices (great linkage during the low carb health push). Sales increased, and we had some fun along the way —I loved when we had their Dalmatian jump off the Bud truck to join the Miller delivery guy.

The head-to-head battle approach is not one that will go away, as of 2009 brands like Apple were still taking jabs at Microsoft (more indirectly via the PC callout) and Dunkin' Donuts was trying to battle Starbucks for coffee drinkers. This tactic will always be present and can be a great way for a brand to create short-term spikes in product sales. Just make sure to keep it lighthearted; when it gets "mean," the general public will be turned off.

Part two of the question regarding ambush marketing at events has some similarities to the advertising battles listed above, but gets more directly into the experiential space. Yes, the Miller and Pepsi examples above were head-to-head battles, but they were not grounded in the philosophy of "ambush." No element of surprise was in the dialogue; it was a war and not a sneak attack. Companies pay millions of dollars to sponsor sporting events or partner with teams; they expect the consumer to walk away and remember what brands helped support the amazing event they may have just witnessed. They want consumers to understand that without the sponsors many teams could not afford the athletes on the roster or the special perks and amenities in the stadium/arena. Sponsors want to be exclusive in their category, and they do not want to share the stage. I have been on both sides of this battle; I have ambushed and been the ambushee. Either way it sucks for the ambushee.

While running my first marathon in New York during the mid '90s, I was very aware of the presence that Nike had throughout the race course. For example, at mile 14, they had bought an out-of-home placement across an overpass that said something like "You could turn back now, but it would be even longer than just finishing." After all these years, it still sticks in my head. I was looking for the next one along the course in my personal game of "Where's Waldo?" to avoid the pain I was feeling throughout my body. The reason I bring it up: I know Nike was not the sponsor, but even if you paid me, I could not tell you the name of the sneaker company that was.

Nike has always been the master of the ambush. I was at the Summer Olympics in Atlanta where Nike had one of the most visited attractions near the Olympic Village. Key word this time: near. They could not be in the village with Coke, Swatch, and other sponsors because they were crashing the event. They had handed out banners for waving at sporting events and covered the city with messages using their athletes. I am not sure of the price tag, but I will venture a guess that they avoided a $50+ million bill from the Olympic Committee and delivered the same net effect with under $10 million. Even on the medal stand four years earlier in Barcelona, Nike athletes from the original "Dream Team" (most notably Michael Jordan) created a stir when they covered up the Reebok logos on their warm up uniforms to avoid revealing the marks of the competitor. I don't think this was an ambush, but it was very symbolic of Nike's power nonetheless.

Ambushing at events is not for everyone; if you go down this path, be prepared to face lawsuits, cease and desist orders, and angry event organizers who try to put a stop to your actions. They may not know you're coming, but they will do anything they can to stop you from completing your guerilla attack.

Q: ARE THERE ANY SPECIAL CONSIDERATIONS THAT SHOULD BE TAKEN WHEN MARKETING TO KIDS?

JASON MILETSKY
THE AGENCY PERSPECTIVE

Let's put any laws aside for this question, because laws make the answer too easy. That is, it'd be very easy for me to simply discuss laws that protect children as the only considerations that marketers have to keep in mind. This really is more of a moral issue—the need for brands to market to kids responsibly. There absolutely must be a high bar set here because the audience is more impressionable and more easily swayed than adults—and with marketing to an impressionable audience comes the responsibility of doing so ethically.

One of the first things I was told when my agency started working with Hershey's (we handle Internet marketing for various brands) was that we had to be vigilant about avoiding marketing to children directly due to childhood-obesity issues. I have to admit: For a brand that could clearly benefit from marketing directly to kids, I really admire their commitment to *not*. Because the only thing easier than taking candy from a baby is making that baby want some candy in the first place.

But Hershey's (and others) aside, brands have forever marketed directly to children, and they will continue to do so. I mean, how many TV commercials have you seen showing kids playing with action figures against a background of a dense jungle or a dramatic cityscape, with heart-pounding music and adrenaline-pumping close-up shots of well-lit superheroes and their ultra-sleek vehicles? Usually, these commercials make the toys look so cool I'm tempted to pick one or two up for myself. It's easy to see how kids could be swayed by advertising like this. These ads aren't selling toys; they're selling action and adventure. What kids *don't* see is that the toys will look just a smidge different against a terrain of ceramic kitchen tile and the music playing in the background is nothing more dramatic than a vacuum cleaner, a screaming baby sister, and some anonymous cartoon with the volume jacked.

There's no question that marketing to kids means walking a fine line between forging an emotional connection and cult indoctrination. Kids' tastes may be changing, and they are definitely maturing faster than we did when we were kids (the old Atari can't exactly compete with PlayStation, and our popularity was judged by real friends, not by page views), but that doesn't mean kids have the emotional or intellectual capacity to see through the propaganda found in advertising the same way most adults can. Nor can they really comprehend the cost/value of the products they see—potentially creating a hardship for parents who are more financially strapped and forced to say "no" more often.

It can, however, be tough to know exactly where that line should be drawn. Case in point: Once, after taking my four-year-old cousin, Gabriella, to one of those Chuck E. Cheese look-alikes at the mall, we passed a Build-a-Bear Workshop store. Of course she wanted to go in, and of course I couldn't say no to her—although I confess I didn't know what the store was all about. So we walked in, and there was a wall of different unstuffed bears and animals for her to choose from. Most of them were between $9 and $12—not bad, actually. I figured I would blow that and more trying to win one for her at a carnival. She chose her bear, after which we were shuttled through a series of stations—one to pick out a heart for it (because if the bear doesn't have a heart, how can it love you?), one to stuff the bear, one to sew it shut, one to "wash" him, etc. So far so good. But then we got sucked in, because a bear can't go around naked, now can it? Naturally, we had to pick out clothes. And shoes. And accessories. And pajamas. And of course, all these goodies were at eye-level for a four year old. Thankfully, I was able to distract her from seeing the adoption center, where no doubt I'd have had to pay another $20 for a piece of paper confirming that the bear was officially hers. I already had piece of paper just like that: my receipt for $118.

I'm still not sure how I feel about all that, or whether I consider it responsible marketing. On the one hand, it's brilliant. My hat's off to whoever came up with the concept. Getting people to fork over that kind of change for a stuffed animal when they could buy one at Target for the cost of one bear shoe is pure genius. And there is the experience to consider: Gabriella had a great time! On the other hand, when it was over, all I remember seeing was a lot of really happy kids—and a lot of really despondent parents. I guess I can't say Build-a-Bear did anything wrong; at some point, I have to take responsibility as a caretaker for knowing what I'm getting into and learning to say no.

To be fair, I believe that for the most part, marketers are responsible in their approach to children. There are certain campaigns that may be questionable (the M&M's characters are definitely kid-friendly, even if the situations they find themselves in are usually more adult-oriented) and even ridiculous (kids shouldn't even know that *Grand Theft Auto* exists, much less be tempted to play it), but as an industry, I believe marketers and the brands they represent do a good job taking the high road.

MICHAEL HAND

THE CLIENT PERSPECTIVE

There are definitely considerations that need to be deliberated when marketing toward kids; issues that go beyond what is legal and deal more with what is ethical. Children are consumers, just like their adult counterparts, but they come to the shopping experience with a different level of education and individual experience. They do not have the same level of knowledge, decision making capability, and reasoning skills to differentiate right from wrong in all cases. These facts alone require marketers to proceed in a way that does not take advantage of these perceived inabilities for their own selfish gain. Marketers need to avoid abusing the power of influence with these young minds and craft messages that are socially responsible, while also touting their product benefits.

On a personal note, I have spent a significant portion of my career trying really hard to avoid marketing to kids. (Not because I do not like kids, but because my jobs precluded such practice.) In the beer industry, we had strict guidelines and legal restrictions that were in place to make sure we had no imagery or messages that were deemed as targeting drinkers under the age of 21. We also had rules about where our media messages could run based on viewership levels across demographics. We pulled reports on every single ad that aired and looked at the corresponding audience composition numbers. If certain shows were defined as reaching a high percentage of under-age drinkers, we immediately pulled future placements from that particular show.

In the candy industry, it is assumed that we sit around a table eating chocolate bars in a conference room and imagine ways to create marketing messages that go after first- and second-grade kids. This is exceptionally far from the truth. Self-imposed guidelines, formed across a variety of packaged goods behemoths, are in place that prohibit us from creating and placing such messages. In fact, next time you check out the Hershey's Web site, make sure to click through to the "Privacy Policy" at the bottom of the page. As part of the Children's Advertising Review Unit (CARU), a strong ethical stance is taken on marketing to youngsters. All aspects of the work are designed to be "accessible and safe for kids of all ages" but really focus on children over the age of 13. At Hershey's, we did not put games on our Web sites because it was assumed that kids would be the only ones to play them, despite countless research studies showing the average age of "gamers" being over 18. We also developed point of sale with the intention of stopping mom in the aisle of a grocery store, not her child. It sounds counterintuitive based on what is perceived as the pattern of consumption behavior, but the focus was on influencing the gatekeeper of the home, not the child.

If your company does target the young adult or tween (8–12 year olds) consumer base, there are a number of things to keep top of mind as you develop marketing elements. First, despite other companies' policies to avoid these consumers, a lot of potential money is in play when talking to this group and trying to drive increased purchase frequency and volume. The tween group alone influences overall annual purchases (self and adults) of greater than $500 billion, while playing a hand in the box office success of animated films that carry a PG rating, the music sales of youth oriented artists like Miley Cyrus, and exercising a major influence on apparel and auto sales (source: *USA Weekend*, 8/10/08). The shift from Disney television to the big screen for the release of *High School Musical 3* is a shining example of the power this group has in influencing the American culture: It was tweens that helped drive the film to number one at the box office with an opening weekend of more than $42 million in October 2008 (the third highest opening weekend in the history of October film releases). The film went on to gross more than $90 million in the U.S. and another $150 million in foreign markets (source: www.boxofficemojo.com), not to mention the additional sales of soundtracks and merchandise.

The most important consideration for marketers (and retailers as well) to be concerned about is that marketing to kids must be done in a respectful way. Whether communicating with this group online (where they spend an obscene amount of time each day) or via other media forums, messages need to be informative and fun while also avoiding that fine line of "crossing into adult content." Marketers need to make sure they are compliant with all legal guidelines that have been put in place with respect to the privacy of children and potential for viewing "harmful material," and must ensure compliance with both the COPA and COPPA legal acts. Establishing a strong relationship with this audience today can have a major impact on a marketer's profitability for many years to come.

Q: • SHOULD BRANDS CREATE LINE
• EXTENSIONS? HOW MANY IS TOO MANY?

JASON MILETSKY
THE AGENCY PERSPECTIVE

Both. The more your brand name appears on shelves, the more recognizable it will be. That's just simple math. But that doesn't necessarily mean you're opening yourself up to new audiences. It's possible, of course, that brand extensions will attract new markets that you may not have reached otherwise, but they need to be extended into the right areas—areas where a close association can be made between the new product category and the brand promise. Otherwise, the brand can quickly become diluted and lose its meaning.

First, let's just make sure we're all on the same page with what a brand extension is—or at least how I define it—because it's not necessarily as obvious as one may think. Products often come in different flavors, sizes, and varieties; these are *not* line extensions. Hefty, for example, may sell trash bags in a 10 pack or a 24 pack, tall or regular size, with handles or without. These are product or line extensions, not brand extensions. But if you were to walk into the kitchenware aisle and see a line of Hefty baking trays, *that* would be a brand extension. It's applying a recognizable brand name—its reputation and what it stands for—to an entirely different line and type of products. In this case, Hefty would be leveraging its brand image as strong and durable to create an impression in consumers' minds that the baking trays are similarly strong and durable.

But the more that a brand name is used on different lines of products, the more it's possible to dilute its value. Spread anything over a larger surface and it's going to get thinner and lose its substance. As more extensions are added, the brand will come to represent more promises and personalities and will need be meaningful to new markets. That's a lot to ask. Eventually, the brand will need to represent so much it'll end up not representing anything at all.

In order for it to work, the brand has to be firmly established and the extensions need to be well thought out. The Hefty example before was fictional and for illustrative purposes only (to my knowledge, Hefty does not have a line of baking trays). But there are plenty of examples of companies that have extended their brand thoughtfully and successfully. Arm & Hammer, long known for making the orange box of baking soda in everyone's refrigerator, successfully extended its brand into oral healthcare. In fact, in a true testament to power of branding, Arm & Hammer's toothpaste (which I use myself) tastes simply awful the first dozen or so times you use it. But taste doesn't matter because the brand is so closely associated with cleanliness that consumers automatically believe in the effectiveness of the product. Virgin, whose brand has been associated with innovation and, to a certain extent, irreverence, has successfully lent its name to music, air travel, and cell-phone service.

A few years back, I watched an interview with TV Donald Trump on some talk show. Trump has done an amazing job of creating a highly visible brand from his name. The Trump brand is synonymous with entrepreneurship, 1980s-style big-business deals, real estate, and the art of making money. So it makes sense that the Trump name isn't only on top of high-rise apartment buildings, casinos, and hotels, but on the Trump University online school (which has further extended into a book series), a luxury magazine, and more. Anyway, during the interview, Trump was talking about his new line of—wait for it—steaks. Steaks? Really? I don't know if they're doing well—maybe they are. I mean, Trump has about a gazillion more dollars than I've got, so obviously he's done a few things right. But this was one brand extension that just seemed like a stretch (unless, of course, we're talking about steak and cheese...).

MICHAEL HAND
THE CLIENT PERSPECTIVE

 Should? I am not sure if they should because every brand is different, but they certainly can find some value in it. The "art" of the line extension has been mastered by very few successful companies. It is too easy to start the line extension process (new flavors, new package sizes, added ingredients, etc.) and then be in a situation where it becomes a crutch for your sales organization whenever they are hungry for new news. Line extensions serve a distinct purpose and often drive initial trial, but do not fool yourself into believing that a simple in-and-out burst of activity will translate to long-term health—there is an illusion of growth, but it is not truly sustainable volume. "In and outs" will likely only confuse consumers to your brand equity. When a line extension does not go well, the repercussions are felt by the anchor brand and you need to make sure you are comfortable tackling that risk. For every Diet Coke built off the Coke platform and name, you may get a Vanilla Coke that hits well with only a small portion of the marketplace but ultimately diverts your brand focus and message.

Customers are not as loyal as they used to be, and choices are everywhere in every category. I am of the mindset that a line extension only will be successful if you are creating it to fill a new need that is unaddressed in the market. They should not be used to take on a competitor's advantage that happens to be a gap in your own portfolio. In this scenario, you will be better off creating a new equity instead of drafting off of yourself. You always need to be sure that a line extension does not open the door for your loyal users to leave your brand— retention of your core is key and cannibalization must be avoided.

A better approach may be to segment the market by stages of the consumers' life and see if you can optimize the product mix for each user, as opposed to simply adding more flavors or product inclusions. An example of this that I have experienced firsthand is in both the baby and dog food aisles of the local grocer. After my first child was born and switched to eating "real" food, I was amazed at the varieties I could find. But rather than just sell against themselves, companies like Gerber outlined the path for me and explained why "Carrots stage #1" was different than "Carrots stage #2" and made it important to my decision process. I look at this less as a line extension and more as consumer education of core products. Extensions included the appropriate finger foods, snacks, cereals, juices, and treats that went along with each stage and eventually filled my shopping cart. In the pet food aisle, I quickly realized that the food I gave my black lab as a puppy was not the same "formula" she needed when she was 10 and had already been through two knee surgeries. I found IAMS did a tremendous job of "extending" their brand into various profiles to hit consumer demand. Again, matched with treats and other items, my total spending increased.

I have also seen firsthand how overextending can be detrimental to brand health and profitability. Just because you have the manufacturing ability to make a bizarre flavored item does not mean you should actually bring it to market; 22 varieties/flavors of any one brand is not a good thing. Do your homework in advance and make sure the market needs what you plan to send into the store. The taste profile or package must be believable and on strategy.

Q: • Is "Going Green" for Real?
• Or Is It Just a Fad?

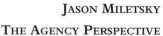

What's your perspective on this question?
Let us know at PerspectivesOnMarketing.com.

Jason Miletsky
The Agency Perspective

 Okay, I know I'm going to catch some real shit for at least part of my answer to this question, but screw it, I'm going to write what I believe. Actually, considering the extreme political differences between me and my lovely and remarkably brilliant editor (hello Kate), I'll be surprised if this answer even gets printed. So here is it, plain and simple: There are two camps when it comes to global warming and the environment. There's the one camp that's really loud about "going green" and uses scientific evidence in an attempt to prove that man is wreaking havoc on the Earth and if we don't change our ways now we're headed for imminent doom. Me? I'm in the other camp—the much quieter group that finds more credibility in scientific reports that prove humans have had no measurable effect on the environment. But the other guys are way better organized; under the leadership of Al Gore, this group has used the media to market its stance incredibly effectively. If you don't believe me, check out the commercial on YouTube starring that dude from *ER*, speaking on behalf of the World Wildlife Fund. It shows two polar bears (one of them is a baby, of course, because what's cuter than a baby polar bear?) standing on a small piece of ice and then diving into the water in search of, well, a *bigger* piece of ice. It all seems very sad, sure to elicit endless "awwws." But it's the *music*, folks! Replace the sad background from the "Songs to Die By" CD with something out of a Peter Sellers flick, and you've got yourself a couple of much happier looking polar bears. But you gotta hand it to them—it's great marketing!

But this is a marketing book, not a treatise on climate change. I'm not a scientist, and I'm not going to waste pages here reprinting scientific analyses that support my beliefs. (Be happy! I'm saving trees!) I'm here to give the agency's perspective on marketing issues. So even though I think all this climate-change stuff is a bunch of bullshit, the "go green" movement has taught me a valuable lesson: Going green is going nowhere. It's here to stay.

I used to believe the whole going-green thing was a fad—that it would go away as soon as we had something else to think about. I figured the environment would be fine as soon as it was no longer in the spotlight. The real solution, I used to joke, was to use federal money to encourage Britney Spears to start partying again. If only our Hollywood actors would keep behaving badly, we'd get tired of talking about polar bears and carbon dioxide and leave the world alone to spin through space in peace. Well, apparently I was wrong. Watching the housing and financial markets collapse in 2008 might not have been as entertaining as watching Lindsay Lohan's career spiral out of control, but those stories did dominate headlines—and still this damned go-green thing wouldn't go away.

And it's not going to, because going green is the perfect issue. It's more personal than, say, giving money to a cause that helps homeless people. Climate change is everywhere and affects all of us—our kids, our grandkids, our pets, and the *future of the whole freaking universe*. It's also easy for people to do next to nothing (like buy a product that is eco-friendly) and fool themselves they're actually making a contribution. Plus, it's got a powerful, organized movement behind it.

I do think, though, it'll die down. Eventually, we'll have some major legislation aimed at saving the planet, and people will think they don't have to think so much about it, which will open the door for the next great cause. (Sorry PETA, it won't be you. Fish won't be called "sea kittens," and we'll still eat veal.) But we're still a ways away from that—and going green will never vanish completely. So for brands looking to connect with consumers: Like it or not, it's time to start the office-recycling program and slap a "We're Green" sticker on your packaging or you, too, could end up on the endangered species list.

MICHAEL HAND
THE CLIENT PERSPECTIVE

⤶ I was one of the biggest skeptics out there. I never thought this "green" thing was really going to amount to much. Yeah, the world would always have a bunch of "tree huggers" who ran around and stood in front of bulldozers in

Birkenstocks to save their neighborhood forest or who floated around the world's oceans in rafts trying to stop oil drilling and prevent large fishing boats from dropping their nets near dolphins. But in my mind, they were the minority. They were the "crazy" ones. As it turns out, I was wrong. Those particular tactics certainly were a bit extreme, but the world has definitely taken notice of the "green movement," albeit in a less dramatic way. When a former Vice President of the United States (Al Gore) adapts a PowerPoint presentation into a movie (and wins an Academy Award) about global warming that nets almost $50 million at the box office, you can be sure the issue is here to stay. I am not going to say that I am a card-carrying "greenie" myself, but from a marketing perspective, you need to take this group seriously.

Every marketer is jumping on the bandwagon and touting themselves as "environmentally friendly" and made with more "sustainable" materials/ingredients. Those marketers who don't make the jump will be left behind as consumers across the globe worry about helping to "save the world" one plastic bottle and recycled package at a time. It has also become a fashion statement to show your environmental friendliness by sporting bold, iconic markings on your eco-friendly garb to show off to your peers. More and more consumers are shopping at their local grocers with canvas bags, and celebrities are showing up on awards show red carpets stepping out from a Prius rather than a stretch Hummer Limousine.

What started as a simple mantra to "Reduce, Reuse, Recycle" is now backed by governmental regulation. Stronger enforcement that ranges from elimination of plastic bag usage at grocery stores in San Francisco to emissions controls on automobiles across the United States is now commonplace. Think about it: The United States alone uses approximately 100 billion plastic bags annually, and petroleum-based plastics are not biodegradable. This means that not one plastic bag will ever decompose. That is a serious problem. If you thought that paper bag usage was much better, guess again. According to the *Washington Post*, the production of paper bags generates 70 percent more air pollutants and 50 times more water pollutants than the production of plastic bags. I guess we are screwed either way.

Honda continues to stand out as one of the top eco-friendly brands in the world. For decades they have been seeking ways to help the environment through advanced technology and innovative new products. These products range from one of the first hybrids on the market (Insight) to the newest generation of emissions-free vehicles (FCX Clarity). The American Council for an Energy-Efficient Economy has recognized Honda for having the "greenest" vehicle on the planet (Civic GX) and placed three additional vehicles on their most environmentally conscious list. This has become just another deficit the US automakers are facing in the long uphill battle to regain market share.

Another great example is footwear manufacturer Timberland, who is placing "nutritional labels" on each shoe box that includes information about where the shoes were made and the manpower it took to produce them. On the inside of each box, Timberland challenges the purchaser with a simple question, "What kind of footprint will you leave?" The reason this type of message is so effective is that it puts the decision back in the consumer's hands and gets them to take an active role in change. They point out that the purchase is only half of the equation.

As a marketing person, I can tell you that we in the industry are thinking harder about how we produce our materials and keeping a tighter watch on waste from the client side. Major corporations have instituted waste measures in packaging runs and work with third parties to re-purpose all their scrap for other production needs. They are using more recycled materials in the development of point of sale displays at the printing stage and trying to limit their use of coatings and varnish to cut back on pollutants. These are all positive steps, but most marketers also know that about one-third of consumers don't relate to environmental messages. Marketers will make continued changes, but don't expect an overnight shift to screaming about the topic.

Q: FROM A MARKETING PERSPECTIVE, IS IT IMPORTANT FOR A BRAND TO CONNECT WITH THE LOCAL COMMUNITY?

JASON MILETSKY

THE AGENCY PERSPECTIVE

The goal of a successful brand-building campaign is to improve a brand's reputation among its consumer base and increase its exposure. Ultimately, the reputation will be built on how well a company consistently fulfills its brand promise and maintains an emotional connection with its audience. This is why a brand can build exposure quickly through marketing, but gains trust more slowly as its reputation is developed over time.

That being stated, I think this question can be more easily answered by looking at it from another direction: Will a brand seriously suffer if it's *not* connected to the local community? I recently drove through my town and spotted a large sign on the fence surrounding a local park announcing an upcoming golf tournament to benefit a cancer fund that was sponsored by Buick. Having this question in the back of my mind, I started keeping my eyes open for other similar signs and noticed that, well, I really didn't notice any. I didn't see a Windex Walk-a-Thon advertised anywhere, nor did I see any church carnivals paid for by Sun Microsystems. And I didn't think less of those brands—or of any of the millions of other brands—for being absent. In fact, I would never have even noticed that those companies weren't openly involved in my community if I hadn't happened to have this question on my mind.

Of course, there are more ways to get involved in a community than just sponsoring events. There are the ad buys in high-school newspapers wishing seniors good luck before they graduate; there are checks written to a local children's carnival; there are donations of the corporate luxury suite at the local football stadium for an upcoming game to raise money at a school auction; the list goes on. But regardless of how many ways brands can be involved on the local level, there will always be far more brands that *don't* get involved—and those brands will still survive and very possibly thrive.

I think local involvement makes more sense for some companies than others. I mentioned that golf outing sponsored by Buick; that makes sense because Buick has a number of local dealerships that may benefit. Undoubtedly, this particular sponsorship was secured by a local dealership who paid for it through some kind of co-op advertising fund. Large restaurant chains that rely on local consumers would also be natural candidates for strong community involvement; beyond the relatively inexpensive marketing they'd receive, being more involved creates a warm and fuzzy feeling. Over time, townspeople may even forget how the big, bad TGI Friday's drove the local family-owned bar on the corner out of business. In these situations, involvement makes a lot of sense—but even then it probably couldn't be considered vital to survival or even profitability.

So I guess my point is that I'm all for philanthropy, and I believe in giving back and supporting the community. But while I think it's a wonderful gesture for brands to get involved and I believe that community activism can help improve a brand's reputation as well as provide good body copy for press releases, I don't believe it's absolutely necessary for a brand to be super involved on the local level. I believe that like any other marketing opportunity, brands need to measure the cost versus the expected return. They must determine whether a strong local push will really be worth the investment, providing substantial returns (measured either by sales, brand perception, brand exposure, or some other device).

MICHAEL HAND
THE CLIENT PERSPECTIVE

I have always been a firm believer in the importance of making sure the community knows you appreciate their role in your success. Clients may not see a lot of financial upside in having the locals on their side, but trust me—they will see a lot of downside if the local community is against them. Effective efforts start with a few basic principles:

- **Get involved and have a voice.** Support the local schools, sports teams, holiday parades, marching band car washes, hospitals, churches, and community groups. A donation to help the high school football team get new uniforms will pay for itself in the sheer value of good will before the team even kicks off in the season opener. Make sure executives take part in town hall meetings and local elections. Get employees to volunteer for local charities and give a little something back via fundraising efforts. Listen to what people in the community are saying they need and react accordingly.

- **Be a "neighbor."** Contributions need to be more than just financial. Open your doors to the community through job opportunities, continued learning, and public forums to tell them what you have planned. For example, if you want to widen the road outside of the plant entrance so that trucks can maneuver the turns better, just let the locals know before they read it in the paper or see the construction crew.

If you are a smaller company and other similar size entities exist in the community, look for ways to partner and provide special offers. Focus on those potential consumers within a 15 minute drive to your door and you will see a long-term benefit. It is human nature to want to support your local shops, provided that they offer good value and reliable service. Smaller companies can also benefit from an annual outreach effort to get feedback on their performance. If residents are familiar with your work, they will be happy to comment in hopes that they will see improved results or, if you are performing well, more of the same. Those not familiar with your service will be intrigued by the fact that you took the time to try and improve.

Even large corporate entities should play up their community roots. Show the town on your Web site and make it a part of your culture. When hiring outside talent, candidates want to know what the local area provides. Strong community relationships can really help tell the story and portray good values.

It is also important to remember that folks in your community know people in other markets as well; they read national newspapers and they watch the news. Do not assume they will bury their heads in the sand and trust you without hesitation. Be open, honest, and don't expect to get a free pass if things take a negative turn in the public forum.

Q: • Is Sports Sponsorship • Worth the Cost?

JASON MILETSKY

THE AGENCY PERSPECTIVE

⤶ As I'm writing this, there's a lingering debate about the wisdom behind Citibank's $400 million naming rights for the NY Mets' new stadium. As of now (early 2009), the stadium is set to be completed soon—and despite intense media and public scrutiny, Citibank seems determined to keep their name on top of the stadium, even if they have to hide behind a "legally binding" contract to do so. And they should. Good for them. Hopefully by the time this book is on the shelves, they won't have caved and succumbed to the pressure.

The problem is that many critics, including certain politicians, think it's irresponsible for Citibank to spend that much for naming rights to a stadium when they received $45 billion in bailout money from the government. That makes sense; clearly, marketing and advertising are just silly hobbies to keep people like me busy during the day. Why would we want to use taxpayer money ("taxpayer money" is the key phrase, apparently, that gets people really riled up) to actually, I don't know, *advertise the business* so that the company might generate a profit sometime in the future? That's so silly! Better to just give them the money to pay down debts and hope that new customers appear through osmosis.

People's naïveté on this issue astounds me. All the news has to do is say "$400 million" and slap a big "taxpayer money" at the end of it, and we're all up in arms. But break it down and look at the benefits:

- It's $400 million over 20 years, which comes out to a far more palatable $20 million per year (considering that commercial time during the Super Bowl runs around $3 million for 30 seconds, $20 million for naming rights to a stadium seems like a bargain.)

- The stadium will seat (or, by the time you're reading this, does seat) 42,500 people. That's 42,500 people sitting in a stadium where they can't escape the Citibank name over the course of 81 home games every year. (That's just for the regular season. If the Mets make it to the post season, there will be even more impressions and heightened national exposure.)

- 42,500 people is nothing compared to the number of people who will watch the games on television (both in and out of New York) and will regularly be exposed to the Citibank name.

- In between games, each and every time a home game is mentioned, the news will refer to the stadium using the Citibank name.

- Baseball isn't the only thing that will go on there; there will be concerts and other events that will put the Citibank name in front of completely different audiences.

- The stadium isn't located in some back alley; it's right on Grand Central Parkway, where God knows how many people will drive past it each and every day, and where who knows how many more people will see it from their airplane windows as they fly in and out of LaGuardia airport, which is pretty much right next door.

For anybody who doesn't believe in the power of the brand and brand-building's ability to translate increased awareness into revenue, well, none of these bullet points will impress you very much. But brand-building does work. It's not just a cute hobby to keep creative types busy all day. The more the brand's name is exposed to its audience, the more it's recognized, trusted, and will remain top of mind.

For people who do believe in the power of branding, sports sponsorships offer some unique opportunities to reach a captured audience that is passionate and emotional about a particular sport and team while significantly increasing the amount of media attention in a positive way. It might seem like a waste to some, but sports are one of our all-time favorite distractions and can be a highly effective means of connecting with consumers.

MICHAEL HAND

THE CLIENT PERSPECTIVE

⤶ Asking the "sports marketing guy" if sponsorship is worth the cost is like asking the Pope if he believes in religion. Of course I believe it is worth the cost, but since this is a book, I am going to guess you are looking for a bit of substance behind that response. In addition, it would not be fair for me to paint the response with really broad strokes of positive support. The reality is that for some companies, sports sponsorship is not worth the investment it takes to do it right. The facts show that sports sponsorship is on the rise despite tough economic times. According to a 2007/2008 study from IEG, the sports category alone was projected to account for 69 percent ($11.6 billion) of the total sponsorship dollars in-market. This marked an increase of greater than 16 percent, and the sixth consecutive year of growth (source: Reuters 1/22/08).

I believe the first step toward your analysis is to set up success criteria for which you will evaluate any potential partnership. You need to hold firm to the process and know that the criteria will be different for each individual organization. Hidden agendas and personal passions must come off the table to be able to evaluate each program on its own merit. Just because you do not watch a particular sport/team does not mean that your target is not interested in it. Let the facts tell the story and guide you.

SUCCESS CRITERIA FOR SPORTS SPONSORSHIP SELECTION

The following is a sample of success criteria/questions you may ask as you prepare for a sports property exploration/selection. This is developed with larger budgets and activation plans in mind, so remember that you may need to adjust according to your size:

Ability to Create a National/Regional Marketing Platform

How far do you want/need to reach?

What type of assets will the property provide as vehicles to get that message out (media, in-arena, added partnerships, etc.)?

Ability to Deliver Against Seasonality/Key Windows of Activation

Do you need activity at a certain time of year?

Do you want a partner with activity all year long/no off season?

Strong Brand/Corporate Vision Alliance

Can you integrate your brand/company into the fabric of the property?

Will the property be focused on a single brand or shared across multiple brands?

Is the demographic appeal broad enough/too broad to cover your primary targets? Will it alienate any of your key consumers/users?

Does the partnership provide growth opportunity if desired?

Does the partner provide local to national potential?

Does the partner provide national to global potential?

Financial Alignment

Are the financial terms flexible?

Do you need/want performance bonus triggers against delivery?

Do you need/want an option year for potential extension?

System Enthusiasm

Will the organization be supportive and rally around the partnership?

Will retail/customer partners get excited about the relationship?

First, you must keep in mind that not all sports sponsorships are multi-million dollar, multi-year agreements. The appeal of sports is that they happen every day around the globe, and range from large global properties (Olympic Games) to strong national leagues (National Football League/Major League Baseball). They include regional and market-specific execution through teams (Milwaukee Brewers/Dallas Cowboys/Indiana Pacers), and they cover every slice of the market across the world (extreme sports, rodeo, racing, fishing, etc.). They can also be broken down to the very local level for direct connection with the community (minor league teams/local colleges). Regardless of your need, every brand or company can line up their target market and find a property that would be the best potential fit. Sports sponsorship can be extremely targeted when used correctly and, in turn, can drive remarkable results. You do need to consider that backing one team could anger the fans of another and that endorsing one athlete connects your brand to his personal decisions (more on this topic will be covered later). Before committing to this, however, an organization really needs to establish their activation goals and objectives in advance. You need to have a vision of success in mind first and not try to build it on-the-fly; this will fail miserably (I know because I have made that mistake). It is one thing to cut the check and associate your name with a partner, but what do you plan to do with the property in-market? How will you use it to connect with your consumers and your customers? I have always tried to live by the mantra that for every dollar you spend on the alliance contract, you should plan to spend two dollars to activate against it. It does you little good to have a pile of tickets and exclusive logo rights with no plan in place to use the assets.

This last point leads me to the group of companies that should not pursue sports deals: Companies that buy into deals because the new CEO likes a particular team or select sport never fare well when the results come in. This is not a personal preference selection based on what the executive board watches each night on ESPN. Organizations that have very limited funds and are considering spending all their money on rights alone should shy away from this space. Notice I did not say small budgets: You can certainly make a sponsorship work on a smaller budget, but you need a plan. There are also things that shouldn't be bought, even if they have a price tag. Do not, I repeat, do not sponsor a memorial service or any other event that could be deemed disrespectful by the masses.

Finally, let me exude the virtues of sports for those naysayers and show how sponsoring sports can be worth every penny set aside for it. When the right alliance is formed with a partner, it can be as big as any ad campaign or communication effort. Some of the best activation I have seen in sports partnerships is through companies you have never heard of. NASCAR is full of these examples. The small shipping company or heating/cooling business unit that leverages every asset they are given to entertain potential customers and get people to hear their story at hospitality events are shining examples of doing it right. These groups are using the assets to create a one-of-a-kind experience that fans (and non-fans alike) will cherish forever.

On the global stage, two major properties stand out in my mind as the top draws for both consumer awareness and business-to-business development: The Olympic Games and soccer's FIFA World Cup are the dominant players. These events do not happen every year so the buildup is intense, and for the period of time that the action is taking place on the field, court, or in the pool, viewership and fan enthusiasm is at an all-time high. Coca-Cola's first Olympic sponsorship dates back to 1928, and they continue to reinvent the partnership on a world-wide stage. For the Beijing festivities in 2008, they exploited the packaging graphics tactic to generate added buzz and support the alliance. They brilliantly used special graphics to illustrate how their brand translates across cultures and always reinforced the concept of unity—a principle that is very on brand character and supportive of the "Coke Side of Life" mantra they tout in their U.S. advertising (source: Schawk Press Release, 12/2/08). Again, this is a major expense that could be utilized to do most anything else: open a factory, invest in capital equipment, or even launch a new product. With greater vision, the global partnership platforms can be leveraged and used as a rallying cry for the entire organization while also generating incremental sales. Do you ever watch swimming outside the Olympics? Probably not, but does that mean that Michael Phelps is not a household name and that the entire world is unaware of his amazing accomplishments in Beijing (and as a result are they not aware of his "out of the pool" issues as well)?

The emotional connection made with fans is most important. The issue I cannot stress enough is that it is not the "thing" that you have a partnership with that matters, it is what you do with that "thing" that makes all the difference in the world.

Q: • ARE CELEBRITY ENDORSEMENTS
• WORTH THE EXPENSE?

JASON MILETSKY
THE AGENCY PERSPECTIVE

If there's one thing that's not up for debate, it's how obsessed Americans are as a whole with celebrities. Witness those crappy magazines you see in the checkout line at the grocery store, not to mention the meteoric rise of TMZ online and on television. Combine that with the 64,000-plus videos posted daily on YouTube by people just aching for their 15 minutes of fame, and it becomes clear that celebrities are—and always will be—an integral part of our lives. And that means they'll continue to be a force in marketing.

Using celebrities can be expensive and frustrating. They can be demanding, hard-headed, obnoxious, and impossible to work with. But they can also sell product. Consumers relate to celebrities; in many ways, they admire them. A famous actress changes her hairstyle and suddenly it's a wide-sweeping fad. I'm not a psychiatrist, but my guess is that many people want to feel like they have somewhat of a personal relationship with their favorite celebs—which, in marketing terms, often translates to "He uses Colgate toothpaste, so I'll use Colgate toothpaste." Maybe it's not as clear-cut as that, but on a subconscious level, there's definitely a "Well, if it's good enough for them, it's good enough for me" kind of thing at play. So in that sense, yes. Celebrity endorsements are worth the expense. If a celebrity can make a brand stand out among its competitors and help compel people to buy more product, then there's no question about that celebrity's worth.

277

That said, brands can't simply put a celebrity next to a product and expect magic to happen. (It's never as easy that, is it?) There are certain variables that brands need to consider when working with celebrities:

- **They're human, and they're prone to getting into trouble:** The difference between them and regular people, though, is that when an athlete or celebrity gets into trouble, the media is all over it. And I'm not just talking about Kobe Bryant and the other thugs in the NBA; after all, even Martha Stewart went to jail. (And if one more person tells me that she was just made an example of, so help me…. She was *not* just made an example of; she sold stock she knew was faulty. And in order to sell stock, someone else needs to buy it. Maybe it was you, or your neighbor, or some guy who suddenly can't pay for his kid to go to college because she knowingly sold him faulty stock. But I digress….) And when the superstar gets into trouble, it can immediately reflect badly on the brand.

- **The more exclusive the celebrity is, the better:** When a star endorses too many products at once, it comes off as disingenuous. It might cost a brand more to keep a celebrity to itself, but it could be worth the expense.

- **A celebrity can't replace a good idea or a creative concept:** McDonald's classic "Nothin' but Net" spots, which I discuss in detail later in this book, are a great example of how celebrities can be used well. Same with Nike's "Bo Knows" campaign, or that single great spot with Joe Namath wearing women's stockings. They didn't just rely on the power of the celebrity; they used the celebrities to drive home a winning idea. That's why those spots, and others like them, work.

- **Whatever the star is selling has to be believable:** Remember that campaign with Tiger Woods pitching Buicks? Perfect example. The dude drives around in million-dollar cars. He's not lusting after a Buick. But Michael Jordan wearing Hanes? That made a little more sense. In order for people to buy into a campaign, there has to be a plausible relationship between the celebrity and the product he or she is endorsing. People need to believe that the celebrity could reasonably be expected to use the product even without compensation.

- **Not every athlete can deliver a line like Peyton Manning:** Most of them deliver their lines like Mike Tyson. Athletes in particular may not be the best actors, and brands have to make sure that their spokespeople can, well, *speak*.

In addition to placing them in mass-media spots, brands that use celebrities typically also require access to those stars for a certain number of public appearances, signings, Web contests, and other uses, heightening their exposure in relation to the brand. Considering all this, companies that are aware of the pitfalls and can work around the particular difficulties involved with star endorsements should find that these efforts can provide a solid return.

MICHAEL HAND

THE CLIENT PERSPECTIVE

Athlete and celebrity endorsements are one of the oldest tricks in the book when trying to connect with a hard-to-reach target and can be worth the expense if they are viewed as legitimate users of the product they are helping to sell. Athletes and celebs will balk at these deals and make you go through countless hurdles with agents to get close enough for "real" evaluation, but deep down they have to love these deals. Tiger Woods takes in approximately $100 million a year in endorsements alone. Sure he is busy and wants some time with his growing family, but do you think he is willing to pass up that kind of cash for simply spending three days a year with Gillette, EA Sports, and Tag Heuer?

The first thing you must do when going down this path is conduct a "reality check" test with your key customers and consumers to see if the impact will be substantial enough to justify the cost. You cannot predict sales before a program starts, but you should certainly explore any data that you may have available to you. You should get a good sense of what other brands/products the endorsee works with and confirm that you have no direct conflict. You should check references and make sure that the individual is "good to work with" and can deliver messages on strategy when representing your company in the public eye. You should also look at any data that is available on his or her familiarity, credibility, and appeal with your target audience. Q-scores and the Davie-Brown index can be good sources to get some initial reads.

It can be a match made in heaven, with marketers getting their brand into consumers' minds and celebrities and athletes getting the residual impact of the brand's characteristics associated with them. National Football League quarterback Donovan McNabb built his entire image around TV ads that featured him with his mom for Campbell's Chunky Soup. He was seen as approachable and a guy with strong family values. This is a win-win scenario when he gets his team to the Super Bowl and stays out of trouble in the media. We live in a world where nothing shuts down, and the media scrutiny on these individuals is everywhere: 24 hours a day, camera bulbs are flashing and messages are being posted on bulletin boards and blogs.

Synergy between celeb and product is critical. When Atlanta Falcons quarterback Michael Vick was arrested and eventually jailed for his role in a dog fighting scandal, he left a wake of scorned companies behind him. Rawlings was using him as their face of youth football, and Nike was about to release a new shoe using him as the featured star. The character of the companies involved was questioned and corporate big wigs were quick to create distance. This is the greatest risk you take in endorsement agreements: your brand image and reputation are always at stake.

The best celebrity usage will eventually create an instant brand connection when they perform well on the field or big screen. The demand for celebrity endorsement remains stable despite tough economic factors. Brands like Pepsi, Gatorade, and Nike continue to use athletes to endorse their products with little end in sight. As athletes like Shaquille O'Neal of the NBA and Brett Favre of the NFL write their final chapters, the next generation of LeBron James and Peyton Manning are swooping in to embrace the youth of America in their respective sports. Do you need a successful case study to show the value? Consider that people started trying the new Amp Energy drink product from Pepsi/Mountain Dew simply because NASCAR's Dale Earnhardt Jr. stuck the logo on the hood of his Chevrolet. Within the first year of signing on with Dale Jr., AMP Energy saw remarkable growth in NASCAR markets, growing 127.5 percent in the year; that is the power of endorsement. When the stars align, results can be magical.

It is important to gauge this impact throughout the process; establish research check-ins twice a year to see if the athlete/celebrity is being connected to your brand, and if their involvement is resulting in better purchase behavior. Gauge the interest within your field sales organization and see if the impact is being felt with your key customers. It can be very difficult to isolate the impact of such a deal, but hopefully top line sales are on the rise. Success will ultimately come down to two major factors:

- Do you have the right marriage of brand with celebrity?

- Is the endorsement relationship helping you break through the clutter at retail (and with your customers)?

Q: FOUR OUT OF FIVE DENTISTS AGREE.... HOW MUCH DO THIRD-PARTY ENDORSEMENTS ADD TO BRAND CREDIBILITY?

JASON MILETSKY

THE AGENCY PERSPECTIVE

There are three types of endorsements:

- **The bullshit endorsement:** This is when the endorsement is completely made up—when neither the endorsement nor the person making it is legit. You can usually spot these straight away because the name of the person giving the endorsement is vague. "This is the best product I've ever used! — Diane S., Boston, MA." Diane S.? Really? If you don't got a last name, you don't got an endorsement.

- **The paid endorsement:** People, usually celebrities, are paid to say positive things about a brand.

- **The legit endorsement:** Real people—general consumers or professionals (doctors, dentists, etc.) or organizations—whose names and/or likenesses are actually used provide positive feedback about their experience with a certain brand. These endorsements are given without compensation.

And you know what? To some extent, they can all work. There's confidence in numbers. Nobody wants to be the first one to step out on the frozen lake if there's a chance the ice might be thin. Endorsements give people the security of knowing that others have already walked across the ice and gotten to the other side, safe and sound; they can try a brand feeling a little more sure about it. Maybe even more importantly, endorsements give people an easy out and someone to blame if something goes wrong. (We do love to blame other people for our decisions, don't we?) "Sorry I dragged you to such a bad movie—it got great reviews!"

Until recently, of course, all endorsements were pretty much bullshit, even if the quote given was genuine, unpaid, and made by real people. Collectively, consumers made an unspoken decision to ignore the glaring fact that brands present only the positive statements—the ones that make their case—and ignore any dissenting opinions. When Tide showed us a busy mom claiming that using Tide kept her colors brighter, it was with the unspoken understanding that others had said they preferred *another* brand, but we never got to see or hear anything about it. And there was nothing wrong with that; it's expected that a brand will stack the deck in their favor, promoting only the reviews and endorsements that put them in a positive light.

But the days when we allowed ourselves the bliss of ignorance are gone—brought to an end by Web 2.0. With social media, which has become a routine part of consumers' lives, consumers have worked research into the beginning of the purchasing process, and have worked the leaving of online reviews into the end of the purchasing process. And all these reviews are easily accessible—meaning that brands can't simply rely on paid endorsements, bullshit endorsements, or one-sided stories any longer. It doesn't matter how much money you throw at marketing something positive when a dissenting opinion is only a Google search away. So while endorsements will continue to be a powerful marketing tool, it's more important than ever for brands to live up to their promises and maintain a good enough impression to truly back up their endorsements.

MICHAEL HAND
THE CLIENT PERSPECTIVE

The power of third-party endorsements can be a major influencing factor with select target groups. This practice has always been a tried and true tactic in presidential primary elections for a reason. When a certain candidate is endorsed by a local senator or governor, it sends a signal to the masses that "the person I voted for and that I think is doing a good job likes him/her, so I guess I should as well." It is comical to me when the endorsed candidate loses the primary election and then everybody shifts to the candidate from their party that they were bad mouthing only weeks before. I could write another whole book on marketing in politics, so let's move on.

Two of the groups that feel the impact of the third-party endorsement the most in the United States are elderly people and Hispanics. I vow it will not happen to me when I get old, but I see it frequently throughout my extended family and have discussed it with a number of friends and colleagues; the conversation is astounding. The blind following of a single doctor's feedback and the incredible connection to an "article that I read" blows me away. I am not a psychologist, so I will not try to examine it much further, but I can tell you with conviction that brands using such claims resonate well with this target. If a doctor says it will work, elderly consumers will give it chance; what is there to lose?

Hispanics are not much different in the blind following of such endorsements. The lower the acculturation level of the consumer (thus the lower level of fluency and confidence in using the English language) plays a great factor. The most affected group within this subset is clearly Hispanic moms. These women place great faith in the advertising claims and doctor recommendations that they hear in their daily life. According to the U.S. Census Bureau, this demographic is predicted to have the greatest impact on America's population growth in the coming decade (Hispanics contribute 56 percent of all new population growth in the United States), so it would make sense for marketers to construct messages using third-party endorsements when speaking to these key consumers.

On a minor side note, the phrase used in this question has a direct connection to the next subject on "stretching the truth" (see Question #78, "How Far Can We Stretch the 'Truth' in Marketing?"), but I do want to make an initial comment here. Trident has been using the "four out five dentists" approach since the mid-1960s and, when examined more closely, the phrase really is not an endorsement at all. The television commercials state that "four out of five dentists recommend sugarless gum *for their patients who chew gum.*" They are not saying anything about the fact that most dentists would prefer you not chew gum at all. Nonetheless, this claim has become the benchmark for third-party endorsement in advertising. It has become part of pop culture, even appearing in an episode of top television show *Friends* during their first season with Chandler sarcastically replying to Rachel's "Guess what? Guess what?" question with "The fifth dentist caved, and now they're all recommending Trident?"

Q: • HOW FAR CAN WE STRETCH
   • THE "TRUTH" IN MARKETING?

JASON MILETSKY

THE AGENCY PERSPECTIVE

I never check my mail. Usually what happens is, I go to the mailbox, look at it, and think, "Could there be anything in there I *really* want to look at?" And the answer's always the same: "No." I only get five bills each month, and I pay those online. There's the obligatory holiday card I'm not interested in reading (although I do, of course, look forward to the Hand family Christmas card each winter), some circulars from the local supermarket, and a community newspaper that I'd say was written by sixth graders but I don't want to insult the local middle school. So I just let it pile up until the mailman eventually tracks me down and complains that my mailbox is so stuffed, it's overflowing.

But of course, there are times where I have no choice but to rummage through the pile of envelopes that have accumulated over the course of a month or two (usually when the mailman starts to rant)—and it's then that I remember why I hate the mail in the first place. Inevitably, somewhere among the useless waste of paper is a very official-looking envelope—thin, black and white, perforated, and glued around three sides, with a government-style seal in the upper-left corner, a return address indicating that it's from the Department of Something or Other, and a warning near the bottom that it's a felony to reuse the envelope and that, if convicted of this crime, I'll be subject to a fine of up to $500 and one year in prison. (No doubt I'd have to share a cell with that rat bastard who ripped the big, white tag off his mattress.)

Now, logically, I know this is a piece of crap. But still—you don't mess with the government. So as much as I hate myself for it, I open it. And although the exact subject matter and wording are always different, it's always some kind of formal letter urging me to call immediately to discuss an "important issue." Reading further, the "important issue" is typically that my car warranty is up and they want to sell me ongoing insurance, or that I'm the randomly selected winner of a dream vacation and I just need to hand over my credit card and Social Security number for verification.

Seriously, nothing pisses me off more than this kind of crap. I'm no lawyer, but this tactic seems like it's illegal—although if it is, I'm sure these guys have done their homework and worked through every loophole they can find. And if it *is* legal, I don't consider it "marketing." These companies know there are many people who frighten easily, who don't know how to recognize a scam when they see one, and they're selling a product by deliberately trying to take advantage of that. I honestly don't know how people who work at companies like this can sleep at night.

I think for legitimate brands and marketers, this gets to the crux of the issue. Clearly, this question isn't asking us to outline the legal boundaries of marketing. It's not asking the extent to which we should be held accountable in a court of law for the claims we make, nor is it attempting to say if and when it might be illegal to pull a bait and switch on shoppers. The point is, it may be legal to run campaigns like this—or like the FreeCreditReport.com campaign, where it's only after that annoying prick finishes singing that song that the voiceover guy discloses that the credit report is "free" only if you enroll in some Triple Advantage bullshit, or those campaigns for smoking-cessation products that show case studies of people who've kicked the habit in just a few short weeks but say "Results not typical" in nine-point font at the bottom. (If it's not typical, then why are you showing it? What is typical?) These companies play into people's ongoing desire to quit and, in doing so, get their hopes up for something that the law of averages, by way of the results not being "typical," dictates they won't be able to accomplish—at least not by using this particular product. It may be legal, but that doesn't mean it's right. Maybe some people can justify it to themselves, but I can't. Call me Mary Poppins, but I believe that marketers have a moral responsibility to create an image and send a message without deliberately misleading consumers into believing something that's just not true.

Look, I'm not a prude. I'm not going to say I've never told a lie before, because we all have. Nobody is above exaggerating a point for emphasis or embellishing a story to make it funnier or to make themselves more of the hero. But we all have an internal mechanism that tells us when we've taken that too far. There's a big difference between a guy putting up a profile on a dating Web site and saying he's 190 pounds when he's really 220 and a guy saying he's single when he's actually married. It's a matter of expectation being built and the potential for disappointment. There's no definitive line that says when you've gone too far; you just know. It's no different for brands (except that brands are more accountable when they stretch the truth too far because it requires more pre-planning). Remember the old McDonald's campaign that said, "We love to see you smile," and showed a bunch of bright, happy people behind the counter getting off on giving great service? *Really?* I've never been in a McDonald's in my life where someone behind the counter has even paid attention to me, much less cared about whether or not I smiled. It was a stretch of the truth that really didn't matter very much—the kind of exaggeration that has become so commonplace we barely recognize it anymore. Claims like "New and Improved!" "Great Tasting!" "Long Lasting!" may or may not be true, but people hardly put any stock into them anyway, so they aren't going to hurt anybody. They're benign, general, and expected. They're also a world away from more pointed claims that play on people's fears or longings, designed simply to turn a buck without delivering the goods.

MICHAEL HAND

THE CLIENT PERSPECTIVE

Stretching the "truth" is always a very fine line that you must walk in marketing. As a client, I lean to the side of always being very straightforward and direct in any messages that hit the consumer marketplace. I am of the mindset that "stretching" the realms of reality will come back and bite you if you are not careful. I see this as most difficult when working on retail-centric activation platforms. For example, while working at General Motors, I was involved in developing retail advertising to support month-end blow-out sales, special lease deals, and model year-end inventory offers. All I can say to consumers is make sure you always read the fine print. In many cases, the photo we would use to show the vehicle on "special" did not necessarily match the item you would see in the dealership at the same price. We could show nicer wheels, roof racks, chrome trim, and special paint as long as we stated that the "vehicle shown may include optional equipment." We added fine print and disclaimers that pointed out the details of the pricing structure and models included to get around the "vehicle shown" issue. It existed at the bottom of every print ad, and let's face it, most Americans didn't bother to read it. It was also inserted into our television spots via disclosures at the bottom of screen, again never examined by potential consumers. Our primary goal was to drive showroom traffic, and it worked. The reality is that people did not feel duped by these offers; they just needed an extra push to get them in the door. Sure, some were seeking the price point from our ads and drove off the lot with a lesser equipped model; but most stuck to the image they saw and stepped up the investment it would take to bring that model home. The challenge was getting them in the door and behind the wheel. Illegal—no. Stretched a bit—absolutely.

Regardless of industry, pricing appears to be the biggest culprit on this "stretch of the truth" as far as I am concerned. Personal computers are another shining example of the practice where the image will include large monitors, connected speakers, and beautiful display stands while the actual offer includes none of the above. Some will call this the "bait and switch" approach, and it is unethical on many levels. Have you ever signed up for cable TV and gotten three free months of HBO? Guess what? More than half of the people getting the same offer will forget about the expiration and just start paying full rate in month four. Another "glowing" example: I think I finally finished paying off my college credit cards this year. You know the people on spring break or in the college mailroom pushing zero percent financing for a year like it is the cure for cancer? I fell victim and with no job upon graduation saw the "25 percent jump" in my interest rate kick in. Did they lie to me? No. Was it a bit deceiving? Yes. Was I upset when the rate jumped? You better believe it.

Finally, there is one area where I stand firm that no "stretch" is allowed or should even be considered: health care/drug advertising. I know they read quickly through the warning statements as if they were giving away concert tickets on the radio, but health risks are nothing to "stretch the truth" over. Be straightforward with your consumers and you will keep their trust; this is a sensible long-term strategy.

Q: ARE THERE ANY ETHICAL ISSUES IN THE USE OF SCARE TACTICS IN MARKETING? ("YOU WILL LOSE YOUR MONEY IF..." OR "IT COULD HARM YOUR FAMILY UNLESS...")

JASON MILETSKY

THE AGENCY PERSPECTIVE

ADT, a provider of home-security systems, has one TV spot that always makes me laugh. While getting into bed, a couple hears a noise. The wife freaks, and the husband, in spite of being certain it's nothing, goes to check it out. He barely gets to the staircase when a masked intruder bursts through the door—at which point he runs back to his wife in the bedroom like a little girl. Then the phone rings, and when the wife answers, we see that the person on the other end of the line is a buff, handsome ADT rep, sitting perfectly straight, his chest puffed out, in the dramatic lighting of the corporate office, calling to make sure the couple is okay. You can almost hear the line that he never actually delivers: "I'm calling to make sure you're safe, because clearly your husband is useless." It's unintentionally cheesy, but it works.

The other spots in the campaign are less cheesy; in fact, they can actually be a little jarring to watch. They're very well produced, and even though you know what's coming, the inevitable break-in is pretty powerful. It's a scare tactic, and they don't pull any punches—but theirs is a service that people don't want to think about. They don't want to plan for such an event because it's easy enough to think, "That will never happen to me." In order to get people interested, they have to do more than just tap an emotion; they have to strike a nerve. They need people to watch those spots and easily put themselves and their loved ones in those same situations.

But there has to be a line drawn somewhere. There is a point where things go too far and these tactics become irresponsible. To find that line, the brand has to determine whether the fear they're trying to evoke (even if exaggerated):

- Is necessary to make a point.

- Preys on people who are disadvantaged or may not have the cognitive aptitude or education to understand that they have a choice in making a purchase. (For more on this, refer to my answer to Question #78, "How Far Can We Stretch the 'Truth' in Marketing?"

- Realistically applies to the product or service being sold. For example, there's an easy correlation to be made with break-ins and the need to invoke a sense of fear. There's not such a correlation, though, with a brand like Tic-Tacs.

- Is clearly the best or only means of selling the brand. In other words, are there other ways you could market an effective message?

So yes, there is a place and a need for certain scare tactics in marketing. But using this approach to forge an emotional connection with your audience is a big responsibility with many important considerations.

MICHAEL HAND

THE CLIENT PERSPECTIVE

The problem with this question is that it groups all marketing efforts that use scare tactics into one common bucket. The reality is that this is not the case. I do feel that poor ethics comes into play for some, but I also feel that a sense of fear can make a tremendous impact with the consumer and is needed to drive action in select circumstances.

Let me first talk to the use of scare tactics in a negative way and with questionable motives. Most of the folks in this group are the losers you see on cable TV infomercials in the middle of the night or those who bombard you with direct mail efforts passing themselves off as somebody else. This group targets the elderly and looks for ways to sell unnecessary items or policies that people cannot always afford. I also take major issue when I open my own mailbox during the week and I get a letter telling me that a "recall may be outstanding" on my car. If only I had company X looking out for me via their warranty plan nothing will be left for me to worry about—talk about sneaky. Is there a recall out? No. Am I now calling bullshit on this group for hacking into a database that contained my Vehicle Identification Number and home address? You bet I am. Slightly above this group in the ethical conversation are the people on TV showing you how infested your air ducts are or how much it will cost to fix your pipes should the inevitable underground burst take place. They thrive on getting people to fear the worst and coerce them into making an expensive service decision without a realistic sense of the likelihood they have of said problem occurring.

Scare tactics that get you to sit up and take notice of issues that are related to serious health and wellness issues are fair game in my book. I feel these executions make for some of the best ads on television, and I see no ethical conflicts at all. Facts are facts, and people should feel free to share even when done in a highly emotional form. I am not a smoker and never have been, but after watching the "Truth" campaign, I find it hard to imagine that anybody who takes a smoke break every day would want to keep the habit. It is no wonder that such powerful ads are needed today considering that, in 1962, Winston was actually selling cigarettes by using *The Flintstones* in television ads. The use of real people in the "Truth" work suffering from cancer of the throat and larynx breathing through a whole in their neck is not a pretty sight. To take the scare tactic a step further in one particular ad, they actually have the man sing a song through his voice box, and it freaks me out (as well as the people on the street in the ad). The "Truth" squad has also extended the idea into viral e-mails and a Web-based platform that shows "scary" facts on cigarettes contents and the impact of smoking. Again, nothing unethical about it, but very moving.

Similar tactics are being used all over the country with issues ranging from drunk driving to gun control to teen pregnancy and sexually transmitted diseases. With life-related issues of this magnitude, you cannot afford to have the facts fall on deaf ears. Fact-based scare tactics work, and they get people's attention; I have no issue with that if they state the truth and save more lives in the process.

Q: FROM A CREATIVE/CONCEPTUAL PERSPECTIVE, HOW DIFFERENT IS B2B MARKETING FROM B2C MARKETING?

JASON MILETSKY
THE AGENCY PERSPECTIVE

Clearly, if the average person is asked to name a brand off the top of their head, they're going to name a consumer brand—Nike, Coke, McDonald's, or something along those lines. Those are the brands that are in our faces all the time—the brands we buy on a regular basis, and the ones we see on TV when we come home at night. But—and I have been beating this drum for a lot of years now and will continue to do so—brand-building is not strictly limited to B2C companies. It's every bit as important for B2B companies to build their brands. In fact, in some respects it's even *more* important due to certain limitations on marketing and there being more at stake with each decision (more on that in a minute).

First, let me lay down two fundamental truths that form the basis for my beliefs about B2B brand-building:

- Brands help to build trust, and the importance of trust is directly proportional to the cost of purchase. That is, the higher the price, the more trust is required.

- B2B means "business to business," not "bricks to bricks." Behind every business decision is a real, live person with his or her own unique personality and a life outside of the office. We market to people, not to buildings.

Brand managers and marketing directors often forget that even in a sales environment of negotiated prices, personal relationships, and potentially longer sales cycles, the brand still plays a heightened role in purchasing decisions. The people behind those decisions are real people—and like any market, those people often share very similar characteristics. But they shouldn't be confused with their jobs. For example, if you're looking to reach HR directors, chances are you'll be reaching a largely female audience over the age of 45. But just because they run HR departments doesn't mean they're boring or that they love HR as a rule.

They are people with real feelings who have families, go out with friends, and want to be entertained like anybody else. These are the very same people that Dove soap tries to reach by strengthening their brand, so why should a payroll company put in any less effort when trying to get them to choose their company as a vendor?

Because of the expense and potential for waste (waste being people the marketer isn't interested in reaching), B2B brands don't usually have the luxury of using mass-media tools such as television for marketing purposes. Once in awhile you may see some B2B company advertising on a Sunday morning political talk show, but these are few and far between; and more than likely, they're trying to pique the interest of potential investors, not potential customers. With marketing avenues usually limited to online and offline trade-publication advertising, direct mail, or trade shows, the brand becomes that much more important and provides that much more of an advantage to the salespeople who actively try to close various accounts. Most industries are pretty small, and word about vendors and even individual players gets around quickly; so how the brand is perceived and how easily it's recognized may be the deciding factor in getting a contract or being passed over for someone seen as more reliable.

Once again, the trust issue becomes a greater factor when more money is at stake, and the brand is what tells the decision makers whether their money will be well-spent. Plus—and this is an important distinction—decision-makers are not spending their own money. They're spending their *company's* money—and will be responsible for explaining how they've spent it. That means they won't necessarily be looking for the lowest price around; they'll be looking for the smartest buy. The wrong decision could mean the difference between getting a promotion—or remaining employed—and not.

In my agency's marketing of JVC Professional—the B2B arm of the electronics giant, which sells professional-grade cameras and display equipment to other companies and studios—the toughest hurdle we've had to overcome is the overarching belief by the market that "Nobody ever got fired for buying Sony." The Sony brand has become synonymous with quality and innovation, and the feeling is that purchasing Sony products is not only beneficial, it's safe. Buying anything else—JVC, Panasonic, Sharp, anything—would be taking a chance with your budget and your job. You don't fight that just with lower prices; you fight it by building a better brand.

MICHAEL HAND
THE CLIENT PERSPECTIVE

↳ My experience working on business-to-business marketing initiatives is far less extensive than my experience working on business-to-consumer programs, but I will attempt to frame my thoughts on the major differences. My first instinct was to say that they are actually quite the same; after all, you are talking to *people* who make purchasing decisions in both scenarios. People are people; you should be able to connect with them regardless of the item you are pushing. On some levels this is true, but the complexity of the two approaches divides them on many factors.

First, in consumer marketing efforts the person making the purchase usually does not *need* to buy your product or service. They do not have to have a new car, need to eat a Reese's Peanut Butter Cup, or get expanded cable with all the premium channels. They are making an emotional purchase, and your creative approach needs to captivate them and draw them to your brand. In business efforts, the person making the call will likely *need* to make the purchase. He or she will need to buy printer paper, get fax service, or fill the vending machines with snacks and drinks. Their choice is more about who to make the purchase from and what value is the supplier providing to their company. This removes the hurdle of creating demand: You simply need to fill the void. Business purchases are also typically rooted in the bottom line, which is an entirely different conceptual perspective to start from.

Second, most consumer buyers will not take the time to get all the details you have to offer. Yes, they will go to a Web site and research some large purchases that they are planning, but most buying decisions are spontaneous and made using top of mind opinions they have formed from your marketing efforts or friend's feedback. This drives the importance of creating high-level brand awareness and, more importantly, brand relevance. The business buyer's decisions are more calculated and planned out. The buyer will read the excruciating details and take time to make the "right" call, not simply the emotional one. They thrive on information and will keep asking for more data to justify their selection. The business purchase cycle also takes place over a much longer period of time, often involving a larger unit volume in the final transaction. Due to the extended time factor, part of the decision process often becomes the partnership or relationship the sales team has made with the buyer.

Finally, consumers will usually make a buying decision on their own or with only their spouse (or parent) present for the transaction. They trust their own instincts and know they are spending their own money. This requires creative work focused on the empowered individual, not an entire group. The individual will deal with the consequences if the results are flawed. The business buyer, on the other hand, will use a team in his or her decision-making approach. They will often ask for references or for a trial period to use the item in advance before making a commitment. Business teams also have multiple functional experts who will weigh in on the final purchase. If you are looking for an IT solution, a team of programmers is likely to cast a vote. If contemplating a new copier, everyone from the administrative staff to office services team will offer advice and counsel.

As you can see, the underlying theme of producing high quality goods and services will always win in the end. However, the creative message and process of connecting is quite different in the business to consumer and business to business selling scenario. The theme of emotion versus function is ever present.

Q: INTERNAL MARKETING: WHAT'S THE BEST WAY TO JAZZ UP THE WORKFORCE, AND IS IT EVEN WORTH THE EFFORT?

JASON MILETSKY
THE AGENCY PERSPECTIVE

Let me tackle part two of that question first: Absolutely! Employees should be the biggest advocates of your brand. But you can't expect them to have that sense of pride and loyalty simply because they cash a paycheck with your logo. Ongoing internal efforts must be undertaken to familiarize the workforce with what your brand is really about—the promise, the personality, what makes your brand unique in the market. You want your employees to live the brand and to reinforce the brand values at all consumer touch points.

Internal marketing doesn't have to be crazy expensive, and it doesn't necessarily have to run parallel with or even greatly reflect any external, consumer-facing marketing efforts. There are a number of ways that companies can market to their employees and get them to live the brand:

- **Give new hires a "brand overview" book:** This book should discuss the brand, its promise, its personality, the market, and how each employee plays a role in creating a positive consumer experience. This should be required reading so that all new employees start with a full understanding of what the brand is about and how their own actions can affect consumers.

For more information on this, check out *Perspectives on Managing Employees*, which discusses in detail how to get all employees to be a bigger part of the consumer experience.

- **Set up specific training sessions:** These sessions should teach employees about the brand—what it is, how it works, and why it's important. This is especially true for employees who will directly interact with customers, to make them aware of how the brand is perceived on the outside. They should be trained in the type of language and attitude that should be used during customer interactions, what their specific role is in fulfilling the brand promise, and how their behavior can add to or detract from the brand personality.

- **Make proper use of office wall space:** Floral prints or paintings of landscapes are nice, but your office isn't a New Jersey diner. Use your wall space for internal promotional purposes. Using the brand look and feel, create prints that display the products or services your company sells, announce the brand values, or promote an internal campaign (discussed in a moment). If your company does any print advertising, have the agency make poster-sized reprints of each ad and hang them around the office so that employees who may never see these ads in their published form can see how the brand is being marketed on the outside. Maybe make a montage of positive consumer feedback received either through regular mail or e-mail. The point is, every company has wall space available that should be used to somehow promote the brand. But whatever you do with it, please, for the sake of all that is good in the world, no more of those horrible Successories posters. Seriously, enough with those. If you have some in your office, put this book away and go take them down. You'll thank me later.

- **Circulate an internal newsletter:** Sending this out weekly is probably too aggressive, but monthly or quarterly newsletters should be doable. Let employees know what's happening around the company, any good news, new initiatives that are taking place, etc. As always, keep the design, tone, and look and feel reflective of the brand, and make sure to include sections that celebrate the brand itself—how individuals within the company are living the brand and examples of how each employee is helping to improve the consumer experience. Printed versions of newsletters are always good, but HTML e-mail blasts also work if you're looking to reduce internal marketing costs.

- **Hold town hall meetings:** While these can be extravagant, they don't need to be. A town hall meeting can be held in your company's cafeteria, a local theater, or the ballroom of a nearby hotel. It's a chance for all the employees from a single office or region to get together and intermingle for a day. Seeing that there's a lot more to their company than what happens in their own office or cubicle will help them feel as though they are part of something bigger. More importantly, it gives key executives a chance to talk to everyone at once, fill people in on important news, and promote the brand firsthand to everyone in attendance. The more people feel like they are truly a part of the company, the more likely they'll be to really live the brand. Town hall meetings might reduce the workday by one, but you'll get it all back in increased productivity in the long run by having a more engaged workforce.

■ **Promote the brand through the corporate intranet:** If you don't have an intranet, get one. Give employees the chance to go online and get updates and information—anything that will make them feel more connected to the brand and your company. Design the site to reflect the brand. Use language that promotes it in a positive way and provide articles and stories that prove that living the brand results in a better experience for everybody, both in and out of the company. Blogs written by the brand or marketing manager are a great way to get messages about the brand across; these people might blog in a conversational way about core brand values and provide tips on how employees can live the brand in his or her position within the company.

■ **Create computer wallpapers and screen savers:** This might be a simple idea, but repetition is one of the key ingredients to successful advertising. So keep the brand in front of company employees by making it the first thing they see when they turn on their monitors in the morning, and the first thing they come back to when they return to their computers after being away for a short while.

■ **Communicate to employees through department managers:** The single most important effort a brand or marketing manager can make is to get department managers on board with the brand. Larger companies in particular can make appropriate use of these managers, each of whom will have the ability to influence a large number of employees under their supervision. If the brand is about being buttoned up, focused, and dedicated to taking a proactive approach, for example, then these traits need to be demonstrated in the behavior of each manager. It would be counter-productive for a manager in this type of company to consistently come in late, dress in jeans and golf shirts, and take a "que sera, sera" kind of approach to meeting deadlines. Executives should take extra care to properly explain the brand promise and personality to each manager and provide insight as to how each manager can further promote the brand to the employees in their supervision.

■ **Wrap all internal brand communications under a finite campaign theme:** Consumer marketing efforts are more effective when they are organized and delivered according to a specific timeline, with pre-established goals. The same goes for internal marketing strategies. While the goals may not be directly related to revenue, they can be pegged to track specific employee behavior or involvement in internal activities, or even in increased production. Create a specific creative campaign theme for all communications.

(I'm not a fan of cheesy marketing in general, but internal campaign themes may be the one exception. Themes like "We Are One" or "Yes We Can" are actually appropriate for internal communication efforts, even if they are the marketing equivalent to Velveeta.) Roll out efforts over time, communicate the campaign through wall art and newsletters, and make sure there is a call to action, such as taking part in a contest or internal promotion (discussed in the next bullet point).

■ **Engage employees with contests and promotions:** You're not going to be trying to get your employees to purchase a product, but it's still important to get them engaged in your brand. Use internal marketing to get employees to participate in contests with small prizes awarded to winners, with winners being highlighted on the intranet and newsletter. These contests don't need to be complex—they can be anything from collecting names and selecting random winners to asking employees to submit their new ideas for products or external marketing messages. Whatever you do, do it with the idea in mind to get employees involved.

MICHAEL HAND
THE CLIENT PERSPECTIVE

⤶ No matter how big or small your company is, it is always critical to make sure that the people you employ have positive feelings about the overall organization. People may want to go home and kick the dog every once in awhile because job satisfaction is waning or because they had a bad day, but they should always be in a position to recite positive things about the company culture to their friends, family, and neighbors. It is worth the effort to "jazz things up" because a happy employee is a more productive employee. When somebody truly believes in the mission, vision, and values of the place where they collect a paycheck, they are more willing to put in extra time and genuinely treat budget items like it was their own money—*in many ways it is.*

For starters, the best way to get them excited is to keep them informed of all happenings. Employees want to be in the know and not find out about things in the newspaper; they want to feel valued enough to be informed. If you get employees excited first, the energy will spread to the people they speak with on sales calls and in meetings; your customers and business partners will feel the positive force. Hold informal "town hall" meetings to alert folks to what they may see or hear and always open the floor to questions that people have. Yes, you may get some stupid questions (the saying is not true that no question is stupid), but if people care enough to ask, then treat it seriously. You should also have an area on the company intranet site where folks can submit questions to senior leaders and have those responses posted for all to see. The theme needs to be about empowering your employees to voice their ideas and concerns. When somebody feels empowered to make a difference, they look harder to find solutions, not additional problems.

Connectivity and breaking down silos is the next major objective to keep the group functioning as a team and not just a collective group of individuals. You are trying to build a "family" if you can, and thus you need to encourage people to care about one another. Create a company softball team, encourage Friday Happy Hour events, or have a company fundraiser to get people working together outside the office environment. You can even reward folks for carpooling together to work with special parking spots—it's good for the environment and it gets people interacting right from the start of the day. Teams that enjoy each other's company and have good chemistry in the office can make a major difference when a big work project is on a tight deadline.

Another way to motivate folks is through "free" stuff. These items can range from T-shirts and hats that feature a new tagline to tickets for local sporting events. All that stuff you get from vendors after pitch meetings and have no use for— here is your opportunity to put it to good use. If a new campaign is about to hit the airwaves, drop a sample of the featured product (or your client's) on everybody's desk before they show up for work on Monday morning. Give them an opportunity to see the creative first and thank them for the effort they provide. The power of thank you is bigger than most people will ever acknowledge.

Finally, don't get cheap with your employees. It is so un-motivating when an employee is asked to chip in $15 to keep water stocked in the fridge; either supply the water or get rid of the fridge. In big companies, times are certainly getting tight, but the negative signal sent over a $500 expense will bite you in the ass. Keep people in the office excited—they are the evangelists for all things you believe in. They need to walk out of the office each day with pride.

Q: KEY CHANGES (SUCH AS MATERIALS OR INGREDIENTS) HAVE BEEN MADE TO A PRODUCT IN MID-CAMPAIGN. NOW WHAT?

JASON MILETSKY
THE AGENCY PERSPECTIVE

Well, the good news is we'll get to bill more. The bad news is...well, there really is no "bad" news. There's just an extreme challenge ahead of you—and you're going to earn every additional dollar five times over.

These situations are inevitable. No matter how much planning there is ahead of time, no matter how many signatures have been given by all the right people, companies might still make significant changes to key components at the worst possible time. But dealing with this is no different from dealing with any other emergency: You have to have a plan, you have to have good leadership, you have to take decisive action—and you have to do all of it fast. Did it take you months to put the campaign together? Well guess what: You're going to be making changes a *lot* faster than that! But it should all be manageable. In most cases, you'd have to be completely asleep at the wheel to be blindsided by a change that significant.

The first thing to do is take a full assessment of the situation. Campaigns don't always focus on specific details like ingredients or materials. Very often, brand-oriented campaigns focus more on the personality of the brand, which is unlikely to be radically different regardless of the change that's been made. This may mean that you don't have all that much to do in terms of changing the brand after all. Even if the change is such that it would benefit the brand to market it more heavily, as long as it hasn't made the core campaign message null and void, you can breathe a little easier. In this case, use the PR team to spread the message of the improvement through the media first while you figure out the best way to change the marketing campaign. In the meantime, though, the campaign can just keep running as is.

That's really the best-case scenario. The worst-case scenario is that the change that's been made has rendered your campaign inaccurate. Marketing that a brand is made with real fruit juice becomes an outright lie when the product-development department takes cost-saving measures to replace real juice with some chemical compound. Fortunately, companies rarely move that quickly, and the people who work in them are never very quiet, so as soon as anyone with decision-making power even starts to toy with the idea of making a key change, the marketing department will catch wind of it. This will at least slow the production of future campaign elements and give everyone the chance to put together a contingency plan—just in case.

When the shit does come down, all current spots need to be canceled (there will likely be kill fees for ending media contracts early), and new production will need to be pushed through immediately. You need to reassemble the team and get new creative developed—often without benefit of market-testing it beforehand. Once again, the PR department should step in and fill in any holes while the campaign is stalled. Meanwhile, marketing components that can be completed or updated more quickly, such as the Web site, should be taken care of as fast as possible.

Revamping a campaign in mid-stride will be the true test of the agency. This is where the creative director and the account managers need to be brilliant on their very first swing of the bat. There's not going to be time for a lot of back and forth with the client. Most importantly, this is where the politics of the client/agency relationship have to be put aside and swift, actionable decisions have to be made. For the benefit of the brand, each party needs to speak its mind honestly and someone needs to just make an executive decision. It's all doable, but the team on both sides of the fence had better be ready to really roll up their sleeves and get to work.

MICHAEL HAND
THE CLIENT PERSPECTIVE

 Wouldn't it be great if everything stayed the same and changes never happened? We could just set a plan, start the process, and then sit back and put it all on auto pilot. Well wake up buddy, the only constant in life is change. You better be prepared for it, and you better embrace it when it comes. Product changes happen, sometimes when you least expect it. You simply need to rally the troops and figure out how to communicate it. In all campaigns, there will be a time when things get slightly derailed and problems arise. Do not complain about it or blame others for it, just figure out how to find solutions. Don't jump to conclusions; take a deep breath and assess what is happening with a clear head.

As a client, I ask that you get a core team together at the agency and brainstorm ways to salvage the existing work (assuming it is performing well). Include creative team members and strategic planners, this cannot be purely a creative solve or purely a factual solve—the goal is to create the best revised work in totality.

Per my previous comment, I need you to bring me recommendations and solutions. Do not just tell me what cannot be done.

I also need you to tell me what it will cost to have your recommendations implemented. Nothing bothers me more than hearing a series of ideas to solve a problem without having a budget to review in the process. Eighty percent of the time, clients and agency partners end up picking the most expensive solution because they never really looked at all the options or they were time-pressured into making a quick decision. I beg the agency every day not to force me into a single stream of thought: show me all the facts.

As the client, you need to remain proactive in helping as well. It is your job to get all the facts and make sure the changes that have taken place can be clearly articulated. You also need to prepare any necessary management team members for the fact that you will need additional support in decision making and approvals. Too many times, you will push the agency to deliver revisions quickly and with rush charges, only to sit and wait on the back end for somebody to make a final call on the new work.

Finally, as the client, you need to keep a positive attitude throughout the stressful period. Be optimistic that the changes are for the better and look at this as an opportunity to improve. Flexibility and willingness to embrace change are skills that will make you a valuable player on any business unit.

Q: • CAN YOU TAKE THE MESSAGE GLOBAL?
• SHOULD YOU?

JASON MILETSKY
THE AGENCY PERSPECTIVE

Before you can say whether the message can and should be taken global, you first have to figure out whether the product or service can be provided to a global audience. Is there distribution in place? Is the product or service desirable in other parts of the world? Does the company have the infrastructure to operate globally? Even if the answer to all of these (and similar) questions is yes, the budget still has to be there to support a global marketing campaign—and none of these are questions that the agency can answer.

If a brand truly is global and needs to reach a worldwide audience, then yes, a message can be taken global—but that doesn't mean it should be. In fact, in most cases, a one-size-fits-all effort with respect to messaging simply doesn't work. Cultures vary greatly in terms of their tastes, sensibilities, senses of humor, what they find offensive, what they consider appropriate, how they shop, how they spend, and the types of messages that they're likely to respond to. Personally, I think the best approach for a global brand is to work with a single lead agency to oversee all specific efforts throughout the world, with each region handled either by the agency's own office in that territory or a local agency that they've partnered with to set appropriate strategy and messaging.

MICHAEL HAND
THE CLIENT PERSPECTIVE

Creating a global platform can be an extremely difficult endeavor, but it is one that can reap great rewards when done well. The ability to move a message across continents is something that takes careful planning, solid execution, and seamless integration. The decision to make this leap is for each individual brand to decide, but if you are currently unsure and questioning whether or not to make the move, you are probably *not* ready yet and need to do some more homework. This is an effort that needs to be made with great conviction. The jump to global stature does not just happen because your company has formed an international alliance that gets your product or service on more shelves or because you purchased a smaller company with manufacturing operations in a city with a name you cannot pronounce. You need to travel extensively to emerging markets and find the consumer drivers for your product across various cultures to confirm there is a market fit.

As a client, your overarching objective is to create a strong enough identity for your brand or product that it can translate to any market, but you can never assume that your current message is the correct one to handle that. The key is having a message that is truly ownable and creates a competitive point of difference while remaining grounded in self-identity. (How do you like that for marketing speak?) The core message must have deep universal meaning and provide consumer connectivity in different countries. As you look at your brand image, you need to determine what part of your DNA resonates with targeted users globally. Then when you craft the full selling story, ask yourself: Are global consumers attracted to your brand color palette or logo? Do they register the unique font treatment, or do they go right to your tag line/message? Are you providing a better product experience than the competition? You need to know where to start the global reinvention from.

In an effort to provide a working example, let's assume you work on a youth-oriented brand that is founded on the principles of enthusiasm, seeking "new" experiences, and self-discovery. Regardless of the product iconography, you have a strong foundation for success that is rooted in a common human truth. You may be quite surprised to find that this idea platform can travel to multiple markets and that, regardless of time zone, it connects in a highly emotional way. You also need to make sure that the iconography is worthy of travel through cultures.

Before I stray too far from the original question, the original ask was can you take a message global? In basic terms, the answer is yes. Companies like Pepsi and McDonald's continue to hone these insights as they rapidly expand their footprint on a global scale. They are focused on delivering a consistent product experience while also reinforcing consistent global values.

Lacking a common global message does not exclude you from launching items in multiple locations around the world. Many successful marketers find it a better use of financial resources to mine for insights in one country and produce the best work for that focused audience, rather than trying to cross multiple markets with a watered down "common" message that may not be as clear to select groups. The Buick Motor Division of General Motors is a shining example of this approach. Buick's introduction into China at a more premium price point has caused a bit of a stir in Detroit office corridors. While the corporation struggles greatly and the elimination of model lines is considered, Buick stays alive because of their success overseas at a premium price point.

Now that I have attempted to answer the question "Should you take your message global?"let me outline a few key global campaign advantages and challenges.

GLOBAL CAMPAIGN ADVANTAGES

- Consistency of brand imagery/iconography
- Cost savings in creative production
- Enhanced brand equity
- Larger geographic footprint to leverage assets

GLOBAL CAMPAIGN CHALLENGES

- Integration model is complex
- Consumer relevance can vary within countries
- Variables in socio-economic model by market
- Different competitive set of brands/products to battle could challenge positioning

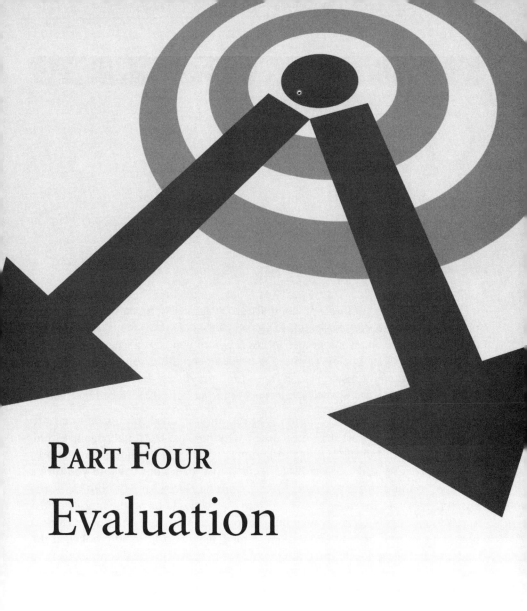

PART FOUR
Evaluation

Q: Is the Integrated Agency Model Something That Works for Everybody?

Michael Hand
The Client Perspective

⤶ Finding one common model that can be applied across a variety of disciplines is never an easy task. On a personal level, I (as a client) applaud the attempts to develop an integrated solution where you can place one direct call to your "integrated agency partner" and have everything solved. By design it eliminates the countless hours of repeating everything that you see and feel with multiple retained agencies, but it is hard to say if it really is more effective.

I had a former boss who swore never to run an integrated solution at any company he was ever a part of. When asked why he was so strongly against it, he would return the question with another question. If you just bought a beautiful piece of property and were ready to build your dream house, would you hire a plumber to build the entire thing? How about an electrician? In both cases, the answer was typically an emphatic no. Sure they could both get the house erected and it would likely be fairly well built, but you know that the masonry work is not going to be at its best, and the house may likely be a little bit crooked at the foundation. People develop an expertise for a reason; even general contractors have strengths they are better suited for. The client/agency world can draw numerous head-to-head comparisons as outlined. Would you hire an Internet agency to build your entire orchestrated marketing plan and positioning platforms? Would the media guys be asked to write the copy for an ad? Neither are good solutions.

When you lock into one agency for an integrated plan, you are often stuck with only one way of thinking through the solution development process. This singular point of view in most cases is no match for what a collection of functional experts could deliver within the same budget. Also, you need to address your own corporate team's design to support such a model. Look yourself in the mirror and decide how you would align with the integrated model and if you have the ability to break down any existing silos that are already in place.

The integrated model can only work if all the client's agency partners already have a strong working relationship and they are willing to designate a lead partner to whom they will report. In this model, the client will funnel conversation and direction through a single point of contact and assume that the others will be comfortable taking the direction and delivering results.

In large agency networks, this can be an easier task, with compensation models and hierarchical structures already built in. But when you have a variety of independent partners or partners from various agency parents, this is never a good choice. My suggestion is to seek strong integration through shared ownership of execution, but to not put all your eggs into one agency basket. Integration may be your intention, but disconnection may be the result.

JASON MILETSKY
THE AGENCY PERSPECTIVE

I'm a bit thrown by the word "everybody" here. Didn't they teach us in SAT class that we should immediately eliminate any answer that was all-inclusive? But, okay. While I'm sure there are cases where the integrated agency model would not be the best choice for a brand, and as much as I think the word "integrated" is overused, I think that in the large majority of cases, clients will greatly benefit from an integrated approach.

The biggest benefit, of course, is that an integrated agency can consider multiple means of marketing communication when developing a strategy, theoretically creating a fuller, more complete attack plan. An agency that specializes in public relations, for example, isn't likely to address a client's needs with any solution other than standard PR strategies. Similarly, an agency that focuses on traditional marketing may not be aware of Web 2.0 tools, or how they can effectively be used to achieve the client's goals. Worse yet, these types of specialty agencies may be prone to downplaying other forms of marketing—not because they believe those other forms of marketing are truly wrong for the brand, but because selling their specialty better suits their own purposes. Integrated agencies, on the other hand, have less of a reason to push one form of marketing over another because they're collecting the revenue regardless.

Additionally, integrated agencies are more capable of mounting a multi-faceted strategy that reaches audiences through a variety of different angles. Depending on the market in question, there may often be a benefit to choreographing an approach that, for example, reaches people first through TV and print, followed shortly after by the release of a viral component, and supported throughout by a steady public-relations campaign.

Finally, an integrated agency can handle more production services in-house, meaning that the creative integrity of all marketing efforts can remain intact. Working through a single source also means that clients should have more seamless and regular communications, lower costs, and less concern about working within tight timeframes. Of course, a viable case can be made for working with a specialist, such as potentially higher levels of expertise within one marketing category, but on the whole, I believe the integrated approach will almost always serve smart, aggressive brands far better.

Q: How Honest Is Too Honest?

MICHAEL HAND

THE CLIENT PERSPECTIVE

Can you really be too honest? I know that people have feelings, and as we all know, nobody likes to be the bearer of bad news, but should you really not share the full truth when you are in a business relationship? I think full disclosure is a necessity for any future success, and if something is amiss, it needs to be addressed in a timely manner. Avoiding this uncomfortable conversation will only turn a small concern today into a larger concern down the road.

It can be especially difficult to inform an agency (or a client for that matter) that their work is not up to par or that the attitude they project leaves no one motivated to work with them. Too often, client/agency reviews are filled with cozy compliments or the "it would be nice to start doing XYZ" type of conversations. The gentler side of human nature prevails and people feel it is better to give a good or neutral performance review than to be candid about the areas that really need improvement. Some folks would rather avoid the conversation completely and just hope that the problems go away. The reality is that the problems can get so big they eventually explode and force a more dramatic change. These meetings should be held quarterly in an agency/client relationship (twice a year is the minimum, and an every day, open door policy is preferred), with well-defined steps outlined to achieve acceptable performance and right the ship.

If done right, these reviews can serve as a growth engine for the collective team. Honest feedback gets the focus on the issues, not the superficial problems that offer little in relationship building. In many cases the client (or agency) will not see value in the mundane babble and therefore will not commit the appropriate amount of time to getting things right. Agencies should demand honest feedback to ensure there are no surprises later, and clients should expect to hear candid feedback as well.

As you know, it is always easier to be honest when things are going well. On the flip side, it can be tremendously hard to voice displeasure and then sit down face-to-face to discuss the issues. The feedback needs to be unbiased and should be supported by more than one person's point of view to validate the concerns. You can't criticize something "just because" and then not have any "suggestions" for how to address the problem; you need to share an action plan and set up regular work sessions to discuss the status. Honest feedback requires teams to be solution-oriented and demands that folks have short memories and are not easily flustered. If needed, there are plenty of consulting groups waiting in the wings to mediate the talks and make sure you don't get too honest.

JASON MILETSKY

THE AGENCY PERSPECTIVE

Crazy People. Dudley Moore, Daryl Hannah. David Paymer (look him up) stealing the show by just saying "Hello." Arguably one of the funniest freakin' movies ever made, and hands down the best movie about advertising of all time. If you're in the advertising industry and you haven't seen this movie, I don't know… all I can say is you should be ashamed of yourself.

For those who aren't familiar with it: Moore plays Emory, an ad exec, doing creative concepting for a large agency, who comes up with the radical idea of telling the public the truth. "Let's level with people," he implores his co-workers. It's an interesting concept, and it's met with exactly the response you'd expect: "We can't level, you crazy bastard, we're in advertising!" Emory's co-workers promptly commit him to a mental institution; there, with the help of the hospital's patients, Emory develops truth-in-advertising classics such as:

- "Buy Volvos. They're boxy but they're good."

- "You may think phone service stinks since deregulation, but don't mess with us, because we're all you've got. In fact, if we fold, you'll have no damn phones. AT&T: We're tired of taking your crap!"

- "Jaguar: For men who want hand jobs from beautiful women they hardly know."

But is the concept of truth in advertising that crazy? Sadly, yes. I say "sadly" because (and I apologize in advance, but this is somewhat of a hot-button issue for me) honesty is the one thing for which people simply have no tolerance anymore.

We have become such a tight-assed PC society, ready to drag people or companies into court if (heaven forbid) anybody dares to hurt our fragile little feelings, it's become virtually impossible for anybody to speak their minds and say what they really feel. Just imagine what the reaction would be if Weight Watchers ran a campaign with the tag, "Because fat people get laid less." They'd get *annihilated*. Overeaters Anonymous, The Association for the Big and Beautiful, PETA, Al Sharpton, Al Gore, Dr. Phil, you name it—anyone with an opinion and a microphone will be at Weight Watchers' doors with picket signs calling for global boycotts. Hell, I'll probably get annihilated just for writing this! I guarantee that someone will write a scathing review of this book simply because I had the nerve to suggest that campaign even in jest.

Keep in mind: I'm not advocating purposefully trying to hurt anyone's feelings. I'm simply saying that we put so much stock into words, we've become so insecure, that we have almost zero threshold for honesty if it's not what we want to hear. We've all forgotten how to take a joke, how to look at ourselves with any sort of realism, how to shrug things off. There are people in other parts of the world who are brutalized by corrupt police working for oppressive governments who would be *thrilled* if the only problems they had to deal with were words. But that's not the situation here. Words sting more here, and people don't want the truth if that truth is going to hurt. If someone asks "How do you like my new haircut?" they're not asking for the truth; they're fishing for a compliment. Answering "*Wow*. Did you do that on purpose?" or even "It looks okay, but I've seen you look better" isn't allowed.

So to answer the question, marketing isn't about "honesty," because pure, raw honesty doesn't propel a brand forward. Brands, like friends and family, have to tell people what they want to hear (within the confines of what the brand can realistically offer). But *real* truth in advertising? That's just crazy.

Q: HOW OFTEN SHOULD THE CLIENT/AGENCY RELATIONSHIP BE ASSESSED?

MICHAEL HAND

THE CLIENT PERSPECTIVE

There really is no magic number of times that a relationship review needs to be conducted. As it is often said, no two relationships are exactly alike. If you are in an established relationship with a partner and have been working together for some time, formal reviews can be done with less frequency, but they should not be avoided. Too often you hear of the organization that gets a new CMO who comes in and shakes up the entire roster, severing ties with long-standing partners in the process. Many times this is because the "positive" feelings were just talk and no formal document ever existed that illustrated the bang up job being done.

I encourage long-standing teams to have a written review at least once a year to get any concerns on the table and address them head on. It also serves as a good reminder of the things that are working between partners to build the business. The actual format of the document/review is up to the partners, and the level of formality can be as well. I suggest "grading" each functional area (account, creative, strategy, and production) on a numeric scale and leaving ample room for free-flowing comments. (Note: Make sure you use an even numbered scale for your grades—such as 1–4—it will force the fence sitters [those who just pick the middle rating every time] to make a positive/negative call.) The critical thing is to make this a "living and breathing" document. Nobody benefits if the review is completed and then ends up tucked in a drawer. As a client, I am also intrigued by the "pay for performance" compensation model with retained partners. When the assessment format is solidified, you might want to consider putting some of the annual fee in a bonus pool. Poor performance nets the client a 10 percent reduction on annual fee, extraordinary performance earns a 10 percent bonus on top of the base. This type of motivation factor in larger contracts can have quite an impact. Nobody messes around when money is involved.

You could make your review process as simple as using the *Start, Stop, and Continue* model that you discussed in middle school "feelings" classes with the health teacher. What are the things you wish the agency would *start* doing more of to help move the business and increase the overall perception/performance of the work? What are the items that you would like to see the agency *stop* doing, due to negative feedback or the creation of difficult work situations that add limited value? And what are the actions that you would like to see the agency *continue* to utilize, as they drive positive results and enhance the image of the team? Pretty basic really, but you would be surprised how much the dialogue can help if you are not doing something more conventional already.

In a "new" agency/client relationship (less than three years), I suggest more formality in the review process. Let's face it: The average tenure of such relationships appears to be getting shorter all the time. Clients keep looking for the magic bullet and swap agencies like they are changing their underwear. (As a side note, this practice has got to stop. When the business is performing badly, clients need to stop pinning the blame on partners and start tackling the issues head on. Yes, the partnerships may not always be a fit, but the direction usually comes from within the ivory tower at corporate. Address your own issues first before dropping the hammer on a partner.) Assessments here should be conducted at a minimum of twice a year for the first three years and with even greater frequency in the beginning. Agencies should be begging for feedback and clients should be salivating to give it. Getting things right in the first six to eight months is extremely important; it will set the foundation for the future. The reason I suggest keeping this over a three-year period is to get a look at the full picture. Year one will show you how a group handles transition and how they get people thinking about new ideas and using new processes. It will emphasize creative development and look closely at how the account staff works with people. In year two, results of the "physical work" will start to come in and ideas will start to be activated in-market. You will learn how the group reacts to feedback and course corrections midstream to maximize an opportunity. You need to really focus on the "what did we learn" and "how will we evolve" areas in these reviews. Year three will be critical to see any adaptations in practice and also to see how the team has evolved. Ask each other the following question: Are you adjusting the scope and staffing plans to fit the needs of the business? The landscape will change over time and new challenges will surface; you need to make sure you are poised for the task.

This all sounds pretty basic, and it is. But you would be shocked how many agency/client relationships exist without such principles in place. Regardless of which side you sit on, start today by scheduling your next formal review.

JASON MILETSKY

THE AGENCY PERSPECTIVE

It seems to me there are usually four specific times when a relationship assessment happens:

- **When a contract is coming due:** It's pretty normal for there to be at least an informal discussion about the relationship and what, if anything, needs to be improved as the end of the contract period draws near.

- **When a major campaign effort is deemed a failure by client:** In the process of determining what went wrong, when, where, and how, an assessment of the overall relationship is made to see whether there is room to move forward together.

- **A new marketing manager or director comes in:** This person will want to get a handle on the relationship and the players, and will most likely try to find a way to push the existing agency out. (Chances are this person has an existing relationship with another agency that he or she wants to work with again.)

- **After about three years or so:** Even if everything is going well, it just makes sense to take a step back and do a more formal assessment just to make sure that the agency isn't getting stale, is keeping up with any changes in the market, and can keep coming up with fresh, creative ideas.

Doing an assessment doesn't have to mean that the agency is in jeopardy of losing an account or even being put in a position of having to defend itself. I've often found that assessments are done over dinner, where I have been totally confident that the account was ours and would remain that way, but discussed any issues with our account managers and whether the client was comfortable with them. Did they think the process was seamless? Is our team communicating often enough with their team? Things like that. I make sure that any of their concerns are addressed and let them know (subtly—nobody needs to be hit over the head) that the relationship is valued and that we're still looking forward to helping them move their brand ahead.

Nobody should assume that the client/agency relationship assessment is nothing more than a bitch session for the client to complain or make changes to the account. It's also a time where the agency can voice their concerns, including individuals on the client side that may be putting up roadblocks to moving forward, changes that the agency thinks could be made to improve the process, and of course issues regarding billing (invoices not getting paid on time, etc.).

Q: HOW DO YOU MOVE FORWARD WHEN YOU'RE NOT SEEING EYE-TO-EYE?

MICHAEL HAND

THE CLIENT PERSPECTIVE

 An unknown author penned the following inspirational thought that has stuck with me for the past 20 years:

> When things go wrong, as they sometimes will,
>
> When the road you're trudging seems all uphill,
>
> When the funds are low and the debts are high,
>
> And you want to smile, but you have to sigh,
>
> When care is pressing you down a bit,
>
> Rest if you must, but don't you quit.

I'm not sure *exactly* why that quote makes sense for me to insert here, but in an odd way, it answers the question directly. When the process is broken or the two sides simply cannot find a common ground, you may need to step away from the exchange for a minute before you "re-engage" and find the solution to your dilemma. Walking away (or taking a rest as the author mentioned) can be a good way to recharge your internal batteries and reflect on what the real issues are that are driving the impasse. Both groups need to share in the ownership of "finding a solution"; too many clients put this onto the agency only and say "find a way to fix it and get back to me." This tactic never works and only causes a deeper chasm between the parties involved. Leaders need to set aside the appropriate amount of time to talk at length about the concerns and really listen to the conversation. I had a great coach in high school who would always ask, "I know you hear me, but are you really listening?" There is a major disparity between those two verbs and they can make a world of difference in breaking through to find a way out of the mess. You need to feel comfortable speaking your mind in a candid way; biting one's tongue and sweeping the problems into a heaping pile in the corner never works. The communication flow is critical—you can "agree to disagree," but you need to let people know that that is your stance. Client/agency relationships can only thrive when all the problems are on the table and no hidden agendas exist. Remember: Smart people run these relationships, draw from previous experience, and focus less on what is not working and more on what currently is working. Ask yourself and the team, how can we make this situation better? If you are 100 percent committed, then ultimately you should not give up. You need to believe in the people who are on both teams and navigate a way to the resolution.

If all else fails and all legitimate efforts have been exhausted, it may just be time to move on and go your separate ways. Sometimes corporate cultures do not align and sometimes individual personalities can create a riff. You owe it to yourself to search for the solution, but you need to admit when one cannot be found. If the relationship ends, do your best to conclude on amicable terms. Trust me, it is a small world and paths will cross again.

JASON MILETSKY
THE AGENCY PERSPECTIVE

If the disagreement is serious enough, it could mean the end of the relationship completely—but that's pretty extreme. Most client/agency relationships don't end in angry shouting matches. There will, however, be times when the client and the agency don't agree about the exact messaging or the best way to move a campaign forward. It's bound to happen. But I think it's up to the agency to keep these situations from getting out of control.

There are three important things that the agency needs to remember in this scenario:

- Even if you disagree on an important issue, you're not adversaries. Everyone involved shares the same interest: moving forward and doing what's best for the brand.

- No matter how much you know about the brand and market in question, the client will undoubtedly have insight into each that you simply don't have by virtue of the fact they live and breathe it every day.

- The client pays the bills, so at the end of the day, they're the ones making the final decision. Agencies need to judge when continuing their side of the debate will be futile and find a way to accept and show support for the client's ideas.

On that last note, I do believe that if a client is insistent on making a bad decision, the agency should get this in writing. It doesn't need to be anything formal; what I do is simply e-mail the client to confirm exactly what it is we're being directed to do and make one last subtle plea to reconsider, with a request that they e-mail me back approval. I know full well that this last plea will go unheeded, but once they e-mail back their approval, then at least I have something to refer to in the event something goes drastically wrong because of the client's directive and I need to defend myself and the agency.

But it really shouldn't come to that. Like any relationship, there are going to be times when you don't see eye-to-eye, and honestly, that's okay. If you both agreed on everything, the client wouldn't need to hire the agency in the first place. It's healthy to disagree; disagreements allow different ideas to surface. But it's the agency's responsibility to keep it under control, to understand who the real decision-makers are, and to know when it's time to back off.

Q: WHAT IS THE ROLE OF THIRD-PARTY RESEARCH IN EVALUATING MARKETING SUCCESS?

MICHAEL HAND

THE CLIENT PERSPECTIVE

Ahhh, research! You either love it or you hate it, and there appears to be very little middle ground. As a client, the expectation is that you will love it, and having reams of data to pilfer through is a good thing—kind of like a badge of honor. The reality is, though, that having piles of research does you little to no good if you have no idea how to leverage it to your advantage and make the work output better from being more informed. That being said, I agree there is some value in having data points to reference and they can provide context on your brand or product. They can also serve as method of entry when trying to set up the introductory meeting with buyers at your key retailer or with management at a prospective client. However, I feel strongly that you can manipulate data in so many ways to tell "any story" that it has begun to lose some impact with me. Many marketers have begun to use research as a crutch for internal accountability and decision making. Brand managers across America are hiding behind the stacks of data and not really getting to know the "ins and outs" that drive behavior shifts of their products and services. Waiting on the focus group results as the reason for delays in making tough judgment calls is not acceptable in my world. I agree it is important to have some data to inform where you need to be, and I agree that research can be a strong tool after a program is completed to evaluate results and avoid making missteps the next time though the process. I just think marketers need to have conviction, and third-party research too often is used to help people hedge their bets.

Talking to 60 moms across three geographically diverse markets about my upcoming print media plan and packaging redesign might assist me in developing unique ideas for program extensions or help me get a deeper understanding of what is resonating with this important shopper, but do we really feel this information is significant enough to us to shift a design direction completely down a new track? Too much emphasis is being placed on these types of responses.

If you hire smart people who know the consumer and have insight on the marketplace, research should be nothing more than a confirmation of your existing sound strategic thoughts.

JASON MILETSKY
THE AGENCY PERSPECTIVE

I wish I had it in me to give the generic answer—something along the lines of, "Third-party research is a vital component, blah, blah, blah"—but I can't, because that's not always the case. For one thing, a third party isn't always necessary to evaluate a successful marketing effort. The huge majority of marketing is done not by multi–billion-dollar multi-nationals; it's done by aggressive companies of all sizes that are anxious to capture greater market share. Some, many, or even most of these efforts won't be large enough to warrant spending money for a third-party evaluation—money that could instead be used for more marketing. Evaluation of success is important, but typically this can be done through the combined efforts of the client and the agency.

When a third party is hired, however, there are complications of which everyone needs to be aware. I don't want to sound cynical, and I am not distrusting of people in general, but I am a realist, and I've been part of this process enough to know what's up. The term "third party" implies that this outside entity is neutral and can give a completely unbiased opinion. Bullshit. Someone is paying their bills. Somebody hired them, and they will always be at least a little aligned to whomever that was.

Suppose the agency hires a third party to run the evaluation. What are the chances that the results of the evaluation are going to be that the campaign blew and that the client wasted their money? It's not going to happen, because the evaluation company wants the agency to hire them again in the future. It's not much better if the client hires them directly; then the third party will see an opportunity for future work with that company and will not only show results, but make unsolicited recommendations as to how to fix problem areas. (Most likely they can do some of that work themselves, or they have a partnership with an agency they would benefit from passing work on to.)

I have no problem with having a third party come in post-campaign and doing the necessary research to measure results—such as determining the increase in brand recognition—but measuring results is different from determining success. I believe the client alone should determine whether success has been reached and whether the campaign proved worth the expense of time and money.

Q: WHEN AN EFFORT FAILS, ARE CLIENTS EXPECTED TO TAKE A "BLAME THE AGENCY" APPROACH, REGARDLESS OF CIRCUMSTANCES?

MICHAEL HAND
THE CLIENT PERSPECTIVE

I can only guess that my counterpart will answer this question by expressing how clients always blame the agency and how they always look for the easy way out. He will say that clients never take the blame and part of being on the agency side is providing your client with a "retained scapegoat." He will also add that while clients are happy to walk solo to the awards podium and bask in the glow of success, they will throw a knife in your back faster than you can imagine. Is he right? Boy, I hope not.

Circumstances certainly come into play, but pointing fingers is not a good practice regardless of which side of the table you are sitting on. If a football team is not performing well on the field when the season starts, the players start to get blamed for being lazy or not following the game plan that was introduced in training camp. As the season rolls on and the team is still doing poorly (think Detroit Lions 0–16 season in 2008), the blame shifts to the head coach who is responsible for getting the players prepared for a win. You can draw parallels to the "agency blame game." The reality is that the majority of creative agencies are not in the battle alone when it comes to consumer-centric marketing efforts, even if they take some extra heat in the beginning. The *Mad Men* days of smoke filled conference rooms and liquid lunches every Thursday have passed (to be frank, I am not really sure they ever existed outside of television shows and movies). Creative presentations and strategic planning meetings are joint efforts, with clients playing a significant role in every step of the development process. Strategy documents and creative briefs are typically approved up through senior levels of management at most large consumer marketing companies.

Rough cuts and final edits of advertising work are typically being signed off on by the Chief Marketing Officer and approved by everybody but the cleaning staff before they hit the air. This does not mean that blame will not get thrown around if things take a negative turn in the marketplace, but it would be a gross exaggeration to "blame the agency" for any effort that does not produce a desired result. The fact remains that agency partners are equally part of the solution and part of the potential problem. Don't waste your time worrying about whom to blame; focus your time on fixing any problems together.

JASON MILETSKY

THE AGENCY PERSPECTIVE

It's not something we like, but it's absolutely something we expect. Something goes wrong? Blame the agency. That's life in marketing, man. It makes total sense, though. I'd never fault the client as a whole or even the main contact as an individual for throwing us under the bus. This isn't a world where anyone is forgiven easily. Mistakes can prove costly and nobody gets rewarded for being brave enough to say, "It was my fault." So when all hell breaks loose, we look for someone else to blame—and when there's nobody else to blame, we just get pissed off at the world.

With any campaign, there's a lot at stake—time and money, how the brand is being perceived by the market, and wasted opportunities, to name a few things. But in times of crisis, when the numbers look rough and it's clear that all that time, money, and opportunity has been squandered, I can tell you this: Nobody is thinking about the brand. Until the dust settles, everyone's main (albeit private) concern is their job security and/or their bonuses. Because here's the deal: When an effort fails, the guy at the top never just laughs it off and says, "Don't worry about it. We'll get 'em next time!" No, he's going to want answers about why it failed and, most importantly, he's going to want names. Why did it fail? What went wrong? Why didn't someone notice it wasn't working and pull the plug sooner?

When the marketing director's (or whoever your contact is) boss is breathing down his or her neck looking for answers, he or she—really, any human being in that position—is going to try to spread some of that heat over to the agency, which is, after all, their most vulnerable option. After all, the agency probably came up with the ideas, they executed the campaign, and most importantly, they're an easy target because they're not around at all times to defend themselves.

What's really scary is that by the time the client squarely blames the agency for everything from failed campaign creative to breakdowns in the Middle East peace process, they'll have already convinced themselves that their accusations are accurate and their recollection about how meetings and initiatives went down is correct. Memory is a scary thing—it's so easily manipulated.

Even though it's not exactly on topic, I want to touch on who really *is* to blame when a campaign fails. There are absolutely times where the agency is at fault, especially in instances where an error was made or a deadline was missed. But I don't believe the agency should shoulder the biggest burden simply because the creative didn't connect or the strategy didn't do what everyone thought it would. Agencies aren't just given a blank check and an empty canvas and told to have fun. We're selected through a pretty vigorous screening process based on the client's opinion of our past work with other brands and the results they believe we can deliver. The agency then presents a number of strategies and concepts derived from information provided from the client (the target demo, goals, key statistics, etc.). There's always client input, which is somehow worked in, and then the client signs off on everything after they're satisfied with the direction they've collectively decided to take.

So is bad creative grounds for firing an agency after a campaign crashes and burns? Sure. It probably wouldn't make sense to invest further in an agency that isn't producing results when the client could instead give another agency a crack at it. But that doesn't mean the agency is at fault in the campaign's demise. The campaign was developed in conjunction with the client, even if all the client did was sign off on it.

Q: WHEN AN EFFORT FAILS, ARE AGENCIES EXPECTED TO PUT THE BEST SPIN ON THE RESULTS? HOW DOES THIS AFFECT TRUE SUCCESS EVALUATION?

MICHAEL HAND

THE CLIENT PERSPECTIVE

I am a big fan of the "glass is half full" approach, but I also look for a sense of reality when conducting assessments of my team's work. If an effort fails, I want to discover the positive elements within it and find a way to repeat that portion again and again. I want to look at which aspects of a program did not work and dig deeper into the *why*. The objective of moving forward is to avoid making the same mistakes the next time around. I do not want the agency to spin the results and give me a misperception of the final work. This gets back to the "honesty" issue that was discussed earlier in the book (see Question #85, "How Honest Is Too Honest?").

You should also give strong consideration to developing a common "scorecard" approach to standardize the evaluation process. Do not force the client or agency to reinvent the wheel when evaluating every effort that goes out the door. Establish some internal benchmarks and key areas to look at and measure for effectiveness. The existing database and historical knowledge will point out any glaring problems. No "spin" should come into play on these factors; because they should be tightly measured data points that are not open to "interpretation," they will be facts (such as unit sales, consumer impressions, brand awareness, samples distributed, sales velocity, increased retail support, and so on).

Personally, I prefer to have an independent third party be the gatekeeper of performance results. On a traditional promotional effort, the fulfillment agency (who has no vested interest in the creative execution) provides data on entries and provides feedback on what worked successfully to drive involvement and what did not. In an advertising campaign, I prefer to use an outside firm to track consumer awareness levels and ad likability scores. When all the results come in, it is time to sit down and address the changes required for improvement in the next phase.

When the outcomes are manipulated, it is hard to make an "apples to apples" comparison across programs; you do not know which areas were artificially inflated and which were a truthful reflection of the work. For this reason alone, you need to keep the post-evaluation straightforward. When it is all said and done, most marketers are going to look at the sales results for the given time period a campaign or program was in-market and let those numbers be the judge and jury of success.

JASON MILETSKY
THE AGENCY PERSPECTIVE

We wouldn't be human if we didn't try to spin failed efforts to look more positive. But agencies haven't exactly cornered the market on this practice. I think putting bad news in the best possible light is as human as gasping for breath when there's no air left.

Nobody wants to deliver bad news. After all, we all know what happens to the messenger. And the truth is, there's always some good news to find in any situation. It's natural to try to fluff that up a bit or somehow cushion the blow before dropping the ax. I often tell my business partner that something we need to buy will cost $4,000 just to let her freak out about it a bit. She then feels a lot better when I tell her the actual cost is only $2,500, which suddenly doesn't sound so bad. We've all done that in one variation or another.

The real question is whether this spin has any kind of effect on evaluating whether a marketing effort has been successful. As long as no false information is being presented (there's absolutely no excuse for an agency to inflate numbers that they may have access to, like Web traffic analytics), then no, I don't believe that spinning news in a more positive light will diminish anyone's ability to accurately evaluate the success of a campaign. But—and this is a big but—that success must be measured in the right way. In other parts of this book, I've made it clear that I believe all goals should be based on realistic numbers—either a percentage increase in consumer recall of the brand, sales, or Web traffic—at the outset of any marketing effort so that everyone is clear on how success will be measured. If you've taken the time to do this (and sadly, many people don't), then the presentation of news won't matter, because the numbers will speak for themselves. Two plus two, no matter how you explain it, will always equal four.

Q: IT'S TIME TO SIGN THE NEXT YEAR OF YOUR AGREEMENT. HOW DO YOU ADDRESS CHANGES IN THE BUSINESS PLAN AND THE TIMEFRAME FOR GETTING THINGS DONE?

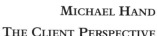

MICHAEL HAND
THE CLIENT PERSPECTIVE

Every year when the agency contract comes up for renewal, the same things happen. First, you agree that this year will be different. You will start the process earlier, and it will go smoothly because everybody wants to make it a priority. Next, you reconcile the hours it took during the previous cycle to get the work done and try to dive deep into the places where you missed your original forecast. Hopefully, you have very few surprises in this conversation because you should be looking at these numbers on a quarterly basis already. However, as a client, I have to laugh a bit here because I have never gone through this reconciliation exercise and found that I "underutilized" my agency partners. In fact, in every case I have "abused the privilege" of having a retainer and unfairly compensated my partner by adding projects to the scope or producing more complex projects that require more time. Yeah, I'm a jerk—I get it.

Flash forward a few weeks and now you are into the conversations regarding the next year's scope and resource (financial and human) allocation. Having just completed the exercise of finding out you overworked the staff and that the recent time frame was beyond maxed out, the client will tell the agency that their hourly forecast for next year needs to come down by 10 percent due to financial reductions at corporate across the board. And get this…we want to add a few more projects that slipped through the cracks at this stage last year. HA! I wish this was a joke, but around small tables in marketing directors' offices around the country this exact conversation is happening every December.

I point out the month of the year to illustrate another point. Both parties involved have likely vowed to get the contract done earlier this year so that the agency does not have payment issues through the first quarter (can't get paid until the contract is signed). Again, the laughter ensues. The contract banter will take place until February on the hours portion, and I have not even started to talk about the involvement of your legal team and the "new" terms and conditions that will need to be shared. Sounds great, doesn't it? Finally, the deal will get done after a few months of stress and a lot of nights losing sleep wondering if the numbers can actually work.

To address changes in the business plan that come up, you need to go back to that point where the 10 percent reduction was requested. The agency needs to stand firm on what can be accomplished, and they need to use historical data to prove it. I suggest that clients and agency partners agree to remove complete projects from the scope of work if they need to "hit a number." The exercise of reducing hours from each individual project will never hold up when the time comes; once the project starts, the agency will be expected to finish it, and it is not likely they will see a favorable hourly closing balance. Both sides also need to remain committed to reviewing the hourly reports on a regular basis to make sure that "scope creep" does not happen over time.

Regarding the time it takes to get the contract done, my advice is to not hold your breath and do your best to remain patient. Corporations are spending a lot of money on the agency resources they retain and will want to get involved in the details. I would suggest negotiating an addendum to extend the existing agreement for three months with an agreement to reconcile over/under payments by April. I hate to sound so negative on the process, but both sides need to be realistic and set expectations far in advance.

JASON MILETSKY

THE AGENCY PERSPECTIVE

Unfortunately, the creative aspect of marketing is only one part of the process. There's also the business part, mired in proposals, negotiations, and contracts. It's the part of the process where both the client and the agency need to walk away from the table feeling like they've each won—the client feeling comfortable that they'll get the work they need accomplished for the money they're spending, and the agency feeling they're getting adequately compensated for their expertise and work.

After the first year, both parties should have a pretty good idea of how much work is really involved with the account, what the deadlines really are, and what value the agency is really bringing to the table. All these can very easily be underestimated before the initial contract is drawn up. Marketing efforts often take twists and turns midstream, and it can be hard to guess how the exact dynamics of a new client/agency relationship will play out. During the process of renewing the contract after the first year, however, it becomes much easier to assess the situation. This is the opportunity for both parties to discuss whether they feel the agreement they have is fair—and if not, what changes need to be made. In the event the business plan on the client side has changed, resulting in the need for new deliverables to match the plan's updated objectives, new fees and a new project plan can be outlined using previous years as the foundation for revisions.

The keys to doing this successfully are for each party to bang out a new contract together with the understanding that they are partners, not adversaries, and to understand what the other is bringing to the table. The client is bringing revenue to the agency, and the agency is providing their experience and unique marketing talents to the client. Neither is easily replaceable, and there is value for each in maintaining a strong relationship. If you are realistic about needs and pricing and enter into a new contract with a mind toward being as fair as possible, both the client and the agency should be able to work through any adjustments in the business plan and new deliverables.

Q: Do You Need to Defend Your Relationship Every Day from Competitive Agencies?

MICHAEL HAND

THE CLIENT PERSPECTIVE

I hate to say it, but, yes. Never turn your back on a competitor, especially in today's marketplace. This is a tough environment for both agencies and clients, and economic indicators show that it will not be getting better anytime soon. Every client is looking for additional ways to save money and secure more efficient spending levels for the work that is delivered. Clients are closely monitoring their own headcount reductions and the need to outsource some of the everyday support functions to which they have grown accustomed. Any edge a brand/product/service can find to win in the market is being sought. Even the client who is very happy with their current relationship will listen to competitive pitches to get some additional insights and ideas on what they could do differently.

New business pitches never stop, and cold calls are becoming an everyday occurrence. From an agency perspective, the new client hunt is more intense than ever. You need to be out hustling to find new opportunities. Think about it, if you are out trying to make things happen with new business development, you can assume the competition will be also. Tools like social media and blogging have quickly become excellent strategies to get an agency's "brand" in front of new faces, and the selling never really stops. It can be expensive to chase new business, but dropping a "general/non-spam" message out regularly for the masses to "get to know you" is never a bad idea. As a client, if your company is fortunate enough to garner any good publicity from its stock market performance or sales figures, you can guarantee that your phone will start ringing with prospective agency partners who attack like sharks when they see blood in the water. Current agencies heed my warning: Defend, defend, defend!

Finally, clients are always looking for ways to consolidate if possible, so remember that the guy you are currently "sharing best practices with" as part of an integrated business model could become the enemy tomorrow. It is always easier for a client to find ways to expand their current business with an existing agency partner than to get a new one; we all know these facts. Think about it:

The guy doing trade promotions on an agency roster today will be looking to exploit his relationships and take over/expand into national promotions and then look to add Web design and potentially advertising. Be prepared.

JASON MILETSKY
THE AGENCY PERSPECTIVE

 Absolutely, but the trick is to defend without being defensive—not an easy task. Agencies have to understand that their clients are constantly being approached by other agencies that are eager to steal them away. It's just the nature of the game—and the larger the client, the more competition there's going to be.

So how does an agency defend against their competition without it negatively affecting their work? The key is to understand the different kinds of competition they'll be facing and how they should effectively respond to each. So as a service to the community, I've assembled a list of each type of competition an agency will face (and you'll face them all), along with the best way of defending yourself from the threat they pose. Trust me, this list alone is worth the price of this book:

- **The Competition: The ongoing threat from unknowns.** Every day, your client gets phone calls, e-mail blasts, direct-mail packages, or other correspondence from other agencies they've never heard of, all trying to set up a meeting to make a case for their services.

- **Your Defense:** Honestly, short of installing a mole as your client contact's admin to intercept mail and phone calls, there's nothing you can do to stop this from happening. Your best—and only—defense is to simply do a great job, stay in constant contact, reinforce the relationship, and do it all consistently. Also, look for ways to "marry" your client into you through back-end Web tools or anything else that would ultimately make it tough to sever ties. Your client doesn't want to interview unknowns, so don't give them a reason to stray.

- **The Competition: The threat of ambush from other retained agencies.** This is one of the most dangerous threats, and agencies need to keep their eyes wide open for both subtle and overt attacks. Most large companies have many agencies working for them. Sometimes their services overlap, sometimes they don't. Often, these agencies are forced to work together on a variety of projects. And while it might seem like everyone is playing nicely together in the sandbox, most of these agencies are looking to either take the work you've been assigned for themselves or pass it on to someone else they would rather work with.

- **Your Defense:** In this situation, you need to play both defense and offense. Defensively, don't give other agencies a chance to call you out to the client. In other words, take extra-special care to make sure there are absolutely no errors in any of your work and that every deadline is hit without going over budget. (If you can come in under budget and look like a hero, even better.) Other agencies on the roster will quickly exploit any errors on your part to make a case against you. At the same time, you have to be on the offensive, playing the same game they are. Keep your eyes open for any opportunities to take work away from them, either for yourself or for partners who you're more confident won't sabotage you. Make subtle references to any mistakes they may have made—especially if you can point out to your client that you were able to keep things on track regardless of their error. It might seem like a dick move, but it's marketing. It has to be competitive before it can be creative.

- **The Competition: Friends or family who suddenly show interest.** This is the area where you'll be most vulnerable. The key decision-maker on the client side has a newly graduated nephew who's gotten a job as a graphic designer at a small agency, and in an effort to show off his worth to his new employers, he calls his brand-manager uncle and asks if he has any work. Brand-manager uncle (your client contact) may only give his nephew's agency a small project, but it's still a project, and it still gives another agency a chance to show their stuff.

- **Your Defense:** First, accept that there's not a whole lot you're going to be able to do to keep this train from moving forward. The best you'll be able to do is slow it down and maybe steer it in a direction where it won't run you over. So the one thing you *shouldn't* try to do is keep your client from passing work on to the agencies their friends or family work for. Instead, try to take the lead role in an effort to contain any potential damage. Chances are, your client is only passing off work out of obligation, but will otherwise consider this a pain in his ass that he'd rather not deal with. Offer to oversee any projects that are given to this other agency. That way, you can keep their role limited and keep their interaction with your client closely guarded.

- **The Competition: The wandering eye of the squeaky wheel.** If you're working with a larger client—or any client where there happen to be a lot of people involved in making marketing decisions—then you're most likely going to have a squeaky wheel in the crowd—a person who doesn't want to work with you. Maybe he or she voted against you during the hiring process and was ignored. Maybe that person has his or her own favorite agency and wants to bring them in, and you're blocking the way. Or maybe he or she just really can't stand the person who hired you and would love to see you fail just to watch his or her co-worker crash and burn along with you. Whatever the reason, this person will most likely exist, and he or she will be waiting for any opportunity to undermine your work.

- **Your Defense:** The first thing you have to do is identify this individual. This person will be easy to notice; he or she is the one who'll sit in meetings with arms folded, arguing against pretty much every point you make. One way or another, this person will make himself or herself known. Once you've identified the squeaky wheel, take a three-pronged approach. First, make sure you keep him or her involved in communications as much as you can, and always double-check any work that he or she will see. If you're going to make a mistake, don't make it in front of this person; don't give him or her a reason to make waves. Second, call him or her out to your main contact. I don't mean you should take a Cindy Brady tattletale approach; I'm just saying that at some point, when you have some alone time with your main contact, you should casually ask about the squeaky wheel. Mention that you get the sense that he or she may not be on board with working with your agency. Chances are your contact will already know about it and will tell you why, but if not, bringing it to his or her attention will help negate any complaints the squeaky wheel may lodge about you. Lastly, do what you can to be friends with the squeaky wheel. Take him or her out to a lunch, or just pull him or her aside after a meeting and ask what he or she specifically would like to see as part of the marketing efforts. If you make the squeaky wheel feel like you're interested in including his or her ideas, he or she will be less likely to undermine your work.

- **The Competition: The threat of mutiny among the crew.** If you have one or two people who have formed a strong, ongoing relationship with the client over a long period of time, there's always the threat that these employees could leave to join a competitor or go and start their own agency, bringing the client with them.

- **Your Defense:** Don't rely on client contracts to keep the client with you; they'll find a way out of them. And *definitely* don't let a non-compete agreement signed by your employees lull you into a false sense of security; they're notoriously tough to enforce and expensive to defend legally. The best way to defend against this is to spread the wealth a little. Make sure multiple people at the agency have made connections with numerous people on the client side, making it harder for them to break away. Also, if you're a manager or an agency owner, it wouldn't hurt you to treat your employees well and make sure they feel appreciated; that way they'll be less inclined to leave you in the first place.

Q: • WHEN IS IT TIME TO END THE
• RELATIONSHIP AND MOVE ON?

MICHAEL HAND
THE CLIENT PERSPECTIVE

Ending a relationship, especially one that has been long-standing, is never an easy thing to do. The marketplace is filled with business challenges, and for an agency, the new business development area is ultra-competitive right now. Agencies need to work a lot harder to gain new business than they do to maintain the business that they currently have, so ending anything can be a bitter pill to swallow, assuming the client pays you on time and treats you with respect. Sitting on the client side of the equation is not much different, but you certainly have a little more of the "control" on your side when deciding whether or not to keep the relationship moving forward. The motivating factor that drives the decision to end a client/agency relationship is not much different than the motivating factor to end any relationship in your life. Issues such as trust, ability to get done what is agreed upon in scope, faith in delivering strong results/new thinking, and the ability to grow together as partners stand out in this list.

Both parties involved in any partnership must compromise and trust one another in order to succeed. Success comes from both parties doing their best for the sake of the business and checking egos at the door. If one of the partners is not committed to delivering their best, then the other partner should consider moving on. Both financial and human resources are involved in this equation and neither should be wasted when things have started to fall apart. The more drawn out the process, the harder it will be to end on good terms. Be fair, be realistic, and try to avoid surprises. Nobody wants to read an article in a trade publication to find out their job is in jeopardy. In addition, if you are looking to "fire" the client, you better make sure you have delivered solid results before parting ways. You can agree to disagree, but you need to be working to drive results at all times and outsiders will see right through an agency resignation when the work has not been up to par.

When the decision is made that you should part ways, the situation needs to be handled professionally and with tact. Just like a personal "break up," the following considerations must be given.

- **Don't do it over the phone.** As a client, you need to conduct the conversation yourself, and you should have the conversation in person. Your business partner should never be shocked by news like this, assuming you have already been putting plans in place to rectify existing concerns, but you need to respect their feelings and hear any additional issues.

- **Pick an appropriate place for the conversation.** You need to pick a place where feelings can be expressed openly and candidly; this will likely not be an easy chat. You owe the agency an opportunity to talk about why you are letting them go (or to tell the client why you are resigning the account). Making the agency travel in for the "break up" is also wrong.

- **Schedule a time to reconnect.** People need time to process the finality of a relationship conclusion, so schedule a time to follow up within 48 hours to discuss anything else that may have surfaced. Hearing bad news and having a constructive discussion about it can provide a great learning experience for both partners. When the conversation concludes, wish your counterpart good luck with their business—and mean it.

- **Stick with your decision.** It is easy to second guess yourself when things start off with difficulty between you and your new partner, but remember that you parted ways with the old crew for a reason. It is easy to fall back into your old routine, but stay committed to charting a new path.

- **Do not burn bridges.** Do not diminish any one person's character and always remember that the world is small; it is likely you will cross paths again. Sometime down the line, your commitment to ending things in a respectable way will pay off.

JASON MILETSKY
THE AGENCY PERSPECTIVE

Ideally, never. But being more of a realist than an idealist, I know that "never" might be little long. Personally, I've been a bit spoiled in my agency career. We have clients that have been with us for the better part of a decade and our relationship is still going strong. But I think—I'm not positive, so don't quote me—that the average client/agency relationship lasts about three years.

In most cases, the end of a relationship is going to come from the client, not the agency. The loss of a client means the loss of revenue, which could mean having to let good employees go. So it takes a pretty extreme situation for the agency to cut ties. I can only think of a few instances where this might occur:

- **The client is just a complete dick, and prone to verbally abusing agency employees:** Personally, I can take it. Say what you want to me if it makes you feel better, and we can all move on and get back to work. But as I mentioned in my answer to Question #2, "What Makes a Client a Good Client?" the first time a client verbally abuses one of my employees and attacks them personally will pretty much be the last time that client gets any work done by my agency. I don't care how much value you bring. There's never an excuse for behaving like that.

- **They take forever to pay their bills:** If they're 30 days late now and then, fine. It's not great, but it's okay. But if they're 90 days overdue on a regular basis, there's only so much of that we can take before we decide it's just not worth having to chase them down and wondering whether they're ever going to pay us.

- **The client wants to increase our responsibilities but decrease the budget:** I'm not sure this needs much of an explanation....

I can't speak for the client (which is why I'm writing my side of this book from the agency perspective), but I can name at least some reasons why a client would decide to end a relationship:

- They're just not happy with the work that was done or the results that were ultimately achieved.

- They feel like they've been the victims of a bait-and-switch, where the A-team came in and made the pitch but the C-team was assigned to the account after the contract was signed.

- The agency does a crappy job of communicating with the client.

- A team the client likes is changing—for example, some key people on the agency side have resigned—opening the door for the client to search for a new agency.

- A new marketing director is hired on the client side and wants to bring in his or her own favorite agency.

Personally, it doesn't matter if it's tennis, chess, or clients: I hate to lose. Losing clients is inevitable, but that doesn't mean anyone on the agency side has to like it—and it certainly doesn't mean there isn't room to try to keep it from happening. If it's an account the agency wants to keep, part of the agency's job is to look for red flags along the way and keep the relationship going as long as possible.

Q: CAN WE REALLY DETERMINE AN ROI?

MICHAEL HAND

THE CLIENT PERSPECTIVE

Of all the questions being bantered about in the halls of major corporations across America, this one seems to be getting the most attention lately. Marketing is fast becoming a results-driven department within the broader corporate structure. The days of going on guts and instinct are no longer acceptable to the corner office. Executives are looking for answers to the age old question of how a program has performed in the past and how they can predict the future by selecting only the projects that will net the best results. Marketing teams are huddling with sales teams and then bringing in their research groups to banter about a number of approaches that will deliver the figures in question. Simply put, everybody wants to be more profitable and everybody wants to pick the right elements of the marketing mix to drive that end result. I can tell you firsthand that every person has developed some metric that works for them, but in totality these metrics are flawed and can be challenged in many ways. Problem is, chief executive officers and chief financial officers will not rest until they have an effective indicator.

Based on the medium, some analytics are further developed than others. For example, your larger CPG companies likely have formulas in their database where they can plug in total distribution/reach and timing information on a free standing insert (FSI) to get a sense of what the redemption rates will be. They can take that purchase rate and compare it to like periods in previous years and decipher what is "incremental volume" as opposed to standard rate of purchase and traffic on a given item. Newspaper ads and direct mail campaigns can probably be looked at in a similar way. When I worked at General Motors, we knew exactly what kind of volume we could deliver when we dropped a direct mail offer customized for a specific audience. When the monthly numbers looked in jeopardy, we knew we could look at folks with leases expiring in the coming three months, offer each of them "bonus cash" to pull ahead the purchase decision, and bank the net sales at a certain percentage rate. This was never a cheap proposition because it took a broad reach to net stronger results, but we dusted off the tactic at least three times a year for our older models in the lineup.

Other areas of the marketing mix are a lot more "squishy" when it comes to measuring results. The process of calculating an ROI is more art than it is science and has left many puzzled and seeking better data. Big corporations run advertising all the time, and it tends to be the largest line item in most teams' budgets, but are they effectively measuring the return on investment on this major brand awareness driver? The bigger question that needs to be solved is whether "extra sales now" is really the basis for determining an ROI. Consideration needs to be given to the profit margin versus the sales price and certainly some credit should be given to the long-term impact/value that a customer can provide if he becomes a loyalist in the process.

Fundamentally, I think the ROI debate is flawed. Consumers do not live in a bubble, and they are not exposed to only one part of your marketing mix; they interact with your brand all the time and are impacted by a multitude of those messages. You can focus an effort through one medium, but the influence of all the components is what drives your return on investment. Bottom line, ROI is more than a process of doing math; its calculation is an important spoke in the marketing wheel that needs to be rooted in strategic insights and development. It will drive a results-oriented mindset and get employees talking to each other.

JASON MILETSKY
THE AGENCY PERSPECTIVE

It's not just possible, it's necessary. A lot of people outside of the industry think that marketing is all about being creative and coming up with new ideas. (I love it when I tell someone about an account I'm working on and they respond by saying, "Hey, I have a great slogan for that company," because of course my job is just that easy and all it really takes is a great *slogan*. Ugh.) People don't realize that behind the fun, creative part, there are numbers, statistics, and goals. If you don't determine whether you've achieved a positive ROI, marketing efforts become just haphazard and random.

As far as I'm concerned, when it comes to marketing a brand, nothing of any significance should be done without knowing *why* it's being done and what the specific numeric goals are. Campaigns take time and money, and represent the brand's opportunity to speak to its market. If mistakes are made, then these opportunities might be missed. The market might not be reached, competition could gain market share, or even worse, the wrong campaign could damage the brand. One way or another, every campaign effort needs to be measured.

The important thing is to set the right goals. Brand campaigns, for example, aren't necessarily meant to generate sales—at least, not directly. They're meant to penetrate the minds of the market and keep the audience constantly aware of the brand so that its promise and personality are increasingly recognizable and they instantly understand what to expect from the brand (even if they've never had direct contact with it personally).

Because the purpose of a brand campaign is to generate awareness, basing goals on increased sales is probably not the best way to measure success. Building exposure and trust in a brand takes time. The more consumers are exposed to a brand, the more they'll start to trust it, which will eventually lead to increased sales—but it's not going to happen overnight. Plus, there are other things that need to be considered when setting goals, such as the role that sales people, store designers, and other factors play. An aggressive brand campaign may get people through the door, but after that it's up to the brand to make the sale.

Instead, the best way to measure a brand campaign is to base goals on something that is needed and that the campaign can realistically accomplish. Getting more people through the doors of a retail store is a good goal, as is getting more people to visit a Web site. (Each of these, and other goals like them, should have hard numbers attached. I'm just using "Get more people through the door" for illustrative purposes.) An even better goal is to base success on brand exposure and perception among the target market, measured through exacting pre- and post-campaign research.

Q: BRAND RECOGNITION AND CUSTOMER SENTIMENT HAVE IMPROVED, BUT SALES HAVEN'T. IS THE CAMPAIGN STILL A SUCCESS?

MICHAEL HAND

THE CLIENT PERSPECTIVE

I wish I could say the answer to this question is yes, but I cannot. Every brand/product/service wants to see their brand recognition and customer sentiment increase; these are strong measures of a brand's health. The problem is that we work within a business model that is 100 percent focused on delivering business results—and that means more sales. Even with the strongest insights and message structure, if sales results are not coming along for the ride, then you will need to look for an alternate way to deliver the campaign. The exception to this hard and fast judgment would be if different expectations were set as part of the objectives development from the start.

Ad agencies should always set targets in advance and sign up for the "agreed upon" goals in the creative brief (it is highly unlikely you will ever get to change the goals, but you should debate if needed). Without goals and objectives, both agencies and clients can lean on trivial facts like the poor weather or incompetent training staff for the lack in sales volume. Both agency and client need to agree on a vision for success, with the client saying in clear and concise terms, "This is what we want to achieve." When goals are signed off on, you have established accountability for both sides to deliver against. You can also monitor results on a regular basis, as opposed to waiting for the end of the year to find out if you passed or failed.

The fact remains: Great brand-building ads that make consumers feel good about your products do not always result in double-digit sales growth. The product itself needs to be great, the product needs to have a strong presence at retail, and you need to stay committed to investing in it. These are the ways to ensure long-term sales health. Building recognition is good, increasing sentiment is even better, but they mean nothing without sales volume.

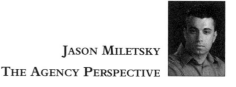

JASON MILETSKY

THE AGENCY PERSPECTIVE

Maybe, maybe not. Ultimately, yes, revenue needs to be generated and brand building campaigns need to contribute to that. But just because the needle doesn't move and the cash register isn't ringing doesn't mean anyone should suddenly conclude that the campaign crashed and burned. There are a few variables that need to be considered before that determination can be made:

- **What were the pre-established goals of the campaign?** If the goals that everyone agreed on prior to execution were to increase sales, then no, the campaign did not succeed if sales have stayed flat. But there are other goals to shoot for that might not be revenue-based. Maybe the goal was to increase brand recognition, or to improve consumers' perception of the brand, or to successfully and smoothly introduce a new brand look and feel. Success for these types of goals would more likely be measured by comparing pre-campaign market research with post-campaign market research, and may receive a stamp of approval without even looking at sales figures.

- **Has the brand been pulling its weight?** The agency can only market the brand. We can't fulfill the brand promise. Any problems a company faces that might be harming their brand and negatively affecting consumer sentiment could be too powerful a deterrent for even the best marketing to overcome. (But don't pay too much attention to this bullet point; it flies in the face of the "blame the agency" route that brands are famous for taking when things go wrong.)

- **Is there are a secondary component that's not being considered properly?** I once had a client who was unhappy with us because they got very few new leads from a brand campaign that we developed for them. In response, we pointed out that throughout the campaign, traffic to their Web site had increased significantly—and we had recommended from the beginning that they improve their site (which was developed by another agency before we were retained, and was truly awful). So it's entirely possible that the campaign worked but the Web site failed.

- **Is there a human component that's failing to do its job?** If you run a B2B direct-mail campaign, but the salespeople who call recipients afterward screw up on the phone, that's not the campaign's fault; it's the salespeople's. Similarly, a marketing campaign could increase traffic to a retail store, but if the cashiers are unfriendly or the selection is weak or the store is dirty? Well, those problems will contribute to poor sales, but be completely unrelated to any campaign effort.

Of course, flat sales could also be the result of a poor campaign. Believe me, I'm not saying the agency can't be at fault or that the campaign may not be effective. I'm just saying you may need to be consider other reasons before any final judgment is made.

PART FIVE
Just for Fun

Q: • IS SUPER BOWL ADVERTISING • WORTH THE MONEY?

JASON MILETSKY
THE AGENCY PERSPECTIVE

It's the largest audience in the world for a single telecast, typically tripling the obscene number of people who tune in for the *American Idol* finale. It gets a cross-section of sports fans and people who just want to be part of the festivities. Men, women, and children watch it. Maybe most importantly, ever since Apple's *1984* watershed commercial had its one and only TV airing during the Super Bowl, the game has become the single annual instance when people watch TV as much for the commercials as they do for the game itself. Indeed, in most cases, people are still talking about the commercials days after they've stopped talking about the game. And don't forget about the amazing amount of media attention and publicity they receive in the weeks before and after the game. Plus, the commercials will be seen on the Web for a long time afterward.

So all the pieces are there. If a 30-second spot cost a dollar, then there's no question about its worth. The question of worth only comes up here because of the extreme price, which is closing in on the $3 million mark for half a minute—and this doesn't include the production costs, which can be tremendous; people expect the best during the Super Bowl. But the cost for the spots is where it is because of basic free-market economics; it's the point where supply meets demand.

Not every brand can afford this kind of price tag, and even though there have been instances when entire brands have been launched from the Super Bowl, like Monster.com, it can be a crap shoot. Considering the fact that consumers have easy access to funny and shocking video clips through social media, I'm doubtful that I'd recommend any brand with a very limited budget overextend themselves and gamble on a one-shot deal. It's a lot harder to be memorable today than it used to be, so if you blow it, you're screwed.

But it's hard to argue with the numbers. According to *AdvertisingAge* magazine, the results that some brands have seen have just been outrageous. After one Super Bowl, CareerBuilder saw an increase in job applications by 68 percent; Audi increased Web traffic by 200 percent for a full month after the game; E-Trade increased new, funded accounts by 32 percent a week after the game; and GoDaddy.com points to the Super Bowl (where it has advertised since 2005) for its rise from 16 percent market share to an astonishing 46 percent worldwide.

I'm sure there are painful stories as well, where Super Bowl advertising ended up failing and harming the brand. My guess would be that in those cases, the business model or the commercial itself was more to blame than the venue. There's no stage in the world that's better for marketers to reach their audience. So for larger brands and brands that have the capital, there is absolutely a sound argument that can be made for Super Bowl spots being worth the money.

MICHAEL HAND

THE CLIENT PERSPECTIVE

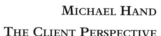 Super Bowl I aired on two networks in 1967, where they charged an average rate of $40,000 for a 30-second spot that was seen by more than 50 million combined viewers. Flash forward to 2008, and the average rate, according to Nielsen Media Research, jumped to a rather staggering $2.7 million per 30 seconds to hit more than 97 million viewers on an early Sunday evening. I know it sounds like a lot of cash (well, it more than sounds like it—it is a lot of cash), but the reality is that the Super Bowl could be one of the best bargains in media. No, I am not doing drugs and I am not on prescription medication while crafting this response. The fact remains that no other television broadcast commands as much dedicated attention in sheer viewers and ancillary coverage of the commercials as the Super Bowl.

The Super Bowl not only provides a solid platform of total viewership, it provides one of the only venues that I can think of where people will literally tune in just for the ads. For football fans and non-football fans alike, the Super Bowl has become an "unofficial" holiday in America, with consumers spending outrageously to host parties and eat guacamole like avocados were going away forever. In fact, beer manufacturers rank Super Bowl weekend as the top selling beer occasion outside the Memorial Day to Labor Day window. The action on the field is certainly important, but shows like *Today* and *Good Morning America* feature stories just about the ads, Web-site traffic increases tremendously, and water cooler talk is at fever pitch. The talk is split between conversations on zone blitz defenses and chats about the celebrity appearing in an ad for an insurance company.

Ads in the Big Game can certainly bolster the presence of industry leaders, but it can also be a great venue to build brand awareness overnight for a new company or product. The game remains a strategic play for companies like godaddy.com and E-trade who are trying to build their Web-based businesses in a challenging economy. It can also be used by a division within a company, like Volvo Trucks, who historically spent almost their entire annual marketing budget for one ad in the game to keep their name in the consideration set with their target market.

In January 2009, *AdAge* revealed a series of mind-blowing figures related to recent Super Bowl ad placements: a few highlights include the following:

- After the 2008 game, Cars.com saw brand awareness increase 12 percent, Audi saw web traffic increase 200 percent in the first 30 days post-game, and CareerBuilder.com saw a 68 percent surge over the three months that followed a comical ad featuring monkeys in an office setting.

- Go Daddy, who ran some "revealing" content featuring race car driver Danica Patrick, received more than $11.5 million in free publicity after having the original ad rejected for sexual content by the censorship board.

- Beer behemoth Anheuser-Busch garnered 21 million online views of their ads within the first week of the game.

From these facts alone, I stand behind my statement that Super Bowl advertising is worth every penny (just don't run a crappy ad).

Q: • What Is the Best Viral
• Campaign Ever Run?

Jason Miletsky
The Agency Perspective

The concept of a viral campaign is that the marketing gets done by enticing people to pass the campaign around to their friends, co-workers, and family. This is usually done through e-mail. By and large, these campaigns don't amount to anything more than a one-off video of something silly that makes the rounds for a couple of days and then is quickly forgotten.

Personally, I like viral campaigns that have more creativity and are developed around an actual concept. There are a few that spring to mind, but only one that I have referenced over and over again when I discuss the power of going viral: Burger King's "Subservient Chicken" Web site, which I mentioned in my answer to Question #55, "How Powerful Is Viral Marketing? Can Viral Marketing Be a Planned Effort, Given That It Relies So Heavily on Consumer Involvement?"

The site (SubservientChicken.com—check it out; it's still up and running) features a plain black background with a single video area in the center and text box below it. The video shows a guy in a chicken suit standing in the middle of a living room. Visitors can tell the guy what to do by typing their command in the text field. So if you type, "Do five jumping jacks," the guy will do five jumping jacks and wait for the next request. The people who created the site did a really great job—they basically thought of and filmed everything people could possibly tell a guy in a chicken suit alone in a room to do, logged it all in a database, and the site pulls the right clip based on keywords used in the visitor's text. And you know what? It's crazy addictive. The first time I was there, I must have spent close to an hour making this guy do stuff. And I must have sent the link on to at least five other people (and I'm being conservative in that estimate). Clearly I wasn't the only one anxious to pass the site around; the numbers have become legendary. Within a week, the site had more than 20 million visitors.

What I really like about this campaign is that it was fun and viral, but with a point. Making the guy do whatever you want underscores Burger King's long-standing "Have It Your Way" theme while introducing a new line of chicken products. The campaign became so well known that it morphed into a second round of creative, in which two guys in chicken suits had a staged fight on DirecTV. For me, nothing on the viral side of life has come close to being as memorable at BK's SubservientChicken.com effort.

MICHAEL HAND
THE CLIENT PERSPECTIVE

I feel a bit pathetic admitting this, but I struggled to think of any outstanding viral campaigns when I first read this question. My counterpart probably has a million references on this one, but unfortunately I was at a bit of a loss. I tend to think of viral campaigns as in-and-out activity, and in most cases, it does not show up on my radar screen. They might drive a program spike, but the Web-based nature of the program does not stand out in my mind.

The one viral program that does come to me was an entry I was going to submit for the best single ad of all time question earlier (in fact, I had written it there and moved it here when I saw this follow-up question). Carlton Draught's "Big Ad" was an award winning television ad that did an awesome job of ridiculing the blockbuster, cinematic commercials that companies have been pushing for the past decade. But when I thought about it more and then did some high-level research, the online facts show that a viral push is what drove its awareness and created its pass along. What sparked it for me was the fact that I never saw the ad on television, it was passed on from a co-worker. In the ad, what appear to be two rival armies (one in red and one in yellow) march toward each other in what looks like a movie scene directly lifted from the *Braveheart;* I actually expected to see Mel Gibson pop onto the screen. The armies sing in an opera-esque manner with lyrics such as "It's a big ad, it's so freaking—HUGE." The visual composition of the armies ends up forming a glass of beer and a human body, with the beer eventually going down the body's throat as robed men dance in jubilation.

According to information that I was able to find after the fact, the ad was distributed via the Internet two weeks prior to being made available for the television networks. Just 24 hours after the ad's release, the "Big Ad" had been downloaded 162,000 times, and within two weeks it had been seen by more than one million viewers in 132 countries. The viral release was so successful that the television media budget was reduced for fears the ad would be overexposed (source: Times Online-UK, 7/25/07). By all definitions of success, this viral campaign truly was "big."

Q: WHAT IS THE BEST USE OF ATHLETE OR CELEBRITY ENDORSEMENT?

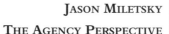

JASON MILETSKY

THE AGENCY PERSPECTIVE

Well, the guy in me immediately wants to give the nod to Maria Sharapova for her endorsement of…well, just about anything. Who cares? She's just amazing to look at. But base-male tendencies aside, I have scoured my mind for what I really think would qualify as "the best." I considered Pepsi's use of Michael Jackson back in the day, some of the work Nike did with Tiger Woods (much better, by the way, than how Accenture uses Tiger Woods), and even the classic Coke ad with Mean Joe Greene giving his jersey to the kid after the game. But no matter what I thought about, I kept coming back to one campaign.

I know what the answer *should* be, by the way. The answer should be Nike's use of Michael Jordan back when they unveiled their Air Jordan line. If there was ever proof that aligning your brand with a celebrity could work, this was it. But based on creativity and just pure fun, I gotta go with McDonald's "Nothin' But Net" campaign. This classic campaign, which first appeared during the Super Bowl in the early 1990s, featured Michael Jordan and Larry Bird (who were both still active NBA players at the time) playing a game of H-O-R-S-E, with the winner receiving a Big Mac. The two basketball stars (who were also pretty good actors in their own right) started off in a gymnasium, calling their own shots, ending each by saying "Nothin' but net." The shots were fairly easy at first (well, easy for them) but got increasingly difficult until they were standing on top of a skyscraper, still shooting into the same basket in the gym, and still making every shot. It was funny, and played on the amazing dominance of Jordan and Bird—you almost believed they really could make those shots! The campaign kind of fell apart when Charles Barkley joined the cast, but seeing Jordan and Bird playing off each other? That's got to be a slam dunk. (Sorry for the cheesy ending.)

MICHAEL HAND

THE CLIENT PERSPECTIVE

Many people question using athletes or celebrities to endorse a brand, fearing the brand will not form its own identity and simply become nothing more than an extension of the spokesperson or simply draft off of their equity base. I can understand this thought process; however, I feel differently about the practice. As long as the balance of brand to celebrity is carefully crafted with the brand still the star, then it can work. If you have a brand that is looking to become more contemporary or have a role in pop culture, the connection to the cachet of sports and entertainment is something that not many other placements will provide you. This tactic can also be highly successful in providing disruption value with viewers, as many television audiences are enamored with famous people.

You need to be careful and make sure that no matter how big the "celebrity name," you do thorough research into their background and make sure they will be a strong fit with your primary target audience. Many times you get an anxious director or vice president who wants to just get the deal done and does not bother to conduct a detailed background check. Endorsing a product launch with a celebrity can be destroyed very quickly if the celebrity ends up on the news for beating his girlfriend or doing something else that is equally offensive—you need to have a plan B to resolve such an issue quickly.

You also need to make sure that you select a celebrity to work with who is not overexposed. He or she needs to drive value incrementally and ensure that the advertising does not simply blend into the background noise. It is assumed most of these guys will endorse anything to cash a paycheck (and some will); you need to find the right one.

This leads to a few of my favorite endorsement relationships. First, I absolutely love William Shatner's work for Priceline. Shatner has become the James Bond of budget travel with his quirky motions and odd facial expressions. He has made it fun to find a "good travel deal" and the persona plays off the brand's image in a very complementary way.

My other favorites include

- Michael Jordan for Nike—it is hard to avoid a reference to the guy whose entire image was defined by a dunk from the free throw line in a pair of shoes named after him. Jordan went on to multiple deals (McDonald's, Rayovac batteries, and Hanes to name a few), but he will always be seen as a Nike guy first.

- John Madden has taken his position as a football expert and found a way to turn it into gold. His endorsement and name entitlement of EA Sports professional football title is the most sought after gaming experience every year; not bad for a guy in his 70s and perfect for a company that wants to have a little attitude and free spirit.

Q: • WHAT IS THE BEST SINGLE
• AD EVER PRODUCED?

JASON MILETSKY
THE AGENCY PERSPECTIVE

I'm going to admit something that nobody in advertising is supposed to admit—at least, not out loud. I didn't like Apple's *1984* spot. I know it put them on the map, and I know all the stats that prove how effective it was, and I know that it's sacrilegious to say anything negative about it. After all, there are certain things you're supposed to just accept in life: Led Zeppelin's *Stairway to Heaven* is the greatest song ever written, *The Godfather* is the greatest movie ever made, and Apple's *1984* is the single greatest commercial ever produced. But I'm sorry, I just don't dig it. It's good and well-produced for its time, but it just isn't what everyone seems to make it out to be.

So what *do* I consider the best single ad to be? I came up with two that I had a hard time deciding between, but finally decided that I had to name one the winner. So first, the runner up: Honda's "Cog" spot. I'm not going to spend a lot of time describing this spot. I can't do it justice. But I definitely recommend you check it out on YouTube. Basically, it's like the old game of Mousetrap or a series of dominoes set up to fall over. Starting with a simple gear rolling down a plank, a chain reaction made up of car parts is set in motion until the reveal at the end shows a fully assembled Honda, accompanied by a voiceover that asks, "Isn't it nice when things just...work?" It's a full two minutes, and it's addicting to watch—there's just no way to watch it only halfway through. It's fun, engaging, and well worth the payoff at the end.

I know I didn't do the "Cog" spot enough credit, but if you think I undersold that, there is absolutely no way I can do justice to what I consider to be the best ad ever made: Campbell Soup's "Foster Child" spot. It's been a long time since I've seen it, so I may have some of the details wrong, but basically the spot opens with a social worker standing with a small girl on the porch of what will be the girl's new home. The child, clutching a teddy bear, looks sad and scared. The foster mother answers the door and tries to talk to the girl, but the child won't respond. Before leaving, the social worker tries to reassure the dispirited foster mom that the little girl will come around; she just needs time. So the foster mom goes to the kitchen and makes a bowl of Campbell's soup, which she takes to the little girl in her room, hoping to create some sort of connection. But the little girl still won't look at her; she just clings to her teddy bear even more tightly. Completely dejected, the foster mom turns to leave. She's one foot out the door when the little girl says, "My mommy used to fix me this soup."

Are they fucking *kidding* me? Seriously—I didn't shed a tear at the end of *Love Story*. In fact, the only time I've ever gotten teary at a movie was at the end of *Rudy*. But there I was, all watery-eyed at the end of a 30-second commercial. Unreal. Campbell's did an amazing job tapping into a powerful emotion. (By the way, if the spot sounds depressing, it really isn't. There's a nice payoff at the very end, where the foster mother, fighting back tears, answers, "My mother used to make it for me, too," and the foster mom and little girl bond. But my eyes stop being dry as soon as the little girl delivers her line.) My hat goes off to anybody who can evoke an emotion out of me in only 30 seconds.

MICHAEL HAND

THE CLIENT PERSPECTIVE

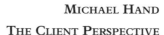 Most of the best known advertising critics will say without any hesitation that the best television ad ever produced was "1984," which introduced Americans to the Apple Macintosh computer for the first time. It had everything that a big ad needs to get your attention: It was in the Super Bowl, it was directed by a high-powered Hollywood movie team (led by Ridley Scott), and it had both tremendous drama and hype. To make this ad even more special, it never appeared on television again after this event.

The storyline provided depth of character with its direct link to the George Orwell novel of the same name, where Big Brother is watching every move and forcing (practically celebrating) social conformity. The overcast industrial setting set the tone as the heroine of the spot—an Olympian-like female runner—entered the scene carrying an oversized hammer. While she is chased by faceless people in black uniforms, Big Brother rambles on about the need to stick with the status quo—until she launches her hammer into the Big Brother master screen and destroys it. Peace is restored and people are free to express themselves openly.

The commercial concludes with an introduction date on the screen and the phrase "You'll see why 1984 won't be like 1984." Powerful stuff. I can imagine the guys around the chips and dip looking up and saying "Holy Crap!" while another turns to his buddy with a glazed look and says, "What just happened?" Not many ads can get that type of reaction. Unlike the critics, I will not call it the best ever; but I will give it mention on my short list.

As I thought harder about this question, a few favorites came to my mind:

- **"Aaron Burr"—Got Milk? campaign.** How great is this ad? As a functional message it portrays the product (milk) as hero that is just out of reach. You watch in pain (granted you are laughing through the pain) for this guy surrounded by the contest trivia answer and unable to speak. I guess we should all have milk on hand for such an occasion.

- **"Frogs"—Budweiser.** I am not the biggest fan of the product portfolio coming out of the St. Louis brewery (my Milwaukee connection runs deep), but you need to hand it to these guys. They have made some classic ads and this is one of the best. All young adult male consumers (and even some awkward older ones) were croaking their brand name in bars across the globe. It is a smart ad, and high on my list next to the first two Bud Bowl events.

- **"When I Grow Up"—Monster.** Every day people go home from work and feel sorry for themselves because aspects of their jobs suck. This ad took all the inner thoughts running through their heads and made them public. It was suddenly OK to be looking for more than "middle management." Best part, they used kids to tell the story of what they had to look forward to. Very funny, but also a very powerful statement.

- **"If You Let Me Play"—Nike.** This is another great use of kids to tell a story, albeit a more emotional one. I'm not sure I truly appreciated this ad before I had a daughter of my own, but it certainly hits home now. For all the testosterone that Nike throws around and athlete endorsement money they spend, this is the best I have seen from the Portland office.

Q: WHAT IS THE WORST CAMPAIGN EVER RUN?

JASON MILETSKY

THE AGENCY PERSPECTIVE

This is a particularly tough question to answer, because the really bad campaigns probably proved so awful that they disappeared before they ever seeped into our consciousness at all. So I'm sure there are some I should be considering that just aren't coming to me. But I have to admit, as soon as I read this question, there was one huge campaign that immediately came to mind.

First, though, I want to briefly nominate a runner up for worst campaign: Microsoft's "I'm a PC" campaign. Okay, maybe this isn't *so* terrible that it deserves to be listed as one of the worst ever, but it's pretty bad, and it was current as I was writing this, so it happened to be top of mind. Why Microsoft, with, like, what, 92 percent market share, would play into Apple's hands and not only further legitimize them, but make them seem even cooler than they already did is just beyond me. Yes, Apple's "I'm a Mac" campaign brilliantly made themselves look like the choice of the young, hip, and cool while making PCs look like the choice of *Dungeon & Dragons* players everywhere. But Microsoft would have been far better off countering with their own unique campaign than trying to use Apple's own creative against them. Maybe it worked (I haven't seen any numbers that prove success or failure), but to me it looked a little like Microsoft was a pouty child who had gotten his feelings hurt. At the very least, if they were determined to go that route, they should have done a better job at their messaging. Of all the people looking proudly into the camera saying, "I'm a PC," none of them were nearly as cool as the dude who plays the Apple in the "I'm a Mac" ads. Seriously, what was with the guy who said, "I'm a PC, and I'm a human being. Not a human doing, not a human thinking, a human being." What the hell can that possibly mean? I think I'd rather be a Mac, thank you very much.

But that's only the runner-up. Here's my vote for the worst campaign ever: AT&T's mLife campaign. One day, back in late 2002, I was driving to Manhattan. As I approached the Lincoln Tunnel, I passed a billboard that asked, "What is mLife?" (or something like that). That was my first glimpse into a campaign that I immediately knew would play out badly. There was no logo on the billboard or in any of the TV, billboard, or print ads that followed. The Web site also offered few clues—just teasers leading up to a grand reveal during the Super Bowl. Was it a new religion? A new form of yoga? Gee, what could it possibly be? I don't remember the actual Super Bowl commercial in great detail, but the mystery was finally solved: mLife was a far-reaching effort by AT&T to re-brand their wireless services. The "m" stood for "mobile," and mLife was how we were all going to be living in the future.

On one level, I suppose it worked; I've read that immediately after the spot aired, their site logged in close to 700,000 unique visitors, and reports were that the traffic actually overwhelmed the servers and the site was down for a bit. (This could be wrong, but since it doesn't change my opinion of the campaign, I'm not going to bother looking it up.) But it doesn't matter. What was silly about the whole thing was that AT&T and their agency assumed that people had the relative intelligence of an avocado—that we could easily be spoon-fed a new term, would accept it into our vernacular, would refer to mLife in casual conversation with friends, and would basically hand ownership of the letter "m" to AT&T. Please. It was way too heavy-handed and obvious, like someone giving himself a nickname. (Remember the Maestro on *Seinfeld*?) It's not like the iPod, iPhone, or iMac, which are names of products. mLife's biggest problem was with the word "life." It wanted people to refer to their own lifestyles with a brand name. Sorry, not gonna happen. Again, I haven't seen any actual numbers, so I have no official knowledge as to whether this campaign achieved its goals. But considering that the letter "m" still exists, safe and sound in relative freedom from any association with AT&T, I'll make the educated guess that the campaign was a complete failure. I wonder if the people who came up with this ad gem still cringe when they see the relative ease with which Apple took ownership of the letter "i… ."

MICHAEL HAND

THE CLIENT PERSPECTIVE

I always feel a little bad when I vote for the "worst" of anything. Sure, I have an opinion, but I do not really know what the objective of the program was or what went on behind the closed door of a conference room to know if I am being a fair judge. (For example, I know many folks who rip the Buick and Tiger Woods work without knowing the full story or business results.) However, some commercial work just does not appeal to me and simply does not make sense in my mind. With that as a little background, I have selected two campaigns that I flat out do not/did not understand.

First, my vote for the worst ongoing advertising campaign is the Geico Caveman work. I really just think they are stupid ads, and I see absolutely no linkage back to the insurance industry whatsoever. Here is a company with another talking icon (the Geico Gekko) who actually appeals to a broad cross section of people, yet they keep running this idiotic crap. Please tell me that people do not watch these ads and find them amusing; I will need to question America's appreciation for comedy if that is the case. They are not good, and they are not very clever either. What do people see in this? (By the way, who was the person who thought making this into a TV sitcom for ABC was a good idea? I hope people got fired for that ridiculous decision. No surprise that it was cut after only a few episodes —wow!)

The other body of work that I simply did not understand was the work from Quiznos' Subs that featured a creature that looked like a rat as a "mascot." How is showing a singing rat (I now understand it was a "sponge monkey") appeal-ing to people when talking about food? Seriously? Again, somebody approved this ad to go on air. Somebody from the client side thought it was a good idea, and somebody on the agency side actually agreed to present the work. I can visualize the account guy going back and telling the creative team that the client wants to produce their idea, even they must have thought it was a joke. According to comments from Quiznos' management team after the ads were pulled, Web-site traffic was at an all-time high and they reported "mixed" "like-ability" responses with some fans really loving the spots. I can't get over the fact that they were trying to sell me a sub with a rodent; it symbolized all things unsanitary to me and made me run from Quiznos' outlets.

Q: What Is the Best Campaign Ever Run?

What's your perspective on this question?
Let us know at PerspectivesOnMarketing.com.

Jason Miletsky
The Agency Perspective

I *love* great advertising. I really do. And there are so many amazing campaigns that could vie for the title of best ever. The "Got Milk" campaign is clearly a contender, as are the Pepsi Challenge, the Energizer Bunny, Mastercard's "Priceless" campaign, and some of the older, classic efforts like the "Please Don't Squeeze the Charmin" ads with Mr. Whipple or Calgon's "Ancient Chinese Secret" ads. I could go spend the better part of this book just going down the list of all the amazing marketing campaigns I've admired over the years.

Having said all of that, my choice for best ad campaign ever might surprise people. I'm sure I'll get plenty of e-mail or comments on the blog about how ridiculous I'm being. Keep in mind, my choice has nothing to do with results, and it's not about the best single ad ever. So here it goes. My choice for best campaign ever, among all the other possible candidates, is Bud Light's "Real Men of Genius" campaign.

This campaign was originally named "Real American Heroes," but Bud Light respectfully changed the name to "Real Men of Genius" after 9/11 so as not to offend the real heroes who rightly deserved our collective admiration during that time. But while the name of the campaign may have changed, its humor and attitude have not. The campaign, which debuted in 1999, features a powerfully voiced announcer humorously touting a nameless individual or group of people whose contributions to the world or activities in their everyday lives couldn't be less pointless. Mr. Tiny Dog Clothing Manufacturer, Mr. Professional Sports Leg Cramp Rubber Outer, and Mr. Handlebar Mustache Wearer Guy are just some of the more than 100 spots that have been produced over the last decade.

Each spot is hilarious, with the announcer playing up the associated achievements while a fantastically cheesy backup singer chimes in to support each point. They say nothing at all about the product—nothing about its taste or the calories it contains—they're just pure brand building through humor and, in a sense, self-deprecation.

As much as I wanted to choose a TV campaign for the answer to this question, I kept coming back to these Bud Lights radio spots. (Supposedly there were two TV spots in this campaign, but I've never seen them.) Talk about getting a reaction! Not only do I turn the radio volume up when these spots come on, but I'll end any conversation going on so I can listen intently until the commercial is over. Considering that radio commercials are usually my opportunity to change the station, pop in a CD, or make a cell-phone call, any campaign that can stop me in my tracks and make me listen to every second has got to be among the best ever.

MICHAEL HAND
THE CLIENT PERSPECTIVE

I really wrestled with this question more than I thought I would. The catch for me was to focus on true "campaigns." I did not want to speak to the single ad that broke through and made a ton of noise in the market, but was not a part of a continued messaging platform. I wanted to include work that was extended into multiple forms of media and was not only TV-centric. As I listed my favorite ads and elicited some help from friends and colleagues, one glaring observation rose to the top: Almost all of the things I liked had an enhanced level of integration built in. I could not pick just one, so the following are some of my all time favorites (not ranked in any particular order):

- **Nike—Just Do It.** This body of work from the mid-80s really struck an emotional chord with me. They found a way to capture the passion and determination of athletes through their products. The print work was outstanding, and I loved the story builds with great athletes of every era (do an online search for Barry Sanders and Nolan Ryan examples to see my point). The line was all over clothing and integrated into everything Nike did. Awesome.

- **Marlboro—The Marlboro Man.** I do not smoke, never have. But this guy was a bad ass. With legal changes in the world of cigarette advertising, the Marlboro Man has really not been that active in recent years. But true to the mark of any great campaign, he is still referenced today on a regular basis. You would see him in-store and on billboards, always looking cool and in control.

- **Absolut Vodka—The Bottle.** The main thing here was simplicity. No TV ads at all. They turned print advertising into an art form. In the '80s and '90s you could walk into a college dorm room and find Absolut ads torn from magazines and taped to the wall. The reference to unique landmarks always created a little buzz. I particularly liked the Brooklyn Bridge ad with bottles cut into the arches. This is campaign excellence in my book.

- **Miller Lite—Tastes Great...Less Filling.** Yes, I worked at Miller, so I have a little bias toward their work. The truth is that this work had been off the air for years when I got there. I just think the classic television ads with the all-stars were fantastic. Again staying power is key; the fact that college football stadiums will still get a chant going across buildings that seat 80,000 is a salute to greatness.

- **Mastercard—Priceless.** This is another campaign that strikes the emotional nerve in people. They took an everyday transaction that you could use any credit card to make and turned it into part of a "priceless" moment. This really is brand building at its finest. The baseball ads get me choked up every time; and a number of the "mock" priceless ads on the Internet are truly hilarious.

- **Energizer Batteries—Bunny.** If there is one consumer benefit you want to hear from a battery manufacturer, it is that they last longer than the other guys. These executions used pictures of a pink bunny wearing shades to tell the story of how they just keep on going and going. This icon became so strong it was incorporated into the actual package design; not many spokescharacters can make that claim.

- **ESPN—This is Sportscenter.** As a sports fan, I can tell you that ESPN has become all things sports to most men in America. Whether it is the multiple networks across cable, the relationship with ABC, or the strength they have on the Web, you imagine a place in Bristol, CT that is like Willy Wonka's Chocolate Factory for guys. The ads make the biggest stars feel human, and what's not to like about the Brewers' Sausages racing through the cubicles?

- **Las Vegas—What Happens Here.** Vegas has forever been known as the city of sin, and it was deemed as true negative. A place only for degenerate gamblers, Elvis impersonators, and late-night drive-through weddings, Vegas was not (and never will be) known for its moral compass. This campaign turned that negative into a positive and made the unique storylines something of legend and worthy of consideration for any travelers' next weekend jaunt.

CLOSING REMARKS

JASON MILETSKY

There you have it. Everything you could ever need to know about marketing. Well, not really. Marketing is so full of twists, turns, dead-ends, and forks in the road that that there's always something new to learn. As I wrote this book, I found that with each question I answered, a dozen more came to mind. It's amazing that executing a successful idea is about so much more than just being creative. It's about understanding the mood and sentiment of the marketplace —and the mood and sentiment of the client. After all, that's what marketing comes down to: forging, managing, and maintaining relationships.

But while we couldn't cover absolutely every marketing-related topic in a single book, I hope that I was at least able to give you a glimpse into how the people on the agency side see our industry. There's a delicate balance that we all seek between executing the best possible campaigns that we can while at the same time dodging insufferable egos (our own and the clients'), cutting through the inevitable politics, targeting audiences in an ever-changing consumer landscape, and ultimately trying to keep accounts with us for as long as possible. For agencies, the creative part of marketing is tempered by the realities of business, and our perspectives on every aspect of communication will always be influenced by that reality.

None of that means that there isn't room for a shitload of fun! This is marketing, man. You can't do this job without passion and energy. Marketing is a chance to see ideas start off as vague concepts tossed out haphazardly during a brainstorming meeting and then be a part of giving them shape and bringing them to life. I haven't experienced much in my life that comes close to that sense of fulfillment.

I appreciate the time you've taken to read this book. Sincerely, thank you. It was a lot of hard work to put together and involved many long, introspective nights trying to figure out what I really believe (not just what I've gotten used to saying at pitch meetings). I set out to teach, and ended up learning a lot myself. I hope you did as well.

MICHAEL HAND

Okay, let me have it. You disagree with my take on "green" issues and you think my selections for the best ads in history were way off. Or maybe you support my idea of ongoing agency review meetings and think it was brilliant how I outlined the death of print media as we know it. (Was the use of the word "brilliant" a bit much?) Regardless of where you stand on these individual issues, I really hope you enjoyed reading the work.

Throughout the writing process it became very clear to me that the chasm dividing clients and agency partners is a somewhat fictional one. Both sides understand what it takes to deliver great work and both sides want to be successful in the market for the brands/products they support.

It was a challenge pulling together this book, and it made me think about where I stand on various topics from both a strategic and creative point of view. It even made me contemplate a career move away from the client side to see how the other half really lives. The process of achieving the end goal may vary, but everybody's heart is in the same place. I hope I was able to provide a perspective that illustrates the importance of people in this undertaking. As a client, you can get very caught up in the research data, brand architecture pyramids, and ROI calibration documents, but you fall into a death spiral where you start to do marketing via PowerPoint and Excel spreadsheets. Hopefully this book has shown that it needs to be about much more than data and theory when you are bringing ideas to life.

The world of marketing is undergoing an amazing evolution and new ways to connect with consumers surface every day. You could walk into a store or turn on the TV right now and be confronted with hundreds of additional examples to prove or discredit any point made by me or my counterpart in this text, and I think that is an amazing thing. Regardless of your personal level of involvement in the world of marketing, I hope we have opened your eyes to the ways we each think about and approach the marketplace.

I know the debates have only begun and I am sure I will have plenty of future discussions on the topics raised in this book (and the hundreds of new questions that surfaced while writing). Whether it be over a breakfast meeting or a beer, I look forward to the ongoing dialog and I hope to keep the conversation lively. (I can promise you that I will likely drop an "f bomb" at some point in the conversation; please don't be offended.) This is the "work stuff" that keeps me up at night, and I hope my kids grow up to find something they are equally passionate about.

I walk away from this experience with a deeper respect for the hard work it takes to be both a good client and a good agency partner. I have rediscovered my love for the challenges of this business and have a stronger-than-ever belief in the people it takes to make it all happen. I leave you with one final reminder as you embark upon your own journey: Have fun, make your own mistakes, respect your business partners, love your family, and find your own joys. For me, that joy will include family movie night and a spirited conversation with my kids about who is the coolest Power Ranger.

INDEX

A

B

trademarks, 84–85
  brands and, 93
  guidelines for using, 100
  projects and campaigns honoring, 148
training
  billing for training costs, 57
  employees, sessions for, 296
Trident, 283
Trump, Donald, 263
Trump University online school, 263
trust
  and brand-building, 158
  brand promises and, 113–114
  and B2B marketing, 292
truth
  in advertising, 312–313
  stretching the "truth" in marketing, 284–287
tuna, dolphin-safe, 246–247
TV. *See* television
tween group, marketing to, 261
Twitter, 200
typeface for brand names, 100
Tyson, Mike, 278

U

Under Armour (UA), 93, 109
US Weekly, 183
USA Today Ad Meter, 43, 166
USA Weekend, 261

V

variable pricing by client size, 28–29
vendor, agency as, 67–69
verbal appreciation, importance of, 65–66
verbally abusive clients, 336
Verizon, 171
Vick, Michael, 279–280
victories, celebrating, 10
video. *See also* streaming video
  conferencing, 70–72
  DVRs (digital video recorders), 166, 170, 172
  sharing sites, 198
viral marketing, 193–196
  social-media releases (SMRs) and, 207–208
  successful campaigns, 347–348
Virgin America, 104–105
Volvo, 97
  Trucks, 346

W

Wal-Mart, 187, 223
  "Game Time" theme, 216–217
  power of, 219–221
  pricing and, 235
Wal-Mart Effect, 185
Wall Street Journal, 194
Washington Post, 267
Web sites. *See also* Internet
  design of, 127
  leveraging online space, 189
  loyalty programs, 228
  navigation requirements, 189
  organization of, 189
  returning to site, encouraging, 189
  searching the Web, 200–201
Webkinz, 199
WebTV, 198
Weight Watchers, 313
Welch, Jack, 105
Werden, Nick, 53
Wesley, Chris, 46–47
"When I Grow Up" ad (Monster), 354
Wikipedia, 165
  on promotion, 184
Wikis, 189
Winkler, Donald, 39
winning awards, 51–54
Winston cigarettes, 290
Woods, Tiger
  and Buick, 156–157, 204, 278–279, 357
  and EA Sports, 156, 279
  and Nike, 156, 349
World Wildlife Fund, 265
worst campaign ever run, 355–357

X–Y

XM Radio, 179

Yahoo! and video-conferencing, 71
YouTube, 198, 200, 265
  celebrity endorsements and, 277
  "Cog" ad (Honda), 352
  viral marketing and, 194

Here is a preview of five questions from another book in the *Perspectives On...* series

Now available!

PERSPECTIVES™ ON
Increasing Sales

- Tested methods for improving sales and building client relationships
- Topics include prospecting, negotiation tactics, communication, and more
- Hear what the sales expert and the buyer have to say—authors have not collaborated

THE SALES EXPERT
MARVIN N. MILETSKY

THE PURCHASING AGENT
JAMES A. CALLANDER

Q: Is It Okay to Stretch the Truth to Win an Account?

Marvin Miletsky
The Sales Perspective

What's your perspective on this question?
Let us know at PerspectivesOnSales.com.

There's a major difference between stretching the truth and outright lying—and anyone who tells you that salespeople can be successful without stretching the truth a bit is, well, outright lying. And anyone who outright lies to sell *anything*—even the idea that salespeople never need to stretch the truth—will inevitably get caught in his or her own trap.

Case in point: A few years back, my organization was competing with another company—our only real competitor—for a large order for an item my company had manufactured for years. But suddenly, a third company arrived on the scene. Their sales manager bid for the work that we knew should be ours, telling the customer that although his company had never made the item before, their manufacturing department had created samples that had passed independent laboratory testing and were ready to be produced. He also offered much faster delivery at a substantially lower cost. The customer bought this guy's story, got what they wanted faster, and saved a bundle of cash. All was well with their world…until the bottom dropped out. It turned out the sales manager from the other company had outright lied. His company had neither produced nor tested any of these units. His scheme was to obtain the order first and then produce the product. Ultimately, the product they produced failed miserably. The buyer won the resulting court case, and we supplied our product as a replacement—and at a higher price than our original quote.

In the end, these bold sorts of lies will come back to haunt you more often than not. Salespeople live and die by their reputation, and nothing will tear down a reputation faster than getting caught in a lie. That being said, there will be times when a little manipulation of the truth is unavoidable. In a perfect world—one with no competition—it'd be great to tell the customer the truth at all times and let the chips fall where they may. But the world's not perfect. Competition does exist, and if the customer's decision comes down to some minor point, then stretching the truth is just a necessary part of sales survival.

Some people may argue that a lie is a lie, no matter how you look at it—that "stretching the truth" is merely a euphemism. But anyone who's read Dante's *Inferno* knows that hell has a lot of levels, and not all sins are equal. The difference between stretching the truth and outright lying is that stretching the truth retains some level of honesty, and can be explained away rather easily in the event you are questioned. For example, suppose a potential customer has already indicated that he's satisfied with your price, but he's concerned that you won't be able to deliver on time. He needs a sample in two weeks, and you know it probably won't be done in less than three; so, you tell your client that you're confident you can ship product in two weeks to obtain the order. If you end up shipping it late, it'd be fairly easy to provide a rational excuse to cover yourself—after all, you only have to buy yourself a little extra time. Besides, a good stretch of the truth can even serve as motivation: Tell the factory that story, and it's very possible they may speed things up and find a way to make good on your promise.

Of course, while embellishing the truth can be justified, a good salesperson knows when not to do it. The previous delivery scenario, for instance, becomes a much different story if the product is needed before Christmas for a holiday sale, but the delivery can't possibly arrive until after the new year.

Your need to stretch the truth will diminish over time as relationships with customers mature. You'll know their timelines and sensibilities, and be better able to anticipate their needs—allowing you to rely on pure honesty more often. But there will always be situations that force you to stretch the truth. Find the line between embellishment and lying, and use it judiciously.

JAMES CALLANDER
THE CUSTOMER PERSPECTIVE

I do not recommend stretching the truth to win an order or to attempt to impress a client. The relationship between the salesperson and the client is important, and must be managed carefully. Your customer relies on you to provide accurate information; your failure to do so jeopardizes that relationship. The fact is, your client has any number of choices when it comes to filling a need, of which you're only one.

Suppose a customer comes to you with a request that's both time sensitive and important to the purchasing agent and his organization. Your proposal quotes a price that is slightly higher than that of your competitor—but you've stretched the truth with respect to how quickly you can deliver the product, promising a lead time that is much faster than your competition's. The customer chooses to contract with you, paying more to receive the product in the specified time-frame.

You may think you are taking a calculated risk when you fudge the delivery time, but you have no control over how long it will take for your proposal to go through your client's purchasing organization. Any delays on this front will start a domino effect, making it that much more difficult for you to meet your client's deadline. And when the product doesn't show up when you said it would, the customer is going to hold you accountable for the delay. Not only will the amount of time you spend expediting, communicating your findings, and ultimately paying for premium freight cost you more in the long run, your customer will see through your excuses and possibly remove you from consideration for future sales opportunities.

From the customer's point of view, the success of any transaction is measured in direct dollars as well as in time lost in the event issues arise as a result of a purchase. If a customer's purchasing decision was based on truthful information, then those engaged in the decision-making process will bear the ill effect of a poor purchasing decision. If, however, the decision to procure a product or service from you or your company was based on information given in an untruthful or misleading manner, then you, too, will also be affected. Not only will any dividends connected to the sale be eroded, but your ability to conduct future business with the customer will disappear as well. You simply cannot afford for your image to take a hit by less-than-truthful comments or statements.

Besides, even without stretching the truth, issues will arise from missed dead-lines, pricing errors, shipping delays, or damages. It happens—and you'll have to deal with the fallout. When you do, you'll want your client to trust you to resolve the issue quickly, honestly, and professionally. How can we trust if we've been lied to?

I recommend that you ground yourself in truth. Never put yourself in a position that raises a moral or ethical question. If you don't base your dealings on truthfulness, your chances of establishing and maintaining a solid customer base will be greatly reduced—if not eliminated completely. Is it okay to stretch the truth to win a sale? No! Wouldn't you rather be a person your customers trust—the one customers want to have handling their requests? I know that's the kind of salesperson that I want to work with.

Q: HOW MUCH TIME SHOULD YOU ALLOW FOR A MEETING AND HOW LONG SHOULD IT TAKE?

JAMES CALLANDER
THE CUSTOMER PERSPECTIVE

In general, you should allow for no more than one hour, although how much time you actually need may vary. If the meeting is one-on-one, then you might not need a whole hour. And if you are meeting with a group of people, you may need the full hour, but don't expect the meeting to last longer than that (unless it's a training class; these can be longer, depending on the topic). Of course, if you've made contact with multiple people at a company, then you might spend more than one hour there because you'll be attending multiple appointments.

More important than the visit's duration is its quality. First and foremost, showing up unprepared to discuss a specific business item, be it one-on-one or in front of a group, will not help you grow your business or your relationship with your client. Get your message clear in your mind and identify what needs to happen for this meeting to be considered a success. Second, especially if you are meeting one-on-one with a customer, observe his or her demeanor carefully. If he or she seems warm and inviting, make an attempt to socialize for a moment. This can assist you in connecting with your customer, which in turn progresses your relationship. (Be ready, though, to shift to your message at a moment's notice.) If, however, your client is more intent on getting down to business, you'll want to launch right into your message. Prompt presentation of the essentials also allows time for you to ask your client whether other groups or people in the office might be able to employ your services. Of course, there are no guarantees you'll have the chance to ask questions such as these or that the person will provide the information you're asking for; if this happens, you'll want to conclude your visit promptly, thanking your customer for his or her time. Before you go, however, look for a reason to schedule another appointment. Use a request made or a question asked by the client or an observation made by you during the meeting to open the door for the next meeting.

The same points apply if you are meeting with a group. You must still arrive with your message and expectations clear in your mind, and you must assess the demeanor of the group to determine how to proceed. In addition, though, you must be prepared in the event various members of the group want to discuss different things and allow for the exchange of ideas from different directions. This is a good problem to have—that is, any of those present who are active in a meeting (i.e., asking questions) are obviously very interested, which is a good thing (in most meetings, people can't wait to get out of them)—*if* you can manage to stay focused. You'll also want to allocate sufficient time for the group to ask questions and comment on the material presented. In addition to enabling them to more fully understand your presentation, this can offer you tremendous insight on the client's staff and provide an opportunity for you to offer support.

So how do you determine whether to dive right into your message (which you are of course ready to deliver at any moment) or to enjoy a few minutes of socializing? Body language is one way:

- If your client is sitting with arms and legs crossed, then he or she will more than likely want to get right into the discussion. Additionally, he or she may be a bit more close-minded about whatever it is you want to convey and require more convincing on your part.

- If your customer is relaxed in his or her chair, you can expect him or her to be more friendly and inviting, as well as more open to taking a few minutes to be social. In this case, you don't need to cut right to the chase; take the opportunity to probe your client a bit in an off-topic discussion. But be mindful of the time so you don't overstay your welcome.

- If the person you are visiting is leaning forward in his or her chair with his or her arms resting on a desk, that person is very interested in you and, more importantly, the reason for your visit. (Note that most people don't start an appointment in this position, but move to it based on their interest.) In this case, in addition to conveying your message, you may also be able to discuss items *not* related to your visit—most notably, who else in the customer's office might find it beneficial to meet with you. Additionally, in this situation, you should be able to ask probing questions to confirm the client's interest.

Another way to assess how quickly you should get to the meat of your message is by assessing your client's attitude. Is the person smiling? Is he or she frowning?

- If your client is smiling, you should be able to take a few minutes for social conversation before getting to the point.

- If your client is frowning, you can bet that person has something on his or her mind. Regardless of whether the person is frowning because of you or is preoccupied with another issue, you can reasonably assume that the meeting will be short. In this case, you'll need to get right into the reason for your visit.

- If your client seems visibly upset, I doubt anything you say or do will be effective. In this scenario, it might actually be best to attempt to reschedule.

Of course, not all sales calls will relate to a specific item of business. You might have more than one reason to visit. Whether you are able to delve into these additional areas depends to a large extent on your client's willingness to allow the meeting to continue. If my day is full of tasks and appointments, I may simply not be able to deviate from my schedule. If I'm taking calls or allowing others to interrupt your visit, you can bet my time is extremely short or other pressing issues are a priority for my day, distracting me from your visit. If this is the case, get your message across right then and there.

Managing your time—and guarding that of your clients—is tremendously important to becoming successful in sales. Spending too much time at any one client can negatively affect business in other areas. By keeping your sales calls to one hour or less per call, you can make more calls per day, increasing your opportunities to grow your business.

MARVIN MILETSKY
THE SALES PERSPECTIVE

More often than not, it's safe to assume that no one really wants to attend a sales presentation. So if you've set up a meeting with a customer—prospective or existing—try to keep that in mind. Make sure to respect the time that's been granted you. Don't do what I did once when presenting to a group of potential clients: Before getting to the heart of the meeting, I broke the ice with some small talk about the big game that had been played the day before. Before I knew it, an in-depth and lengthy discussion ensued, with all the Monday morning quarterbacks in the room putting their own two cents in—until the main person I had come to target got up, politely explained that our meeting had run past the time he had budgeted for, apologized for the fact that he had another pressing meeting to attend, thanked me for coming, and left. (He did mention that he thought his team would do better the following Sunday.) My meeting was over before it really ever got off the ground; without my main focus in attendance, its continuation was an effort in futility.

You're not the social director on a cruise ship, and these people are not your pals. They represent your future paychecks. Your success is not measured in the time you spend with them, but in the sales that are produced as a result of the presentation you've made. Take control of the meeting right from the outset and keep your focus on the reason you're there. Understand, too, that you might be talking to a medium to large audience, with not all in attendance as interested as you are in what is being said or shown.

So how do you control a meeting? Here's some advice for running meetings, based on some of my experiences:

- Introduce yourself with a warm smile and let your audience know how much you appreciate their attendance.

- As you get ready to start, while shuffling papers or arranging samples or literature, make some off-the-cuff remark in a conversational tone—but nothing that will cause a debate or an in-depth discussion to break out. The weather and traffic problems are safe; there really can't be much disagreement on either.

- Continue the conversation while adjusting your papers, business cards, or literature. This should happen as people are entering the room, before they've settled down into their seats. The idea is to stall until everyone is in the room; it's very difficult to start a presentation while people are still filing in. It disrupts the continuity of the presentation, and inevitably you'll lose the attention of those who were already seated when you try to bring the late arrivals up to speed. After everyone has seen and heard your human side, pick the moment to start your presentation.

- In the beginning of the meeting, try not to get into individual conversations with people. Leave that for after the meeting or some later date during a follow-up visit.

- During the presentation, it's as important to sell yourself as it is your product or service. Relax, talk to the participants—but don't lecture them. State what brought you there in the first place; identify the need they have that you have come to satisfy.

- With the foundation set, go straight to your solution. Hit them with the grabber. Show your product or the new innovation that will meet their needs. Share how your company can help them tackle their problems. Don't be another me-too vendor or the low-price-on-the-street type. You are a salesperson; you've got to have something exciting to say about your product, services, or company that will give them reason to see you again—and you've got to get it out fast! Otherwise, you'll lose them to boredom.

- After you've succeeded in making your point(s), field any questions, listen to any comments, and give them the freedom to end the meeting at their convenience. Before they do, however, thank them all for their attention and make sure you all understand what the next step should be.

One more piece of advice, based on another of one of my early blunders: Take care to avoid damaging the meeting space. I once gave a presentation in a conference room that had a beautiful mahogany table. I had brought more than a dozen samples of industrial products made of various metals to show, so I set them out on the table. After the meeting, which went great, I noticed that my samples had scratched the table. I felt really terrible. There wasn't much I could do about it, although I did apologize to the contact who arranged the meeting and I offered to pay for any repairs. It was an innocent mistake, but one that really threatened the success of the meeting. These days, I carry around a little piece of carpeting to set samples on.

If you keep these points in mind, your audience will know what to expect from you at the next meeting. And when that meeting occurs, those initial barriers will have been broken, and a more relaxed atmosphere can start to present itself. But please, no discussions of politics, sports, or religion. It's all about the sale!

Q: THE CLIENT IS IN A BIND AND NEEDS A PRODUCT OR SERVICE IN AN EMERGENCY. SHOULD THE PRICE GO UP?

What's your perspective on this question?
Let us know at PerspectivesOnSales.com.

MARVIN MILETSKY

THE SALES PERSPECTIVE

Take a good hard look at the cost structure for the products or services you produce using controlled methods. Now take a look at the extra money your company has to spend to produce the same product under emergency circumstances, and you'll realize that not only *should* the price go up, it *must*. It doesn't make a whole lot of sense to satisfy a rush requirement that costs you money, does it?

Even when you think you've accounted for all the additional costs, there are subtle ones that may not even register. One is the cost of breaking the normal flow of your business to satisfy a rush requirement. For example, you might interrupt another requirement that you're working on in order to handle the emergency. Inevitably, you'll return to the original job and find that the time you took to handle the emergency has put you behind schedule. You can't let this customer down, meaning you'll have to take extraordinary measures to catch up, which can mean added personnel or overtime—for which, of course, you can't charge your current customer. All this is to say that emergency production is costly and unproductive and should be avoided if at all possible.

I was once in a manufacturing business that catered mainly to contractors and industrial users. They were not the best planners, and frequently relied on last-minute orders to save their hides. Eventually, we came up with a way to combat the steady stream of "emergencies" that seemed to permeate our business: we instituted a flat "emergency services" charge on all rush orders, above and beyond the charges for the material or service we were going to provide. By the negative responses we got, you'd have thought the world was coming to an end.

We were told that these charges were unfair—and lots of other things, many of which don't belong in print. The amazing thing was, many asked what the normal delivery would be without those charges and were quite satisfied with the standard delivery we offered. Even if we asked whether they wanted air freight as part of the service, they informed us that standard delivery arrangements would be satisfactory. The moral of the story is, make sure you're dealing with a true emergency before you commit to the service.

There's a tenet that selling price is often based upon what the market will bear—and during emergency situations, the market can bear a little more. But I'm not encouraging you to be usurious. You're not in business to handle a single order; your relationship with your customer is built through your total service to them under standard and non-standard conditions. The emergency service you provide for customers should pay dividends in developing and keeping their loyalty in the future. Follow-up calls to see how things went and whether their experience with your company was positive should be made. Keep the service you provided fresh in their minds; it could play a role in breaking a tie in the future. Just remember that a relationship is two-sided. The same response and pricing should not be given to someone using you for this emergency only. You've done your due diligence in trying to court this target, but now, during their hour of need, you become convenient. Make a very handsome profit, serve them well, and try to use this as a stepping-stone for future business—but don't count on it, as they've demonstrated in the past that they already have their standard suppliers lined up.

JAMES CALLANDER
THE CUSTOMER PERSPECTIVE

As a client, I have to manage and satisfy the needs of both management and co-workers. When an emergency arises, my first priority is making the deadline for availability as needed. The second priority is the price. If I can receive product or service within the time allotted from only one vendor, I am willing to pay more to make that happen. If two or more vendors can handle the timing, then price can be a major factor in who gets the order.

If you are faced with a client emergency, you must find the answers to these questions in your attempts to determine your price strategy:

- **Why is the client in this situation and what is expected of you in your attempts to serve the client?** Knowing this enables you to respond in a way most likely to meet the need. At the same time, understanding exactly what is expected provides direction necessary to escalate the proper response within your busy schedule and that of others needed to support the inquiry. If you require others in your organization to assist in managing the solution, then the price should reflect the time and effort you and others put forth in submitting the final offer. What is required internally to satisfy the client's request often helps determine your markup. Things like special handling, expedited delivery, and technical support all play a role in determining the final price. Extensive effort on your part and that of others you need to manage a solution should not be free.

Clients that ask for support to a time-sensitive request that do not accept enhanced costs become a nuisance to the rest of your client base. Let's face it: The last thing you need is to drop everything to support a client that doesn't value your time. Keep this in mind if you find that one of your clients repeatedly cries wolf.

■ **Is the product or service readily available?** Regardless of the urgency of an inquiry I send to vendors, if the product or service is readily available, your chance to raise the price is limited. If your competitors can provide the same or equal item immediately, then you have no advantage to offer. If, however, you have an exclusive selection or if sole-source capability permits you to raise your price to support my need, then I might not be thrilled to pay more, but I will be forced to balance cost versus time issues in my decision.

When I'm dealing with a situation that requires immediate support from my vendors, I'm usually attempting to fix a problem that has popped up unexpectedly. This forces me to lean on my vendors to work under pressure as I am doing. Those vendors who understand this and rise to the challenge do so with a sense of expectation—specifically, that an order will be the result of the vendor's ability to provide the necessary solution in the established timeframe.

Gathering the right information and evaluating your ability to handle the client emergency is the starting point. Once you have determined what you can do to address the problem, your attention should shift to developing your price. The amount of effort, the exclusivity of your offering, and the handling and or expediting required to deliver must all be weighed when determining whether you should expect to increase your margin. Do not forget, however, that in most cases, you are not the only vendor contacted by the client to help with the inquiry.

Client emergency requests are a constant part of doing business. You never know when an emergency is coming, but I am confident you will deal with them regularly. (Any type of next-day or second-day-air requirements applied to your client's request should raise the red flag.) How you handle the challenge can affect your business both positively and negatively.

Q: THE CLIENT HAS CALLED THE SALESPERSON'S BLUFF. CAN THE SALESPERSON STILL BACKTRACK AND SAVE FACE?

MARVIN MILETSKY

THE SALES PERSPECTIVE

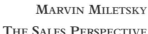

A wife returns home to find her husband in bed with another woman and demands to know who she is. He responds by asking her "what woman? There's no woman in this bed, you're imagining it!" Deny, deny, deny! That's the joke; unfortunately that's not real life.

As we go forward in our pursuit of business, there might be times that we have to embellish our stories or even make some sort of bluff in order to close. And as with anything we do that stretches the truth or at least rearranges it, we stand the possibility of being caught. I can't say that bluffing is a sales technique, but I'm sure that I've done it more than once. In the end, I really have had to be creative in certain circumstances in order to close an order, and the art of misdirection has been included. It's never anything I plan ahead to do, but when push comes to shove, I would rather bluff in an effort to get the order than walk away without giving it that good ole college try. Before you even consider such a tack, make sure you know the prospect well enough to be able to survive if you are caught. Try never to consider the person you're trying to deal with as an imbecile. He probably didn't get to his position of authority by being a fool, so don't treat him as one.

I can remember bluffing my way into an order by telling the prospect that we'd require six weeks to satisfy his needs and that the only way we could succeed was by starting immediately on it. My bluff landed me the order, and all was well with my world. That was until my company shipped the merchandise within a week, as we had the material available at the time of our offer and I had neglected to coordinate with the shipping department that we hold these items for several weeks. There was another time that I urged a prospect to act swiftly on his decision because a competitor of his had also been inquiring about the same product, and we had only enough to fill one requirement. My ploy worked, and I got the order away from a competitor of mine and at a higher price due to my bluff. My strategy was exposed the very next week when an employee from the competing company hired on to my customer's company and exposed the fact that his original company was never interested in my material in the first place. Who could have known?

In the rare occasions that my bluff has been caught, I found myself having to face the music with my clients. We've discussed the importance of building a relationship that usually has as its foundation the component of trust. Based on the circumstances, I was unable to actually come clean and admit that I was bluffing or embellishing. I apologized for leading my customer astray and attributed it to poor information I had received when we had originally discussed their project. I took total blame rather than try to blame others in my organization because, I told them, no matter what, it was my responsibility to get everything right, no matter who gave me the information. In our discussion of the situation, I have always tried to get the upper hand by speaking in a confident yet apologetic voice. I also have brought the discussion to a quick end by getting into some other business topic, perhaps a new product or service we have just introduced.

There have been times when the end of this discussion has occurred with the customer still a little leery and suspicious and not quite accepting my story. There's little you can do at this point other than to be contrite and let the conversation come to its natural end. I've actually never had a circumstance where the bluff was so outlandish that we couldn't recover from it. Hold your bluffs to a minimum; the more often you try, the harder it gets to recover if you do actually get caught.

JAMES CALLANDER
THE CUSTOMER PERSPECTIVE

You can backtrack from any statement, and you will from time to time. For example, when information based on current circumstances changes, then you should inform your client. But you should never try to play games with your clients. What do you hope to gain by inviting trouble? Your client is looking to you for guidance through any lengthy process associated with an order. They use the information you provide for planning and scheduling. You must keep this information clean and to the point, and not overstate your capabilities.

Bluffs typically are one of three types:

- **Bluffs about availability:** Your proposal indicates delivery is four weeks; you know it is closer to six. When week four rolls around and your client has scheduled installation based on your proposal date, guess who is going to have a bad day? That's right: you! And what do you think will happen if your client knows that the information you've provided in your proposal is bogus? They are not going to let it slide; they will ask you directly about how you can make a six-week item ship in four.

- **Bluffs about terms:** On most vendor proposals, the payment terms are typically net 30 days. When the dollars become excessive or there are terms on which the client must insist, however, both parties must negotiate. That is, the client needs better terms on large-dollar orders. If you as the vendor insist on standard payment terms, the client will certainly wonder whether you are bluffing with regard to holding firm on the terms, whether you simply don't know what you can provide, or whether you have even asked your management for guidance. Regardless of the reason, the client will look to other vendors to negotiate better terms. And once that happens, you will have lost your competitive edge—at which point there is no backtracking or saving face. Worse, it will likely become a source of resentment for the client and may color their opinion of you in future dealings. I doubt the client will be anything but cordial, but they will not easily forget, either. If you are ever presented with this situation by one of your clients, I suggest communicating with your management for direction.

- **Bluffs about price:** Clients have various tools, some precise and others more like barometers, for determining the current market value of their inquiry—meaning that the vendor who inflates prices is usually easy to spot. Clients who see a vendor trying to make a fast buck tend to challenge the proposal to uncover why costs exceed their estimate; the explanation given by the vendor weighs heavy on the client's acceptance. If the client is not satisfied with the answer, the vendor may get the order at the requested price, but future consideration could suffer. To save face, the vendor could decide to adjust pricing to satisfy the client, which will go a long way toward maintaining trust built up with the client.

Q: • CAN YOU WORK TOGETHER IN
       • SPITE OF A PERSONALITY CONFLICT?

JAMES CALLANDER

THE CUSTOMER PERSPECTIVE

One of my first tasks before beginning a project in a new city is to establish accounts with vendors to support our office and materials needs. This requires me to do research in the local area to find the right logistical support ahead of time. During this process, I typically contact 20 or 30 vendors to discuss what we are looking for and evaluate their capabilities. Inevitably, some vendors struggle to grasp our needs and expectations. How they handle this gives me my first clue as to whether I will likely experience a personality conflict with this vendor. If the vendor manages the situation properly, I can overlook their initial difficulty grasping our needs for the moment and move on. But if the vendor becomes difficult—for example, if the individual assigned to our account is unwilling to accommodate our method of conducting business—this usually signals that there are more problems ahead. Would this be considered a personality conflict? It sure feels like one. Obviously, being new to us, the vendor might be apprehensive at first. I can understand that. But if I am asking for nothing more than for that vendor to help resolve an issue and all I get are arguments, I doubt very seriously I will need that vendor's phone number again.

Personality conflicts are based on perceptions that are rooted in emotion and tend to get in the way of conducting business. Personality conflicts can be difficult to overcome, but the fact is, clients can typically look to several different vendors for any product or service they require. Put another way, if a personality conflict arises between a client and a vendor, the vendor is usually the party that must make concessions. If there is a rift between the client buyer and the salesperson calling on that buyer, then the salesperson had better find a way to clear things up—for example, removing any emotional triggers from his or her communications. If he or she fails to do so, the chances of that salesperson continuing to sell to that client are marginal at best. If the issue is left up to the client to resolve, they will look to other vendors to fill the gap. The goal in sales is to book an order; salespeople should focus on achieving this goal every day. That means reacting to situations in a manner that is acceptable to the client.

MARVIN MILETSKY
THE SALES PERSPECTIVE

Although you'll probably encounter lots of people with similar personalities during your career, no two will be exactly the same—and just because one person takes to you does not guarantee that another will. In fact, you might be welcomed like a long-lost family member by one person and as an enemy by another—and you're still the same person! One thing's for sure: There are no guarantees that your clients will like you. (Of course, there's also no guarantee that you're going to take to the person on the other side of the desk—but in that case, you'll almost always have to find some way of dealing with him or her. After all, that person can always find someone else to deal with, either within your company or at a competitor, with whom he or she can get along.) Just remember: In sales, it's never about you. It's about your clients and satisfying their needs. Adjusting your personality to meet their requirements is something you're going to have to decide to do or move on.

> One thing I've learned through experience is to be a good listener. I always try to allow the customer to set the tone for our conversation and fall into place with his or her direction.

Still, there are going to be people who just don't take to you no matter what you do. You'll see it in their reaction when you call, in the difficulty you have making an appointment, or in your inability to land any orders (or orders beyond the ones you know are the leftovers). You may ultimately need to decide whether you're wasting your precious time with someone who doesn't appear to want to enter into any short- or long-range business relationship with you—*ever*. Here's an expression you've heard before: Cut your losses and move on! Don't burn any bridges, but put these people on your lowest-priority list. Spend more time with clients with whom you have at least some chance for success. By the way, that guy with the attitude just might have done you a world of good. By signaling to you that you ought not waste any of your precious time on him, he enables you to spend more time with those prospects who are easier to get along with and will give you at least a fighting chance for success.

> Remember: You don't have to become friends with your client in order to do business. A cordial but professional relationship can do wonders.

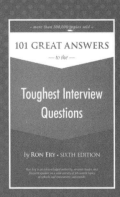
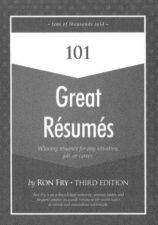